Workouts

in

Intermediate Microeconomics

Fourth Edition

Workouts in
Intermediate Microeconomics
Fourth Edition

Theodore C. Bergstrom

University of Michigan

Hal R. Varian

University of California at Berkeley

W. W. Norton & Company • New York • London

Copyright © 1996, 1993, 1990, 1987 by Theodore C. Bergstrom and
Hal R. Varian

ISBN 0-393-96843-X

W. W. Norton & Company , Inc., 500 Fifth Avenue, New York, N.Y. 10110
http://www.wwnorton.com
W. W. Norton & Company Ltd., 10 Coptic Street, London WC1A 1PU

2 3 4 5 6 7 8 9 0

Contents

Quizzes

Preface

Persons or objects that are held in low esteem are often renamed in hopes of making them less unpopular. Undertakers are called morticians and then funeral directors. Schoolteachers are called instructors and then educators. Exercise books become workbooks and then study guides. But if the old reality doesn't change, the new name eventually becomes as disagreeable as the old, and another euphemism must be sought. This "workout book" is really an exercise book. But anyone who has endured a dozen or more years of school has been tormented by so many hopelessly insipid and boring "exercise books" as to no longer notice the apt metaphor of exercise in "exercise book." In this book we try to devise mental "workouts" that are lively stimuli for economics students who want to develop skill and agility in thinking about economics. As with physical exercise, there seems to be no way of becoming good at economics without a lot of time and hard work. But hard work, mental or physical, needn't be boring. We hope this workbook is not. If worst comes to worst, somebody can always try a new exercise book called *Economic Aerobics*.

Readers of sedentary inclination in physical matters may find even metaphorical workouts exhausting. To such readers we suggest an alternative interpretation of the title. It could be a work out book as in "Work out the odd numbered problems in Chapter 11."

In these problems we occasionally make thought-voyages to other planets that feature fantastic economic customs very different from those familiar on earth. Our purpose is not to prepare you for space travel; we know of no plans to send economists into space. It turns out that in economics, as in all of science, a playful imagination is a powerful instrument for understanding. Don't worry though, we have tried to include some boring problems for those of you who plan to be bank inspectors or university administrators.

Getting Started

Students often tell us, "I read the textbook and I thought I understood it, but when I try to do the problems, I don't know where to start." Indeed it is a lot easier to passively "learn" a concept than to try to apply it. But the main reason for learning the tools of economic theory is so that you can apply them, and the best way we know to develop the skill of applying ideas is to do lots of problems.

Don't be discouraged if you can't solve every problem when you first see it. In most chapters you will find some problems that are pretty easy and some that are very challenging, even for advanced students. To help you get started, at least one and sometimes several problems are worked out for you at the beginning of each chapter. You will find that many problems are written in such a way as to guide you toward the answer by taking one little step at a time. Also, you will find the answers to the even-numbered problems in the back of the book. We suggest that you work several of the even-numbered problems, checking your answers against the answers in the back and then try your hand at some of the odd-numbered ones.

One thing you should do to get started is to get together some colored pens or pencils. In most chapters you will find several problems that ask you to draw graphs. We urge you to do a lot of these. Even if you know how a graph should look because you have seen it in the textbook, you should get your pencil out and draw it. One of the first things that most practicing economists do when they start to work on an economic problem is draw some diagrams. Not only does looking at a diagram help you to understand many economic ideas, but drawing the diagram with your own hand often helps to fix it in your brain. In the graphical problems we ask you to use specific colors to draw certain lines. We ask for blue, black, and red ink. We are not just being fussy when we ask you to do this. You will find that your graphs are a lot clearer and more informative if you use different colors for the different lines. We have requested specific colors so that if somebody grades your paper, he or she will be able to tell at a glance if you have the figure right.

We've indicated the difficulty of each problem with a score from 0 to 2 and have marked the problems that need calculus. In general the mathematics used in the problems is pretty elementary, mostly simple algebra. When we use calculus it is only very simple calculus. But despite the elementary nature of the mathematics, the problems do require some effort—like any good workout.

Multiple-Choice Quiz Bank

In the back of the book, you will find a multiple-choice quiz bank to the back of the book that provides extra opportunities for practice. Each of these multiple-choice questions is designed to be quite easy to do if you have mastered the corresponding question in the main text of *Workouts*.

Instructors who have adopted *Workouts* for their course can get a free copy of a Norton's test generating software, *Norton TestMaker*. *TestMaker* will generate new versions of the quiz problems in the back of the book, which have the same internal logic, but different numerical values. This can be used to make additional problems for students to practice on or make short quizzes that can be used to check that students have mastered the material in *Workouts*.

Grading quizzes is quick and reliable because the quizzes are multiple-choice and can be graded electronically. In our course, we tell the students to work through all the quiz questions for each chapter, either by themselves or with a study group. Then during the term we have a short in-class quiz approximately every other week. Since the quiz questions are based on homework questions with different numbers, students who have done their homework find it easy to do well on the quizzes.

What's New in the Fourth Edition

In the fourth edition we have added a new chapter on Information Technology and new problems on price discrimination and product bundling.

Acknowledgments

In writing this workout book, we have shamelessly borrowed problems from several of our colleagues, students, and friends at the University of Michigan. To us, this seems only fair, since over the years, we have also caused them many problems. Our benefactors include the following individuals: Greg Acs, Mark Bagnoli, Angela Bills, Larry Blume, Severin Borenstein, Charlie Brown, John Cross, John Fountain, Aaron Fried, Jan Gerson, Roger Gordon, Otis Gilley, Debra Holt, Gordon Karels, John Miller, Peter Morgan, John Ries, Sharon Parrott, Richard Porter, Chris Proulx, Arthur Robson, Ephraim Sadka, Steve Salant, Hyun Shinn, Oz Shy, Carl Simon, Alasdair Smith, Frank Stafford, Harvey Steele, Effluvia Stench, Joe Swierzbinski, and Paul Walker.

Some readers may think that they notice connections between characters in our problems and colleagues or other living persons who might happen to have similar names or characteristics. Let us assure you that any such relation is entirely accidental. The characters in our problems are all simple-minded creatures with very narrow interests.

Workouts
in
Intermediate Microeconomics
Fourth Edition

The Market

Introduction. The problems in this chapter examine some variations on the apartment market described in the text. In most of the problems we work with the true demand curve constructed from the reservation prices of the consumers rather than the "smoothed" demand curve that we used in the text.

Remember that the reservation price of a consumer is that price where he is just indifferent between renting or not renting the apartment. At any price below the reservation price the consumer will demand one apartment, at any price above the reservation price the consumer will demand zero apartments, and exactly at the reservation price the consumer will be indifferent between having zero or one apartment.

You should also observe that when demand curves have the "staircase" shape used here, there will typically be a *range* of prices where supply equals demand. Thus we will ask for the the highest and lowest price in the range.

1.1 (3) Suppose that we have 8 people who want to rent an apartment. Their reservation prices are given below. (To keep the numbers small, think of these numbers as being daily rent payments.)

$$\begin{array}{rccccccccc} \text{Person} & = & A & B & C & D & E & F & G & H \\ \text{Price} & = & 40 & 25 & 30 & 35 & 10 & 18 & 15 & 5 \end{array}$$

(a) Plot the market demand curve in the following graph. (Hint: When the market price is equal to some consumer i's reservation price there will be two different quantities of apartments demanded, since consumer i will be indifferent between having or not having an apartment.)

Price

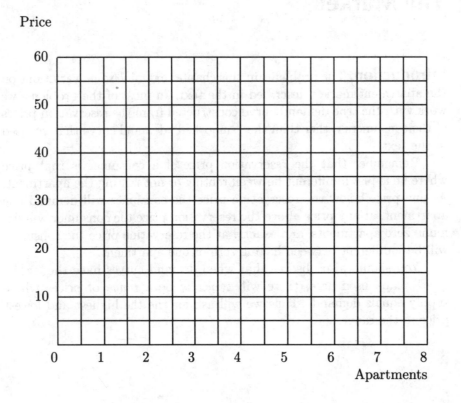

(b) Suppose the supply of apartments is fixed at 5 units. In this case there is a whole range of prices that will be equilibrium prices. What is the highest price that would make the demand for apartments equal to 5

units?_____.

(c) What is the lowest price that would make the market demand equal

to 5 units?_____.

(d) With a supply of 4 apartments, which of the people A–H end up

getting apartments?_____.

(e) What if the supply of apartments increases to 6 units. What is the

range of equilibrium prices?_____.

1.2 (3) Suppose that there are originally 5 units in the market and that 1 of them is turned into a condominium.

(a) Suppose that person A decides to buy the condominium. What will be the highest price at which the demand for apartments will equal the supply of apartments? What will be the lowest price? Enter your answers in column A, in the table. Then calculate the equilibrium prices of apartments if B, C, ..., decide to buy the condominium.

Person	A	B	C	D	E	F	G	H
High price								
Low price								

(b) Suppose that there were two people at each reservation price and 10 apartments. What is the highest price at which demand equals supply?

_____ Suppose that one of the apartments was turned into a condominium. Is that price still an equilibrium price?_____.

1.3 (2) Suppose now that a monopolist owns all the apartments and that he is trying to determine which price and quantity maximize his revenues.

(a) Fill in the box with the maximum price and revenue that the monopolist can make if he rents 1, 2,..., 8 apartments. (Assume that he must charge one price for all apartments.)

Number	1	2	3	4	5	6	7	8
Price								
Revenue								

(b) Which of the people A–F would get apartments?_____.

(c) If the monopolist were required by law to rent exactly 5 apartments, what price would he charge to maximize his revenue?_____.

(d) Who would get apartments?_____.

(e) If this landlord could charge each individual a different price, and he knew the reservation prices of all the individuals, what is the maximum revenue he could make if he rented all 5 apartments?_____.

(f) If 5 apartments were rented, which individuals would get the apartments?_____.

1.4 (2) Suppose that there are 5 apartments to be rented and that the city rent-control board sets a maximum rent of $9. Further suppose that people A, B, C, D, and E manage to get an apartment, while F, G, and H are frozen out.

(a) If subletting is legal—or, at least, practiced—who will sublet to whom in equilibrium? (Assume that people who sublet can evade the city rent-control restrictions.)_____

_____.

(b) What will be the maximum amount that can be charged for the sublet payment?_____.

(c) If you have rent control with unlimited subletting allowed, which of the consumers described above will end up in the 5 apartments?_____

_____.

(d) How does this compare to the market outcome?_____.

1.5 (2) In the text we argued that a tax on landlords would not get passed along to the renters. What would happen if instead the tax was imposed on renters?

(a) To answer this question, consider the group of people in Problem 1. What is the maximum that they would be willing to pay to the landlord if they each had to pay a $5 tax on apartments to the city? Fill in the box below with these reservation prices.

Person	A	B	C	D	E	F	G	H
Reservation Price								

(b) Using this information determine the maximum equilibrium price if there are 5 apartments to be rented._____.

(c) Of course, the total price a renter pays consists of his or her rent plus the tax. This amount is_____.

(d) How does this compare to what happens if the tax is levied on the landlords?_____.

Budget Constraint

Introduction. These workouts are designed to build your skills in describing economic situations with graphs and algebra. Budget sets are a good place to start, because both the algebra and the graphing are very easy. Where there are just two goods, a consumer who consumes x_1 units of good 1 and x_2 units of good 2 is said to consume the *consumption bundle*, (x_1, x_2). Any consumption bundle can be represented by a point on a two-dimensional graph with quantities of good 1 on the horizontal axis and quantities of good 2 on the vertical axis. If the prices are p_1 for good 1 and p_2 for good 2, and if the consumer has income m, then she can afford any consumption bundle, (x_1, x_2), such that $p_1 x_1 + p_2 x_2 \leq m$. On a graph, the *budget line* is just the line segment with equation $p_1 x_1 + p_2 x_2 = m$ and with x_1 and x_2 both nonnegative. The budget line is the boundary of the *budget set*. All of the points that the consumer can afford lie on one side of the line and all of the points that the consumer cannot afford lie on the other.

If you know prices and income, you can construct a consumer's budget line by finding two commodity bundles that she can "just afford" and drawing the straight line that runs through both points.

Example: Myrtle has 50 dollars to spend. She consumes only apples and bananas. Apples cost 2 dollars each and bananas cost 1 dollar each. You are to graph her budget line, where apples are measured on the horizontal axis and bananas on the vertical axis. Notice that if she spends all of her income on apples, she can afford 25 apples and no bananas. Therefore her budget line goes through the point $(25, 0)$ on the horizontal axis. If she spends all of her income on bananas, she can afford 50 bananas and no apples. Therfore her budget line also passes throught the point $(0, 50)$ on the vertical axis. Mark these two points on your graph. Then draw a straight line between them. This is Myrtle's budget line.

What if you are not told prices or income, but you know two commodity bundles that the consumer can just afford? Then, if there are just two commodities, you know that a unique line can be drawn through two points, so you have enough information to draw the budget line.

Example: Laurel consumes only ale and bread. If she spends all of her income, she can just afford 20 bottles of ale and 5 loaves of bread. Another commodity bundle that she can afford if she spends her entire income is 10 bottles of ale and 10 loaves of bread. If the price of ale is 1 dollar per bottle, how much money does she have to spend? You could solve this problem graphically. Measure ale on the horizontal axis and bread on the vertical axis. Plot the two points, $(20, 5)$ and $(10, 10)$, that you know to be on the budget line. Draw the straight line between these points and extend the line to the horizontal axis. This point denotes the amount of ale Laurel can afford if she spends all of her money on ale. Since ale costs 1 dollar a bottle, her income in dollars is equal to the largest number of bottles she can afford. Alternatively, you can reason as follows. Since the bundles $(20, 5)$ and $(10, 10)$ cost the same, it must be that giving up 10 bottles of ale makes her able to afford an extra 5 loaves of bread. So bread costs twice as much as ale. The price of ale is 1 dollar, so the price of bread is 2 dollars. The bundle $(20, 5)$ costs as much as her income. Therefore her income must be $20 \times 1 + 5 \times 2 = 30$.

When you have completed this workout, we hope that you will be able to do the following

- Write an equation for the budget line and draw the budget set on a graph when you are given prices and income or when you are given two points on the budget line.

- Graph the effects of changes in prices and income on budget sets.

- Understand the concept of *numeraire* and know what happens to the budget set when income and all prices are multiplied by the same positive amount.

- Know what the budget set looks like if one or more of the prices is negative.

- See that the idea of a "budget set" can be applied to constrained choices where there are other constraints on what you can have, in addition to a constraint on money expenditure.

2.1 (0) You have an income of $40 to spend on two commodities. Commodity 1 costs $10 per unit, and commodity 2 costs $5 per unit.

(a) Write down your budget equation._____.

(b) If you spent all your income on commodity 1, how much could you

buy?_____.

(c) If you spent all of your income on commodity 2, how much could you

buy?_____ Use blue ink to draw your budget line in the graph below.

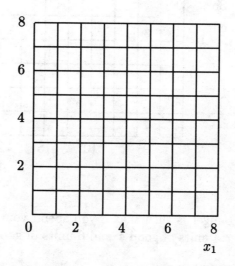

(d) Suppose that the price of commodity 1 falls to $5 while everything

else stays the same. Write down your new budget equation. _____

_____ On the graph above, use red ink to draw your new budget
line.

(e) Suppose that the amount you are allowed to spend falls to $30, while
the prices of both commodities remain at $5. Write down your budget

equation. _____ Use black ink to draw this budget line.

(f) On your diagram, use blue ink to shade in the area representing commodity bundles that you can afford with the budget in Part (e) but could
not afford to buy with the budget in Part (a). Use black ink or pencil to
shade in the area representing commodity bundles that you could afford
with the budget in Part (a) but cannot afford with the budget in Part
(e).

2.2 (0) On the graph below, draw a budget line for each case.

(a) $p_1 = 1$, $p_2 = 1$, $m = 15$. (Use blue ink.)

(b) $p_1 = 1$, $p_2 = 2$, $m = 20$. (Use red ink.)

(c) $p_1 = 0$, $p_2 = 1$, $m = 10$. (Use black ink.)

(d) $p_1 = p_2$, $m = 15p_1$. (Use pencil or black ink. Hint: How much of good 1 could you afford if you spend your entire budget on good 1?)

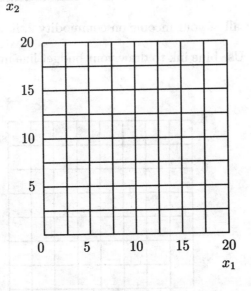

2.3 (0) Your budget is such that if you spend your entire income, you can afford either 4 units of good x and 6 units of good y or 12 units of x and 2 units of y.

(a) Mark these two consumption bundles and draw the budget line in the graph below.

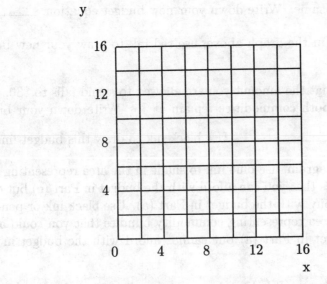

(b) What is the ratio of the price of x to the price of y?_____.

(c) If you spent all of your income on x, how much x could you buy?

_____.

(d) If you spent all of your income on y, how much y could you buy?

_____.

(e) Write a budget equation that gives you this budget line, where the price of x is 1._____.

(f) Write another budget equation that gives you the same budget line, but where the price of x is 3._____.

2.4 (1) Murphy was consuming 100 units of X and 50 units of Y. The price of X rose from 2 to 3. The price of Y remained at 4.

(a) How much would Murphy's income have to rise so that he can still exactly afford 100 units of X and 50 units of Y?_____.

2.5 (1) If Amy spent her entire allowance, she could afford 8 candy bars and 8 comic books a week. She could also just afford 10 candy bars and 4 comic books a week. The price of a candy bar is 50 cents. Draw her budget line in the box below. What is Amy's weekly allowance?_____.

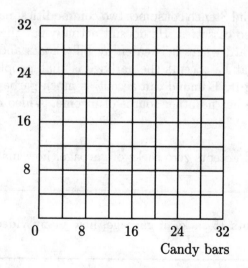

Comic books

Candy bars

2.6 (0) In a small country near the Baltic Sea, there are only three commodities: potatoes, meatballs, and jam. Prices have been remarkably stable for the last 50 years or so. Potatoes cost 2 crowns per sack, meatballs cost 4 crowns per crock, and jam costs 6 crowns per jar.

(a) Write down a budget equation for a citizen named Gunnar who has an income of 360 crowns per year. Let P stand for the number of sacks of potatoes, M for the number of crocks of meatballs, and J for the number of jars of jam consumed by Gunnar in a year._____.

(b) The citizens of this country are in general very clever people, but they are not good at multiplying by 2. This made shopping for potatoes excruciatingly difficult for many citizens. Therefore it was decided to introduce a new unit of currency, such that potatoes would be the *numeraire*. A sack of potatoes costs one unit of the new currency while the same relative prices apply as in the past.

(c) In terms of the new currency, what is the price of meatballs?_____.

(d) In terms of the new currency, what is the price of jam?_____.

(e) What would Gunnar's income in the new currency have to be for him to be exactly able to afford the same commodity bundles that he could afford before the change?_____.

(f) Write down Gunnar's new budget equation._____ Is Gunnar's budget set any different than it was before the change?_____

2.7 (0) Edmund Stench consumes two commodities, namely garbage and punk rock video cassettes. He doesn't actually eat the former but keeps it in his backyard where it is eaten by billy goats and assorted vermin. The reason that he accepts the garbage is that people pay him $2 per sack for taking it. Edmund can accept as much garbage as he wishes at that price. He has no other source of income. Video cassettes cost him $6 each.

(a) If Edmund accepts zero sacks of garbage, how many video cassettes can he buy?_____.

(b) If he accepts 15 sacks of garbage, how many video cassettes can he buy?_____.

(c) Write down an equation for his budget line._____.

(d) Draw Edmund's budget line and shade in his budget set.

Garbage

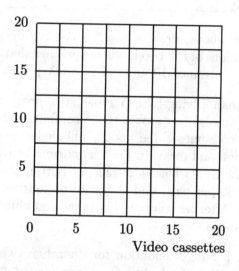

Video cassettes

2.8 (0) If you think Edmund is odd, consider his brother Emmett. Emmett consumes speeches by politicians and university administrators. He is paid $1 per hour for listening to politicians and $2 per hour for listening to university administrators. (Emmett is in great demand to help fill empty chairs in public lectures because of his distinguished appearance and his ability to refrain from making rude noises.) Emmett consumes one good for which he must pay. We have agreed not to disclose what that good is, but we can tell you that it costs $15 per unit and we shall call it Good X. In addition to what he is paid for consuming speeches, Emmett receives a pension of $50 per week.

Administrator speeches

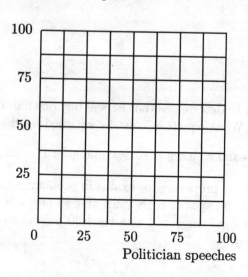

Politician speeches

(a) Write down a budget equation stating those combinations of the three commodities, Good X, hours of speeches by politicians (P), and hours of speeches by university administrators (A) that Emmett could afford to

consume per week._____.

(b) On the graph above, draw a two-dimensional diagram showing the locus of consumptions of the two kinds of speeches that would be possible for Emmett if he consumed 10 units of Good X per week.

2.9 (0) Jonathan Livingstone Yuppie is a prosperous lawyer. He has, in his own words, "outgrown those confining two-commodity limits." Jonathan consumes three goods, unblended Scotch whiskey, designer tennis shoes, and meals in French gourmet restaurants. The price of Jonathan's brand of whiskey is $20 per bottle, the price of designer tennis shoes is $80 per pair, and the price of gourmet restaurant meals is $50 per meal. After he has paid his taxes and alimony, Jonathan has $400 a week to spend.

(a) Write down a budget equation for Jonathan, where W stands for the number of bottles of whiskey, T stands for the number of pairs of tennis shoes, and M for the number of gourmet restaurant meals that he

consumes._____.

(b) Draw a three-dimensional diagram to show his budget set. Label the intersections of the budget set with each axis.

(c) Suppose that he determines that he will buy one pair of designer tennis shoes per week. What equation must be satisfied by the combinations of

restaurant meals and whiskey that he could afford?_____.

2.10 (0) Martha is preparing for exams in economics and sociology. She has time to read 40 pages of economics and 30 pages of sociology. In the same amount of time she could also read 30 pages of economics and 60 pages of sociology.

(a) Assuming that the number of pages per hour that she can read of either subject does not depend on how she allocates her time, how many pages of sociology could she read if she decided to spend all of her time on sociology and none on economics? _____ (Hint: You have two points on her budget line, so you should be able to determine the entire line.)

(b) How many pages of economics could she read if she decided to spend all of her time reading economics?_____.

2.11 (1) Harry Hype has $5,000 to spend on advertising a new kind of dehydrated sushi. Market research shows that the people most likely to buy this new product are recent recipients of M.B.A. degrees and lawyers who own hot tubs. Harry is considering advertising in two publications, a boring business magazine and a trendy consumer publication for people who wish they lived in California.

Fact 1: Ads in the boring business magazine cost $500 each and ads in the consumer magazine cost $250 each.

Fact 2: Each ad in the business magazine will be read by 1,000 recent M.B.A.'s and 300 lawyers with hot tubs.

Fact 3: Each ad in the consumer publication will be read by 300 recent M.B.A.'s and 250 lawyers who own hot tubs.

Fact 4: Nobody reads more than one ad, and nobody who reads one magazine reads the other.

(a) If Harry spends his entire advertising budget on the business publication, his ad will be read by _____ recent M.B.A.'s and by _____ lawyers with hot tubs.

(b) If he spends his entire advertising budget on the consumer publication, his ad will be read by _____ recent M.B.A.'s and by _____ lawyers with hot tubs.

(c) Suppose he spent half of his advertising budget on each publication. His ad would be read by _____ recent M.B.A.'s and by _____ lawyers with hot tubs.

(d) Draw a "budget line" showing the combinations of number of readings by recent M.B.A.'s and by lawyers with hot tubs that he can obtain if he spends his entire advertising budget. Does this line extend all the way to the axes?_____ Sketch, shade in, and label the budget set, which includes all the combinations of MBA's and lawyers he can reach if he spends *no more than* his budget.

(e) Let M stand for the number of instances of an ad being read by an M.B.A. and L stand for the number of instances of an ad being read by a lawyer. This budget line is a line segment that lies on the line with equation _____ With a fixed advertising budget, how many readings by M.B.A.'s must he sacrifice to get an additional reading by a lawyer with a hot tub?_____.

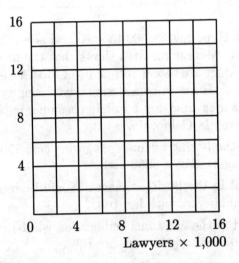

M.B.A.'s × 1,000

Lawyers × 1,000

2.12 (0) On the planet Mungo, they have two kinds of money, blue money and red money. Every commodity has two prices—a red-money price and a blue-money price. Every Mungoan has two incomes—a red income and a blue income.

In order to buy an object, a Mungoan has to pay that object's red-money price in red money and its blue-money price in blue money. (The shops simply have two cash registers, and you have to pay at both registers to buy an object.) It is forbidden to trade one kind of money for the other, and this prohibition is strictly enforced by Mungo's ruthless and efficient monetary police.

- There are just two consumer goods on Mungo, ambrosia and bubble gum. All Mungoans prefer more of each good to less.
- The blue prices are 1 bcu (bcu stands for blue currency unit) per unit of ambrosia and 1 bcu per unit of bubble gum.
- The red prices are 2 rcus (red currency units) per unit of ambrosia and 6 rcus per unit of bubble gum.

(a) On the graph below, draw the red budget (with red ink) and the blue budget (with blue ink) for a Mungoan named Harold whose blue income is 10 and whose red income is 30. Shade in the "budget set" containing all of the commodity bundles that Harold can afford, given its* two budget constraints. Remember, Harold has to have enough blue money *and* enough red money to pay both the blue-money cost and the red-money cost of a bundle of goods.

Bubble gum

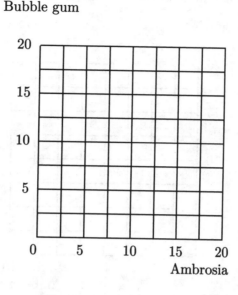

Ambrosia

(b) Another Mungoan, Gladys, faces the same prices that Harold faces and has the same red income as Harold, but Gladys has a blue income of 20. Explain how it is that Gladys will not spend its entire blue income no matter what its tastes may be. (Hint: Draw Gladys's budget lines.)

_____

_____.

(c) A group of radical economic reformers on Mungo believe that the currency rules are unfair. "Why should everyone have to pay two prices for everything?" they ask. They propose the following scheme. Mungo will continue to have two currencies, every good will have a blue price and a red price, and every Mungoan will have a blue income and a red income. But nobody has to pay both prices. Instead, everyone on Mungo must declare itself to be either a Blue-Money Purchaser (a "Blue") or a Red-Money Purchaser (a "Red") before it buys anything at all. Blues must make all of their purchases in blue money at the blue prices, spending only their blue incomes. Reds must make all of their purchases in red money, spending only their red incomes.

Suppose that Harold has the same income after this reform, and that prices do not change. Before declaring which kind of purchaser it will be, Harold contemplates the set of commodity bundles that it could afford by making one declaration or the other. Let us call a commodity bundle

_____

* We refer to all Mungoans by the gender-neutral pronoun, "it." Although Mungo has two sexes, neither of them is remotely like either of ours.

"attainable" if Harold can afford it by declaring itself to be a "Blue" and buying the bundle with blue money or if Harold can afford the bundle by declaring itself to be a "Red" and buying it with red money. On the diagram below, shade in all of the attainable bundles.

Bubble gum

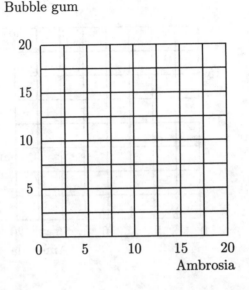

Ambrosia

2.13 (0) Are Mungoan budgets really so fanciful? Can you think of situations on earth where people must simultaneously satisfy more than one budget constraint? Is money the only scarce resource that people use up when consuming?_____

_____

_____

_____.

Preferences

Introduction. In the previous section you learned how to use graphs to show the set of commodity bundles that a consumer can afford. In this section, you learn to put information about the consumer's preferences on the same kind of graph. Most of the problems ask you to draw indifference curves.

Sometimes we give you a formula for the indifference curve. Then all you have to do is graph a known equation. But in some problems, we give you only "qualitative" information about the consumer's preferences and ask you to sketch indifference curves that are consistent with this information. This requires a little more thought. Don't be surprised or disappointed if you cannot immediately see the answer when you look at a problem, and don't expect that you will find the answers hiding somewhere in your textbook. The best way we know to find answers is to "think and doodle." Draw some axes on scratch paper and label them, then mark a point on your graph and ask yourself, "what other points on the graph would the consumer find indifferent to this point?" If possible, draw a curve connecting such points, making sure that the shape of the line you have drawn reflects the features required by the problem. This gives you one indifference curve. Now pick another point that is preferred to the first one you drew and draw an indifference curve through it.

Example: Jocasta loves to dance and hates housecleaning. She has strictly convex preferences. She prefers dancing to any other activity and never gets tired of dancing, but the more time she spends cleaning house, the less happy she is. Let us try to draw an indifference curve that is consistent with her preferences. There is not enough information here to tell us exactly where her indifference curves go, but there is enough information to determine some things about their shape. Take a piece of scratch paper and draw a pair of axes. Label the horizontal axis "Hours per day of housecleaning." Label the vertical axis "Hours per day of dancing." Mark a point a little ways up the vertical axis and write a 4 next to it. At this point, she spends 4 hours a day dancing and no time housecleaning. Other points that would be indifferent to this point would have to be points where she did more dancing *and* more housecleaning. The pain of the extra housekeeping should just compensate for the pleasure of the extra dancing. So an indifference curve for Jocasta must be upward sloping. Because she loves dancing and hates housecleaning, it must be that she prefers all the points above this indifference curve to all of the points on or below it. If Jocasta has strictly convex preferences, then it must be that if you draw a line between any two points on the same indifference curve, all the points on the line (except the endpoints) are preferred to the endpoints. For this to be the case, it must be that the indifference curve slopes upward ever more steeply as you move to the right along it.

You should convince yourself of this by making some drawings on scratch paper. Draw an upward-sloping curve passing through the point $(0,4)$ and getting steeper as one moves to the right.

When you have completed this workout, we hope that you will be able to do the following

- Given the formula for an indifference curve, draw this curve, and find its slope at any point on the curve.

- Determine whether a consumer prefers one bundle to another or is indifferent between them, given specific indifference curves.

- Draw indifference curves for the special cases of perfect substitutes and perfect complements.

- Draw indifference curves for someone who dislikes one or both commodities.

- Draw indifference curves for someone who likes goods up to a point but who can get "too much" of one or more goods.

- Identify weakly preferred sets and determine whether these are convex sets and whether preferences are convex.

- Know what the marginal rate of substitution is and be able to determine whether an indifference curve exhibits "diminishing marginal rate of substitution."

- Determine whether a preference relation or any other relation between pairs of things is transitive, whether it is reflexive, and whether it is complete.

3.1 (0) Charlie likes both apples and bananas. He consumes nothing else. The consumption bundle where Charlie consumes x_A bushels of apples per year and x_B bushels of bananas per year is written as (x_A, x_B). Last year, Charlie consumed 20 bushels of apples and 5 bushels of bananas. It happens that the set of consumption bundles (x_A, x_B) such that Charlie is indifferent between (x_A, x_B) and $(20, 5)$ is the set of all bundles such that $x_B = 100/x_A$. The set of bundles (x_A, x_B) such that Charlie is just indifferent between (x_A, x_B) and the bundle $(10, 15)$ is the set of bundles such that $x_B = 150/x_A$.

(a) On the graph below, plot several points that lie on the indifference curve that passes through the point $(20, 5)$, and sketch this curve, using blue ink. Do the same, using red ink, for the indifference curve passing through the point $(10, 15)$.

(b) Use pencil to shade in the set of commodity bundles that Charlie weakly prefers to the bundle $(10, 15)$. Use blue ink to shade in the set of commodity bundles such that Charlie weakly prefers $(20, 5)$ to these bundles.

Bananas

Apples

For each of the following statements about Charlie's preferences, write "true" or "false."

(c) $(30,5) \sim (10,15)$._____.

(d) $(10,15) \succ (20,5)$._____.

(e) $(20,5) \succeq (10,10)$._____.

(f) $(24,4) \succeq (11,9.1)$._____.

(g) $(11,14) \succ (2,49)$._____.

(h) A set is convex if for any two points in the set, the line segment between them is also in the set. Is the set of bundles that Charlie weakly prefers to $(20,5)$ a convex set?_____.

(i) Is the set of bundles that Charlie considers inferior to $(20,5)$ a convex set?_____.

(j) The slope of Charlie's indifference curve through a point, (x_A, x_B), is known as his marginal _____ of _____ at that point.

(k) Remember that Charlie's indifference curve through the point $(10, 10)$ has the equation $x_B = 100/x_A$. Those of you who know calculus will remember that the slope of a curve is just its derivative, which in this case is $-100/x_A^2$. (If you don't know calculus, you will have to take our word for this.) Find Charlie's marginal rate of substitution at the point,

$(10, 10)$._____.

(l) What is his marginal rate of substitution at the point $(5, 20)$?_____

_____.

(m) What is his marginal rate of substitution at the point $(20, 5)$?_____

_____.

(n) Do the indifference curves you have drawn for Charlie exhibit diminishing marginal rate of substitution?_____.

3.2 (0) Ambrose consumes only nuts and berries. Fortunately, he likes both goods. The consumption bundle where Ambrose consumes x_1 units of nuts per week and x_2 units of berries per week is written as (x_1, x_2). The set of consumption bundles (x_1, x_2) such that Ambrose is indifferent between (x_1, x_2) and $(1, 16)$ is the set of bundles such that $x_1 \geq 0$, $x_2 \geq 0$, and $x_2 = 20 - 4\sqrt{x_1}$. The set of bundles (x_1, x_2) such that $(x_1, x_2) \sim (36, 0)$ is the set of bundles such that $x_1 \geq 0$, $x_2 \geq 0$ and $x_2 = 24 - 4\sqrt{x_1}$.

(a) On the graph below, plot several points that lie on the indifference curve that passes through the point $(1, 16)$, and sketch this curve, using blue ink. Do the same, using red ink, for the indifference curve passing through the point $(36, 0)$.

(b) Use pencil to shade in the set of commodity bundles that Ambrose weakly prefers to the bundle $(1, 16)$. Use red ink to shade in the set of all commodity bundles (x_1, x_2) such that Ambrose weakly prefers $(36, 0)$ to these bundles. Is the set of bundles that Ambrose prefers to $(1, 16)$ a

convex set?_____.

(c) What is the slope of Ambrose's indifference curve at the point $(9, 8)$? (Hint: Recall from calculus the way to calculate the slope of a curve. If you don't know calculus, you will have to draw your diagram carefully

and estimate the slope.)_____.

(d) What is the slope of his indifference curve at the point $(4, 12)$?_____

_____.

Berries

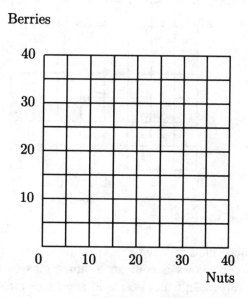

Nuts

(e) What is the slope of his indifference curve at the point $(9, 12)$?_____

_____ at the point $(4, 16)$?_____.

(f) Do the indifference curves you have drawn for Ambrose exhibit diminishing marginal rate of substitution?_____.

(g) Does Ambrose have convex preferences?_____.

3.3 (0) Shirley Sixpack is in the habit of drinking beer each evening while watching "The Best of Bowlerama" on TV. She has a strong thumb and a big refrigerator, so she doesn't care about the size of the cans that beer comes in, she only cares about how much beer she has.

(a) On the graph below, draw some of Shirley's indifference curves between 16-ounce cans and 8-ounce cans of beer. Use blue ink to draw these indifference curves.

8-ounce cans

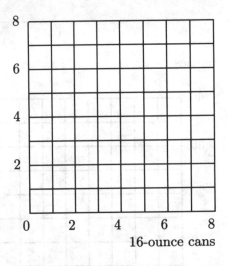

16-ounce cans

(b) Lorraine Quiche likes to have a beer while she watches "Masterpiece Theatre." She only allows herself an 8-ounce glass of beer at any one time. Since her cat doesn't like beer and she hates stale beer, if there is more than 8 ounces in the can she pours the excess into the sink. (She has no moral scruples about wasting beer.) On the graph above, use red ink to draw some of Lorraine's indifference curves.

3.4 (0) Elmo finds himself at a Coke machine on a hot and dusty Sunday. The Coke machine requires exact change—two quarters and a dime. No other combination of coins will make anything come out of the machine. No stores are open, no one is in sight. Elmo is so thirsty that the only thing he cares about is how many soft drinks he will be able to buy with the change in his pocket, the more he can buy, the better. While Elmo searches his pockets, your task is to draw some indifference curves that describe Elmo's preferences about what he finds.

Dimes

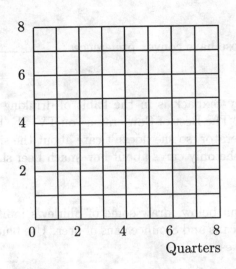

Quarters

(a) If Elmo has 2 quarters and a dime in his pockets, he can buy 1 soft drink. How many soft drinks can he buy if he has 4 quarters and 2 dimes?

_____.

(b) Use red ink to shade in the area on the graph consisting of all combinations of quarters and dimes that Elmo thinks are just indifferent to having 2 quarters and 1 dime. (Imagine that it is possible for Elmo to have fractions of quarters or of dimes, but, of course, they would be useless in the machine.) Now use blue ink to shade in the area consisting of all combinations that Elmo thinks are just indifferent to having 4 quarters and 2 dimes. Notice that Elmo has indifference "bands," not indifference curves.

(c) Does Elmo have convex preferences between dimes and quarters?

_____.

(d) Does Elmo always prefer more of both kinds of money to less?_____

(e) Does Elmo have a bliss point?_____.

(f) If Elmo had arrived at the Coke machine on a Saturday, the drugstore across the street would have been open. This drugstore has a soda fountain that will sell you as much Coke as you want at a price of 4 cents an ounce. The salesperson will take any combination of dimes and quarters in payment. Suppose that Elmo plans to spend all of the money in his pocket on Coke at the drugstore on Saturday. On the graph above, use pencil or black ink to draw one or two of Elmo's indifference curves between quarters and dimes in his pocket. (For simplicity, draw your graph as if Elmo's fractional quarters and fractional dimes are accepted at the corresponding fraction of their value.) Describe these new indifference

curves in words._____.

3.5 (0) Randy Ratpack hates studying both economics and history. The more time he spends studying either subject, the less happy he is. But Randy has strictly convex preferences.

(a) Sketch an indifference curve for Randy where the two commodities are hours per week spent studying economics and hours per week spent studying history. Will the slope of an indifference curve be positive or

negative?_____.

(b) Do Randy's indifference curves get steeper or flatter as you move from

left to right along one of them?_____.

Hours studying history

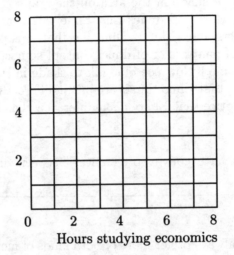

Hours studying economics

3.6 (0) Flossy Toothsome likes to spend some time studying and some time dating. In fact her indifference curves between hours per week spent studying and hours per week spent dating are concentric circles around her favorite combination, which is 20 hours of studying and 15 hours of dating per week. The closer she is to her favorite combination, the happier she is.

(a) Suppose that Flossy is currently studying 25 hours a week and dating 3 hours a week. Would she prefer to be studying 30 hours a week and

dating 8 hours a week? _____ (Hint: Remember the formula for the distance between two points in the plane?)

(b) On the axes below, draw a few of Flossy's indifference curves and use your diagram to illustrate which of the two time allocations discussed above Flossy would prefer.

Hours dating

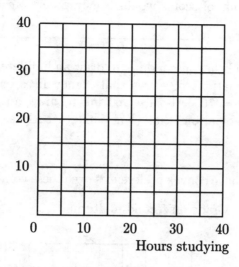

Hours studying

3.7 (0) Joan likes chocolate cake and ice cream, but after 10 slices of cake, she gets tired of cake, and eating more cake makes her less happy. Joan always prefers more ice cream to less. Joan's parents require her to eat everything put on her plate. In the axes below, use blue ink to draw a set of indifference curves that depict her preferences between plates with different amounts of cake and ice cream. Be sure to label the axes.

(a) Suppose that Joan's preferences are as before, but that her parents allow her to leave anything on her plate that she doesn't want. On the graph below, use red ink to draw some indifference curves depicting her preferences between plates with different amounts of cake and ice cream.

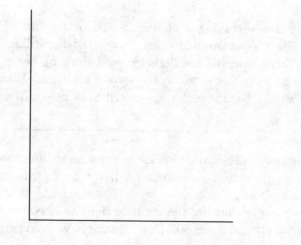

3.8 (0) Professor Goodheart always gives two midterms in his communications class. He only uses the higher of the two scores that a student gets on the midterms when he calculates the course grade.

(a) Nancy Lerner wants to maximize her grade in this course. Let x_1 be her score on the first midterm and x_2 be her score on the second midterm. Which combination of scores would Nancy prefer, $x_1 = 20$ and $x_2 = 70$

or $x_1 = 60$ and $x_2 = 50$?_____.

(b) On the graph below, use red ink to draw an indifference curve showing all of the combinations of scores that Nancy likes exactly as much as $x_1 = 20$ and $x_2 = 70$. Also use red ink to draw an indifference curve showing the combinations that Nancy likes exactly as much as $x_1 = 60$ and $x_2 = 60$.

(c) Does Nancy have convex preferences over these combinations?_____.

Grade on second midterm

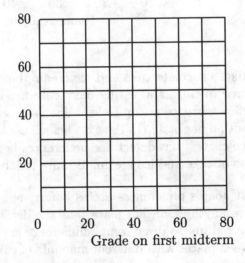

Grade on first midterm

(d) Nancy is also taking a course in economics from Professor Stern. Professor Stern gives two midterms. Instead of discarding the lower grade, Professor Stern discards the higher one. Let x_1 be her score on the first midterm and x_2 be her score on the second midterm. Which combination of scores would Nancy prefer, $x_1 = 20$ and $x_2 = 70$ or $x_1 = 60$ and

$x_2 = 50$?_____.

(e) On the graph above, use blue ink to draw an indifference curve showing all of the combinations of scores on her econ exams that Nancy likes exactly as well as $x_1 = 20$ and $x_2 = 70$. Also use blue ink to draw an indifference curve showing the combinations that Nancy likes exactly as well as $x_1 = 60$ and $x_2 = 50$. Does Nancy have convex preferences over

these combinations?_____.

3.9 (0) Mary Granola loves to consume two goods, grapefruits and avocados.

(a) On the graph below, the slope of an indifference curve through any point where she has more grapefruits than avocados is −2. This means that when she has more grapefruits than avocados, she is willing to give

up _____ grapefruit(s) to get one avocado.

(b) On the same graph, the slope of an indifference curve at points where she has fewer grapefruits than avocados is −1/2. This means that when she has fewer grapefruits than avocados, she is just willing to give up

_____ grapefruit(s) to get one avocado.

(c) On this graph, draw an indifference curve for Mary through bundle $(10A, 10G)$. Draw another indifference curve through $(20A, 20G)$.

Grapefruits

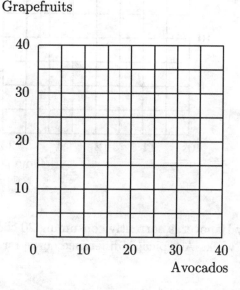

Avocados

(d) Does Mary have convex preferences?_____.

3.10 (2) Ralph Rigid likes to eat lunch at 12 noon. However, he also likes to save money so he can buy other consumption goods by attending the "early bird specials" and "late lunchers" promoted by his local diner. Ralph has 15 dollars a day to spend on lunch and other stuff. Lunch at noon costs \$5. If he delays his lunch until t hours after noon, he is able to buy his lunch for a price of $\$5 - t$. Similarly if he eats his lunch t hours before noon, he can buy it for a price of $\$5 - t$. (This is true for fractions of hours as well as integer numbers of hours.)

(a) If Ralph eats lunch at noon, how much money does he have per day to spend on other stuff?_____.

(b) How much money per day would he have left for other stuff if he ate at 2 P.M.?_____.

(c) On the graph below, use blue ink to draw the broken line that shows combinations of meal time and money for other stuff that Ralph can just afford. On this same graph, draw some indifference curves that would be consistent with Ralph choosing to eat his lunch at 11 A.M.

Money

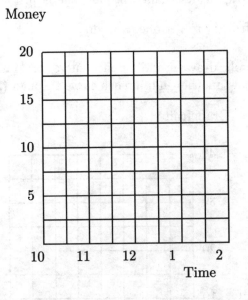

Time

3.11 (0) Henry Hanover is currently consuming 20 cheeseburgers and 20 Cherry Cokes a week. A typical indifference curve for Henry is depicted below.

Cherry Coke

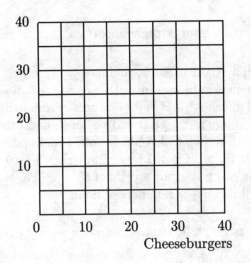

Cheeseburgers

(d) If someone offered to trade Henry one extra cheeseburger for every Coke he gave up, would Henry want to do this?_____.

(e) What if it were the other way around: for every cheeseburger Henry gave up, he would get an extra Coke. Would he accept this offer?_____

_____.

(f) At what rate of exchange would Henry be willing to stay put at his current consumption level?_____.

3.12 (1) Tommy Twit is happiest when he has 8 cookies and 4 glasses of milk per day. Whenever he has more than his favorite amount of either food, giving him still more makes him worse off. Whenever he has less than his favorite amount of either food, giving him more makes him better off. His mother makes him drink 7 glasses of milk and only allows him 2 cookies per day. One day when his mother was gone, Tommy's sadistic sister made him eat 13 cookies and only gave him 1 glass of milk, despite the fact that Tommy complained bitterly about the last 5 cookies that she made him eat and begged for more milk. Although Tommy complained later to his mother, he had to admit that he liked the diet that his sister forced on him better than what his mother demanded.

(a) Use black ink to draw some indifference curves for Tommy that are consistent with this story.

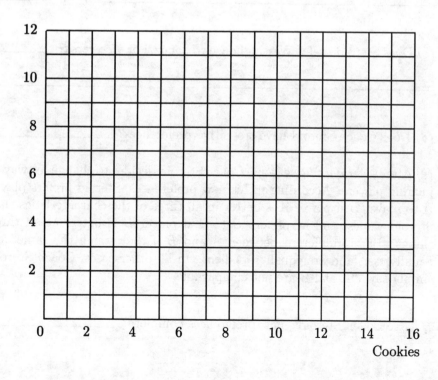

Milk

Cookies

(b) Tommy's mother believes that the optimal amount for him to consume is 7 glasses of milk and 2 cookies. She measures deviations by absolute values. If Tommy consumes some other bundle, say, (c, m), she measures his departure from the optimal bundle by $D = |7 - m| + |2 - c|$. The larger D is, the worse off she thinks Tommy is. Use blue ink in the graph above to sketch a few of Mrs. Twit's indifference curves for Tommy's consumption. (Hint: Before you try to draw Mrs. Twit's indifference curves, we suggest that you take a piece of scrap paper and draw a graph of the locus of points (x_1, x_2) such that $|x_1| + |x_2| = 1$.)

3.13 (0) Coach Steroid likes his players to be big, fast, and obedient. If player A is better than player B in two of these three characteristics, then Coach Steroid prefers A to B, but if B is better than A in two of these three characteristics, then Steroid prefers B to A. Otherwise, Steroid is indifferent between them. Wilbur Westinghouse weighs 340 pounds, runs very slowly, and is fairly obedient. Harold Hotpoint weighs 240 pounds, runs very fast, and is very disobedient. Jerry Jacuzzi weighs 150 pounds, runs at average speed, and is extremely obedient.

(a) Does Steroid prefer Westinghouse to Hotpoint or vice versa?_____

_____.

(b) Does Steroid prefer Hotpoint to Jacuzzi or vice versa?_____

_____.

(c) Does Steroid prefer Westinghouse to Jacuzzi or vice versa?_____

_____.

(d) Does Coach Steroid have transitive preferences?_____.

(e) After several losing seasons, Coach Steroid decides to change his way of judging players. According to his new preferences, Steroid prefers player A to player B if player A is better in all three of the characteristics that Steroid values, and he prefers B to A if player B is better at all three things. He is indifferent between A and B if they weigh the same, are equally fast, and are equally obedient. In all other cases, Coach Steroid simply says "A and B are not comparable."

(f) Are Coach Steroid's new preferences complete?_____.

(g) Are Coach Steroid's new preferences transitive?_____.

(h) Are Coach Steroid's new preferences reflexive?_____.

3.14 (0) The Bear family is trying to decide what to have for dinner. Baby Bear says that his ranking of the possibilities is (honey, grubs, Goldilocks). Mama Bear ranks the choices (grubs, Goldilocks, honey), while Papa Bear's ranking is: (Goldilocks, honey, grubs). They decide to take each pair of alternatives and let a majority vote determine the family rankings.

(a) Papa suggests that they first consider honey vs. grubs, and then the winner of that contest vs. Goldilocks. Which alternative will be chosen?

_____.

(b) Mama suggests instead that they consider honey vs. Goldilocks and then the winner vs. grubs. Which gets chosen?_____.

(c) What order should Baby Bear suggest if he wants to get his favorite food for dinner?_____.

(d) Are the Bear family's "collective preferences," as determined by voting, transitive?_____.

3.15 (0) Olson likes strong coffee, the stronger the better. But he can't distinguish small differences. Over the years, Mrs. Olson has discovered that if she changes the amount of coffee by more than one teaspoon in her six-cup pot, Olson can tell that she did it. But he cannot distinguish differences smaller than one teaspoon per pot. Where A and B are two different cups of coffee, let us write $A \succ B$ if Olson prefers cup A to cup B. Let us write $A \succeq B$ if Olson either prefers A to B, or can't tell the difference between them. Let us write $A \sim B$ if Olson can't tell the difference between cups A and B. Suppose that Olson is offered cups A, B, and C all brewed in the Olsons' six-cup pot. Cup A was brewed using 14 teaspoons of coffee in the pot. Cup B was brewed using 14.75 teaspoons of coffee in the pot and cup C was brewed using 15.5 teaspoons of coffee in the pot. For each of the following expressions determine whether it is true of false.

(a) $A \sim B$._____.

(b) $B \sim A$._____.

(c) $B \sim C$. _____.

(d) $A \sim C$. _____.

(e) $C \sim A$. _____.

(f) $A \succeq B$. _____.

(g) $B \succeq A$. _____.

(h) $B \succeq C$. _____.

(i) $A \succeq C$. _____.

(j) $C \succeq A$. _____.

(k) $A \succ B$. _____.

(l) $B \succ A$. _____.

(m) $B \succ C$. _____.

(n) $A \succ C$. _____.

(o) $C \succ A$. _____.

(p) Is Olson's "at-least-as-good-as" relation, $\succeq$, transitive?_____.

(q) Is Olson's "can't-tell-the difference" relation, $\sim$, transitive?_____.

(r) is Olson's "better-than" relation, $\succ$, transitive._____.

Utility

Introduction. In the previous chapter, you learned about preferences and indifference curves. Here we study another way of describing preferences, the *utility function*. A utility function that represents a person's preferences is a function that assigns a utility number to each commodity bundle. The numbers are assigned in such a way that commodity bundle (x, y) gets a higher utility number than bundle (x', y'), if and only if the consumer prefers (x, y) to (x', y'). If a consumer has the utility function $U(x_1, x_2)$, then she will be indifferent between two bundles if they are assigned the same utility.

If you know a consumer's utility function, then you can find the indifference curve passing through any commodity bundle. Recall from the previous chapter that when good 1 is graphed on the horizontal axis and good 2 on the vertical axis, the slope of the indifference curve passing through a point (x_1, x_2) is known as the *marginal rate of substitution*. An important and convenient fact is that *the slope of an indifference curve is minus the ratio of the marginal utility of good 1 to the marginal utility of good 2*. For those of you who know even a tiny bit of calculus, calculating marginal utilities is easy. To find the marginal utility of either good, you just take the derivative of utility with respect to the amount of that good, treating the amount of the other good as a constant. (If you don't know any calculus at all, you can calculate an approximation to marginal utility by the method described in your textbook. Also, at the beginning of this section of the workbook, we list the marginal utility functions for commonly encountered utility functions. Even if you can't compute these yourself, you can refer to this list when later problems require you to use marginal utilities.)

Example: Arthur's utility function is $U(x_1, x_2) = x_1 x_2$. Let us find the indifference curve for Arthur that passes through the point $(3, 4)$. First, calculate $U(3, 4) = 3 \times 4 = 12$. The indifference curve through this point consists of all (x_1, x_2) such that $x_1 x_2 = 12$. This last equation is equivalent to $x_2 = 12/x_1$. Therefore to draw Arthur's indifference curve through $(3, 4)$, just draw the curve with equation $x_2 = 12/x_1$. At the point (x_1, x_2), the marginal utility of good 1 is x_2 and the marginal utility of good 2 is x_1. Therefore Arthur's marginal rate of substitution at the point $(3, 4)$ is $-x_2/x_1 = -4/3$.

Example: Arthur's uncle, Basil, has the utility function $U^*(x_1, x_2) = 3x_1 x_2 - 10$. Notice that $U^*(x_1, x_2) = 3U(x_1, x_2) - 10$, where $U(x_1, x_2)$ is Arthur's utility function. Since U^* is a positive multiple of U minus a constant, it must be that any change in consumption that increases U will also increase U^* (and vice versa). Therefore we say that Basil's utility function is a *monotonic increasing transformation* of Arthur's utility function. Let us find Basil's indifference curve through the point $(3, 4)$. First we find that $U^*(3, 4) = 3 \times 3 \times 4 - 10 = 26$. The indifference curve passing through this point consists of all (x_1, x_2) such that $3x_1x_2 - 10 = 26$. Simplify this last expression by adding 10 to both sides of the equation and dividing both sides by 3. You find $x_1x_2 = 12$, or equivalently, $x_2 = 12/x_1$. This is exactly the same curve as Arthur's indifference curve through $(3, 4)$. We could have known in advance that this would happen, because if two consumers' utility functions are monotonic increasing transformations of each other, then these consumers must have the same preference relation between any pair of commodity bundles.

When you have finished this workout, we hope that you will be able to do the following

- Draw an indifference curve through a specified commodity bundle when you know the utility function.

- Calculate marginal utilities and marginal rates of substitution when you know the utility function.

- Determine whether one utility function is just a "monotonic transformation" of another and know what that implies about preferences.

- Find utility functions that represent preferences when goods are perfect substitutes and when goods are perfect complements.

- Recognize utility functions for commonly studied preferences such as perfect substitutes, perfect complements, and other kinked indifference curves, quasilinear utility, and Cobb-Douglas utility.

4.0 Warm Up Exercise. This is the first of several "warm up exercises" that you will find in *Workouts*. These are here to help you see how to do calculations that are needed in later problems. The answers to *all* warm up exercises are in your answer pages. If you find the warm up exercises easy and boring, go ahead—skip them and get on to the main problems. You can come back and look at them if you get stuck later.

This exercise asks you to calculate marginal utilities and marginal rates of substitution for some common utility functions. These utility functions will reappear in several chapters, so it is a good idea to get to know them now. If you know calculus, you will find this to be a breeze. Even if your calculus is shaky or nonexistent, you can handle the first three utility functions just by using the definitions in the textbook. These three are easy because the utility functions are linear. If you do not know any calculus, fill in the rest of the answers from the back of the workbook and keep a copy of this exercise for reference when you encounter these utility functions in later problems.

$u(x_1, x_2)$	$MU_1(x_1,x_2)$	$MU_2(x_1,x_2)$	$MRS(x_1,x_2)$
$2x_1 + 3x_2$			
$4x_1 + 6x_2$			
$ax_1 + bx_2$			
$2\sqrt{x_1} + x_2$			
$\ln x_1 + x_2$			
$v(x_1) + x_2$			
$x_1 x_2$			
$x_1^a x_2^b$			
$(x_1 + 2)(x_2 + 1)$			
$(x_1 + a)(x_2 + b)$			
$x_1^a + x_2^a$			

4.1 (0) Remember Charlie from Chapter 3? Charlie consumes apples and bananas. We had a look at two of his indifference curves. In this problem we give you enough information so you can find *all* of Charlie's indifference curves. We do this by telling you that Charlie's utility function happens to be $U(x_A, x_B) = x_A x_B$.

(a) Charlie has 40 apples and 5 bananas. Charlie's utility for the bundle $(40, 5)$ is $U(40, 5) =$_____ The indifference curve through $(40, 5)$ includes all commodity bundles (x_A, x_B) such that $x_A x_B =$_____

So the indifference curve through $(40, 5)$ has the equation $x_B =$_____

_____ On the graph below, draw the indifference curve showing all of the bundles that Charlie likes exactly as well as the bundle $(40, 5)$.

Bananas

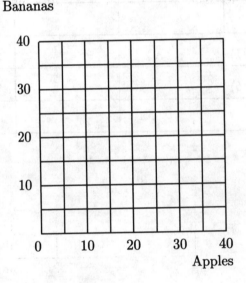

Apples

(b) Donna offers to give Charlie 15 bananas if he will give her 25 apples. Would Charlie have a bundle that he likes better than $(40, 5)$ if he makes this trade?_____ What is the largest number of apples that Donna could demand from Charlie in return for 15 bananas if she expects him to be willing to trade or at least indifferent about trading?_____ (Hint: If Donna gives Charlie 15 bananas, he will have a total of 20 bananas. If he has 20 bananas, how many apples does he need in order to be as well-off as he would be without trade?)

4.2 (0) Ambrose, whom you met in the last chapter, continues to thrive on nuts and berries. You saw two of his indifference curves. One indifference curve had the equation $x_2 = 20 - 4\sqrt{x_1}$, and another indifference curve had the equation $x_2 = 24 - 4\sqrt{x_1}$, where x_1 is his consumption of nuts and x_2 is his consumption of berries. Now it can be told that Ambrose has quasilinear utility. In fact, his preferences can be represented by the utility function: $U(x_1, x_2) = 4\sqrt{x_1} + x_2$.

(a) Ambrose originally consumed 9 units of nuts and 10 units of berries. His consumption of nuts is reduced to 4 units, but he is given enough berries so that he is just as well-off as he was before. After the change,

how many units of berries does Ambrose consume?_____.

(b) On the graph below, indicate Ambrose's original consumption and sketch an indifference curve passing through this point. As you can verify, Ambrose is indifferent between the bundle (9,10) and the bundle (25,2). If you doubled the amount of each good in each bundle, you would have bundles (18,20) and (50,4). Are these two bundles on the same indifference

curve as each other?_____   (Hint: How do you check whether two bundles are indifferent when you know the utility function?)

Berries

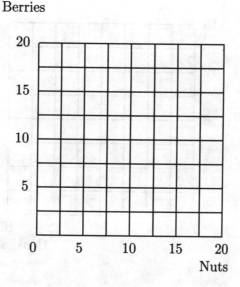

Nuts

(c) What is Ambrose's marginal rate of substitution, $MRS(x_1, x_2)$, when

he is consuming the bundle $(9, 10)$? (Give a numerical answer.)_____
What is Ambrose's marginal rate of substitution when he is consuming

the bundle $(9, 20)$?_____.

(d) We can write a general expression for Ambrose's marginal rate of substitution when he is consuming commodity bundle (x_1, x_2). This is

$MRS(x_1, x_2) =$_____   Although we always write $MRS(x_1, x_2)$ as a function of the two variables, x_1 and x_2, we see that Ambrose's utility function has the special property that his marginal rate of substitution

does not change when the variable _____ changes.

4.3 (0) Burt's utility function is $U(x_1, x_2) = (x_1 + 2)(x_2 + 6)$, where x_1 is the number of cookies and x_2 is the number of glasses of milk that he consumes.

(a) What is the slope of Burt's indifference curve at the point where he is consuming the bundle $(4, 6)$?_____ Use pencil or black ink to draw a line with this slope through the point $(4, 6)$. (Try to make this graph fairly neat and precise, since details will matter.) The line you just drew is the *tangent line* to the consumer's indifference curve at the point $(4, 6)$.

(b) The indifference curve through the point $(4, 6)$ passes through the points (_____,0), (7,_____), and (2,_____). Use blue ink to sketch in this indifference curve. Incidentally, the equation for Burt's indifference curve through the point $(4, 6)$ is $x_2 = $_____.

Glasses of milk

Cookies

(c) Burt currently has the bundle $(4, 6)$. Ernie offers to give Burt 9 glasses of milk if Burt will give Ernie 3 cookies. If Burt makes this trade, he would have the bundle _____ Burt refuses to trade. Was this a wise decision?_____ Mark the bundle $(1, 15)$ on your graph.

(d) Ernie says to Burt, "Burt, your marginal rate of substitution is -2. That means that an extra cookie is worth only twice as much to you as an extra glass of milk. I offered to give you 3 glasses of milk for every cookie you give me. If I offer to give you more than your marginal rate of substitution, then you should want to trade with me." Burt replies, "Ernie, you are right that my marginal rate of substitution is -2. That means that I am willing to make *small* trades where I get more than 2

glasses of milk for every cookie I give you, but 9 glasses of milk for 3 cookies is too big a trade. My indifference curves are not straight lines, you see." Would Burt be willing to give up 1 cookie for 3 glasses of

milk?_____ Would Burt object to giving up

2 cookies for 6 glasses of milk?_____.

(e) On your graph, use red ink to draw a line with slope -3 through the point $(4, 6)$. This line shows all of the bundles that Burt can achieve by trading cookies for milk (or milk for cookies) at the rate of 1 cookie for every 3 glasses of milk. Only a segment of this line represents trades that make Burt better off than he was without trade. Label this line segment on your graph AB.

4.4 (0) Phil Rupp's utility function is $U(x, y) = \max\{x, 2y\}$.

(a) On the graph below, use blue ink to draw and label the line whose equation is $x = 10$. Also use blue ink to draw and label the line whose equation is $2y = 10$.

(b) If $x = 10$ and $2y < 10$, then $U(x, y) =$_____ If $x < 10$ and $2y = 10$,

then $U(x, y) =$_____.

(c) Now use red ink to sketch in the indifference curve along which

$U(x, y) = 10$. Does Phil have convex preferences?_____.

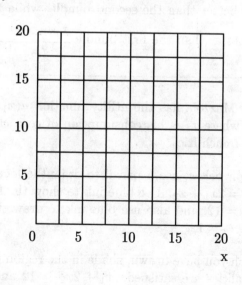

4.5 (0) As you may recall, Nancy Lerner is taking Professor Stern's economics course. She will take two examinations in the course, and her score for the course is the minimum of the scores that she gets on the two exams. Nancy wants to get the highest possible score for the course.

(a) Write a utility function that represents Nancy's preferences over alternative combinations of test scores x_1 and x_2 on tests 1 and 2 respectively.

$U(x_1, x_2) =$ _____.

4.6 (0) Remember Shirley Sixpack and Lorraine Quiche from the last chapter? Shirley thinks a 16-ounce can of beer is just as good as two 8-ounce cans. Lorraine only drinks 8 ounces at a time and hates stale beer, so she thinks a 16-ounce can is no better or worse than an 8-ounce can.

(a) Write a utility function that represents Shirley's preferences between commodity bundles comprised of 8-ounce cans and 16-ounce cans of beer. Let X stand for the number of 8-ounce cans and Y stand for the number

of 16-ounce cans. _____.

(b) Now write a utility function that represents Lorraine's preferences.

_____.

(c) Would the function $u(X, Y) = 100X + 200Y$ represent Shirley's prefer-

ences? _____ Would the utility function $U(x, y) = (5X + 10Y)^2$ rep-

resent her preferences? _____ Would the utility function $U(x, y) =$

$X + 3Y$ represent her preferences? _____.

(d) Give an example of two commodity bundles such that Shirley likes the first bundle better than the second bundle, while Lorraine likes the

second bundle better than the first bundle. _____

_____.

4.7 (0) Harry Mazzola has the utility function $u(x_1, x_2) = \min\{x_1 + 2x_2, 2x_1 + x_2\}$, where x_1 is his consumption of corn chips and x_2 is his consumption of french fries.

(a) On the graph below, use a pencil to draw the locus of points along which $x_1 + 2x_2 = 2x_1 + x_2$. Use blue ink to show the locus of points for which $x_1 + 2x_2 = 12$, and also use blue ink to draw the locus of points for which $2x_1 + x_2 = 12$.

(b) On the graph you have drawn, shade in the region where *both* of the following inequalities are satisfied: $x_1 + 2x_2 \geq 12$ and $2x_1 + x_2 \geq 12$.

At the bundle $(x_1, x_2) = (8, 2)$, one sees that $2x_1 + x_2 =$ _____ and

$x_1 + 2x_2 =$ _____ Therefore $u(8, 2) =$ _____.

(c) Use black ink to sketch in the indifference curve along which Harry's utility is 12. Use red ink to sketch in the indifference curve along which Harry's utility is 6. (Hint: Is there anything about Harry Mazzola that reminds you of Mary Granola?)

French fries

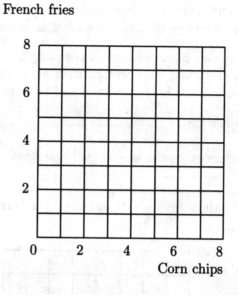

Corn chips

(d) At the point where Harry is consuming 5 units of corn chips and 2 units of french fries, how many units of corn chips would he be willing to

trade for one unit of french fries?_____.

4.8 (1) Vanna Boogie likes to have large parties. She also has a strong preference for having exactly as many men as women at her parties. In fact, Vanna's preferences among parties can be represented by the utility function $U(x, y) = \min\{2x - y, 2y - x\}$ where x is the number of women and y is the number of men at the party. On the graph below, let us try to draw the indifference curve along which Vanna's utility is 10.

(a) Use pencil to draw the locus of points at which $x = y$. What point

on this gives Vanna a utility of 10?_____   Use blue ink to draw the line along which $2y - x = 10$. When $\min\{2x - y, 2y - x\} = 2y - x$,

there are (More men than women, more women than men)?_____

_____ Draw a squiggly red line over the part of the blue line for which $U(x, y) = \min\{2x - y, 2y - x\} = 2y - x$. This shows all the combinations that Vanna thinks are just as good as $(10, 10)$ but where there are (more

men than women, more women than men)?_____   Now draw a blue line along which $2x - y = 10$. Draw a squiggly red line over the part of this new blue line for which $\min\{2x - y, 2y - x\} = 2x - y$. Use pencil to shade in the area on the graph that represents all combinations that Vanna likes at least as well as $(10, 10)$.

(b) Suppose that there are 9 men and 10 women at Vanna's party. Would Vanna think it was a better party or a worse party if 5 more men came to her party?_____.

(c) If Vanna has 16 women at her party and more men than women, and if she thinks the party is exactly as good as having 10 men and 10 women, how many men does she have at the party?_____ If Vanna has 16 women at her party and more women than men, and if she thinks the party is exactly as good as having 10 men and 10 women, how many men does she have at her party?_____.

(d) Vanna's indifference curves are shaped like what letter of the alphabet?_____.

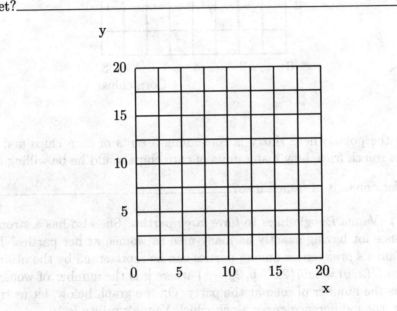

4.9 (0) Suppose that the utility functions $u(x, y)$ and $v(x, y)$ are related by $v(x, y) = f(u(x, y))$. In each case below, write "Yes" if the function f is a positive monotonic transformation and "No" if it is not. (Hint for calculus users: A differentiable function $f(u)$ is an increasing function of u if its derivative is positive.)

(a) $f(u) = 3.141592u.$_____.

(b) $f(u) = 5,000 - 23u.$_____.

(c) $f(u) = u - 100,000.$_____.

(d) $f(u) = \log_{10} u.$_____.

(e) $f(u) = -e^{-u}.$_____.

(f) $f(u) = 1/u.$_____.

(g) $f(u) = -1/u.$_____.

4.10 (0) Martha Modest has preferences represented by the utility function $U(a, b) = ab/100$, where a is the number of ounces of animal crackers that she consumes and b is the number of ounces of beans that she consumes.

(a) On the graph below, sketch the locus of points that Martha finds indifferent to having 8 ounces of animal crackers and 2 ounces of beans. Also sketch the locus of points that she finds indifferent to having 6 ounces of animal crackers and 4 ounces of beans.

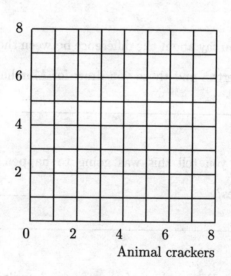

(b) Bertha Brassy has preferences represented by the utility function $V(a, b) = 1{,}000a^2b^2$, where a is the number of ounces of animal crackers that she consumes and b is the number of ounces of beans that she consumes. On the graph below, sketch the locus of points that Bertha finds indifferent to having 8 ounces of animal crackers and 2 ounces of beans. Also sketch the locus of points that she finds indifferent to having 6 ounces of animal crackers and 4 ounces of beans.

Beans

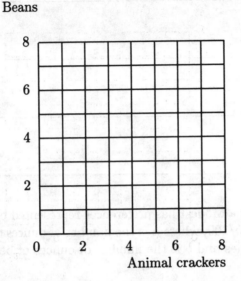

Animal crackers

(c) Are Martha's preferences convex?_____ Are Bertha's?_____

_____.

(d) What can you say about the difference between the indifference curves you drew for Bertha and those you drew for Martha?_____

_____.

(e) How could you tell this was going to happen without having to draw the curves?_____

_____.

4.11 (0) Willy Wheeler's preferences over bundles that contain non-negative amounts of x_1 and x_2 are represented by the utility function $U(x_1, x_2) = x_1^2 + x_2^2$.

(a) Draw a few of his indifference curves. What kind of geometric figure are they?_____ Does Willy have

convex preferences?_____.

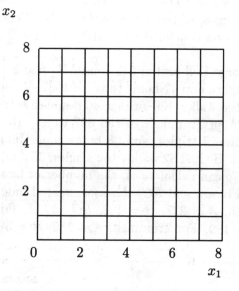

4.12 (0) Calc Joe Bob has a utility function given by $u(x_1, x_2) = x_1^2 + 2x_1x_2 + x_2^2$.

(a) Compute Joe Bob's marginal rate of substitution: $MRS(x_1, x_2) =$

_____.

(b) Joe Bob's straight cousin, Al, has a utility function $v(x_1, x_2) = x_2 + x_1$.

Compute Al 's marginal rate of substitution. $MRS(x_1, x_2) =$_____.

(c) Do $u(x_1, x_2)$ and $v(x_1, x_2)$ represent the same preferences?_____

_____ Can you show that Joe Bob's utility function is a monotonic transformation of Al's? (Hint: Some have said that Joe Bob is square.)

_____.

4.13 (0) The idea of assigning numerical values to determine a preference ordering over a set of objects is not limited in application to commodity bundles. The *Bill James Baseball Abstract* argues that a baseball player's batting average is not an adequate measure of his offensive productivity. Batting averages treat singles just the same as extra base hits. Furthermore they do not give credit for "walks," although a walk is almost as good as a single. James argues that a double in two at-bats is better than a single, but not as good as two singles. To reflect these considerations, James proposes the following index, which he calls "runs created." Let A be the number of hits plus the number of walks that a batter gets in a season. Let B be the number of total bases that the batter gets in the season. (Thus, if a batter has S singles, W walks, D doubles, T triples, and H

home runs, then $A = S+D+T+H+W$ and $B = S+W+2D+3T+4H$.)
Let N be the number of times the batter bats. Then his index of runs
created in the season is defined to be AB/N and will be called his RC.

(a) In 1987, George Bell batted 649 times. He had 39 walks, 105 singles,
32 doubles, 4 triples, and 47 home runs. In 1987, Wade Boggs batted 656
times. He had 105 walks, 130 singles, 40 doubles, 6 triples, and 24 home
runs. In 1987, Alan Trammell batted 657 times. He had 60 walks, 140
singles, 34 doubles, 3 triples, and 28 home runs. In 1987, Tony Gwynn
batted 671 times. He had 82 walks, 162 singles, 36 doubles, 13 triples, and
7 home runs. We can calculate A, the number of hits plus walks, B the
number of total bases, and RC, the runs created index for each of these
players. For Bell, $A = 227$, $B = 408$, $RC = 143$. For Boggs, $A = 305$,
$B = 429$, $RC = 199$. For Trammell, $A = 265$, $B = 389$, $RC = 157$. For

Gwynn, $A =$_____ , $B =$_____ , $RC =$_____.

(b) If somebody has a preference ordering among these players, based only
on the runs-created index, which player(s) would she prefer to Trammell.

_____

(c) The differences in the number of times at bat for these players are
small, and we will ignore them for simplicity of calculation. On the graph
below, plot the combinations of A and B achieved by each of the players.
Draw four "indifference curves," one through each of the four points you
have plotted. These indifference curves should represent combinations of
A and B that lead to the same number of runs-created.

Number of total bases

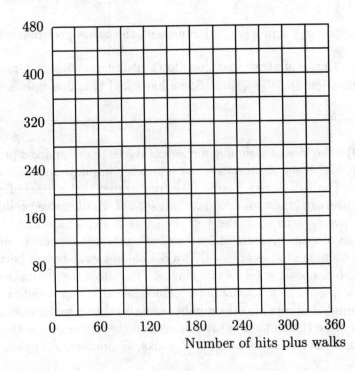

Number of hits plus walks

4.14 (0) This problem concerns the runs-created index discussed in the preceding problem. Consider a batter who bats 100 times and always either makes an out, hits for a single, or hits a home run.

(a) Let x be the number of singles and y be the number of home runs in 100 at bats. Suppose that the utility function $U(x, y)$ by which we evaluate alternative combinations of singles and home runs is the runs created index. Then the formula for the utility function is $U(x, y) =$

_____.

(b) Let's try to find out about the shape of an indifference curve between singles and home runs. Hitting 10 home runs and no singles would give him the same runs created index as hitting _____ singles and no home runs. Mark the points $(0, 10)$ and $(x, 0)$, where $U(x, 0) = U(0, 10)$.

(c) Where x is the number of singles you solved for in the previous part, mark the point $(x/2, 5)$ on your graph. Is $U(x/2, 5)$ greater than or less than or equal to $U(0, 10)$? _____ Is this consistent with the

batter having convex preferences between singles and home runs?_____

_____.

Home runs

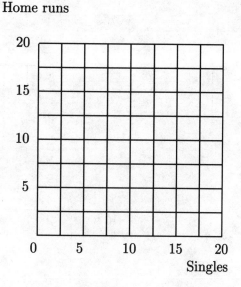

Singles

Chapter 5

Choice

Introduction. You have studied budgets, and you have studied preferences. Now is the time to put these two ideas together and do something with them. In this chapter you study the commodity bundle chosen by a utility-maximizing consumer from a given budget.

Given prices and income, you know how to graph a consumer's budget. If you also know the consumer's preferences, you can graph some of his indifference curves. The consumer will choose the "best" indifference curve that he can reach given his budget. But when you try to do this, you have to ask yourself, "but how do I find the most desirable indifference curve that the consumer can reach?" The answer to this question is "look in the likely places." Where are the likely places? As your textbook tells you, there are three kinds of likely places. These are: (*i*) a tangency between an indifference curve and the budget line; (*ii*) a kink in an indifference curve; (*iii*) a "corner" where the consumer specializes in consuming just one good.

Here is how you find a point of tangency if we are told the consumer's utility function, the prices of both goods, and the consumer's income. The budget line and an indifference curve are tangent at a point (x_1, x_2) if they have the same slope at that point. Now the slope of an indifference curve at (x_1, x_2) is the ratio $-MU_1(x_1, x_2)/MU_2(x_1, x_2)$. (This slope is also known as the marginal rate of substitution.) The slope of the budget line is $-p_1/p_2$. Therefore an indifference curve is tangent to the budget line at the point (x_1, x_2) when $MU_1(x_1, x_2)/MU_2(x_1, x_2) = p_1/p_2$. This gives us one equation in the two unknowns, x_1 and x_2. If we hope to solve for the x's, we need another equation. That other equation is the budget equation $p_1x_1 + p_2x_2 = m$. With these two equations you can solve for (x_1, x_2).*

Example: A consumer has the utility function $U(x_1, x_2) = x_1^2x_2$. The price of good 1 is $p_1 = 1$, the price of good 2 is $p_2 = 3$, and his income is 180. Then, $MU_1(x_1, x_2) = 2x_1x_2$ and $MU_2(x_1, x_2) = x_1^2$. Therefore his marginal rate of substitution is $-MU_1(x_1, x_2)/MU_2(x_1, x_2) = -2x_1x_2/x_1^2 = -2x_2/x_1$. This implies that his indifference curve will be tangent to his budget line when $-2x_2/x_1 = -p_1/p_2 = -1/3$. Simplifying this expression, we have $6x_2 = x_1$. This is one of the two equations we need to solve for the two unknowns, x_1 and x_2. The other equation is the budget equation. In this case the budget equation is $x_1 + 3x_2 = 180$. Solving these two equations in two unknowns, we find $x_1 = 120$ and

---

* Some people have trouble remembering whether the marginal rate of substitution is $-MU_1/MU_2$ or $-MU_2/MU_1$. It isn't really crucial to remember which way this goes as long as you remember that a tangency happens when the marginal utilities of any two goods are in the same proportions as their prices.

$x_2 = 20$. Therefore we know that the consumer chooses the bundle $(x_1, x_2) = (120, 20)$.

For equilibrium at kinks or at corners, we don't need the slope of the indifference curves to equal the slope of the budget line. So we don't have the tangency equation to work with. But we still have the budget equation. The second equation that you can use is an equation that tells you that you are at one of the kinky points or at a corner. You will see exactly how this works when you work a few exercises.

Example: A consumer has the utility function $U(x_1, x_2) = \min\{x_1, 3x_2\}$. The price of x_1 is 2, the price of x_2 is 1, and her income is 140. Her indifference curves are L-shaped. The corners of the L's all lie along the line, $x_1 = 3x_2$. She will choose a combination at one of the corners, so this gives us one of the two equations we need for finding the unknowns x_1 and x_2. The second equation is her budget equation, which is $2x_1 + x_2 = 140$. Solve these two equations to find that $x_1 = 60$ and $x_2 = 20$. So we know that the consumer chooses the bundle $(x_1, x_2) = (60, 20)$.

When you have finished these exercises, we hope that you will be able to do the following

- Calculate the best bundle a consumer can afford at given prices and income in the case of simple utility functions where the best affordable bundle happens at a point of tangency.

- Find the best affordable bundle, given prices and income for a consumer with kinked indifference curves.

- Recognize standard examples where the best bundle a consumer can afford happens at a corner of the budget set.

- Draw a diagram illustrating each of the above types of equilibrium.

- Apply the methods you have learned to choices made with some kinds of nonlinear budgets that arise in real-world situations.

5.1 (0) We begin again with Charlie of the apples and bananas. Recall that Charlie's utility function is $U(x_A, x_B) = x_A x_B$. Suppose that the price of apples is 1, the price of bananas is 2, and Charlie's income is 40.

(a) On the graph below, use blue ink to draw Charlie's budget line. (Use a ruler and try to make this line accurate.) Plot a few points on the indifference curve that gives Charlie a utility of 150 and sketch this curve with red ink. Now plot a few points on the indifference curve that gives Charlie a utility of 300 and sketch this curve with black ink or pencil.

Bananas

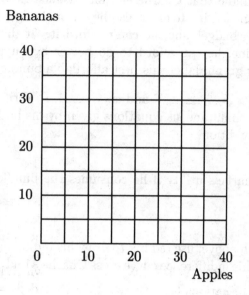

Apples

(b) Can Charlie afford any bundles that give him a utility of 150?_____

_____.

(c) Can Charlie afford any bundles that give him a utility of 300?_____

(d) On your graph, mark a point that Charlie can afford and that gives him a higher utility than 150. Label that point *A*.

(e) Neither of the indifference curves that you drew is tangent to Charlie's budget line. Let's try to find one that is. At any point, (x_A, x_B), Charlie's marginal rate of substitution is a function of x_A and x_B. In fact, if you calculate the ratio of marginal utilities for Charlie's utility function, you will find that Charlie's marginal rate of substitution is $MRS(x_A, x_B) = -x_B/x_A$. This is the slope of his indifference curve at (x_A, x_B). The slope of Charlie's budget line is _____ (give a numerical answer).

(f) Write an equation that implies that the budget line is tangent to an indifference curve at (x_A, x_B). _____ There are many solutions to this equation. Each of these solutions corresponds to a point on a different indifference curve. Use pencil to draw a line that passes through all of these points.

(g) The best bundle that Charlie can afford must lie somewhere on the line you just penciled in. It must also lie on his budget line. If the point is outside of his budget line, he can't afford it. If the point lies inside of his budget line, he can afford to do better by buying more of both goods. On your graph, label this best affordable bundle with an *E*. This happens where $x_A=$_____ and $x_B=$_____ Verify your answer by solving the two simultaneous equations given by his budget equation and the tangency condition.

(h) What is Charlie's utility if he consumes the bundle $(20, 10)$?_____
_____

(i) On the graph above, use red ink to draw his indifference curve through $(20,10)$. Does this indifference curve cross Charlie's budget line, just touch it, or never touch it?_____.

5.2 (0) Clara's utility function is $U(X, Y) = (X+2)(Y+1)$, where X is her consumption of good X and Y is her consumption of good Y.

(a) Write an equation for Clara's indifference curve that goes through the point $(X, Y) = (2, 8)$. $Y =$_____ On the axes below, sketch Clara's indifference curve for $U = 36$.

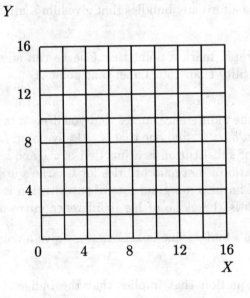

(b) Suppose that the price of each good is 1 and that Clara has an income of 11. Draw in her budget line. Can Clara achieve a utility of 36 with this budget?_____.

(c) At the commodity bundle, (X, Y), Clara's marginal rate of substitution is _____.

(d) If we set the absolute value of the MRS equal to the price ratio, we have the equation_____.

(e) The budget equation is_____.

(f) Solving these two equations for the two unknowns, X and Y, we find $X =$_____ and $Y =$_____.

5.3 (0) Ambrose, the nut and berry consumer, has a utility function $U(x_1, x_2) = 4\sqrt{x_1} + x_2$, where x_1 is his consumption of nuts and x_2 is his consumption of berries.

(a) The commodity bundle $(25, 0)$ gives Ambrose a utility of 20. Other points that give him the same utility are $(16, 4)$, $(9,$_____ $)$, $(4,$ _____ $)$, $(1,$_____ $)$, and $(0,$_____ $)$. Plot these points on the axes below and draw a red indifference curve through them.

(b) Suppose that the price of a unit of nuts is 1, the price of a unit of berries is 2, and Ambrose's income is 24. Draw Ambrose's budget line with blue ink. How many units of nuts does he choose to buy?_____ _____

(c) How many units of berries?_____.

(d) Find some points on the indifference curve that gives him a utility of 25 and sketch this indifference curve (in red).

(e) Now suppose that the prices are as before, but Ambrose's income is 34. Draw his new budget line (with pencil). How many units of nuts will he choose? _____ How many units of berries?_____.

Berries

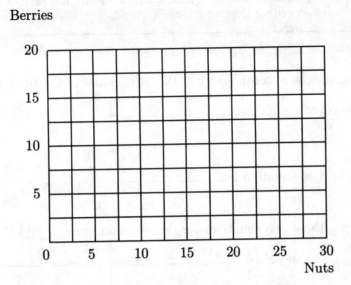

(f) Now let us explore a case where there is a "boundary solution." Suppose that the price of nuts is still 1 and the price of berries is 2, but Ambrose's income is only 9. Draw his budget line (in blue). Sketch the indifference curve that passes through the point $(9, 0)$. What is the slope of his indifference curve at the point $(9, 0)$?_____.

(g) What is the slope of his budget line at this point?_____.

(h) Which is steeper at this point, the budget line or the indifference curve?_____.

(i) Can Ambrose afford any bundles that he likes better than the point $(9, 0)$?_____.

5.4 (1) Nancy Lerner is trying to decide how to allocate her time in studying for her economics course. There are two examinations in this course. Her overall score for the course will be the *minimum* of her scores on the two examinations. She has decided to devote a total of 1,200 minutes to studying for these two exams, and she wants to get as high an overall score as possible. She knows that on the first examination if she doesn't study at all, she will get a score of zero on it. For every 10 minutes that she spends studying for the first examination, she will increase her score by one point. If she doesn't study at all for the second examination she will get a zero on it. For every 20 minutes she spends studying for the second examination, she will increase her score by one point.

(a) On the graph below, draw a "budget line" showing the various combinations of scores on the two exams that she can achieve with a total of 1,200 minutes of studying. On the same graph, draw two or three "indifference curves" for Nancy. On your graph, draw a straight line that goes through the kinks in Nancy's indifference curves. Label the point where this line hits Nancy's budget with the letter *A*. Draw Nancy's indifference curve through this point.

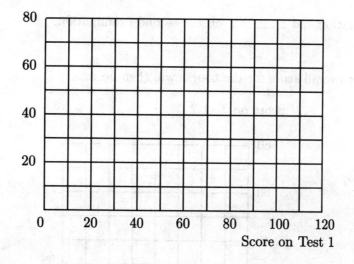

Score on Test 2

Score on Test 1

(b) Write an equation for the line passing through the kinks of Nancy's indifference curves. _____

(c) Write an equation for Nancy's budget line. _____

(d) Solve these two equations in two unknowns to determine the intersection of these lines. This happens at the point $(x_1, x_2) =$_____.

(e) Given that she spends a total of 1,200 minutes studying, Nancy will maximize her overall score by spending _____ minutes studying for the first examination and _____ minutes studying for the second examination.

5.5 (1) In her communications course, Nancy also takes two examinations. Her overall grade for the course will be the *maximum* of her scores on the two examinations. Nancy decides to spend a total of 400 minutes studying for these two examinations. If she spends m_1 minutes studying for the first examination, her score on this exam will be $x_1 = m_1/5$. If she spends m_2 minutes studying for the second examination, her score on this exam will be $x_2 = m_2/10$.

(a) On the graph below, draw a "budget line" showing the various combinations of scores on the two exams that she can achieve with a total of 400 minutes of studying. On the same graph, draw two or three "indifference curves" for Nancy. On your graph, find the point on Nancy's budget line that gives her the best overall score in the course.

(b) Given that she spends a total of 400 minutes studying, Nancy will maximize her overall score by achieving a score of _____ on the first examination and _____ on the second examination.

(c) Her overall score for the course will then be_____.

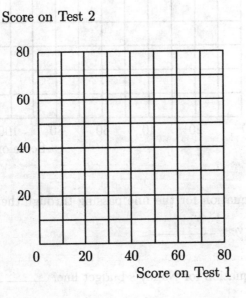

Score on Test 2

Score on Test 1

5.6 (0) Elmer's utility function is $U(x, y) = \min\{x, y^2\}$.

(a) If Elmer consumes 4 units of x and 3 units of y, his utility is_____.

(b) If Elmer consumes 4 units of x and 2 units of y, his utility is_____.

(c) If Elmer consumes 5 units of x and 2 units of y, his utility is_____.

(d) On the graph below, use blue ink to draw the indifference curve for Elmer that contains the bundles that he likes exactly as well as the bundle $(4, 2)$.

(e) On the same graph, use blue ink to draw the indifference curve for Elmer that contains bundles that he likes exactly as well as the bundle $(1, 1)$ and the indifference curve that passes through the point $(16, 5)$.

(f) On your graph, use black ink to show the locus of points at which Elmer's indifference curves have kinks. What is the equation for this

curve?_____.

(g) On the same graph, use black ink to draw Elmer's budget line when the price of x is 1, the price of y is 2, and his income is 8. What bundle

does Elmer choose in this situation?_____.

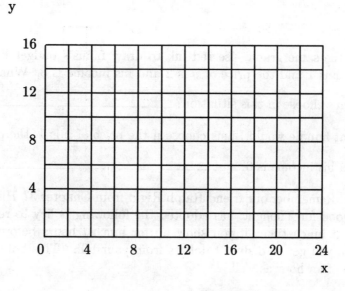

(h) Suppose that the price of x is 10 and the price of y is 15 and Elmer

buys 100 units of x. What is Elmer's income? _____ (Hint: At first you might think there is too little information to answer this question. But think about how much y he must be demanding if he chooses 100 units of x.)

5.7 (0) Linus has the utility function $U(x, y) = x + 3y$.

(a) On the graph below, use blue ink to draw the indifference curve passing through the point $(x, y) = (3, 3)$. Use black ink to sketch the indifference curve connecting bundles that give Linus a utility of 6.

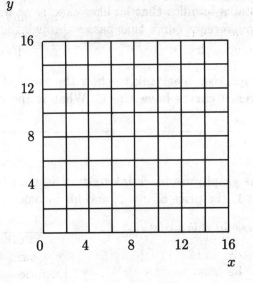

(b) On the same graph, use red ink to draw Linus's budget line if the price of x is 1 and the price of y is 2 and his income is 8. What bundle does Linus choose in this situation?_____.

(c) What bundle would Linus choose if the price of x is 1, the price of y is 4, and his income is 8?_____.

5.8 (2) Remember our friend Ralph Rigid from Chapter 3? His favorite diner, Food for Thought, has adopted the following policy to reduce the crowds at lunch time: if you show up for lunch t hours before or after 12 noon, you get to deduct t dollars from your bill. (This holds for any fraction of an hour as well.)

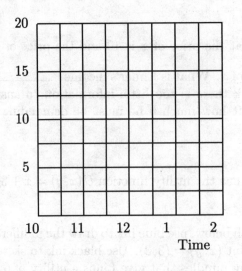

(a) Use blue ink to show Ralph's budget set. On this graph, the horizontal axis measures the time of day that he eats lunch, and the vertical axis measures the amount of money that he will have to spend on things other than lunch. Assume that he has $20 total to spend and that lunch at noon costs $10. (Hint: How much money would he have left if he ate at noon? at 1 P.M.? at 11 A.M.?)

(b) Recall that Ralph's preferred lunch time is 12 noon, but that he is willing to eat at another time if the food is sufficiently cheap. Draw some red indifference curves for Ralph that would be consistent with his choosing to eat at 11 A.M.

5.9 (0) Joe Grad has just arrived at the big U. He has a fellowship that covers his tuition and the rent on an apartment. In order to get by, Joe has become a grader in intermediate price theory, earning $100 a month. Out of this $100 he must pay for his food and utilities in his apartment. His utilities expenses consist of heating costs when he heats his apartment and air-conditioning costs when he cools it. To raise the temperature of his apartment by one degree, it costs $2 per month (or $20 per month to raise it ten degrees). To use air-conditioning to cool his apartment by a degree, it costs $3 per month. Whatever is left over after paying the utilities, he uses to buy food at $1 per unit.

Food

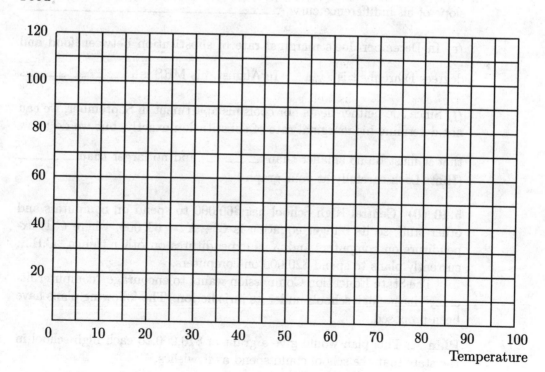

(a) When Joe first arrives in September, the temperature of his apartment is 60 degrees. If he spends nothing on heating or cooling, the temperature in his room will be 60 degrees and he will have $100 left to spend on food.

If he heated the room to 70 degrees, he would have _____ left to spend

on food. If he cooled the room to 50 degrees, he would have _____ left to spend on food. On the graph below, show Joe's September budget constraint (with black ink). (Hint: You have just found three points that Joe can afford. Apparently, his budget set is not bounded by a single straight line.)

(b) In December, the outside temperature is 30 degrees and in August poor Joe is trying to understand macroeconomics while the temperature outside is 85 degrees. On the same graph you used above, draw Joe's budget constraints for the months of December (in blue ink) and August (in red ink).

(c) Draw a few smooth (unkinky) indifference curves for Joe in such a way that the following are true. (*i*) His favorite temperature for his apartment would be 65 degrees if it cost him nothing to heat it or cool it. (*ii*) Joe chooses to use the furnace in December, air-conditioning in August, and neither in September. (*iii*) Joe is better off in December than in August.

(d) In what months is the slope of Joe's budget constraint equal to the

slope of his indifference curve?_____.

(e) In December Joe's marginal rate of substitution between food and

degrees Fahrenheit is _____ In August, his MRS is_____.

(f) Since Joe neither heats nor cools his apartment in September, we can not determine his marginal rate of substitution exactly, but we do know

that it must be no smaller than _____ and no larger than _____ (Hint: Look carefully at your graph.)

5.10 (0) Central High School has $60,000 to spend on computers and other stuff, so its budget equation is $C + X = 60,000$, where C is expenditure on computers and X is expenditures on other things. C.H.S. currently plans to spend $20,000 on computers.

The State Education Commission wants to encourage "computer literacy" in the high schools under its jurisdiction. The following plans have been proposed.

Plan A: This plan would give a grant of $10,000 to each high school in the state that the school could spend as it wishes.

Plan B: This plan would give a $10,000 grant to any high school, so long as the school spends at least $10,000 *more* than it currently spends on computers. Any high school can choose not to participate, in which case it does not receive the grant, but it doesn't have to increase its expenditure on computers.

Plan C: Plan C is a "matching grant." For every dollar's worth of computers that a high school orders, the state will give the school 50 cents.

Plan D: This plan is like plan C, except that the maximum amount of matching funds that any high school could get from the state would be limited to $10,000.

(a) Write an equation for Central High School's budget if plan A is adopted._____ Use black ink to draw the budget line for Central High School if plan A is adopted.

(b) If plan B is adopted, the boundary of Central High School's budget set has two separate downward-sloping line segments. One of these segments describes the cases where C.H.S. spends at least $30,000 on computers. This line segment runs from the point $(C, X) = (70,000, 0)$ to the point

$(C, X) =$ _____.

(c) Another line segment corresponds to the cases where C.H.S. spends less than $30,000 on computers. This line segment runs from $(C, X) =$ _____ to the point $(C, X) = (0, 60,000)$. Use red ink to draw these two line segments.

(d) If plan C is adopted and Central High School spends C dollars on computers, then it will have $X = 60,000 - .5C$ dollars left to spend on other things. Therefore its budget line has the equation _____ _____ Use blue ink to draw this budget line.

(e) If plan D is adopted, the school district's budget consists of two line segments that intersect at the point where expenditure on computers is _____ and expenditure on other instructional materials is_____ _____.

(f) The slope of the flatter line segment is _____ The slope of the steeper segment is _____ Use pencil to draw this budget line.

Thousands of dollars worth of other things

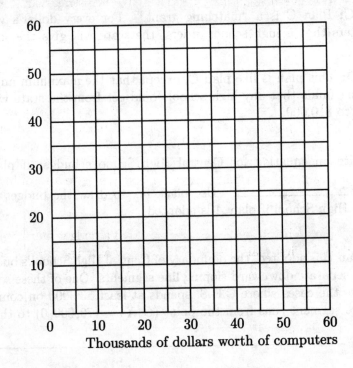

Thousands of dollars worth of computers

5.11 (0) Suppose that Central High School has preferences that can be represented by the utility function $U(C, X) = CX^2$. Let us try to determine how the various plans described in the last problem will affect the amount that C.H.S. spends on computers.

(a) If the state adopts none of the new plans, find the expenditure on computers that maximizes the district's utility subject to its budget constraint. _____.

(b) If plan A is adopted, find the expenditure on computers that maximizes the district's utility subject to its budget constraint. _____.

(c) On your graph, sketch the indifference curve that passes through the point (30,000,40,000) if plan B is adopted. At this point, which is steeper, the indifference curve or the budget line? _____.

(d) If plan B is adopted, find the expenditure on computers that maximizes the district's utility subject to its budget constraint. (Hint: Look at your graph.) _____.

(e) If plan C is adopted, find the expenditure on computers that maximizes the district's utility subject to its budget constraint._____.

(f) If plan D is adopted, find the expenditure on computers that maximizes the district's utility subject to its budget constraint._____.

5.12 (0) The telephone company allows one to choose between two different pricing plans. For a fee of $12 per month you can make as many local phone calls as you want, at no additional charge per call. Alternatively, you can pay $8 per month and be charged 5 cents for each local phone call that you make. Suppose that you have a total of $20 per month to spend.

(a) On the graph below, use black ink to sketch a budget line for someone who chooses the first plan. Use red ink to draw a budget line for someone who chooses the second plan. Where do the two budget lines cross?

_____.

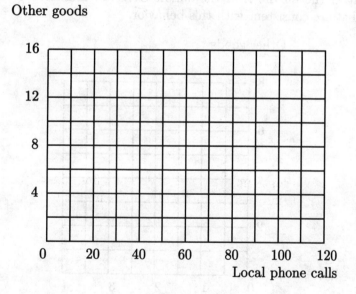

(b) On the graph above, use pencil to draw indifference curves for someone who prefers the second plan to the first. Use blue ink to draw an indifference curve for someone who prefers the first plan to the second.

5.13 (1) This is a puzzle—just for fun. Lewis Carroll (1832-1898), author of *Alice in Wonderland* and *Through the Looking Glass,* was a mathematician, logician, and political scientist. Carroll loved careful reasoning about puzzling things. Here Carroll's Alice presents a nice bit of economic analysis. At first glance, it may seem that Alice is talking nonsense, but, indeed, her reasoning is impeccable.

"I should like to buy an egg, please." she said timidly. "How do you sell them?"

"Fivepence farthing for one—twopence for two," the Sheep replied.

"Then two are cheaper than one?" Alice said, taking out her purse.

"Only you must eat them both if you buy two," said the Sheep.

"Then I'll have one please," said Alice, as she put the money down on the counter. For she thought to herself, "They mightn't be at all nice, you know."

(a) Let us try to draw a budget set and indifference curves that are consistent with this story. Suppose that Alice has a total of 8 pence to spend and that she can buy either 0, 1, or 2 eggs from the Sheep, but no fractional eggs. Then her budget set consists of just three points. The point where she buys no eggs is $(0, 8)$. Plot this point and label it A. On your graph, the point where she buys 1 egg is $(1, 2\frac{3}{4})$. (A farthing is 1/4 of a penny.) Plot this point and label it B.

(b) The point where she buys 2 eggs is _____ Plot this point and label it C. If Alice chooses to buy 1 egg, she must like the bundle B better than either the bundle A or the bundle C. Draw indifference curves for Alice that are consistent with this behavior.

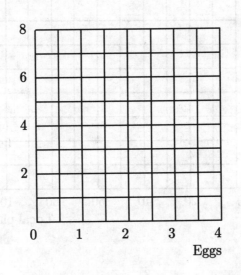

Demand

Introduction. In the previous chapter, you found the commodity bundle that a consumer with a given utility function would choose in a specific price-income situation. In this chapter, we take this idea a step further. We find demand *functions*, which tell us for *any* prices and income you might want to name, how much of each good a consumer would want. In general, the amount of each good demanded may depend not only on its own price, but also on the price of other goods and on income. Where there are two goods, we write demand functions for Goods 1 and 2 as $x_1(p_1, p_2, m)$ and $x_2(p_1, p_2, m)$.*

When the consumer is choosing positive amounts of all commodities and indifference curves have no kinks, the consumer chooses a point of tangency between her budget line and the highest indifference curve that it touches.

Example: Consider a consumer with utility function, $U(x_1, x_2) = (x_1 + 2)(x_2 + 10)$. To find $x_1(p_1, p_2, m)$ and $x_2(p_1, p_2, m)$, we need to find a commodity bundle (x_1, x_2) on her budget line at which her indifference curve is tangent to her budget line. The budget line will be tangent to the indifference curve at (x_1, x_2) if the price ratio equals the marginal rate of substitution. For this utility function, $MU_1(x_1, x_2) = x_2 + 10$ and $MU_2(x_1, x_2) = x_1 + 2$. Therefore the "tangency equation" is $p_1/p_2 = (x_2 + 10)/(x_1 + 2)$. Cross-multiplying the tangency equation, one finds $p_1 x_1 + 2p_1 = p_2 x_2 + 10p_2$.

The bundle chosen must also satisfy the budget equation, $p_1 x_1 + p_2 x_2 = m$. This gives us two linear equations in the two unknowns, x_1 and x_2. You can solve these equations yourself, using high school algebra. You will find that the solution for the two "demand functions" is

$$x_1 = \frac{m - 2p_1 + 10p_2}{2p_1}$$

$$x_2 = \frac{m + 2p_1 - 10p_2}{2p_2}.$$

There is one thing left to worry about with the "demand functions" we just found. Notice that these expressions will be positive only if $m - 2p_1 + 10p_2 > 0$ and $m + 2p_1 - 10p_2 > 0$. If either of these expressions is negative, then it doesn't make sense as a demand function. What happens in this

---

* For some utility functions, demand for a good may not be affected by all of these variables. For example, with Cobb-Douglas utility, demand for a good depends on the good's own price and on income but not on the other good's price. Still, there is no harm in writing demand for Good 1 as a function of p_1, p_2, and m. It just happens that the derivative of $x_1(p_1, p_2, m)$ with respect to p_2 is zero.

case is that the consumer will choose a "boundary solution" where she consumes only one good. At this point, her indifference curve will not be tangent to her budget line.

When a consumer has kinks in her indifference curves, she may choose a bundle that is located at a kink. In the problems with kinks, you will be able to solve for the demand functions quite easily by looking at diagrams and doing a little algebra. Typically, instead of finding a tangency equation, you will find an equation that tells you "where the kinks are." With this equation and the budget equation, you can then solve for demand.

You might wonder why we pay so much attention to kinky indifference curves, straight line indifference curves, and other "funny cases." Our reason is this. In the funny cases, computations are usually pretty easy. But often you may have to draw a graph and think about what you are doing. That is what we want you to do. Think and fiddle with graphs. Don't just memorize formulas. Formulas you will forget, but the habit of thinking will stick with you.

When you have finished this workout, we hope that you will be able to do the following

- Find demand functions for consumers with Cobb-Douglas and other similar utility functions.

- Find demand functions for consumers with quasilinear utility functions.

- Find demand functions for consumers with kinked indifference curves and for consumers with straight-line indifference curves.

- Recognize complements and substitutes from looking at a demand curve.

- Recognize normal goods, inferior goods, luxuries, and necessities from looking at information about demand.

- Calculate the equation of an inverse demand curve, given a simple demand equation.

6.1 (0) Charlie is back—still consuming apples and bananas. His utility function is $U(x_A, x_B) = x_A x_B$. We want to find his demand function for apples, $x_A(p_A, p_B, m)$, and his demand function for bananas, $x_B(p_A, p_B, m)$.

(a) When the prices are p_A and p_B and Charlie's income is m, the equation for Charlie's budget line is $p_A x_A + p_B x_B = m$. The slope of Charlie's indifference curve at the bundle (x_A, x_B) is $-MU_1(x_A, x_B)/MU_2(x_A, x_B) =$

_____ The slope of Charlie's budget line is _____ Charlie's indifference curve will be tangent to his budget line at the point

(x_A, x_B) if the following equation is satisfied, _____.

(b) You now have two equations, the budget equation and the tangency equation, that must be satisfied by the bundle demanded. Solve these two equations for x_A and x_B. Charlie's demand function for apples is $x_A(p_A, p_B, m) =$_____ , and his demand function for bananas is

$x_B(p_A, p_B, m) =$ _____.

(c) In general, the demand for both commodities will depend on the price of both commodities and on income. But for Charlie's utility function, the demand function for apples depends only on income and the price of apples. Similarly, the demand for bananas depends only on income and the price of bananas. Charlie always spends the same fraction of his income on bananas. What fraction is this? _____.

6.2 (0) Douglas Cornfield's preferences are represented by the utility function $u(x_1, x_2) = x_1^2 x_2^3$. The prices of x_1 and x_2 are p_1 and p_2.

(a) The slope of Cornfield's indifference curve at the point (x_1, x_2) is

_____.

(b) If Cornfield's budget line is tangent to his indifference curve at (x_1, x_2), then $\frac{p_1 x_1}{p_2 x_2} =$_____ (Hint: Look at the equation that equates the slope of his indifference curve with the slope of his budget line.) When he is consuming the best bundle he can afford, what fraction of his income does Douglas spend on x_1? _____.

(c) Other members of Doug's family have similar utility functions, but the exponents may be different, or their utilities might be multiplied by a positive constant. If a family member has a utility function $U(x, y) = c x_1^a x_2^b$ where a, b, and c are positive numbers, what fraction of his or her income will that family member spend on x_1? _____.

6.3 (0) Our thoughts return to Ambrose and his nuts and berries. Ambrose's utility function is $U(x_1, x_2) = 4\sqrt{x_1} + x_2$, where x_1 is his consumption of nuts and x_2 is his consumption of berries.

(a) Let us find his demand function for nuts. The slope of Ambrose's indifference curve at (x_1, x_2) is _____ Setting this slope equal to the slope of the budget line, you can solve for x_1 without even using the budget equation. The solution is $x_1 =$_____.

(b) Let us find his demand for berries. Now we need the budget equation. In Part (a), you solved for the amount of x_1 that he will demand. The budget equation tells us that $p_1 x_1 + p_2 x_2 = M$. Plug the solution that you found for x_1 into the budget equation and solve for x_2 as a function of income and prices. The answer is $x_2 = $_____.

(c) When we visited Ambrose in Chapter 5, we looked at a "boundary solution," where Ambrose consumed only nuts and no berries. In that example, $p_1 = 1$, $p_2 = 2$, and $M = 9$. If you plug these numbers into the formulas we found in Parts (a) and (b), you find $x_1 = $_____ , and $x_2 = $_____ Since we get a negative solution for x_2, it must be that the budget line $x_1 + 2x_2 = 9$ is not tangent to an indifference curve when $x_2 \geq 0$. The best that Ambrose can do with this budget is to spend all of his income on nuts. Looking at the formulas, we see that at the prices $p_1 = 1$ and $p_2 = 2$, Ambrose will demand a positive amount of both goods if and only if $M > $_____.

6.4 (0) Donald Fribble is a stamp collector. The only things other than stamps that Fribble consumes are Hostess Twinkies. It turns out that Fribble's preferences are represented by the utility function $u(s,t) = s + \ln t$ where s is the number of stamps he collects and t is the number of Twinkies he consumes. The price of stamps is p_s and the price of Twinkies is p_t. Donald's income is m.

(a) Write an expression that says that the ratio of Fribble's marginal utility for Twinkies to his marginal utility for stamps is equal to the ratio of the price of Twinkies to the price of stamps. _____ (Hint: The derivative of $\ln t$ with respect to t is $1/t$, and the derivative of s with respect to s is 1.)

(b) You can use the equation you found in the last part to show that if he buys both goods, Donald's demand function for Twinkies depends only on the price ratio and not on his income. Donald's demand function for Twinkies is_____.

(c) Notice that for this special utility function, if Fribble buys both goods, then the total amount of money that he spends on Twinkies has the peculiar property that it depends on only one of the three variables m, p_t, and p_s, namely the variable _____ (Hint: The amount of money that he spends on Twinkies is $p_t t(p_s, p_t, m)$.)

(d) Since there are only two goods, any money that is not spent on Twinkies must be spent on stamps. Use the budget equation and Donald's demand function for Twinkies to find an expression for the number of stamps he will buy if his income is m, the price of stamps is p_s and the

price of Twinkies is p_t._____.

(e) The expression you just wrote down is negative if $m < p_s$. Surely it makes no sense for him to be demanding negative amounts of postage stamps. If $m < p_s$, what would Fribble's demand for postage stamps be?

_____ What would his demand for Twinkies be? _____
(Hint: Recall the discussion of boundary optimum.)

(f) Donald's wife complains that whenever Donald gets an extra dollar, he always spends it all on stamps. Is she right? (Assume that $m > p_s$.)

_____.

(g) Suppose that the price of Twinkies is $2 and the price of stamps is $1. On the graph below, draw Fribble's Engel curve for Twinkies in red ink and his Engel curve for stamps in blue ink. (Hint: First draw the Engel curves for incomes greater than $1, then draw them for incomes less than $1.)

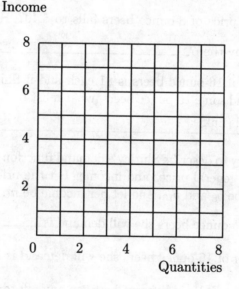

Income

6.5 (0) Shirley Sixpack, as you will recall, thinks that two 8-ounce cans of beer are exactly as good as one 16-ounce can of beer. Suppose that these are the only sizes of beer available to her and that she has $30 to spend on beer. Suppose that an 8-ounce beer costs $.75 and a 16-ounce beer costs $1. On the graph below, draw Shirley's budget line in blue ink, and draw some of her indifference curves in red.

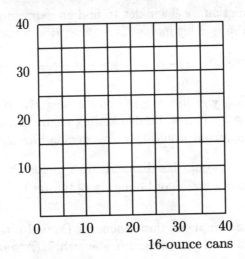

8-ounce cans

16-ounce cans

(a) At these prices, which size can will she buy, or will she buy some of

each?_____.

(b) Suppose that the price of 16-ounce beers remains $1 and the price of

8-ounce beers falls to $.55. Will she buy more 8-ounce beers?_____.

(c) What if the price of 8-ounce beers falls to $.40? How many 8-ounce

beers will she buy then?_____.

(d) If the price of 16-ounce beers is $1 each and if Shirley chooses some 8-ounce beers and some 16-ounce beers, what must be the price of 8-ounce

beers?_____.

(e) Now let us try to describe Shirley's demand function for 16-ounce beers as a function of general prices and income. Let the prices of 8-ounce and 16-ounce beers be p_8 and p_{16}, and let her income be m. If $p_{16} < 2p_8$, then

the number of 16-ounce beers she will demand is _____ If $p_{16} > 2p_8$,

then the number of 16-ounce beers she will demand is _____ If $p_{16} =$

_____ p_8, she will be indifferent between any affordable combinations.

6.6 (0) Miss Muffet always likes to have things "just so." In fact the only way she will consume her curds and whey is in the ratio of 2 units of whey per unit of curds. She has an income of $20. Whey costs $.75 per unit. Curds cost $1 per unit. On the graph below, draw Miss Muffet's budget line, and plot some of her indifference curves. (Hint: Have you noticed something kinky about Miss Muffet?)

(a) How many units of curds will Miss Muffet demand in this situation? _____ How many units of whey?_____.

Whey

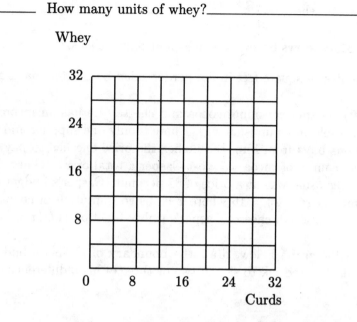

(b) Write down Miss Muffet's demand function for whey as a function of the prices of curds and whey and of her income, where p_c is the price of

curds, p_w is the price of whey, and m is her income. $D(p_c, p_w, m) =$_____

_____ (Hint: You can solve for her demands by solving two equations in two unknowns. One equation tells you that she consumes twice as much whey as curds. The second equation is her budget equation.)

6.7 (1) Mary's utility function is $U(b, c) = b + 100c - c^2$, where b is the number of silver bells in her garden and c is the number of cockle shells. She has 500 square feet in her garden to allocate between silver bells and cockle shells. Silver bells each take up 1 square foot and cockle shells each take up 4 square feet. She gets both kinds of seeds for free.

(a) To maximize her utility, given the size of her garden, Mary should

plant _____ silver bells and _____ cockle shells. (Hint: Write down her "budget constraint" for space. Solve the problem as if it were an ordinary demand problem.)

(b) If she suddenly acquires an extra 100 square feet for her garden, how

much should she increase her planting of silver bells?_____

_____ How much should she increase her planting of cockle shells?

_____.

(c) If Mary had only 144 square feet in her garden, how many cockle shells would she grow?_____.

(d) If Mary grows both silver bells and cockle shells, then we know that the number of square feet in her garden must be greater than_____.

6.8 (0) Casper consumes cocoa and cheese. He has an income of $16. Cocoa is sold in an unusual way. There is only one supplier and the more cocoa one buys from him, the higher the price one has to pay per unit. In fact, x units of cocoa will cost Casper a total of x^2 dollars. Cheese is sold in the usual way at a price of $2 per unit. Casper's budget equation, therefore, is $x^2 + 2y = 16$ where x is his consumption of cocoa and y is his consumption of cheese. Casper's utility function is $U(x, y) = 3x + y$.

(a) On the graph below, draw the boundary of Casper's budget set in blue ink. Use red ink to sketch two or three of his indifference curves.

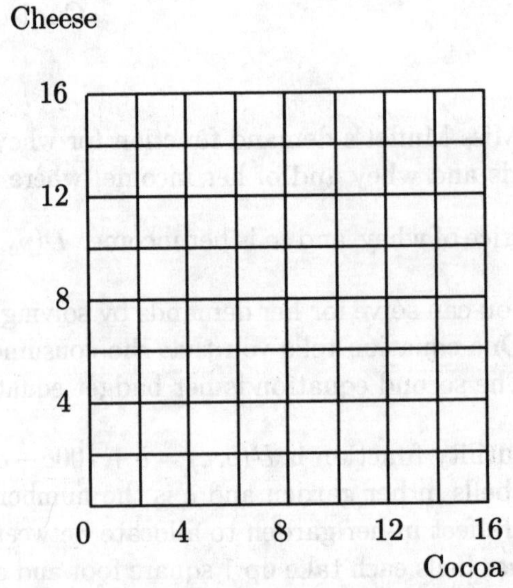

Cheese

(b) Write an equation that says that at the point (x, y), the slope of Casper's budget "line" equals the slope of his indifference "curve."_____

_____ Casper demands _____ units of cocoa and _____ units of cheese.

6.9 (0) Perhaps after all of the problems with imaginary people and places, you would like to try a problem based on actual fact. The U.S. government's Bureau of Labor Statistics periodically makes studies of family budgets and uses the results to compile the consumer price index. These budget studies and a wealth of other interesting economic data can be found in the annually published *Handbook of Labor Statistics*. The tables below report total current consumption expenditures and expenditures on certain major categories of goods for 5 different income groups in the United States in 1961. People within each of these groups all had similar incomes. Group A is the lowest income group and Group E is the highest.

Table 6.1
Expenditures by Category for Various Income Groups in 1961

Income Group	A	B	C	D	E
Food Prepared at Home	465	783	1078	1382	1848
Food Away from Home	68	171	213	384	872
Housing	626	1090	1508	2043	4205
Clothing	119	328	508	830	1745
Transportation	139	519	826	1222	2048
Other	364	745	1039	1554	3490
Total Expenditures	1781	3636	5172	7415	14208

Table 6.2
Percentage Allocation of Family Budget

Income Group	A	B	C	D	E
Food Prepared at Home	26	22	21	19	13
Food Away from Home	3.8	4.7	4.1	5.2	6.1
Housing	35	30			
Clothing	6.7	9.0			
Transportation	7.8	14			

(a) Complete Table 6.2.

(b) Which of these goods are normal goods?_____.

(c) Which of these goods satisfy your textbook's definition of *luxury goods* at most income levels?_____.

(d) Which of these goods satisfy your textbook's definition of *necessity goods* at most income levels?_____.

(e) On the graph below, use the information from Table 6.1 to draw "Engel curves." (Use total expenditure on current consumption as income for purposes of drawing this curve.) Use red ink to draw the Engel curve for food prepared at home. Use blue ink to draw an Engel curve for food away from home. Use pencil to draw an Engel curve for clothing. How does the shape of an Engel curve for a luxury differ from the shape

of an Engel curve for a necessity?_____

_____.

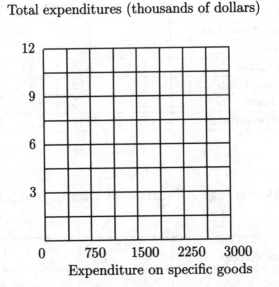

Total expenditures (thousands of dollars)

Expenditure on specific goods

6.10 (0) Percy consumes cakes and ale. His demand function for cakes is $q_c = m - 30p_c + 20p_a$, where m is his income, p_a is the price of ale, p_c is the price of cakes, and q_c is his consumption of cakes. Percy's income is $100, and the price of ale is $1 per unit.

(a) Is ale a substitute for cakes or a complement? Explain._____

_____.

(b) Write an equation for Percy's demand function for cakes where income

and the price of ale are held fixed at $100 and $1._____.

(c) Write an equation for Percy's inverse demand function for cakes where

income is $100 and the price of ale remains at $1._____ At

what price would Percy buy 30 cakes? _____ Use blue ink to draw Percy's inverse demand curve for cakes.

(d) Suppose that the price of ale rises to $2.50 per unit and remains there.

Write an equation for Percy's inverse demand for cakes. _____

_____ Use red ink to draw in Percy's new inverse demand curve for cakes.

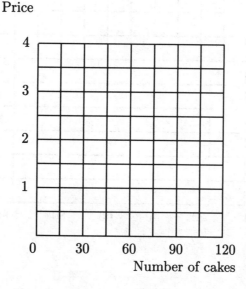

Price

Number of cakes

6.11 (0) Richard and Mary Stout have fallen on hard times, but remain rational consumers. They are making do on $80 a week, spending $40 on food and $40 on all other goods. Food costs $1 per unit. On the graph below, use black ink to draw a budget line. Label their consumption bundle with the letter A.

(a) The Stouts suddenly become eligible for food stamps. This means that they can go to the agency and buy coupons that can be exchanged for $2 worth of food. Each coupon costs the Stouts $1. However, the maximum number of coupons they can buy per week is 10. On the graph, draw their new budget line with red ink.

(b) If the Stouts have homothetic preferences, how much more food will they buy once they enter the food stamp program?_____.

Dollars worth of other things

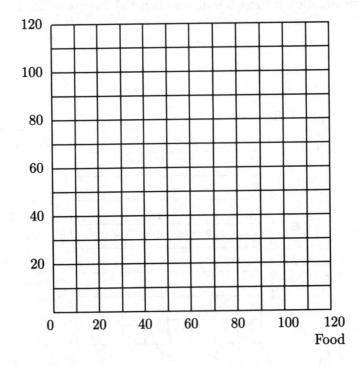

Calculus **6.12 (2)** As you may remember, Nancy Lerner is taking an economics course in which her overall score is the *minimum* of the number of correct answers she gets on two examinations. For the first exam, each correct answer costs Nancy 10 minutes of study time. For the second exam, each correct answer costs her 20 minutes of study time. In the last chapter, you found the best way for her to allocate 1200 minutes between the two exams. Some people in Nancy's class learn faster and some learn slower than Nancy. Some people will choose to study more than she does, and some will choose to study less than she does. In this section, we will find a general solution for a person's choice of study times and exam scores as a function of the time costs of improving one's score.

(a) Suppose that if a student does not study for an examination, he or she gets no correct answers. Every answer that the student gets right on the first examination costs P_1 minutes of studying for the first exam. Every answer that he or she gets right on the second examination costs P_2 minutes of studying for the second exam. Suppose that this student spends a total of M minutes studying for the two exams and allocates the time between the two exams in the most efficient possible way. Will the student have the same number of correct answers on both exams?

_____ Write a general formula for this student's overall score for the

course as a function of the three variables, P_1, P_2, and M, $S =$_____ If this student wants to get an overall score of S, with the smallest possible total amount of studying, this student must spend _____ minutes

studying for the first exam and _____ studying for the second exam.

(b) Suppose that a student has the utility function

$$U(S, M) = S - \frac{A}{2} M^2,$$

where S is the student's overall score for the course, M is the number of minutes the student spends studying, and A is a variable that reflects how much the student dislikes studying. In Part (a) of this problem, you found that a student who studies for M minutes and allocates this time wisely between the two exams will get an overall score of $S = \frac{M}{P_1+P_2}$. Substitute $\frac{M}{P_1+P_2}$ for S in the utility function and then differentiate with respect to M to find the amount of study time, M, that maximizes the

student's utility. $M =$_____ Your answer will be a function of the variables P_1, P_2, and A. If the student chooses the utility-maximizing amount of study time and allocates it wisely between the two exams, he

or she will have an overall score for the course of $S =$_____.

(c) Nancy Lerner has a utility function like the one presented above. She chose the utility-maximizing amount of study time for herself. For Nancy, $P_1 = 10$ and $P_2 = 20$. She spent a total of $M = 1200$ minutes studying for the two exams. This gives us enough information to solve for the variable

A in Nancy's utility function. In fact, for Nancy, $A =$_____.

(d) Ed Fungus is a student in Nancy's class. Ed's utility function is just like Nancy's, with the same value of A. But Ed learns more slowly than Nancy. In fact it takes Ed exactly twice as long to learn anything as it takes Nancy, so that for him, $P_1 = 20$ and $P_2 = 40$. Ed also chooses his amount of study time so as to maximize his utility. Find the ratio of the amount of time Ed spends studying to the amount of time Nancy spends

studying. _____ Will his score for the course be greater than half,

equal to half, or less than half of Nancy's?_____.

6.13 (1) Here is a puzzle for you. At first glance, it would appear that there is not nearly enough information to answer this question. But when you graph the indifference curve and think about it a little, you will see that there is a neat, easily calculated solution.

Kinko spends all his money on whips and leather jackets. Kinko's utility function is $U(x, y) = \min\{4x, 2x + y\}$, where x is his consumption of whips and y is his consumption of leather jackets. Kinko is consuming 15 whips and 10 leather jackets. The price of whips is $10. You are to find Kinko's income.

(a) Graph the indifference curve for Kinko that passes through the point (15, 10). What is the slope of this indifference curve at (15, 10)?_____ _____ What must be the price of leather jackets if Kinko chooses this point?_____ Now, what is Kinko's income?_____.

Leather jackets

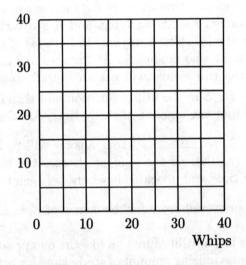

Revealed Preference

Introduction. In the last section, you were given a consumer's preferences and then you solved for his or her demand behavior. In this chapter we turn this process around: you are given information about a consumer's demand behavior and you must deduce something about the consumer's preferences. The main tool is the *weak axiom of revealed preference*. This axiom says the following. If a consumer chooses commodity bundle A when she can afford bundle B, then she will never choose bundle B from any budget in which she can also afford A. The idea behind this axiom is that if you choose A when you could have had B, you must like A better than B. But if you like A better than B, then you will never choose B when you can have A. If somebody chooses A when she can afford B, we say that for her, A is *directly revealed preferred* to B. The weak axiom says that if A is directly revealed preferred to B, then B is not directly revealed preferred to A.

Example: Let us look at an example of how you check whether one bundle is revealed preferred to another. Suppose that a consumer buys the bundle $(x_1^A, x_2^A) = (2, 3)$ at prices $(p_1^A, p_2^A) = (1, 4)$. The cost of bundle (x_1^A, x_2^A) at these prices is $(2 \times 1) + (3 \times 4) = 14$. Bundle $(2, 3)$ is directly revealed preferred to all the other bundles that she can afford at prices $(1, 4)$, when she has an income of 14. For example, the bundle $(5, 2)$ costs only 13 at prices $(1, 4)$, so we can say that for this consumer $(2, 3)$ is revealed preferred to $(1, 4)$.

You will also have some problems about price and quantity indexes. A price index is a comparison of average price levels between two different times or two different places. If there is more than one commodity, it is not necessarily the case that all prices changed in the same proportion. Let us suppose that we want to compare the price level in the "current year" with the price level in some "base year." One way to make this comparison is to compare the costs in the two years of some "reference" commodity bundle. Two reasonable choices for the reference bundle come to mind. One possibility is to use the current year's consumption bundle for the reference bundle. The other possibility is to use the bundle consumed in the base year. Typically these will be different bundles. If the base-year bundle is the reference bundle, the resulting price index is called the *Laspeyres price index*. If the current year's consumption bundle is the reference bundle, then the index is called the *Paasche price index*.

Example: Suppose that there are just two goods. In 1980, the prices were $(1, 3)$ and a consumer consumed the bundle $(4, 2)$. In 1990, the prices were $(2, 4)$ and the consumer consumed the bundle $(3, 3)$. The cost of the 1980 bundle at 1980 prices is $(1 \times 4) + (3 \times 2) = 10$. The cost of this same bundle at 1990 prices is $(2 \times 4) + (4 \times 2) = 16$. If 1980 is treated as the base year and 1990 as the current year, the Laspeyres price ratio is

16/10. To calculate the Paasche price ratio, you find the ratio of the cost of the 1990 bundle at 1990 prices to the cost of the same bundle at 1980 prices. The 1990 bundle costs $(2 \times 3) + (4 \times 3) = 18$ at 1990 prices. The same bundle cost $(1 \times 3) + (3 \times 3) = 12$ at 1980 prices. Therefore the Paasche price index is 18/12. Notice that both price indexes indicate that prices rose, but because the price changes are weighted differently, the two approaches give different price ratios.

Making an index of the "quantity" of stuff consumed in the two periods presents a similar problem. How do you weight changes in the amount of good 1 relative to changes in the amount of good 2? This time we could compare the cost of the two periods' bundles evaluated at some reference prices. Again there are at least two reasonable possibilities, the *Laspeyres quantity index* and the *Paasche quantity index*. The Laspeyres quantity index uses the base-year prices as the reference prices, and the Paasche quantity index uses current prices as reference prices.

Example: In the example above, the Laspeyres quantity index is the ratio of the cost of the 1990 bundle at 1980 prices to the cost of the 1980 bundle at 1980 prices. The cost of the 1990 bundle at 1980 prices is 12 and the cost of the 1980 bundle at 1980 prices is 10, so the Laspeyres quantity index is 12/10. The cost of the 1990 bundle at 1990 prices is 18 and the cost of the 1980 bundle at 1990 prices is 16. Therefore the Paasche quantity index is 18/16.

When you have completed this section, we hope that you will be able to do the following

- Decide from given data about prices and consumption whether one commodity bundle is preferred to another.

- Given price and consumption data, calculate Paasche and Laspeyres price and quantity indexes.

- Use the weak axiom of revealed preferences to make logical deductions about behavior.

- Use the idea of revealed preference to make comparisons of well-being across time and across countries.

7.1 (0) When prices are $(4, 6)$, Goldie chooses the bundle $(6, 6)$, and when prices are $(6, 3)$, she chooses the bundle $(10, 0)$.

(a) On the graph below, show Goldie's first budget line in red ink and her second budget line in blue ink. Mark her choice from the first budget with the label A, and her choice from the second budget with the label B.

(b) Is Goldie's behavior consistent with the weak axiom of revealed preference?_____.

Good 2

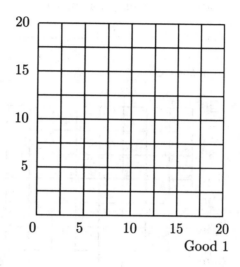

7.2 (0) Freddy Frolic consumes only asparagus and tomatoes, which are highly seasonal crops in Freddy's part of the world. He sells umbrellas for a living, which provides a fluctuating income depending on the weather. But Freddy doesn't mind; he never thinks of tomorrow, so each week he spends as much as he earns. One week, when the prices of asparagus and tomatoes were each $1 a pound, Freddy consumed 15 pounds of each. Use blue ink to show the budget line in the diagram below. Label Freddy's consumption bundle with the letter A.

(a) What is Freddy's income?_____.

(b) The next week the price of tomatoes rose to $2 a pound, but the price of asparagus remained at $1 a pound. By chance, Freddy's income had changed so that his old consumption bundle of (15,15) was just affordable at the new prices. Use red ink to draw this new budget line on the graph

below. Does your new budget line go through the point A? _____

What is the slope of this line?_____.

(c) How much asparagus can he afford now if he spent all of his income

on asparagus?_____.

(d) What is Freddy's income now?_____.

(e) Use pencil to shade the bundles of goods on Freddy's new red budget line that he definitely will *not* purchase with this budget. Is it possible that he would increase his consumption of tomatoes when his budget changes from the blue line to the red one?_____.

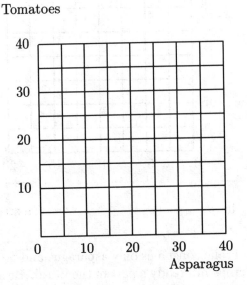

Tomatoes

Asparagus

7.3 (0) Pierre consumes bread and wine. For Pierre, the price of bread is 4 francs per loaf, and the price of wine is 4 francs per glass. Pierre has an income of 40 francs per day. Pierre consumes 6 glasses of wine and 4 loaves of bread per day.

Bob also consumes bread and wine. For Bob, the price of bread is 1/2 dollar per loaf and the price of wine is 2 dollars per glass. Bob has an income of $15 per day.

(a) If Bob and Pierre have the same tastes, can you tell whether Bob is better off than Pierre or vice versa? Explain._____

_____.

(b) Suppose prices and incomes for Pierre and Bob are as above and that Pierre's consumption is as before. Suppose that Bob spends all of his income. Give an example of a consumption bundle of wine and bread such that, if Bob bought this bundle, we would know that Bob's tastes are not the same as Pierre's tastes._____

_____

_____.

7.4 (0) Here is a table of prices and the demands of a consumer named Ronald whose behavior was observed in 5 different price-income situations.

Situation	p_1	p_2	x_1	x_2
A	1	1	5	35
B	1	2	35	10
C	1	1	10	15
D	3	1	5	15
E	1	2	10	10

(a) Sketch each of his budget lines and label the point chosen in each case by the letters A, B, C, D, and E.

(b) Is Ronald's behavior consistent with the Weak Axiom of Revealed

Preference?_____.

(c) Shade lightly in red ink all of the points that you are certain are worse for Ronald than the bundle C.

(d) Suppose that you are told that Ronald has convex and monotonic preferences and that he obeys the strong axiom of revealed preference. Shade lightly in blue ink all of the points that you are certain are *at least as good as* the bundle C.

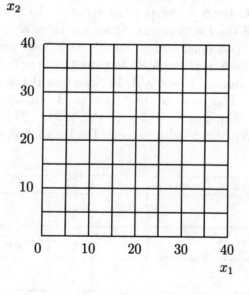

7.5 (0) Horst and Nigel live in different countries. Possibly they have different preferences, and certainly they face different prices. They each consume only two goods, x and y. Horst has to pay 14 marks per unit of x and 5 marks per unit of y. Horst spends his entire income of 167 marks on 8 units of x and 11 units of y. Good x costs Nigel 9 quid per unit and good y costs him 7 quid per unit. Nigel buys 10 units of x and 9 units of y.

(a) Which prices and income would Horst prefer, Nigel's income and prices or his own, or is there too little information to tell? Explain your answer._____

_____.

(b) Would Nigel prefer to have Horst's income and prices or his own, or is there too little information to tell?_____

_____.

7.6 (0) Here is a table that illustrates some observed prices and choices for three different goods at three different prices in three different situations.

Situation	p_1	p_2	p_3	x_1	x_2	x_3
A	1	2	8	2	1	3
B	4	1	8	3	4	2
C	3	1	2	2	6	2

(a) We will fill in the table below as follows. Where i and j stand for any of the letters A, B, and C in Row i and Column j of the matrix, write the value of the Situation-j bundle at the Situation-i prices. For example, in Row A and Column A, we put the value of the bundle purchased in Situation A at Situation A prices. From the table above, we see that in Situation A, the consumer bought bundle $(2, 1, 3)$ at prices $(1, 2, 8)$. The cost of this bundle A at prices A is therefore $(1 \times 2) + (2 \times 1) + (8 \times 3) = 28$, so we put 28 in Row A, Column A. In Situation B the consumer bought bundle $(3, 4, 2)$. The value of the Situation-B bundle, evaluated at the situation-A prices is $(1 \times 3) + (2 \times 4) + (8 \times 2) = 27$, so put 27 in Row A, Column B. We have filled in some of the boxes, but we leave a few for you to do.

Prices/Quantities	A	B	C
A	28	27	
B		32	30
C	13	17	

(b) Fill in the entry in Row i and Column j of the table below with a D if the Situation-i bundle is directly revealed preferred to the Situation-j bundle. For example, in Situation A the consumer's expenditure is \$28. We see that at Situation-A prices, he could also afford the Situation-B bundle, which cost 27. Therefore the Situation-A bundle is directly revealed preferred to the Situation-B bundle, so we put a D in Row A, Column B. Now let us consider Row B, Column A. The cost of the Situation-B

bundle at Situation-B prices is 32. The cost of the Situation-A bundle at Situation-B prices is 33. So, in Situation B, the consumer could not afford the Situation-A bundle. Therefore Situation B is *not* directly revealed preferred to Situation A. So we leave the entry in Row B, Column A blank. Generally, there is a D in Row i Column j if the number in the ij entry of the table in part (a) is less than or equal to the entry in Row i, Column i. There will be a violation of WARP if for some i and j, there is a D in Row i Column j and also a D in Row j, Column i. Do these

observations violate WARP?_____.

Situation	A	B	C
A	—		
B		—	D
C			—

(c) Now fill in Row i, Column j with an I if observation i is *indirectly* revealed preferred to j. Do these observations violate the Strong Axiom

of Revealed Preference?_____.

7.7 (0) It is January, and Joe Grad, whom we met in Chapter 5, is shivering in his apartment when the phone rings. It is Mandy Manana, one of the students whose price theory problems he graded last term. Mandy asks if Joe would be interested in spending the month of February in her apartment. Mandy, who has switched majors from economics to political science, plans to go to Aspen for the month and so her apartment will be empty (alas). All Mandy asks is that Joe pay the monthly service charge of $40 charged by her landlord and the heating bill for the month of February. Since her apartment is much better insulated than Joe's, it only costs $1 per month to raise the temperature by 1 degree. Joe thanks her and says he will let her know tomorrow. Joe puts his earmuffs back on and muses. If he accepts Mandy's offer, he will still have to pay rent on his current apartment but he won't have to heat it. If he moved, heating would be cheaper, but he would have the $40 service charge. The outdoor temperature averages 20 degrees Fahrenheit in February, and it costs him $2 per month to raise his apartment temperature by 1 degree. Joe is still grading homework and has $100 a month left to spend on food and utilities after he has paid the rent on his apartment. The price of food is still $1 per unit.

(a) Draw Joe's budget line for February if he moves to Mandy's apartment and on the same graph, draw his budget line if he doesn't move.

(b) After drawing these lines himself, Joe decides that he would be better off not moving. From this, we can tell, using the principle of revealed preference that Joe must plan to keep his apartment at a temperature of

less than_____.

(c) Joe calls Mandy and tells her his decision. Mandy offers to pay half the service charge. Draw Joe's budget line if he accepts Mandy's new offer. Joe now accepts Mandy's offer. From the fact that Joe accepted this offer we can tell that he plans to keep the temperature in Mandy's

apartment above_____.

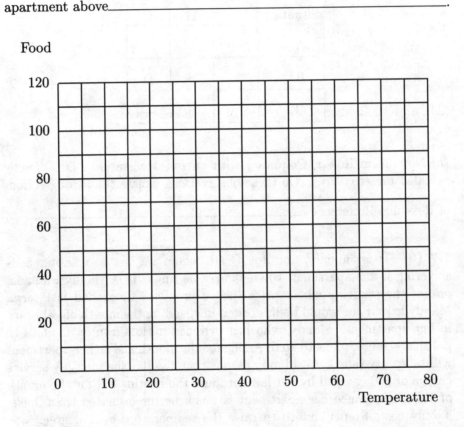

7.8 (0) Lord Peter Pommy is a distinguished criminologist, schooled in the latest techniques of forensic revealed preference. Lord Peter is investigating the disappearance of Sir Cedric Pinchbottom who abandoned his aging mother on a street corner in Liverpool and has not been seen since. Lord Peter has learned that Sir Cedric left England and is living under an assumed name somewhere in the Empire. There are three suspects, R. Preston McAfee of Brass Monkey, Ontario, Canada, Richard Manning of North Shag, New Zealand, and Richard Stevenson of Gooey Shoes, Falkland Islands. Lord Peter has obtained Sir Cedric's diary, which recorded his consumption habits in minute detail. By careful observation, he has also discovered the consumption behavior of McAfee, Manning, and Stevenson. All three of these gentlemen, like Sir Cedric, spend their entire incomes on beer and sausage. Their dossiers reveal the following:

- **Sir Cedric Pinchbottom** — In the year before his departure, Sir Cedric consumed 10 kilograms of sausage and 20 liters of beer per week. At that time, beer cost 1 English pound per liter and sausage cost 1 English pound per kilogram.
- **R. Preston McAfee** — McAfee is known to consume 5 liters of beer and 20 kilograms of sausage. In Brass Monkey, Ontario beer costs 1 Canadian dollar per liter and sausage costs 2 Canadian dollars per kilogram.
- **Richard Manning** — Manning consumes 5 kilograms of sausage and 10 liters of beer per week. In North Shag, a liter of beer costs 2 New Zealand dollars and sausage costs 2 New Zealand dollars per kilogram.
- **Richard Stevenson** — Stevenson consumes 5 kilograms of sausage and 30 liters of beer per week. In Gooey Shoes, a liter of beer costs 10 Falkland Island pounds and sausage costs 20 Falkland Island pounds per kilogram.

(a) Draw the budget line for each of the three fugitives, using a different color of ink for each one. Label the consumption bundle that each chooses. On this graph, superimpose Sir Cedric's budget line and the bundle he chose.

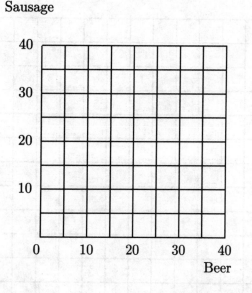

(b) After pondering the dossiers for a few moments, Lord Peter announced. "Unless Sir Cedric has changed his tastes, I can eliminate one of the suspects. Revealed preference tells me that one of the suspects is

innocent." Which one?_____.

(c) After thinking a bit longer, Lord Peter announced. "If Sir Cedric left voluntarily, then he would have to be better off than he was before. Therefore if Sir Cedric left voluntarily and if he has not changed his tastes,

he must be living in_____.

7.9 (1) The McCawber family is having a tough time making ends meet. They spend $100 a week on food and $50 on other things. A new welfare program has been introduced that gives them a choice between receiving a grant of $50 per week that they can spend any way they want, and buying any number of $2 food coupons for $1 apiece. (They naturally are not allowed to resell these coupons.) Food is a normal good for the McCawbers. As a family friend, you have been asked to help them decide on which option to choose. Drawing on your growing fund of economic knowledge, you proceed as follows.

(a) On the graph below, draw their old budget line in red ink and label their current choice C. Now use black ink to draw the budget line that they would have with the grant. If they chose the coupon option, how much food could they buy if they spent all their money on food coupons?

_____ How much could they spend on other things if they bought

no food? _____ Use blue ink to draw their budget line if they choose the coupon option.

Other things

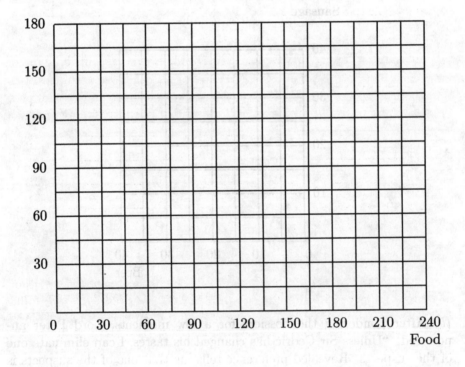

(b) Using the fact that food is a normal good for the McCawbers, and knowing what they purchased before, darken the portion of the black budget line where their consumption bundle could possibly be if they chose the lump-sum grant option. Label the ends of this line segment A and B.

(c) After studying the graph you have drawn, you report to the McCawbers. "I have enough information to be able to tell you which choice to make. You should choose the _____ because_____

_____.

(d) Mr. McCawber thanks you for your help and then asks, "Would you have been able to tell me what to do if you hadn't known whether food was a normal good for us?" On the axes below, draw the same budget lines you drew on the diagram above, but draw indifference curves for which food is not a normal good and for which the McCawbers would be better off with the program you advised them not to take.

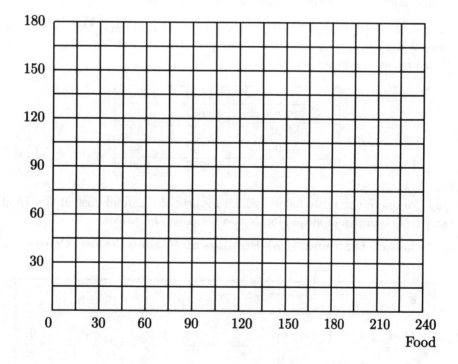

Other things

7.10 (0) In 1933, the Swedish economist Gunnar Myrdal (who later won a Nobel prize in economics) and a group of his associates at Stockholm University collected a fantastically detailed historical series of prices and price indexes in Sweden from 1830 until 1930. This was published in a book called *The Cost of Living in Sweden.* In this book you can find 100 years of prices for goods such as oat groats, hard rye bread, salted codfish, beef, reindeer meat, birchwood, tallow candles, eggs, sugar, and coffee. There are also estimates of the quantities of each good consumed by an average working-class family in 1850 and again in 1890.

The table below gives prices in 1830, 1850, 1890, and 1913, for flour, meat, milk, and potatoes. In this time period, these four staple foods accounted for about 2/3 of the Swedish food budget.

Prices of Staple Foods in Sweden

Prices are in Swedish kronor per kilogram, except for milk, which is in Swedish kronor per liter.

	1830	1850	1890	1913
Grain Flour	.14	.14	.16	.19
Meat	.28	.34	.66	.85
Milk	.07	.08	.10	.13
Potatoes	.032	.044	.051	.064

Based on the tables published in Myrdal's book, typical consumption bundles for a working-class Swedish family in 1850 and 1890 are listed below. (The reader should be warned that we have made some approximations and simplifications to draw these simple tables from the much more detailed information in the original study.)

Quantities Consumed by a Typical Swedish Family

Quantities are measured in kilograms per year, except for milk, which is measured in liters per year.

	1850	1890
Grain Flour	165	220
Meat	22	42
Milk	120	180
Potatoes	200	200

(a) Complete the table below, which reports the annual cost of the 1850 and 1890 bundles of staple foods at various years' prices.

Cost of 1850 and 1890 Bundles at Various Years' Prices

Cost	1850 bundle	1890 bundle
Cost at 1830 Prices	44.1	61.6
Cost at 1850 Prices		
Cost at 1890 Prices		
Cost at 1913 Prices	78.5	113.7

(b) Is the 1890 bundle revealed preferred to the 1850 bundle?_____.

(c) The Laspeyres quantity index for 1890 with base year 1850 is the ratio of the value of the 1890 bundle at 1850 prices to the value of the 1850 bundle at 1850 prices. Calculate the Laspeyres quantity index of staple food consumption for 1890 with base year 1850._____.

(d) The Paasche quantity index for 1890 with base year 1850 is the ratio of the value of the 1890 bundle at 1890 prices to the value of the 1850 bundle at 1890 prices. Calculate the Paasche quantity index for 1890 with

base year 1850._____.

(e) The Laspeyres price index for 1890 with base year 1850 is calculated using 1850 quantities for weights. Calculate the Laspeyres price index for

1890 with base year 1850 for this group of four staple foods._____.

(f) If a Swede were rich enough in 1850 to afford the 1890 bundle of staple

foods in 1850, he would have to spend _____ times as much on these foods as does the typical Swedish worker of 1850.

(g) If a Swede in 1890 decided to purchase the same bundle of food staples that was consumed by typical 1850 workers, he would spend the fraction

_____ of the amount that the typical Swedish worker of 1890 spends on these goods.

7.11 (0) This question draws from the tables in the previous question. Let us try to get an idea of what it would cost an American family at today's prices to purchase the bundle consumed by an average Swedish family in 1850. In the United States today, the price of flour is about $.40 per kilogram, the price of meat is about $3.75 per kilogram, the price of milk is about $.50 per liter, and the price of potatoes is about $1 per kilogram. We can also compute a Laspeyres price index across time and across countries and use it to estimate the value of a current US dollar relative to the value of an 1850 Swedish kronor.

(a) How much would it cost an American at today's prices to buy the bundle of staple food commodities purchased by an average Swedish working

class family in 1850?_____.

(b) Myrdal estimates that in 1850, about 2/3 of the average family's budget was spent on food. In turn, the four staples discussed in the last question constitute about 2/3 of the average family's food budget. If the prices of other goods relative to the price of the food staples are similar in the United States today to what they were in Sweden in 1850, about how much would it cost an American at current prices to consume the same overall consumption bundle consumed by a Swedish working-class

family in 1850?_____.

(c) Using the Swedish consumption bundle of staple foods in 1850 as weights, calculate a Laspeyres price index to compare prices in current

American dollars relative to prices in 1850 Swedish kronor._____ If we use this to estimate the value of current dollars relative to 1850 Swedish kronor, we would say that a U.S. dollar today is worth about

_____ 1850 Swedish kronor.

7.12 (0) Suppose that between 1960 and 1985, the price of all goods exactly doubled while every consumer's income tripled.

(a) Would the Laspeyres price index for 1985, with base year 1960 be

less than 2, greater than 2, or exactly equal to 2? _____ What

about the Paasche price index?_____.

(b) If bananas are a normal good, will total banana consumption in-

crease?_____ If everybody has homothetic preferences, can you determine by what percentage total banana consumption must have in-

creased? Explain._____

_____

_____.

7.13 (1) Norm and Sheila consume only meat pies and beer. Meat pies used to cost $2 each and beer was $1 per can. Their gross income used to be $60 per week, but they had to pay an income tax of $10. Use red ink to sketch their old budget line for meat pies and beer.

Beer

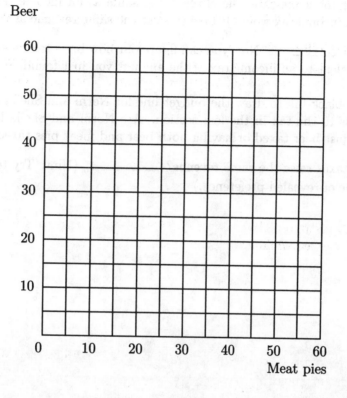

(a) They used to buy 30 cans of beer per week and spent the rest of their income on meat pies. How many meat pies did they buy?_____.

(b) The government decided to eliminate the income tax and to put a sales tax of $1 per can on beer, raising its price to $2 per can. Assuming that Norm and Sheila's pre-tax income and the price of meat pies did not change, draw their new budget line in blue ink.

(c) The sales tax on beer induced Norm and Sheila to reduce their beer consumption to 20 cans per week. What happened to their consumption

of meat pies? _____ How much revenue did this tax

raise from Norm and Sheila?_____.

(d) This part of the problem will require some careful thinking. Suppose that instead of just taxing beer, the government decided to tax *both* beer and meat pies at the *same* percentage rate, and suppose that the price of beer and the price of meat pies each went up by the full amount of the tax. The new tax rate for both goods was set high enough to raise exactly the same amount of money from Norm and Sheila as the tax on

beer used to raise. This new tax collects $_____ for every bottle of beer

sold and $_____ for every meat pie sold. (Hint: If both goods are taxed at the same rate, the effect is the same as an income tax.) How large an income tax would it take to raise the same revenue as the $1 tax

on beer? _____ Now you can figure out how big a tax on each good is equivalent to an income tax of the amount you just found.

(e) Use black ink to draw the budget line for Norm and Sheila that corresponds to the tax in the last section. Are Norm and Sheila better off having just beer taxed or having both beer and meat pies taxed, if both

sets of taxes raise the same revenue? _____ (Hint: Try to use the principle of revealed preference.)

Slutsky Equation

Introduction. It is useful to think of a price change as having two distinct effects, a substitution effect and an income effect. The **substitution effect** of a price change is the change that would have happened *if* income changed at the same time, in such a way that the consumer could exactly afford her old consumption bundle. The rest of the change in the consumer's demand is called the **income effect**. Why do we bother with breaking a real change into the sum of two hypothetical changes? Because we know things about the pieces that we wouldn't know about the whole without taking it apart. In particular, we know that the substitution effect of increasing the price of a good *must* reduce the demand for it. We also know that the income effect of an increase in the price of a good is equivalent to the effect of a *loss* of income. Therefore if the good whose price has risen is a normal good, then both the income and substitution effect operate to reduce demand. But if the good is an inferior good, income and substitution effects act in opposite directions.

Example: A consumer has the utility function $U(x_1, x_2) = x_1 x_2$ and an income of $24. Initially the price of good 1 was $1 and the price of good 2 was $2. Then the price of good 2 rose to $3 and the price of good 1 stayed at $1. Using the methods you learned in Chapters 5 and 6, you will find that this consumer's demand function for good 1 is $D_1(p_1, p_2, m) = m/2p_1$ and her demand function for good 2 is $D_2(p_1, p_2, m) = m/2p_2$. Therefore initially she will demand 12 units of good 1 and 6 units of good 2. If, when the price of good 2 rose to $3, her income had changed enough so that she could exactly afford her old bundle, her new income would have to be $(1 \times 12) + (3 \times 6) = \$30$. At an income of $30, at the new prices, she would demand $D_2(1, 3, 30) = 5$ units of good 2. Before the change she bought 6 units of 2, so the substitution effect of the price change on her demand for good 2 is $5 - 6 = -1$ units. Our consumer's income didn't *really* change. Her income stayed at $24. Her actual demand for good 2 after the price change was $D_2(1, 3, 24) = 4$. The difference between what she actually demanded after the price change and what she would have demanded if her income had changed to let her just afford the old bundle is the income effect. In this case the income effect is $4 - 5 = -1$ units of good 2. Notice that in this example, both the income effect and the substitution effect of the price increase worked to reduce the demand for good 2.

When you have completed this workout, we hope that you will be able to do the following

- Find Slutsky income effect and substitution effect of a specific price change if you know the demand function for a good.

- Show the Slutsky income and substitution effects of a price change on an indifference curve diagram.

- Show the Hicks income and substitution effects of a price change on an indifference curve diagram.
- Find the Slutsky income and substitution effects for special utility functions such as perfect substitutes, perfect complements, and Cobb-Douglas.
- Use an indifference-curve diagram to show how the case of a Giffen good might arise.
- Show that the substitution effect of a price increase unambiguously decreases demand for the good whose price rose.
- Apply income and substitution effects to draw some inferences about behavior.

8.1 (0) Gentle Charlie, vegetarian that he is, continues to consume apples and bananas. His utility function is $U(x_A, x_B) = x_A x_B$. The price of apples is $1, the price of bananas is $2, and Charlie's income is $40 a day. The price of bananas suddenly falls to $1.

(a) Before the price change, Charlie consumed _____ apples and

_____ bananas per day. On the graph below, use black ink to draw Charlie's original budget line and put the label A on his chosen consumption bundle.

(b) If, after the price change, Charlie's income had changed so that he could exactly afford his old consumption bundle, his new income would have been _____ With this income and the new prices, Charlie would

consume _____ apples and _____ bananas. Use red ink to draw the budget line corresponding to this income and these prices. Label the bundle that Charlie would choose at this income and the new prices with the letter B.

(c) Does the substitution effect of the fall in the price of bananas make

him buy more bananas or less bananas? _____ How many

more or less?_____.

(d) After the price change, Charlie actually buys _____ apples and

_____ bananas. Use blue ink to draw Charlie's actual budget line after the price change. Put the label C on the bundle that he actually chooses after the price change. Draw 3 horizontal lines on your graph, one from A to the vertical axis, one from B to the vertical axis, and one from C to the vertical axis. Along the vertical axis, label the income effect, the substitution effect, and the total effect on the demand for bananas. Is the blue line parallel to the red line or the black line that you drew before?

_____.

Bananas

Apples

(e) The income effect of the fall in the price of bananas on Charlie's demand for bananas is the same as the effect of an (increase, decrease)

_____ in his income of $_____ per day. Does the income

effect make him consume more bananas or less? _____ How many

more or how many less?_____.

(f) Does the substitution effect of the fall in the price of bananas make

Charlie consume more *apples* or less? _____ How many more or

less? _____ Does the income effect of the fall in the price of bananas

make Charlie consume more apples or less? _____ What is the total
effect of the change in the price of bananas on the demand for apples?

_____.

8.2 (0) Neville's passion is fine wine. When the prices of all other goods are fixed at current levels, Neville's demand function for high-quality claret is $q = .02m - 2p$, where m is his income, p is the price of claret (in British pounds), and q is the number of bottles of claret that he demands. Neville's income is 7,500 pounds, and the price of a bottle of suitable claret is 30 pounds.

(a) How many bottles of claret will Neville buy?_____.

(b) If the price of claret rose to 40 pounds, how much income would Neville have to have in order to be exactly able to afford the amount of claret and the amount of other goods that he bought before the price change?

_____ At this income, and a price of 40 pounds, how many

bottles would Neville buy?_____.

(c) At his original income of 7,500 and a price of 40, how much claret

would Neville demand?_____.

(d) When the price of claret rose from 30 to 40, the number of bottles

that Neville demanded decreased by _____ The substitution effect (in-

creased, reduced)_____ his demand by _____ bottles and the

income effect (increased, reduced)_____ his demand by_____

_____.

8.3 (0) *Note: Do this problem only if you have read the section entitled "Another Substitution Effect" that describes the "Hicks substitution effect".* Consider the figure below, which shows the budget constraint and the indifference curves of good King Zog. Zog is in equilibrium with an income of \$300, facing prices $p_X = \$4$ and $p_Y = \$10$.

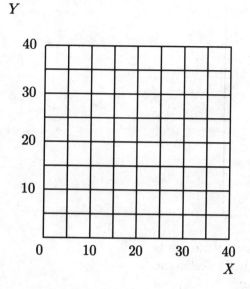

(a) How much X does Zog consume?_____.

(b) If the price of X falls to $2.50, while income and the price of Y stay constant, how much X will Zog consume?_____.

(c) How much income must be taken away from Zog to isolate the Hicksian income and substitution effects (i.e., to make him just able to afford to reach his old indifference curve at the new prices)?_____.

(d) The total effect of the price change is to change consumption from the point _____ to the point_____.

(e) The income effect corresponds to the movement from the point _____ to the point _____ while the substitution effect corresponds to the movement from the point _____ to the point_____.

(f) Is X a normal good or an inferior good?_____.

(g) On the axes below, sketch an Engel curve and a demand curve for Good X that would be reasonable given the information in the graph above. Be sure to label the axes on both your graphs.

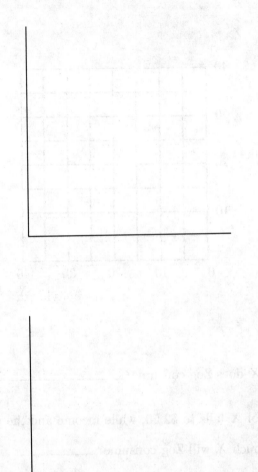

8.4 (0) Maude spends *all* of her income on delphiniums and hollyhocks. She thinks that delphiniums and hollyhocks are perfect substitutes; one delphinium is just as good as one hollyhock. Delphiniums cost $4 a unit and hollyhocks cost $5 a unit.

(a) If the price of delphiniums decreases to $3.00 a unit, will Maude buy more of them? _____ What part of the change in consumption is due to the income effect and what part is due to the substitution effect?

_____.

(b) If the prices of delphiniums and hollyhocks are respectively $p_d = \$4$ and $p_h = \$5$ and if Maude has $120 to spend, draw her budget line in blue ink. Draw the highest indifference curve that she can attain in red ink, and label the point that she chooses as A.

Delphiniums

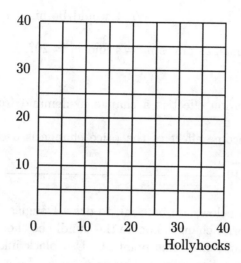

(c) Now let the price of hollyhocks fall to $3 a unit, while the price of delphiniums does not change. Draw her new budget line in black ink. Draw the highest indifference curve that she can now reach with red ink. Label the point she chooses now as B.

(d) How much would Maude's income have to be after the price of hollyhocks fell, so that she could just exactly afford her old commodity bundle

A?_____.

(e) When the price of hollyhocks fell to $3, what part of the change in Maude's demand was due to the income effect and what part was due to

the substitution effect?_____.

8.5 (1) Suppose that two goods are perfect complements. If the price of one good changes, what part of the change in demand is due to the

substitution effect, and what part is due to the income effect?_____

_____.

8.6 (0) Douglas Cornfield's demand function for good x is $x(p_x, p_y, m) = 2m/5p_x$. His income is $1,000, the price of x is $5, and the price of y is $20. If the price of x falls to $4, then his demand for x will change from

_____ to_____.

(a) If his income were to change at the same time so that he could exactly afford his old commodity bundle at $p_x = 4$ and $p_y = 20$, what would his new income be? _____ What would be his demand for x at this new level of income, at prices $p_x = 4$ and $p_y = 20$?_____.

(b) The substitution effect is a change in demand from _____ to _____ The income effect of the price change is a change in demand from _____ to_____.

(c) On the axes below, use blue ink to draw Douglas Cornfield's budget line before the price change. Locate the bundle he chooses at these prices on your graph and label this point A. Use black ink to draw Douglas Cornfield's budget line after the price change. Label his consumption bundle after the change by B.

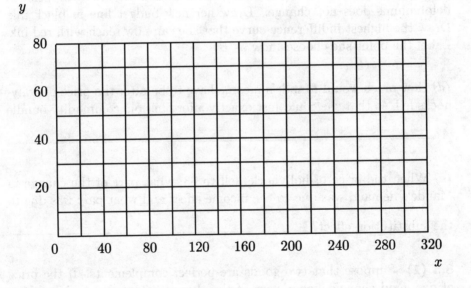

(d) On the graph above, use black ink to draw a budget line with the new prices but with an income that just allows Douglas to buy his old bundle, A. Find the bundle that he would choose with this budget line and label this bundle C.

8.7 (1) Mr. Consumer allows himself to spend $100 per month on cigarettes and ice cream. Mr. C's preferences for cigarettes and ice cream are unaffected by the season of the year.

(a) In January, the price of cigarettes was $1 per pack, while ice cream cost $2 per pint. Faced with these prices, Mr. C bought 30 pints of ice cream and 40 packs of cigarettes. Draw Mr. C's January budget line with blue ink and label his January consumption bundle with the letter *J*.

Ice cream

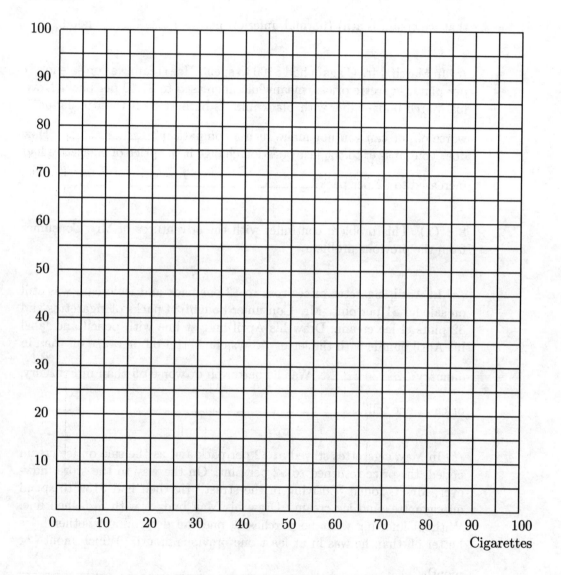

Cigarettes

(b) In February, Mr. C again had $100 to spend and ice cream still cost $2 per pint, but the price of cigarettes rose to $1.25 per pack. Mr. C consumed 30 pints of ice cream and 32 packs of cigarettes. Draw Mr. C's February budget line with red ink and mark his February bundle with the letter *F*. The substitution effect of this price change would make him buy

(less, more, the same amount of) _____ cigarettes and (less, more,

the same amount of) _____ ice cream. Since this is true and the total change in his ice cream consumption was zero, it must be that the income effect of this price change on his consumption of ice cream makes him buy (more, less, the same amount of) _____ ice cream. The income effect of this price change is like the effect of an (increase, decrease) _____ in his income. Therefore the information we have suggests that ice cream is a(n) (normal, inferior, neutral) _____ good.

(c) In March, Mr. C again had $100 to spend. Ice cream was on sale for $1 per pint. Cigarette prices, meanwhile, increased to $1.50 per pack. Draw his March budget line with black ink. Is he better off than in January, worse off, or can you not make such a comparison?_____ How does your answer to the last question change if the price of cigarettes had increased to $2 per pack?_____.

8.8 (1) This problem continues with the adventures of Mr. Consumer from the previous problem.

(a) In April, cigarette prices rose to $2 per pack and ice cream was still on sale for $1 per pint. Mr. Consumer bought 34 packs of cigarettes and 32 pints of ice cream. Draw his April budget line with pencil and label his April bundle with the letter A. Was he better off or worse off than in January?_____ Was he better off or worse off than in February, or can't one tell?_____.

(b) In May, cigarettes stayed at $2 per pack and as the sale on ice cream ended, the price returned to $2 per pint. On the way to the store, however, Mr. C found $30 lying in the street. He then had $130 to spend on cigarettes and ice cream. Draw his May budget with a dashed line. Without knowing what he purchased, one can determine whether he is better off than he was in at least one previous month. Which month or months?_____.

(c) In fact, Mr. C buys 40 packs of cigarettes and 25 pints of ice cream in May. Does he satisfy WARP?_____.

8.9 (2) In the last chapter, we studied a problem involving food prices and consumption in Sweden in 1850 and 1890.

(a) Potato consumption was the same in both years. Real income must have gone up between 1850 and 1890, since the amount of food staples purchased, as measured by either the Laspeyres or the Paasche quantity index, rose. The price of potatoes rose less rapidly than the price of either meat or milk, and at about the same rate as the price of grain flour. So real income went up and the price of potatoes went down relative to other goods. From this information, determine whether potatoes were most likely a normal or an inferior good. Explain your answer._____

_____

_____.

(b) Can one also tell from these data whether it is likely that potatoes were a Giffen good?_____

_____

_____

_____.

8.10 (1) Agatha must travel on the Orient Express from Istanbul to Paris. The distance is 1,500 miles. A traveler can choose to make any fraction of the journey in a first-class carriage and travel the rest of the way in a second-class carriage. The price is 10 cents a mile for a second-class carriage and 20 cents a mile for a first-class carriage. Agatha much prefers first-class to second-class travel, but because of a misadventure in an Istanbul bazaar, she has only $200 left with which to buy her tickets. Luckily, she still has her toothbrush and a suitcase full of cucumber sandwiches to eat on the way. Agatha plans to spend her entire $200 on her tickets for her trip. She will travel first-class as much as she can afford to, but she must get all the way to Paris, and $200 is not enough money to get her all the way to Paris in first class.

(a) On the graph below, use red ink to show the locus of combinations of first- and second-class tickets that Agatha can just afford to purchase with her $200. Use blue ink to show the locus of combinations of first- and second-class tickets that are sufficient to carry her the entire distance from Istanbul to Paris. Locate the combination of first- and second-class miles that Agatha will choose on your graph and label it *A*.

First-class miles

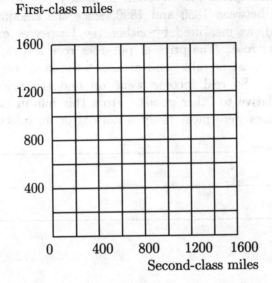

Second-class miles

(b) Let m_1 be the number of miles she travels by first-class coach and m_2 be the number of miles she travels by second-class coach. Write down two equations that you can solve to find the number of miles she chooses to travel by first-class coach and the number of miles she chooses to travel

by second-class coach._____.

(c) The number of miles that she travels by second-class coach is_____

_____.

(d) Just before she was ready to buy her tickets, the price of second-class tickets fell to \$.05 while the price of first-class tickets remained at \$.20. On the graph that you drew above, use pencil to show the combinations of first-class and second-class tickets that she can afford with her \$200 at these prices. On your graph, locate the combination of first-class and second-class tickets that she would now choose. (Remember, she is going to travel as much first-class as she can afford to and still make the 1,500 mile trip on \$200.) Label this point B. How many miles does she travel by

second class now? _____ (Hint: For an exact solution you will have to solve two linear equations in two unknowns.) Is second-class travel a

normal good for Agatha? _____ Is it a Giffen good for her?_____.

8.11 (0) We continue with the adventures of Agatha, from the previous problem. Just after the price change from \$.10 per mile to \$.05 per mile for second-class travel, and just before she had bought any tickets, Agatha misplaced her handbag. Although she kept most of her money in her sock, the money she lost was just enough so that at the new prices, she could exactly afford the combination of first- and second-class tickets that she would have purchased at the old prices. How much money did she lose?

_____ On the graph you started in the previous problem, use black ink to draw the locus of combinations of first- and second-class tickets that she can just afford after discovering her loss. Label the point that she chooses with a C. How many miles will she travel by second class now?_____.

(a) Finally, poor Agatha finds her handbag again. How many miles will she travel by second class now (assuming she didn't buy any tickets before she found her lost handbag)? _____ When the price of second-class tickets fell from \$.10 to \$.05, how much of a change in Agatha's demand for second-class tickets was due to a substitution effect? _____ How much of a change was due to an income effect?_____.

Buying and Selling

Introduction. In previous chapters, we studied the behavior of consumers who start out without owning any goods, but who had some money with which to buy goods. In this chapter, the consumer has an *initial endowment*, which is the bundle of goods the consumer owns before any trades are made. A consumer can trade away from his initial endowment by selling one good and buying the other.

The techniques that you have already learned will serve you well here. To find out how much a consumer demands at given prices, you find his budget line and then find a point of tangency between his budget line and an indifference curve. To determine a budget line for a consumer who is trading from an initial endowment and who has no source of income other than his initial endowment, notice two things. First, *the initial endowment must lie on the consumer's budget line.* This is true because, no matter what the prices are, the consumer can always afford his initial endowment. Second, *if the prices are p_1 and p_2, the slope of the budget line must be $-p_1/p_2$.* This is true, since for every unit of good 1 the consumer gives up, he can get exactly p_1/p_2 units of good 2. Therefore if you know the prices and you know the consumer's initial endowment, then you can always write an equation for the consumer's budget line. After all, if you know one point on a line and you know its slope, you can either draw the line or write down its equation. Once you have the budget equation, you can find the bundle the consumer chooses, using the same methods you learned in Chapter 5.

Example: A peasant consumes only rice and fish. He grows some rice and some fish, but not necessarily in the same proportion in which he wants to consume them. Suppose that if he makes no trades, he will have 20 units of rice and 5 units of fish. The price of rice is 1 yuan per unit, and the price of fish is 2 yuan per unit. The value of the peasant's endowment is $(1 \times 20) + (2 \times 5) = 30$. Therefore the peasant can consume any bundle (R, F) such that $(1 \times R) + (2 \times F) = 30$.

Perhaps the most interesting application of trading from an initial endowment is the theory of labor supply. To study labor supply, we consider the behavior of a consumer who is choosing between leisure and other goods. The only thing that is at all new or "tricky" is finding the appropriate budget constraint for the problem at hand. To study labor supply, we think of the consumer as having an initial endowment of leisure, some of which he may trade away for goods.

In most applications we set the price of "other goods" at 1. The wage rate is the price of leisure. The role that is played by income in the ordinary consumer-good model is now played by "full income." A worker's full income is the income she would have if she chose to take no leisure.

Example: Sherwin has 18 hours a day which he divides between labor and leisure. He can work as many hours a day as he wishes for a wage of $5 per hour. He also receives a pension that gives him $10 a day whether he works or not. The price of other goods is $1 per unit. If Sherwin makes no trades at all, he will have 18 hours of leisure and 10 units of other goods. Therefore Sherwin's initial endowment is 18 hours of leisure a day and $10 a day for other goods. Let R be the amount of leisure that he has per day, and let C be the number of dollars he has to spend per day on other goods. If his wage is $5 an hour, he can afford to consume bundle (R, C) if it costs no more per day than the value of his initial endowment. The value of his initial endowment (his full income) is $10 + (\$5 \times 18) = \$100$ per day. Therefore Sherwin's budget equation is $5R + C = 100$.

9.1 (0) Abishag Appleby owns 20 quinces and 5 kumquats. She has no income from any other source, but she can buy or sell either quinces or kumquats at their market prices. The price of kumquats is four times the price of quinces. There are no other commodities of interest.

(a) How many quinces could she have if she was willing to do without kumquats? _____ How many kumquats could she have if she was willing to do without quinces?_____.

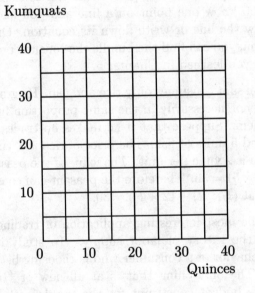

Kumquats

(b) Draw Abishag's budget set, using blue ink, and label the endowment bundle with the letter E. If the price of quinces is 1 and the price of kumquats is 4, write Abishag's budget equation. _____

_____ If the price of quinces is 2 and the price of kumquats is 8, write Abishag's budget equation. _____ What effect does doubling both prices have on the set of commodity bundles that Abishag can afford?_____.

(c) Suppose that Abishag decides to sell 10 quinces. Label her final consumption bundle in your graph with the letter C.

(d) Now, after she has sold 10 quinces and owns the bundle labelled C, suppose that the price of kumquats falls so that kumquats cost the same as quinces. On the diagram above, draw Abishag's new budget line, using red ink.

(e) If Abishag obeys the weak axiom of revealed preference, then there are some points on her red budget line that we can be sure Abishag will not choose. On the graph, make a squiggly line over the portion of Abishag's red budget line that we can be sure she will not choose.

9.2 (0) Mario has a small garden where he raises eggplant and tomatoes. He consumes some of these vegetables, and he sells some in the market. Eggplants and tomatoes are perfect complements for Mario, since the only recipes he knows use them together in a 1:1 ratio. One week his garden yielded 30 pounds of eggplant and 10 pounds of tomatoes. At that time the price of each vegetable was $5 per pound.

(a) What is the monetary value of Mario's endowment of vegetables?

_____.

(b) On the graph below, use blue ink to draw Mario's budget line. Mario ends up consuming _____ pounds of tomatoes and _____ pounds of eggplant. Draw the indifference curve through the consumption bundle that Mario chooses and label this bundle A.

(c) Suppose that before Mario makes any trades, the price of tomatoes rises to $15 a pound, while the price of eggplant stays at $5 a pound.

What is the value of Mario's endowment now? _____ Draw his new budget line, using red ink. He will now choose a consumption bundle

consisting of _____ tomatoes and _____ eggplants.

(d) Suppose that Mario had sold his entire crop at the market for a total of $200, intending to buy back some tomatoes and eggplant for his own consumption. Before he had a chance to buy anything back, the price of tomatoes rose to $15, while the price of eggplant stayed at $5. Draw his

budget line, using pencil or black ink. Mario will now consume _____

pounds of tomatoes and _____ pounds of eggplant.

(e) Assuming that the price of tomatoes rose to \$15 from \$5 before Mario made any transactions, the change in the demand for tomatoes due to the substitution effect was _____ The change in the demand for tomatoes due to the ordinary income effect was _____ The change in the demand for tomatoes due to the endowment income effect was _____ _____ The total change in the demand for tomatoes was_____.

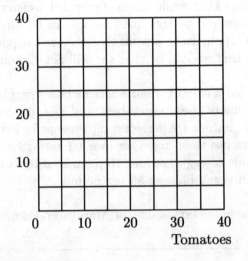

9.3 (0) Lucetta consumes only two goods, A and B. Her only source of income is gifts of these commodities from her many admirers. She doesn't always get these goods in the proportions in which she wants to consume them in, but she can always buy or sell A at the price $p_A = 1$ and B at the price $p_B = 2$. Lucetta's utility function is $U(a, b) = ab$, where a is the amount of A she consumes and b is the amount of B she consumes.

(a) Suppose that Lucetta's admirers give her 100 units of A and 200 units of B. In the graph below, use red ink to draw her budget line. Label her initial endowment E.

(b) What are Lucetta's gross demands for A?_____ And for B?

_____.

(c) What are Lucetta's net demands?_____.

(d) Suppose that before Lucetta has made any trades, the price of good B falls to 1, and the price of good A stays at 1. Draw Lucetta's budget line at these prices on your graph, using blue ink.

(e) Does Lucetta's consumption of good *B* rise or fall?_____ by how much?_____ What happens to Lucetta's consumption of good *A*?_____.

Good B

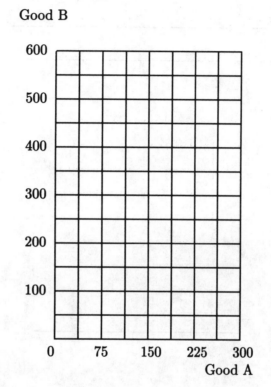

Good A

(f) Suppose that before the price of good *B* fell, Lucetta had exchanged all of her gifts for money, planning to use the money to buy her consumption bundle later. How much good *B* will she choose to consume?_____ How much good *A*?_____.

(g) Explain why her consumption is different depending on whether she was holding goods or money at the time of the price change._____

_____

_____.

9.4 (0) Priscilla finds it optimal not to engage in trade at the going prices and just consumes her endowment. Priscilla has no kinks in her indifference curves, and she is endowed with positive amounts of both goods. Use pencil or black ink to draw a budget line and an indifference curve for Priscilla that would be consistent with these facts. Suppose that the price of good 2 stays the same, but the price of good 1 falls below the level at which Priscilla made no trade. Use blue ink to show her new budget line. Priscilla satisfies the weak axiom of revealed preference. Could it happen that Priscilla will consume less of good 1 than before? Explain._____

_____

_____.

9.5 (0) Potatoes are a Giffen good for Paddy, who has a small potato farm. The price of potatoes fell, but Paddy increased his potato consumption. At first this astonished the village economist, who thought that a decrease in the price of a Giffen good was supposed to reduce demand. But then he remembered that Paddy was a net supplier of potatoes. With the help of a graph, he was able to explain Paddy's behavior. In the axes below, show how this could have happened. Put "potatoes" on the horizontal axis and "all other goods" on the vertical axis. Label the old equilibrium A and the new equilibrium B. Draw a point C so that the Slutsky substitution effect is the movement from A to C and the Slutsky income effect is the movement from C to B. On this same graph, you are also going to have to show that potatoes are a Giffen good. To do this, draw a budget line showing the effect of a fall in the price of potatoes if Paddy didn't own any potatoes, but only had money income. Label the new consumption point under these circumstances by D. (Warning: You probably will need to make a few dry runs on some scratch paper to get the whole story straight.)

9.6 (0) Recall the travails of Agatha, from the previous chapter. She had to travel 1500 miles from Istanbul to Paris. She had only $200 with which to buy first-class and second-class tickets on the Orient Express when the price of first-class tickets was $.20 and the price of second-class tickets was $.10. She bought tickets that enabled her to travel all the way to Paris, with as many miles of first class as she could afford. After she boarded the train, she discovered to her amazement that the price of second-class tickets had fallen to $.05 while the price of first-class tickets remained at $.20. She also discovered that on the train it was possible to buy or sell first-class tickets for $.20 a mile and to buy or sell second-class tickets for $.05 a mile. Agatha had no money left to buy either kind of ticket, but she did have the tickets that she had already bought.

(a) On the graph below, use pencil to show the combinations of tickets that she could afford at the old prices. Use blue ink to show the combinations of tickets that will take her exactly 1,500 miles. Mark the point that she chooses with the letter *A*.

First-class miles

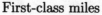

Second-class miles

(b) Use red ink to draw a line showing all of the combinations of first-class and second-class travel that she can afford when she is on the train, by trading her endowment of tickets at the new prices that apply on board the train.

(c) On your graph, show the point that she chooses after finding out about the price change. Does she choose more, less, or the same amount

of second-class tickets?_____.

9.7 (0) Mr. Cog works in a machine factory. He can work as many hours per day as he wishes at a wage rate of w. Let C be the number of dollars he has to spend on consumer goods and let R be the number of hours of leisure that he chooses.

(a) Suppose that Mr. Cog earns $8 an hour and has 18 hours per day to devote to labor or leisure, and suppose that he has $16 of nonlabor income per day. Write an equation for his budget between consumption and leisure. _____ Use blue ink to draw his budget line in the graph below. His initial endowment is the point where he doesn't work, but keeps all of his leisure. Mark this point on the graph below with the letter A. (When your draw your graph, remember that although Cog can choose to work and thereby "sell" some of his endowment of leisure, he cannot "buy leisure" by paying somebody else to loaf for him.) If Mr. Cog has the utility function $U(R, C) = CR$, how many hours of leisure per day will he choose?_____ How many hours per day will he work?

Consumption

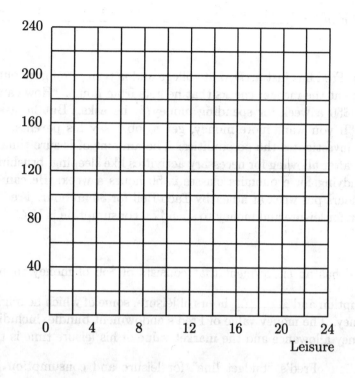

Leisure

(b) Suppose that Mr. Cog's wage rate rose to $12 an hour. Use red ink to draw his new budget line. (He still has $16 a day in nonlabor income.) If Mr. Cog continued to work exactly as many hours as he did before the wage increase, how much more money would he have each day to spend

on consumption?_____ But with his new budget line, he chooses

to work _____ hours, and so his consumption actually increases by

_____

(c) Suppose that Mr. Cog still receives $8 an hour but that his nonlabor income rises to $48 per day. Use black ink to draw his budget line. How

many hours does he choose to work?_____.

(d) Suppose that Mr. Cog has a wage of w per hour and a nonlabor income of m. As before, assume that he has 18 hours to divide between labor and leisure. Cog's budget line has the equation $C + wR = m + 18w$. Using the same methods you used in the chapter on demand functions, find the amount of leisure that Mr. Cog will demand as a function of wages and of nonlabor income. (Hint: Notice that this is just the same as finding the demand for R when the price of R is w, the price of C is 1, and income is $m + 18w$.) Mr. Cog's demand function for leisure is

$R(w, m) =$ _____ Mr. Cog's supply function for labor is therefore

$18 - R(w, m) =$ _____.

9.8 (0) Fred has just arrived at college and is trying to figure out how to supplement the meager checks that he gets from home. "How can anyone live on $50 a week for spending money?" he asks. But he asks to no avail. "If you want more money, get a job," say his parents. So Fred glumly investigates the possibilities. The amount of leisure time that he has left after allowing for necessary activities like sleeping, brushing teeth, and studying for economics classes is 50 hours a week. He can work as many hours per week at a nearby Taco Bell for $5 an hour. Fred's utility function for leisure and money to spend on consumption is $U(C, L) = CL$.

(a) Fred has an endowment that consists of $50 of money to spend on

consumption and _____ hours of leisure, some of which he might "sell" for money. The money value of Fred's endowment bundle, including both his money allowance and the market value of his leisure time is therefore

_____ Fred's "budget line" for leisure and consumption is like a budget line for someone who can buy these two goods at a price of $1 per

unit of consumption and a price of _____ per unit of leisure. The only difference is that this budget line doesn't run all the way to the horizontal axis.

(b) On the graph below, use black ink to show Fred's budget line. (Hint: Find the combination of leisure and consumption expenditures that he could have if he didn't work at all. Find the combination he would have if he chose to have no leisure at all. What other points are on your graph?) On the same graph, use blue ink to sketch the indifference curves that give Fred utility levels of 3,000, 4,500, and 7,500.

(c) If you maximized Fred's utility subject to the above budget, how

much consumption would he choose?_____ (Hint: Remember how to solve for the demand function of someone with a Cobb-Douglas utility function?)

(d) The amount of leisure that Fred will choose to consume is _____

hours. This means that his optimal labor supply will be _____ hours.

Consumption

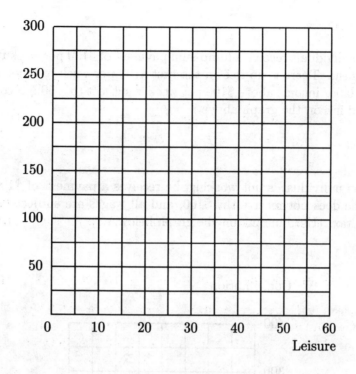

9.9 (0) George Johnson earns \$5 per hour in his job as a truffle sniffer. After allowing time for all of the activities necessary for bodily upkeep, George has 80 hours per week to allocate between leisure and labor. Sketch the budget constraints for George resulting from the following government programs.

(a) There is no government subsidy or taxation of labor income. (Use blue ink on the graph below.)

Consumption

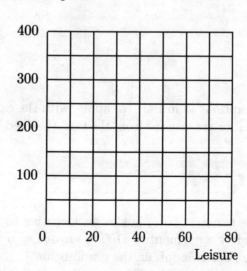

(b) All individuals receive a lump-sum payment of $100 per week from the government. There is no tax on the first $100 per week of labor income. But all labor income above $100 per week is subject to a 50% income tax. (Use red ink on the graph above.)

(c) If an individual is not working, he receives a payment of $100. If he works he does not receive the $100, and all wages are subject to a 50% income tax. (Use blue ink on the graph below.)

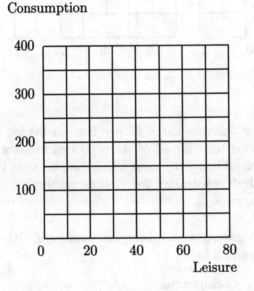

(d) The same conditions as in Part (c) apply, with the exception that the first 20 hours of labor are exempt from the tax. (Use red ink on the graph above.)

(e) All wages are taxed at 50%, but as an incentive to encourage work, the government gives a payment of $100 to anyone who works more than 20 hours a week. (Use blue ink on the graph below.)

Consumption

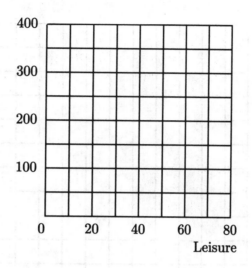

9.10 (0) In the United States, real wage rates in manufacturing have risen steadily from 1890 to the present. In the period from 1890 to 1930, the length of the work week was reduced dramatically. But after 1930, despite continuing growth of real wage rates, the length of the work week has stayed remarkably constant at about 40 hours per week.

Hourly Wages and Length of Work Week in U.S. Manufacturing, 1890-1983

Sources: *Handbook of Labor Statistics, 1983* and *U.S. Economic History*, by Albert Niemi (p. 274). Wages are in 1983 dollars.

Year	Wage	Hours Worked
1890	1.89	59.0
1909	2.63	51.0
1920	3.11	47.4
1930	3.69	42.1
1940	5.27	38.1
1950	6.86	40.5
1960	8.56	39.7
1970	9.66	39.8
1983	10.74	40.1

(a) Use these data to plot a "labor supply curve" on the graph below.

Hourly wage rate (in 1983 dollars)

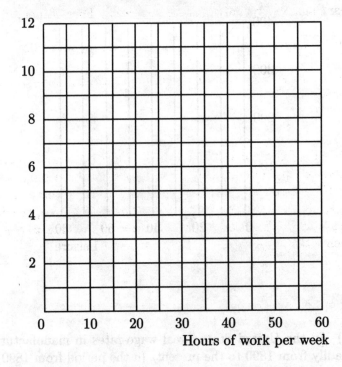

Hours of work per week

(b) At wage rates below $4 an hour, does the workweek get longer or

shorter as the wage rate rises?_____.

(c) The data in this table could be consistent with workers choosing
how many hours a week to work, given the wage rate? An increase in
wages has both an endowment income effect and a substitution effect.

The substitution effect alone would make for a (longer, shorter) _____

_____ workweek. If leisure is a normal good, the endowment income

effect tends to make people choose (more, less)_____ leisure and

a (longer, shorter) _____ workweek. At wage rates below $4 an

hour, the (substitution, endowment income) _____ effect
appears to dominate. How would you explain what happens at wages

above $4 an hour?_____

_____.

(d) Between 1890 and 1909, wage rates rose by _____ percent, but weekly earnings rose by only _____ percent. For this period, the gain in earnings (overstates, understates) _____ the gains in worker's wealth, since they chose to take (more, less) _____ leisure in 1909 than they took in 1890.

9.11 (0) Professor Mohamed El Hodiri of the University of Kansas, in a classic tongue-in-cheek article "The Economics of Sleeping," *Manifold*, vol. 17, 1975, offered the following analysis. "Assume there are 24 hours in a day. Daily consumption being x and hours of sleep s, the consumer maximizes a utility function of the form $u = x^2 s$, where $x = w(24 - s)$, with w being the wage rate."

(a) In El Hodiri's model, does the optimal amount of sleeping increase, decrease, or stay the same as wages increase?_____.

(b) How many hours of sleep per day is best in El Hodiri's model?

_____.

9.12 (0) Wendy and Mac work in fast food restaurants. Wendy gets $4 an hour for the first 40 hours that she works and $6 an hour for every hour beyond 40 hours a week. Mac gets $5 an hour no matter how many hours he works. Each has 80 hours a week to allocate between work and leisure and neither has any income from sources other than labor. Each has a utility function $U = cr$, where c is consumption and r is leisure. Each can choose the number of hours to work.

(a) How many hours will Mac choose to work?_____.

(b) Wendy's budget "line" has a kink in it at the point where $r =$_____ and $c =$_____ Use blue ink for the part of her budget line where she would be if she does not work overtime. Use red ink for the part where she would be if she worked overtime.

Consumption

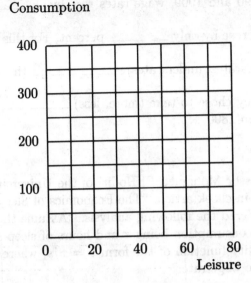

(c) The blue line segment that you drew lies on a line with equation

_____ The red line that you drew lies on a line with equation

_____ (Hint: For the red line, you know one point on the line
and you know its slope.)

(d) If Wendy was paid $4 an hour no matter how many hours she worked,

she would work _____ hours and earn a total of _____ a week.
On your graph, use black ink to draw her indifference curve through this
point.

(e) Will Wendy choose to work overtime?_____ What is the best

choice for Wendy from the red budget line? $(c, r) =$_____ How

many hours a week will she work?_____.

(f) Suppose that the jobs are equally agreeable in all other respects. Since
Wendy and Mac have the same preferences, they will be able to agree

about who has the better job. Who has the better job3.5in_____
(Hint: Calculate Wendy's utility when she makes her best choice. Calculate what her utility would be if she had Mac's job and chose the best
amount of time to work.)

9.13 (1) Wally Piper is a plumber. He charges $10 per hour for his work
and he can work as many hours as he likes. Wally has no source of income
other than his labor. He has 168 hours per week to allocate between labor

and leisure. On the graph below, draw Wally's budget set, showing the various combinations of weekly leisure and income that Wally can afford.

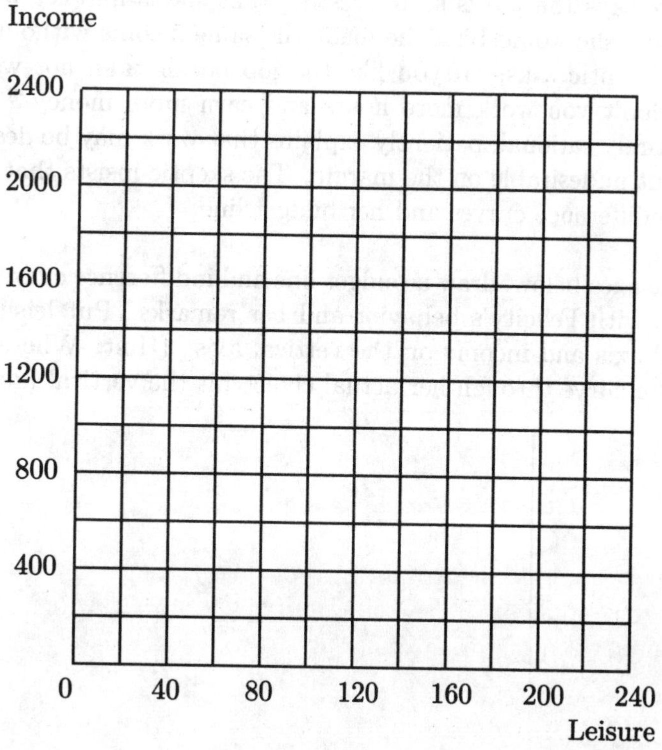

Income

(a) Write down Wally's budget equation. _____.

(b) While self-employed, Wally chose to work 40 hours per week. The construction firm, Glitz and Drywall, had a rush job to complete. They offered Wally $20 an hour and said that he could work as many hours as he liked. Wally still chose to work only 40 hours per week. On the graph you drew above, draw in Wally's new budget line.

(c) Wally has convex preferences and no kinks in his indifference curves. On the graph, draw indifference curves that are consistent with his choice of working hours when he was self-employed and when he worked for Glitz and Drywall.

(d) Glitz and Drywall were in a great hurry to complete their project and wanted Wally to work more than 40 hours. They decided that instead of paying him $20 per hour, they would pay him only $10 an hour for the first 40 hours that he worked per week and $20 an hour for every hour of "overtime" that he worked beyond 40 hours per week. On the graph that you drew above, use red ink to sketch in Wally's budget line with this pay schedule. Draw the indifference curve through the point that Wally chooses with this pay schedule. Will Wally work more than 40 hours or

less than 40 hours per week with this pay schedule? _____.

9.14 (1) Felicity loves her job. She is paid $10 an hour and can work as many hours a day as she wishes. She chooses to work only 5 hours a day. She says the job is so interesting that she is happier working at this job than she would be if she made the same income without working at all. A skeptic asks, "If you like the job better than not working at all, why don't you work more hours and earn more money?" Felicity, who is entirely rational, patiently explains that work may be desirable on average but undesirable on the margin. The skeptic insists that she show him her indifference curves and her budget line.

(a) On the axes below, draw a budget line and indifference curves that are consistent with Felicity's behavior and her remarks. Put leisure on the horizontal axis and income on the vertical axis. (Hint: Where does the indifference curve through her actual choice hit the vertical line $l = 24$?)

9.15 (2) Dudley's utility function is $U(C, R) = C - (12 - R)^2$, where R is the amount of leisure he has per day. He has 16 hours a day to divide between work and leisure. He has an income of $20 a day from nonlabor sources. The price of consumption goods is $1 per unit.

(a) If Dudley can work as many hours a day as he likes but gets zero wages for his labor, how many hours of leisure will he choose?_____.

(b) If Dudley can work as many hours a day as he wishes for a wage rate of $10 an hour, how many hours will he choose to work? (Hint: Write down Dudley's budget constraint. Solve for his labor supply. Remember that the amount of labor he wishes to supply is 16 minus his demand for leisure.)_____.

(c) If Dudley's nonlabor income decreased to $5 a day, how many hours would he choose to work?_____.

(d) Suppose that Dudley has to pay an income tax of 20 percent on all of his income, and suppose that his before-tax wage remained at $10 an hour and his before-tax nonlabor income was $20 per day; how many

hours would he choose to work?_____.

Intertemporal Choice

Introduction. The theory of consumer saving uses techniques that you have already learned. In order to focus attention on consumption over time, we will usually consider examples where there is only one consumer good, but this good can be consumed in either of two time periods. We will be using two "tricks." One trick is to treat *consumption in period 1* and *consumption in period 2* as two distinct commodities. If you make period-1 consumption the **numeraire**, then the "price" of period-2 consumption is the amount of period-1 consumption that you have to give up to get an extra unit of period-2 consumption. This price turns out to be $1/(1+r)$, where r is the interest rate.

The second trick is in the way you treat income in the two different periods. Suppose that a consumer has an income of m_1 in period 1 and m_2 in period 2 and that there is no inflation. The total amount of period-1 consumption that this consumer could buy, if he borrowed as much money as he could possibly repay in period 2, is $m_1 + \frac{m_2}{1+r}$. As you work the exercises and study the text, it should become clear that the consumer's budget equation for choosing consumption in the two periods is always

$$c_1 + \frac{c_2}{1+r} = m_1 + \frac{m_2}{1+r}.$$

This budget constraint looks just like the standard budget constraint that you studied in previous chapters, where the price of "good 1" is 1, the price of "good 2" is $1/(1+r)$, and "income" is $m_1 + \frac{m_2}{(1+r)}$. Therefore if you are given a consumer's utility function, the interest rate, and the consumer's income in each period, you can find his demand for consumption in periods 1 and 2 using the methods you already know. Having solved for consumption in each period, you can also find saving, since the consumer's saving is just the difference between his period-1 income and his period-1 consumption.

Example: A consumer has the utility function $U(c_1, c_2) = c_1 c_2$. There is no inflation, the interest rate is 10%, and the consumer has income 100 in period 1 and 121 in period 2. Then the consumer's budget constraint $c_1 + c_2/1.1 = 100 + 121/1.1 = 210$. The ratio of the price of good 1 to the price of good 2 is $1 + r = 1.1$. The consumer will choose a consumption bundle so that $MU_1/MU_2 = 1.1$. But $MU_1 = c_2$ and $MU_2 = c_1$, so the consumer must choose a bundle such that $c_2/c_1 = 1.1$. Take this equation together with the budget equation to solve for c_1 and c_2. The solution is $c_1 = 105$ and $c_2 = 115.50$. Since the consumer's period-1 income is only 100, he must borrow 5 in order to consume 105 in period 1. To pay back principal and interest in period 2, he must pay 5.50 out of his period-2 income of 121. This leaves him with 115.50 to consume.

You will also be asked to determine the effects of inflation on consumer behavior. The key to understanding the effects of inflation is to see what happens to the budget constraint.

Example: Suppose that in the previous example, there happened to be an inflation rate of 6%, and suppose that the price of period-1 goods is 1. Then if you save $1 in period 1 and get it back with 10 percent interest, you will get back $1.10 in period 2. But because of the inflation, goods in period 2 cost 1.06 dollars per unit. Therefore the amount of period-1 consumption that you have to give up to get a unit of period-2 consumption is $1.06/1.10 = .964$ units of period-2 consumption. If the consumer's money income in each period is unchanged, then his budget equation is $c_1 + .964c_2 = 210$. This budget constraint is the same as the budget constraint would be if there were no inflation and the interest rate were r, where $.964 = 1/(1+r)$. The value of r that solves this equation is known as the **real rate of interest**. In this case the real rate of interest is about .038. When the interest rate and inflation rate are both small, the real rate of interest is closely approximated by the difference between the **nominal interest rate**, (10% in this case) and the inflation rate (6% in this case.), that is, $.038 \sim .10 - .06$. As you will see, this is not such a good approximation if inflation rates and interest rates are large.

10.1 (0) Peregrine Pickle consumes (c_1, c_2) and earns (m_1, m_2) in periods 1 and 2 respectively. Suppose the interest rate is r.

(a) Write down Peregrine's intertemporal budget constraint in present value terms_____.

(b) If Peregrine does not consume anything in period 1, what is the most he can consume in period 2? _____ This is the (future value, present value) of his endowment._____.

(c) If Peregrine does not consume anything in period 2, what is the most he can consume in period 1? _____ This is the (future value, present value) of his endowment. _____ What is the slope of Peregrine's budget line?_____.

10.2 (0) Molly has a Cobb-Douglas utility function $U(c_1, c_2) = c_1^a c_2^{1-a}$, where $0 < a < 1$ and where c_1 and c_2 are her consumptions in periods 1 and 2 respectively. We saw earlier that if utility has the form $u(x_1, x_2) = x_1^a x_2^{1-a}$ and the budget constraint is of the "standard" form $p_1 x_1 + p_2 x_2 = m$, then the demand functions for the goods are $x_1 = am/p_1$ and $x_2 = (1-a)m/p_2$.

(a) Suppose that Molly's income is m_1 in period 1 and m_2 in period 2. Write down her budget constraint in terms of present values._____

_____.

(b) We want to compare this budget constraint to one of the standard form. In terms of Molly's budget constraint, what is p_1?_____ What is p_2?_____ What is m?_____.

(c) If $a = .2$, solve for Molly's demand functions for consumption in each period as a function of m_1, m_2, and r. Her demand function for consumption in period 1 is: $c_1 =$_____ Her demand function for consumption in period 2 is: $c_2 =$_____.

(d) An increase in the interest rate will _____ her period-1 consumption. It will _____ her period-2 consumption and _____ _____ her savings in period 1.

10.3 (0) Nickleby has an income of $2,000 this year, and he expects an income of $1,100 next year. He can borrow and lend money at an interest rate of 10%. Consumption goods cost $1 per unit this year and there is no inflation.

Consumption next year in 1,000s

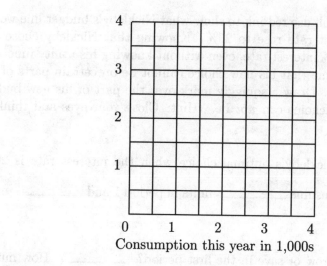

Consumption this year in 1,000s

(a) What is the present value of Nickleby's endowment? _____

What is the future value of his endowment? _____ With blue ink, show the combinations of consumption this year and consumption next year that he can afford. Label Nickleby's endowment with the letter *E*.

(b) Suppose that Nickleby has the utility function $U(C_1, C_2) = C_1 C_2$. Write an expression for Nickleby's marginal rate of substitution between consumption this year and consumption next year. (Your answer will be

a function of the variables C_1, C_2.)_____.

(c) What is the slope of Nickleby's budget line? _____ Write an equation that states that the slope of Nickleby's indifference curve is equal to the slope of his budget line when the interest rate is 10%.

_____ Also write down Nickleby's budget equation._____

_____.

(d) Solve these two equations. Nickleby will consume _____ units

in period 1 and _____ units in period 2. Label this point *A* on your diagram.

(e) Will he borrow or save in the first period? _____ How much?

_____.

(f) On your graph use red ink to show what Nickleby's budget line would be if the interest rate rose to 20%. Knowing that Nickleby chose the point *A* at a 10% interest rate, even without knowing his utility function, you can determine that his new choice cannot be on certain parts of his new budget line. Draw a squiggly mark over the part of his new budget line where that choice can *not* be. (Hint: Close your eyes and think of WARP.)

(g) Solve for Nickleby's optimal choice when the interest rate is 20%.

Nickleby will consume _____ units in period 1 and _____ units in period 2.

(h) Will he borrow or save in the first period? _____ How much?

_____.

10.4 (0) Decide whether each of the following statements is true or false. Then explain why your answer is correct, based on the Slutsky decomposition into income and substitution effects.

(a) "If both current and future consumption are normal goods, an increase in the interest rate will necessarily make a saver save more." _____

_____

_____ .

(b) "If both current and future consumption are normal goods, an increase in the interest rate will necessarily make a saver choose more consumption in the second period." _____

_____ .

10.5 (1) Laertes has an endowment of $20 each period. He can borrow money at an interest rate of 200%, and he can lend money at a rate of 0%. (Note: If the interest rate is 0%, for every dollar that you save, you get back $1 in the next period. If the interest rate is 200%, then for every dollar you borrow, you have to pay back $3 in the next period.)

(a) Use blue ink to illustrate his budget set in the graph below. (Hint: The boundary of the budget set is not a single straight line.)

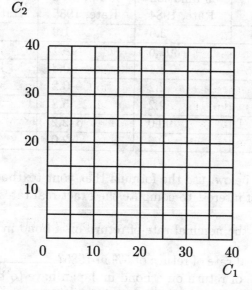

(b) Laertes could invest in a project that would leave him with $m_1 = 30$ and $m_2 = 15$. Besides investing in the project, he can still borrow at 200% interest or lend at 0% interest. Use red ink to draw the new budget set in the graph above. Would Laertes be better off or worse off by investing in this project given his possibilities for borrowing or lending? Or can't one tell without knowing something about his pref-

erences? Explain._____

_____.

(c) Consider an alternative project that would leave Laertes with the endowment $m_1 = 15$, $m_2 = 30$. Again suppose he can borrow and lend as above. But if he chooses this project, he can't do the first project. Use pencil or black ink to draw the budget set available to Laertes if he chooses this project. Is Laertes better off or worse off by choosing this project than if he didn't choose either project? Or can't one tell without knowing more about his pref-

erences? Explain._____

_____

_____.

10.6 (0) The table below reports the inflation rate and the annual rate of return on treasury bills in several countries for the years 1984 and 1985.

Inflation Rate and Interest Rate for Selected Countries

Country	% Inflation Rate, 1984	% Inflation Rate, 1985	% Interest Rate, 1984	% Interest Rate, 1985
United States	3.6	1.9	9.6	7.5
Israel	304.6	48.1	217.3	210.1
Switzerland	3.1	0.8	3.6	4.1
W. Germany	2.2	−0.2	5.3	4.2
Italy	9.2	5.8	15.3	13.9
Argentina	90.0	672.2	NA	NA
Japan	0.6	2.0	NA	NA

(a) In the table below, use the formula that your textbook gives for the exact real rate of interest to compute the exact real rates of interest.

(b) What would the nominal rate of return on a bond in Argentina have

to be to give a real rate of return of 5% in 1985?_____ What would the nominal rate of return on a bond in Japan have to be to give a real

rate of return of 5% in 1985?_____.

(c) Subtracting the inflation rate from the nominal rate of return gives a good approximation to the real rate for countries with a low rate of inflation. For the United States in 1984, the approximation gives you

_____ while the more exact method suggested by the text gives you

_____ But for countries with very high inflation this is a poor approximation. The approximation gives you _____ for Israel in 1984,

while the more exact formula gives you _____ For Argentina in 1985, the approximation would tell us that a bond yielding a nominal rate

of _____ would yield a real interest rate of 5%. This contrasts with

the answer _____ that you found above.

Real Rates of Interest in 1984 and 1985

Country	1984	1985
United States		
Israel		
Switzerland		
W. Germany		
Italy		

10.7 (0) We return to the planet Mungo. On Mungo, macroeconomists and bankers are jolly, clever creatures, and there are two kinds of money, red money and blue money. Recall that to buy something in Mungo you have to pay for it twice, once with blue money and once with red money. Everything has a blue-money price and a red-money price, and nobody is ever allowed to trade one kind of money for the other. There is a blue-money bank where you can borrow and lend blue money at a 50% annual interest rate. There is a red-money bank where you can borrow and lend red money at a 25% annual interest rate.

A Mungoan named Jane consumes only one commodity, ambrosia, but it must decide how to allocate its consumption between this year and next year. Jane's income this year is 100 blue currency units and no red currency units. Next year, its income will be 100 red currency units and no blue currency units. The blue currency price of ambrosia is one b.c.u. per flagon this year and will be two b.c.u.'s per flagon next year. The red currency price of ambrosia is one r.c.u. per flagon this year and will be the same next year.

(a) If Jane spent all of its blue income in the first period, it would be enough to pay the blue price for _____ flagons of ambrosia. If Jane saved all of this year's blue income at the blue-money bank, it would have _____ b.c.u.'s next year. This would give it enough blue currency to pay the blue price for _____ flagons of ambrosia. On the graph below, draw Jane's blue budget line, depicting all of those combinations of current and next period's consumption that it has enough blue income to buy.

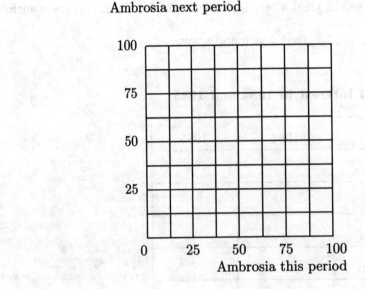

(b) If Jane planned to spend no red income in the next period and to borrow as much red currency as it can pay back with interest with next period's red income, how much red currency could it borrow?_____.

(c) The (exact) real rate of interest on blue money is _____ The real rate of interest on red money is_____.

(d) On the axes below, draw Jane's blue budget line and its red budget line. Shade in all of those combinations of current and future ambrosia consumption that Jane can afford given that it has to pay with both currencies.

Ambrosia next period

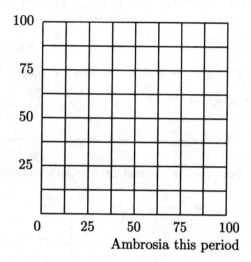

Ambrosia this period

(e) It turns out that Jane finds it optimal to operate *on* its blue budget line and *beneath* its red budget line. Find such a point on your graph and mark it with a C.

(f) On the following graph, show what happens to Jane's original budget set if the blue interest rate rises and the red interest rate does not change. On your graph, shade in the part of the new budget line where Jane's new demand could possibly be. (Hint: Apply the principle of revealed preference. Think about what bundles were available but rejected when Jane chose to consume at C before the change in blue interest rates.)

Ambrosia next period

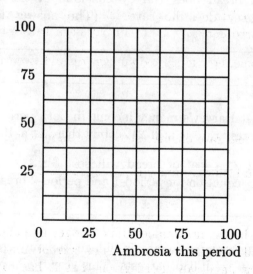

Ambrosia this period

10.8 (0) Mr. O. B. Kandle will only live for two periods. In the first period he will earn $50,000. In the second period he will retire and live on his savings. His utility function is $U(c_1, c_2) = c_1 c_2$, where c_1 is consumption in period 1 and c_2 is consumption in period 2. He can borrow and lend at the interest rate $r = .10$.

(a) If the interest rate rises, will his period-1 consumption increase, decrease, or stay the same?_____

_____.

(b) Would an increase in the interest rate make him consume more or less in the second period?_____

_____.

(c) If Mr. Kandle's income is zero in period 1, and $ 55,000 in period 2, would an increase in the interest rate make him consume more, less, or the same amount in period 1?_____.

10.9 (1) Harvey Habit's utility function is $U(c_1, c_2) = \min\{c_1, c_2\}$, where c_1 is his consumption of bread in period 1 and c_2 is his consumption of bread in period 2. The price of bread is $1 per loaf in period 1. The interest rate is 21%. Harvey earns $2000 in period 1 and he will earn $1,100 in period 2.

(a) Write Harvey's budget constraint in terms of future value, assuming no inflation._____.

(b) How much bread does Harvey consume in the first period and how much money does he save? (The answer is not necessarily an integer.)_____

_____.

(c) Suppose that Harvey's money income in both periods is the same as before, the interest rate is still 21%, but there is a 10% inflation rate.

Then in period 2, a loaf of bread will cost $_____ Write down Harvey's budget equation for period-1 and period-2 bread, given this new

information._____.

10.10 (2) In an isolated mountain village, the only crop is corn. Good harvests alternate with bad harvests. This year the harvest will be 1,000 bushels. Next year it will be 150 bushels. There is no trade with the outside world. Corn can be stored from one year to the next, but rats will eat 25% of what is stored in a year. The villagers have Cobb-Douglas utility functions, $U(c_1, c_2) = c_1 c_2$ where c_1 is consumption this year, and c_2 is consumption next year.

(a) Use red ink to draw a "budget line," showing consumption possibilities for the village, with this year's consumption on the horizontal axis and next year's consumption on the vertical axis. Put numbers on your graph to show where the budget line hits the axes.

(b) How much corn will the villagers consume this year? _____

_____ How much will the rats eat?_____ How much corn

will the villagers consume next year?_____.

(c) Suppose that a road is built to the village so that now the village is able to trade with the rest of the world. Now the villagers are able to buy and sell corn at the world price, which is $1 per bushel. They are also able to borrow and lend money at an interest rate of 10%. On your graph, use blue ink to draw the new budget line for the villagers. Solve

for the amount they would now consume in the first period _____ and

the second period_____.

(d) Suppose that all is as in the last part of the question except that there is a transportation cost of $.10 per bushel for every bushel of grain hauled into or out of the village. On your graph, use black ink or pencil to draw the budget line for the village under these circumstances.

10.11 (0) The table below records percentage interest rates and inflation rates for the United States in some recent years. Complete this table.

Inflation and Interest in the United States, 1965-1985

Year	1965	1970	1975	1978	1980	1985
CPI, Start of Year	38.3	47.1	66.3	79.2	100.0	130.0
CPI, End of Year	39.4	49.2	69.1	88.1	110.4	133
% Inflation Rate	2.9	4.3	4.2	11.3		
Nominal Int. Rate	4.0	6.4	5.8	7.2	11.6	7.5
Real Int. Rate	1.1	2.1	1.6			

(a) People complained a great deal about the high interest rates in the late 70s. In fact, interest rates had never reached such heights in modern times. Explain why such complaints are misleading._____

_____

_____.

(b) If you gave up a unit of consumption goods at the beginning of 1985 and saved your money at interest, you could use the proceeds of your saving to buy _____ units of consumption goods at the beginning of 1986. If you gave up a unit of consumption goods at the beginning of 1978 and saved your money at interest, you would be able to use the proceeds of your saving to buy _____ units of consumption goods at the beginning of 1979.

10.12 (1) Marsha Mellow doesn't care whether she consumes in period 1 or in period 2. Her utility function is simply $U(c_1, c_2) = c_1 + c_2$. Her initial endowment is $20 in period 1 and $40 in period 2. In an antique shop, she discovers a cookie jar that is for sale for $12 in period 1 and that she is certain she can sell for $20 in period 2. She derives no consumption benefits from the cookie jar, and it costs her nothing to store it for one period.

(a) On the graph below, label her initial endowment, E, and use blue ink to draw the budget line showing combinations of period-1 and period-2 consumption that she can afford if she doesn't buy the cookie jar. On the same graph, label the consumption bundle, A, that she would have if she did not borrow or lend any money but bought the cookie jar in period 1, sold it in period 2, and used the proceeds to buy period-2 consumption. If she cannot borrow or lend, should Marsha invest in the cookie jar?

_____.

(b) Suppose that Marsha can borrow and lend at an interest rate of 50%. On the graph where you labelled her initial endowment, draw the budget line showing all of the bundles she can afford if she invests in the cookie jar and borrows or lends at the interest rate of 50%. On the same graph use red ink to draw one or two of Marsha's indifference curves.

Period-2 consumption

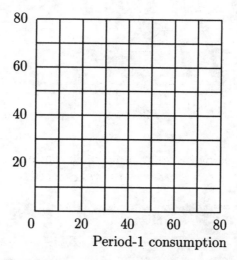

Period-1 consumption

(c) Suppose that instead of consumption in the two periods being perfect substitutes, they are perfect complements, so that Marsha's utility function is $\min\{c_1, c_2\}$. If she can not borrow or lend, should she buy the cookie jar? _____ If she can borrow and lend at an interest rate of 50%, should she invest in the cookie jar?_____ If she can borrow or lend as much at an interest rate of 100%, should she invest in the cookie jar?_____.

Asset Markets

Introduction. The fundamental equilibrium condition for asset markets is that in equilibrium the rate of return on all assets must be the same. Thus if you know the rate of interest and the cash flow generated by an asset, you can predict what its market equilibrium price will be. This condition has many interesting implications for the pricing of durable assets. Here you will explore several of these implications.

Example: A drug manufacturing firm owns the patent for a new medicine. The patent will expire on January 1, 1996, at which time anyone can produce the drug. Whoever owns the patent will make a profit of $1,000,000 per year until the patent expires. For simplicity, let us suppose that profits for any year are all collected on December 31. The interest rate is 5%. Let us figure out what the selling price of the patent rights will be on January 1, 1993. On January 1, 1993, potential buyers realize that owning the patent will give them $1,000,000 every year starting 1 year from now and continuing for 3 years. The present value of this cash flow is

$$\$\frac{1,000,000}{(1.05)} + \frac{1,000,000}{(1.05)^2} + \frac{1,000,000}{(1.05)^3} \sim \$2,723,248.$$

Nobody would pay more than this amount for the patent since if you put $2,723,248 at 5% interest, you could collect $1,000,000 a year from the bank for 3 years, starting 1 year from now. The patent wouldn't sell for less than $2,723,248, since if it sold for less, one would get a higher rate of return by investing in this patent than one could get from investing in anything else. What will the price of the patent be on January 1, 1994? At that time, the patent is equivalent to a cash flow of $1,000,000 in 1 year and another $1,000,000 in 2 years. The present value of this flow, viewed from the standpoint of January 1, 1994, will be

$$\$\frac{1,000,000}{(1.05)} + \frac{1,000,000}{(1.05)^2} \sim \$1,859,310.$$

A slightly more difficult problem is one where the cash flow from an asset depends on how the asset is used. To find the price of such an asset, one must ask what will be the present value of the cash flow that the asset yields if it is managed in such a way as to maximize its present value.

Example: People will be willing to pay $15 a bottle to drink a certain wine this year. Next year they would be willing to pay $25, and the year after that they would be willing to pay $26. After that, it starts to deteriorate and the amount people are willing to pay to drink it falls. The interest rate is 5%. We can determine not only what the wine will sell for but also when it will be drunk. If the wine is drunk in the first year, it would have to sell for $15. But no rational investor is going to sell the wine for

$15 in the first year, because it will sell for $25 one year later. This is a 66.66% rate of return, which is better than the rate of interest. When the interest rate is 5%, investors are willing to pay at least $25/1.05 = $23.81 for the wine. So investors must outbid drinkers, and none will be drunk this year. Will investors want to hold onto the wine for 2 years? In 2 years, the wine will be worth $26, so the present value of buying the wine and storing it for 2 years is $26/(1.05)^2 = 23.58. This is less than the present value of holding the wine for 1 year and selling it for $25. So, we conclude that the wine will be drunk after 1 year. Its current selling price will be $23.81, and 1 year from now, it will sell for $25.

11.0 Warm Up Exercise. Here are a few problems on present values. In all of the following examples, assume that you can both borrow and lend at an annual interest rate of r and that the interest rate will remain the same forever.

(a) You would be indifferent between getting $1 now and _____ dollars, one year from now, because if you put the dollar in the bank, then one year from now you could get back _____ dollars from the bank.

(b) You would be indifferent between getting _____ dollar(s) one year from now and getting $1/(1 + r)$ dollars now, because _____ deposited in the bank right now would enable you to withdraw principal and interest worth $1.

(c) For any $X > 0$, you would be indifferent between getting _____ _____ dollars right now and $X one year from now. The present value of $X received one year from now is _____ dollars.

(d) The present value of an obligation to pay $X one year from now is _____ dollars.

(e) The present value of $X, to be received 2 years from now, is _____ _____ dollars.

(f) The present value of an asset that pays X_t dollars t years from now is _____ dollars.

(g) The present value of an asset that pays $\$X_1$ one year from now, $\$X_2$ in two years, and $\$X_{10}$ ten years from now is _____ _____ dollars.

(h) The present value of an asset that pays a constant amount, $\$X$ per year forever can be computed in two different ways. One way is to figure out the amount of money you need in the bank so that the bank would give you $\$X$ per year, forever, without ever exhausting your principal. The annual interest received on a bank account of _____ dollars will be $\$X$. Therefore having _____ dollars right now is just as good as getting $\$X$ a year forever.

(i) Another way to calculate the present value of $\$X$ a year forever is to evaluate the infinite series, _____ This series is known as a _____ series. Whenever $r > 0$, this sum is well defined and is equal to_____.

(j) If the interest rate is 10%, the present value of receiving $1,000 one year from now will be, to the nearest dollar, _____ The present value of receiving $1,000 a year forever, will be, to the nearest dollar, _____.

(k) If the interest rate is 10%, what is the present value of an asset that requires you to pay out $550 one year from now and will pay you back $1210 two years from now?_____ dollars.

11.1 (0) An area of land has been planted with Christmas trees. On December 1, ten years from now, the trees will be ready for harvest. At that time, the standing Christmas trees can be sold for $1,000 per acre. The land, after the trees have been removed, will be worth $200 per acre. There are no taxes or operating expenses, but also no revenue from this land until the trees are harvested. The interest rate is 10%.

(a) What can we expect the market price of the land to be?_____
_____.

(b) Suppose that the Christmas trees do not have to be sold after 10 years, but could be sold in any year. Their value if they are cut before they are 10 years old is zero. After the trees are 10 years old, an acre of trees is worth $1000 and its value will increase by $100 per year for the next 20 years. After the trees are cut, the land on which the trees stood can always be sold for $200 an acre. When should the trees be cut to maximize the present value of the payments received for trees and land?

_____ What will be the market price of an acre of land?

_____.

11.2 (0) Publicity agents for the Detroit Felines announce the signing of a phenomenal new quarterback, Archie Parabola. They say that the contract is worth $1,000,000 and will be paid in 20 installments of $50,000 per year starting one year from now and with one new installment each year for next 20 years. The contract contains a clause that guarantees he will get all of the money even if he is injured and cannot play a single game. Sports writers declare that Archie has become an "instant millionaire."

(a) Archie's brother, Fenwick, who majored in economics, explains to Archie that he is not a millionaire. In fact, his contract is worth less than half a million dollars. Explain in words why this is so.

_____

_____.

Archie's college course on "Sports Management" didn't cover present values. So his brother tried to reason out the calculation for him. Here is how it goes:

(b) Suppose that the interest rate is 10% and is expected to remain at 10% forever. How much would it cost the team to buy Archie a perpetuity that would pay him and his heirs $1 per year *forever*, starting in 1 year?

_____.

(c) How much would it cost to buy a perpetuity that paid $50,000 a year

forever, starting in one year?_____.

In the last part, you found the present value of Archie's contract if he were going to get $50,000 a year forever. But Archie is not going to get $50,000 a year forever. The payments stop after 20 years. The present value of Archie's actual contract is the same as the present value of a contract that pays him $50,000 a year forever, but makes him pay back $50,000 each year, forever, starting 21 years from now. Therefore you can find the present value of Archie's contract by subtracting the present value of $50,000 a year forever, starting 21 years from now from the present value of $50,000 a year forever.

(d) If the interest rate is and will remain at 10%, a stream of payments of \$50,000 a year, starting 21 years from now has the same present value as a lump sum of \$_____ to be received all at once, exactly 20 years from now.

(e) If the interest rate is and will remain at 10%, what is the present value of \$50,000 per year forever, starting 21 years from now? _____ (Hint: The present value of \$1 to be paid in 20 years is $1/(1+r)^{20} = .15$.)

(f) Now calculate the present value of Archie's contract._____

_____ .

11.3 (0) Professor Thesis is puzzling over the formula for the present value of a stream of payments of \$1 a year, starting 1 year from now and continuing forever. He knows that the value of this stream is expressed by the infinite series

$$S = \frac{1}{1+r} + \frac{1}{(1+r)^2} + \frac{1}{(1+r)^3} + \ldots,$$

but he can't remember the simplified formula for this sum. All he knows is that if the first payment were to arrive today, rather than a year from now, the present value of the sum would be \$1 higher. So he knows that

$$S + 1 = 1 + \frac{1}{(1+r)} + \frac{1}{(1+r)^2} + \frac{1}{(1+r)^3} + \ldots.$$

Professor Antithesis suffers from a similar memory lapse. He can't remember the formula for S either. But, he knows that the present value of \$1 a year forever, starting right now has to be $1 + r$ times as large as the present value of \$1 a year, starting a year from now. (This is true because if you advance any income stream by a year, you multiply its present value by 1+r.) That is,

$$1 + \frac{1}{(1+r)} + \frac{1}{(1+r)^2} + \frac{1}{(1+r)^3} + \ldots = (1+r)S.$$

(a) If Professor Thesis and Professor Antithesis put their knowledge together, they can express a simple equation involving only the variable S.

This equation is $S + 1 =$_____ Solving this equation, they find

that $S =$_____ .

(b) The two professors have also forgotten the formula for the present value of a stream of $1 per year starting next year and continuing for K years. They agree to call this number $S(K)$ and they see that

$$S(K) = \frac{1}{(1+r)} + \frac{1}{(1+r)^2} + \ldots + \frac{1}{(1+r)^K}.$$

Professor Thesis notices that if each of the payments came 1 year earlier, the present value of the resulting stream of payments would be

$$1 + \frac{1}{(1+r)} + \frac{1}{(1+r)^2} + \ldots + \frac{1}{(1+r)^{K-1}} = S(K) + 1 - \frac{1}{(1+r)^K}.$$

Professor Antithesis points out that speeding up any stream of payments by a year is also equivalent to multiplying its present value by $(1+r)$. Putting their two observations together, the two professors noticed an equation that could be solved for $S(K)$. This equation is $S(K) + 1 -$

$\frac{1}{(1+r)^K} =$ _____ Solving this equation for $S(K)$, they find that

the formula for $S(K)$ is_____.

Calculus **11.4 (0)** You are the business manager of P. Bunyan Forests, Inc., and are trying to decide when you should cut your trees. The market value of the lumber that you will get if you let your trees reach the age of t years is given by the function $W(t) = e^{.20t - .001t^2}$. Mr. Bunyan can earn an interest rate of 5% per year on money in the bank.

The rate of growth of the market value of the trees will be greater

than 5% until the trees reach _____ years of age. (Hint: It follows from elementary calculus that if $F(t) = e^{g(t)}$, then $F'(t)/F(t) = g'(t)$.)

(a) If he is only interested in the trees as an investment, how old should

Mr. Bunyan let the trees get?_____.

(b) At what age do the trees have the greatest market value?_____

_____.

11.5 (0) You expect the price of a certain painting to rise by 8% per year forever. The market interest rate for borrowing and lending is 10%. Assume there are no brokerage costs in purchasing or selling.

(a) If you pay a price of x for the painting now and sell it in a year, how much has it cost you to hold the painting rather than to have loaned the

x at the market interest rate?_____.

(b) You would be willing to pay $100 a year to have the painting on your walls. Write an equation that you can solve for the price x at which you would be just willing to buy the painting_____.

(c) How much should you be willing to pay to buy the painting?_____

_____.

11.6 (2) Ashley is thinking of buying a truckload of wine for investment purposes. He can borrow and lend as much as he likes at an annual interest rate of 10%. He is looking at three kinds of wine. To keep our calculations simple, let us assume that handling and storage costs are negligible.

  • Wine drinkers would pay exactly $175 a case to drink Wine A today. But if Wine A is allowed to mature for one year, it will improve. In fact wine drinkers will be willing to pay $220 a case to drink this wine one year from today. After that, the wine gradually deteriorates and becomes less valuable every year.

  • From now until one year from now, Wine B is indistinguishable from Wine A. But instead of deteriorating after one year, Wine B will improve. In fact the amount that wine drinkers would be willing to pay to drink Wine B will be $220 a case in one year and will rise by $10 per case per year for the next 30 years.

  • Wine drinkers would be willing to pay $100 per case to drink Wine C right now. But one year from now, they will be willing to pay $250 per case to drink it and the amount they will be willing to pay to drink it will rise by $50 per case per year for the next 20 years.

(a) What is the most Ashley would be willing to pay per case for Wine A?_____.

(b) What is the most Ashley would be willing to pay per case for Wine B? _____ (Hint: When will Wine B be drunk?)

(c) How old will Wine C be when it first becomes worthwhile for investors to sell off their holdings and for drinkers to drink it? _____ (Hint: When does the rate of return on holding wine get to 10%?)

(d) What will the price of Wine C be at the time it is first drunk?_____

_____.

(e) What is the most that Ashley would be willing to pay today for a case of Wine *C*? (Hint: What is the present value of his investment if he sells it to a drinker at the optimal time?) Express your answer in exponential notation without calculating it out._____.

11.7 (0) Fisher Brown is taxed at 40% on his income from ordinary bonds. Ordinary bonds pay 10% interest. Interest on municipal bonds is not taxed at all.

(a) If the interest rate on municipal bonds is 7%, should he buy municipal bonds or ordinary bonds?_____.

(b) Hunter Black makes less money than Fisher Brown and is taxed at only 25% on his income from ordinary bonds. Which kind of bonds should he buy?_____.

(c) If Fisher has $1,000,000 in bonds and Hunter has $10,000 in bonds, how much taxes does Fisher pay on his interest from bonds? _____

How much taxes does Hunter pay on his interest from bonds?_____.

(d) The government is considering a new tax plan under which no interest income will be taxed. If the interest rates on the two types of bonds do not change, and Fisher and Hunter are allowed to adjust their portfolios, how much will Fisher's after-tax income be increased? _____

How much will Hunter's after-tax income be increased?_____.

(e) What would the change in the tax law do to the demand for municipal bonds if the interest rates did not change?_____.

(f) What interest rate will new issues of municipal bonds have to pay in order to attract purchasers?_____.

(g) What do you think will happen to the market price of the old municipal bonds, which had a 7% yield originally?_____

_____.

11.8 (0) In the text we discussed the market for oil assuming zero production costs, but now suppose that it is costly to get the oil out of the ground. Suppose that it costs $5 dollars per barrel to extract oil from the ground. Let the price in period t be denoted by p_t and let r be the interest rate.

(a) If a firm extracts a barrel of oil in period t, how much profit does it make in period t?_____.

(b) If a firm extracts a barrel of oil in period $t+1$, how much profit does it make in period $t+1$?_____.

(c) What is the present value of the profits from extracting a barrel of oil in period $t+1$?_____ What is the present value of profit from extracting a barrel of oil in period t?_____.

(d) If the firm is willing to supply oil in each of the two periods, what must be true about the relation between the present value of profits from sale of a barrel of oil in the two periods? _____

Express this relation as an equation._____.

(e) Solve the equation in the above part for p_{t+1} as a function of p_t and r._____.

(f) Is the percentage rate of price increase between periods larger or smaller than the interest rate?_____.

11.9 (0) Dr. No owns a bond, serial number 007, issued by the James Company. The bond pays \$200 for each of the next three years, at which time the bond is retired and pays its face value of \$2,000.

(a) How much is the James bond 007 worth to Dr. No at an interest rate of 10%?_____.

(b) How valuable is James bond 007 at an interest rate of 5%?_____

_____.

(c) Ms. Yes offers Dr. No \$2,200 for the James bond 007. Should Dr. No say yes or no to Ms. Yes if the interest rate is 10%? _____ What if the interest rate is 5%?_____.

(d) In order to destroy the world, Dr. No hires Professor Know to develop a nasty zap beam. In order to lure Professor Know from his university position, Dr. No will have to pay the professor $200 a year. The nasty zap beam will take three years to develop, at the end of which it can be built for $2,000. If the interest rate is 5%, how much money will

Dr. No need today to finance this dastardly program? _____

_____ If the

interest rate was 10% would the world be in more or less danger from

Dr. No?_____.

11.10 (0) Chillingsworth owns a large, poorly insulated home. His annual fuel bill for home heating averages $300 per year. An insulation contractor suggests to him the following options.

Plan A. Insulate just the attic. If he does this, he will permanently reduce his fuel consumption by 15%. Total cost of insulating the attic is $300.

Plan B. Insulate the attic and the walls. If he does this, he will permanently reduce his fuel consumption by 20%. Total cost of insulating the attic and the walls is $500.

Plan C. Insulate the attic and the walls, and install a solar heating unit. If he does this, he will permanently reduce his fuel costs to zero. Total cost of this option is $7,000 for the solar heater and $500 for the insulating.

(a) Assume for simplicity of calculations that the house and the insulation will last forever. Calculate the present value of the dollars saved on fuel from each of the three options if the interest rate is 10%. The present

values are: Plan A? _____ Plan B? _____ Plan C?_____.

(b) Each plan requires an expenditure of money to undertake. The difference between the present value and the present cost of each plan is:

Plan A? _____ Plan B? _____ Plan C?_____

_____.

(c) If the price of fuel is expected to remain constant, which option should he choose if he can borrow and lend at an annual interest rate of 10%?

_____.

(d) Which option should he choose if he can borrow and lend at an annual

rate of 5%?_____.

(e) Suppose that the government offers to pay half of the cost of any insulation or solar heating device. Which option would he now choose at interest rates 10%? _____ 5%?_____.

(f) Suppose that there is no government subsidy but that fuel prices are expected to rise by 5% per year. What is the present value of fuel savings from each of the three proposals if interest rates are 10%? (Hint: If a stream of income is growing at x% and being discounted at y%, its present value should be the same as that of a constant stream of income discounted at $(y-x)$%.) Plan A? _____ Plan B? _____ Plan C? _____ Which proposal should Chillingsworth choose if interest rates are 10%? _____ 5%?_____.

11.11 (1) Have you ever wondered if a college education is financially worthwhile? The U.S. Census Bureau collects data on income and education that throws some light on this question. A recent census publication (Current Population Reports, Series P-70, No. 11) reports the average annual wage income in 1984 of persons aged 35–44 by the level of schooling achieved. The average wage income of high school graduates was $13,000 per year. The average wage income of persons with bachelor's degrees was $24,000 per year. The average wage income of persons with master's degrees was $28,000 per year. The average wage income of persons with Ph.D.'s was $40,000 per year. These income differences probably overstate the return to education itself, because it is likely that those people who get more education tend to be more able those who get less. Some of the income difference is, therefore, a return to ability rather than to education. But just to get a rough idea of returns to education, let us see what would be the return if the reported wage differences are all due to education.

(a) Suppose that you have just graduated from high school at age 18. You want to estimate the present value of your lifetime earnings if you do not go to college but take a job immediately. To do this, you have to make some assumptions. Assume that you would work for 47 years, until you are 65 and then retire. Assume also that you would make $13,000 a year for the rest of your life. (If you were going to do this more carefully, you would want to take into account that people's wages vary with their age, but let's keep things simple for this problem.) Assume that the interest rate is 5%. Find the present value of your lifetime earnings. (Hint: First find out the present value of $13,000 a year forever. Subtract from this the present value of $13,000 a year forever, starting 47 years from now.)

(b) Again, supposing you have just graduated from high school at age 18, and you want to estimate the present value of your life time earnings if you go to college for 4 years and do not earn any wages until you graduate from college. Assume that after graduating from college, you would work for 43 years at $24,000 per year. What would be the present value of your

lifetime earnings?_____.

(c) Now calculate the present value of your lifetime earnings if you get a master's degree. Assume that if you get a master's, you have no earnings for 6 years and then you work for 41 years at $28,000 per year. What

would be the present value of your lifetime income?_____.

(d) Finally calculate the present value of your lifetime earnings if you get a Ph.D. Assume that if you get a Ph.D., you will have no earnings for 8 years and then you work for 39 years at $40,000 per year. What would

be the present value of your lifetime income?_____.

(e) Consider the case of someone who married right after finishing high school and stopped her education at that point. Suppose that she is now 45 years old. Her children are nearly adults, and she is thinking about going back to work or going to college. Assuming she would earn the average wage for her educational level and would retire at age 65, what would be the present value of her lifetime earnings if she does not go to

college?_____.

(f) What would be the present value of her lifetime earnings if she goes

to college for 4 years and then takes a job until she is 65?_____.

(g) If college tuition is $5,000 per year, is it financially worthwhile for her

to go to college? Explain._____

_____.

11.12 (0) As you may have noticed, economics is a difficult major. Are their any rewards for all this effort? The U.S. census publication discussed in the last problem suggests that there might be. There are tables reporting wage income by the field in which one gets a degree. For bachelor's degrees, the most lucrative majors are economics and engineering. The average wage incomes for economists are about $28,000 per year and for engineers are about $27,000. Psychology majors average about $15,000 a year and English majors about $14,000 per year.

(a) Can you think of any explanation for these differences?_____

_____

_____

_____

_____

_____

_____.

(b) The same table shows that the average person with an advanced degree in business earns $38,000 per year and the average person with a degree in medicine earns $45,000 per year. Suppose that an advanced degree in business takes 2 years after one spends 4 years getting a bachelor's degree and that a medical degree takes 4 years after getting a bachelor's degree. Suppose that you are 22 years old and have just finished college. If $r = .05$, find the present value of lifetime earnings for a graduating senior who will get an advanced degree in business and earn the average

wage rate for someone with this degree until retiring at 65. _____

Make a similar calculation for medicine._____.

11.13 (0) On the planet Stinko, the principal industry is turnip growing. For centuries the turnip fields have been fertilized by guano which was deposited by the now-extinct giant scissor-billed kiki-bird. It costs $5 per ton to mine kiki-bird guano and deliver it to the fields. Unfortunately, the country's stock of kiki-bird guano is about to be exhausted. Fortunately the scientists on Stinko have devised a way of synthesizing kiki-guano from political science textbooks and swamp water. This method of production makes it possible to produce a product indistinguishable from kiki-guano and to deliver it to the turnip fields at a cost of $30 per ton. The interest rate on Stinko is 10%. There are perfectly competitive markets for all commodities.

(a) Given the current price and the demand function for kiki-guano, the last of the deposits on Stinko will be exhausted exactly one year from now. Next year, the price of kiki-guano delivered to the fields will have to be $30, so that the synthetic kiki-guano industry will just break even. The owners of the guano deposits know that next year, they would get a net return of $25 a ton for any guano they have left to sell. In equilibrium, what must be the current price of kiki-guano delivered to the

turnip fields? _____

_____ (Hint: In equilibrium,

sellers must be indifferent between selling their kiki-guano right now or at any other time before the total supply is exhausted. But we know that they must be willing to sell it right up until the day, one year from now, when the supply will be exhausted and the price will be $30, the cost of synthetic guano.)

(b) Suppose that everything is as we have said previously except that the deposits of kiki-guano will be exhausted 10 years from now. What must be the current price of kiki-guano? (Hint: $1.1^{10} = 2.59$.)

Uncertainty

Introduction. In Chapter 11, you learned some tricks that allow you to use techniques you already know for studying intertemporal choice. Here you will learn some similar tricks, so that you can use the same methods to study risk taking, insurance, and gambling.

One of these new tricks is similar to the trick of treating commodities at different dates as different commodities. This time, we invent new commodities, which we call *contingent commodities*. If either of two events A or B could happen, then we define one contingent commodity as *consumption if A happens* and another contingent commodity as *consumption if B happens*. The second trick is to find a budget constraint that correctly specifies the set of contingent commodity bundles that a consumer can afford.

This chapter presents one other new idea, and that is the notion of von Neumann-Morgenstern utility. A consumer's willingness to take various gambles and his willingness to buy insurance will be determined by how he feels about various combinations of contingent commodities. Often it is reasonable to assume that these preferences can be expressed by a utility function that takes the special form known as *von Neumann-Morgenstern utility*. The assumption that utility takes this form is called the *expected utility hypothesis*. If there are two events, 1 and 2 with probability π_1 and π_2, and if the contingent consumptions are c_1 and c_2, then the von Neumann-Morgenstern utility function has the special functional form, $U(c_1, c_2) = \pi_1 u(c_1) + \pi_2 u(c_2)$. The consumer's behavior is determined by maximizing this utility function subject to his budget constraint.

Example: You are thinking of betting on whether the Cincinnati Reds will make it to the World Series this year. A local gambler will bet with you at odds of 10 to 1 against the Reds. You think the probability that the Reds will make it to the World Series is $\pi = .2$. If you don't bet, you are certain to have \$1,000 to spend on consumption goods. Your behavior satisfies the expected utility hypothesis and your von Neumann-Morgenstern utility function is $\pi_1 \sqrt{c_1} + \pi_2 \sqrt{c_2}$.

The contingent commodities are *dollars if the Reds make the World Series* and *dollars if the Reds don't make the World Series*. Let c_W be your consumption contingent on the Reds making the World Series and c_{NW} be your consumption contingent on their not making the Series. Betting on the Reds at odds 10 to 1 means that if you bet \$x on the Reds, then if the Reds make it to the Series you make a net gain of \$10x, but if they don't, you have a net loss of \$x. Since you had \$1,000 before betting, if you bet \$x on the Reds and they made it to the Series, you would have $c_W = 1,000 + 10x$ to spend on consumption. If you bet \$x on the Reds and they didn't make it to the Series, you would lose \$x, and you would have $c_{NW} = 1,000 - x$. By increasing the amount $\$x$ that you bet, you can make c_W larger and c_{NW} smaller. (You could also bet against the Reds at the same odds. If you bet $\$x$ against the Reds and they fail to make it to the Series, you make a net gain of $.1x$ and if they make it to the Series, you lose $\$x$. If you work through the rest of this discussion for the case where you bet against the Reds, you will see that the same equations apply, with x being a negative number.) We can use the above two equations to solve for a budget equation. From the second equation, we have $x = 1,000 - c_{NW}$. Substitute this expression for x into the first equation and rearrange terms to find $c_W + 10c_{NW} = 11,000$, or equivalently, $.1c_W + c_{NW} = 1,100$. (The same budget equation can be written in many equivalent ways by multiplying both sides by a positive constant.)

Then you will choose your contingent consumption bundle (c_W, c_{NW}) to maximize $U(c_W, c_{NW}) = .2\sqrt{c_W} + .8\sqrt{c_{NW}}$ subject to the budget constraint, $.1c_W + c_{NW} = 1,100$. Using techniques that are now familiar, you can solve this consumer problem. From the budget constraint, you see that consumption contingent on the Reds making the World Series costs $1/10$ as much as consumption contingent on their not making it. If you set the marginal rate of substitution between c_W and c_{NW} equal to the price ratio and simplify the resulting expression, you will find that $c_{NW} = .16c_W$. This equation, together with the budget equation implies that $c_W = \$4,230.77$ and $c_{NW} = \$676.92$. You achieve this bundle by betting $\$323.08$ on the Reds. If the Reds make it to the Series, you will have $\$1,000 + 10 \times 323.08 = \$4,230.80$. If not, you will have $\$676.92$. (We rounded the solutions to the nearest penny.)

12.1 (0) In the next few weeks, Congress is going to decide whether or not to develop an expensive new weapons system. If the system is approved, it will be very profitable for the defense contractor, *General Statics*. Indeed, if the new system is approved, the value of stock in *General Statics* will rise from $\$10$ per share to $\$15$ a share, and if the project is not approved, the value of the stock will fall to $\$5$ a share. In his capacity as a messenger for Congressman Kickback, Buzz Condor has discovered that the weapons system is much more likely to be approved than is generally thought. On the basis of what he knows, Condor has decided that the probability that the system will be approved is $3/4$ and the probability that it will not be approved is $1/4$. Let c_A be Condor's consumptions if the system is approved and c_{NA} be his consumption if the system is not approved. Condor's von Neumann-Morgenstern utility function is $U(c_A, c_{NA}) = .75 \ln c_A + .25 \ln c_{NA}$. Condor's total wealth is $\$50,000$, all of which is invested in perfectly safe assets. Condor is about to buy stock in *General Statics*.

(a) If Condor buys x shares of stock, and if the weapons system is approved, he will make a profit of $\$5$ per share. Thus the amount he can consume, contingent on the system being approved, is $c_A = \$50,000 + 5x$. If Condor buys x shares of stock, and if the weapons system is not ap-

proved, then he will make a loss of $\$$_____ per share. Thus the amount he can consume, contingent on the system not being approved, is $c_{NA} =$

_____ .

(b) You can solve for Condor's budget constraint on contingent commodity bundles (c_A, c_{NA}) by eliminating x from these two equations. His budget constraint can be written as _____ $c_A +$_____ $c_{NA} = 50,000$.

(c) Buzz Condor has no moral qualms about trading on inside information, nor does he have any concern that he will be caught and punished. To decide how much stock to buy, he simply maximizes his von Neumann-Morgenstern utility function subject to his budget. If he sets his marginal rate of substitution between the two contingent commodities equal to their relative prices and simplifies the equation, he finds that $c_A/c_{NA} =$

_____ (Reminder: Where a is any constant, the derivative of $a \ln x$ with respect to x is a/x.)

(d) Condor finds that his optimal contingent commodity bundle is $(c_A, c_{NA}) =$_____ To acquire this contingent commodity bundle, he must buy _____ shares of stock in *General Statics*.

12.2 (0) Willy owns a small chocolate factory, located close to a river that occasionally floods in the spring, with disastrous consequences. Next summer, Willy plans to sell the factory and retire. The only income he will have is the proceeds of the sale of his factory. If there is no flood, the factory will be worth $500,000. If there is a flood, then what is left of the factory would be worth only $50,000. Willy can buy flood insurance at a cost of $.10 for each $1 worth of coverage. Willy thinks that the probability that there will be a flood this spring is 1/10. Let c_F denote the contingent commodity *dollars if there is a flood* and c_{NF} denote *dollars if there is no flood*. Willy's von Neumann-Morgenstern utility function is $U(c_F, c_{NF}) = .1\sqrt{c_F} + .9\sqrt{c_{NF}}$.

(a) If he buys no insurance, then in each contingency, Willy's consumption will equal the value of his factory, so Willy's contingent commodity bundle will be $(c_F, c_{NF}) =$_____ .

(b) To buy insurance that pays him $\$x$ in case of a flood, Willy must pay an insurance premium of $.1x$. (The insurance premium must be paid whether or not there is a flood.) If Willy insures for $\$x$, then if there is a flood, he gets $\$x$ in insurance benefits. Suppose that Willy has contracted for insurance that pays him $\$x$ in the event of a flood. Then after paying his insurance premium, he will be able to consume $c_F =$_____ If Willy has this amount of insurance and there is no flood, then he will be able to consume $c_{NF} =$_____ .

(c) You can eliminate x from the two equations for c_F and c_{NF} that you found above. This gives you a budget equation for Willy. Of course there are many equivalent ways of writing the same budget equation, since multiplying both sides of a budget equation by a positive constant yields an equivalent budget equation. The form of the budget equation

in which the "price" of c_{NF} is 1, can written as $.9c_{NF}+$_____ $c_F =$

_____.

(d) Willy's marginal rate of substitution between the two contingent commodities, *dollars if there is no flood* and *dollars if there is a flood*, is $MRS(c_{NF}, c_F) = -\frac{.9\sqrt{c_F}}{.1\sqrt{c_{NF}}}$. To find his optimal bundle of contingent commodities, you must set this marginal rate of substitution equal to the

number _____ Solving this equation, you find that Willy will choose

to consume the two contingent commodities in the ratio_____.

(e) Since you know the ratio in which he will consume c_{NF} and c_F, and you know his budget equation, you can solve for his optimal consumption

bundle, which is $(c_{NF}, c_F)=$_____ Willy will buy an in-

surance policy that will pay him _____ if there is a flood. The

amount of insurance premium that he will have to pay is_____.

12.3 (0) Clarence Bunsen is an expected utility maximizer. His preferences among contingent commodity bundles are represented by the expected utility function

$$u(c_1, c_2, \pi_1, \pi_2) = \pi_1\sqrt{c_1} + \pi_2\sqrt{c_2}.$$

Clarence's friend, Hjalmer Ingqvist, has offered to bet him $1,000 on the outcome of the toss of a coin. That is, if the coin comes up heads, Clarence must pay Hjalmer $1,000 and if the coin comes up tails, Hjalmer must pay Clarence $1,000. The coin is a fair coin, so that the probability of heads and the probability of tails are both 1/2. If he doesn't accept the bet, Clarence will have $10,000 with certainty. In the privacy of his car dealership office over at Bunsen Motors, Clarence is making his decision. (Clarence uses the pocket calculator that his son, Elmer, gave him last Christmas. You will find that it will be helpful for you to use a calculator too.) Let Event 1 be "coin comes up heads" and let Event 2 be "coin comes up tails."

(a) If Clarence accepts the bet, then in Event 1, he will have _____

dollars and in Event 2, he will have _____ dollars.

(b) Since the probability of each event is 1/2, Clarence's expected utility for a gamble in which he gets c_1 in Event 1 and c_2 in Event 2 can be described by the formula _____ Therefore Clarence's expected utility if he accepts the bet with Hjalmer will be _____ (Use that calculator.)

(c) If Clarence decides not to bet, then in Event 1, he will have _____ dollars and in Event 2, he will have _____ dollars. Therefore if he doesn't bet, his expected utility will be _____.

(d) Having calculated his expected utility if he bets and if he does not bet, Clarence determines which is higher and makes his decision accordingly.

Does Clarence take the bet?_____.

12.4 (0) It is a slow day at Bunsen Motors, so since he has his calculator warmed up, Clarence Bunsen (whose preferences toward risk were described in the last problem) decides to study his expected utility function more closely.

(a) Clarence first thinks about really *big* gambles. What if he bet his entire $10,000 on the toss of a coin, where he loses if heads and wins if tails? Then if the coin came up heads, he would have 0 dollars and if it came up tails, he would have $20,000. His expected utility if he took the bet would be _____ , while his expected utility if he didn't take the bet would be _____ Therefore he concludes that he would not take such a bet.

(b) Clarence then thinks, "Well, of course, I wouldn't want to take a chance on losing all of my money on just an ordinary bet. But, what if somebody offered me a really good deal. Suppose I had a chance to bet where if a fair coin came up heads, I lost my $10,000, but if it came up tails, I would win $50,000. Would I take the bet? If I took the bet, my expected utility would be _____ If I didn't take the bet, my expected utility would be _____ Therefore I should _____ the bet."

(c) Clarence later asks himself, "If I make a bet where I lose my $10,000 if the coin comes up heads, what is the smallest amount that I would have to win in the event of tails in order to make the bet a good one for me to take?" After some trial and error, Clarence found the answer. You, too, might want to find the answer by trial and error, but it is easier to find

the answer by solving an equation. On the left side of your equation, you would write down Clarence's utility if he doesn't bet. On the right side of the equation, you write down an expression for Clarence's utility if he makes a bet such that he is left with zero consumption in Event 1 and x in Event 2. Solve this equation for x. The answer to Clarence's question

is where $x - 10,000$. The equation that you should write is _____

The solution is $x = $_____.

(d) Your answer to the last part gives you two points on Clarence's indifference curve between the contingent commodities, money in Event 1 and money in Event 2. (Poor Clarence has never heard of indifference curves or contingent commodities, so you will have to work this part for him, while he heads over to the Chatterbox Cafe for morning coffee.) One of these points is where money in both events is $10,000. On the graph below, label this point, A. The other is where money in Event 1 is zero

and money in Event 2 is _____ On the graph below, label this point B.

Money in Event 2 ($\times 1,000$)

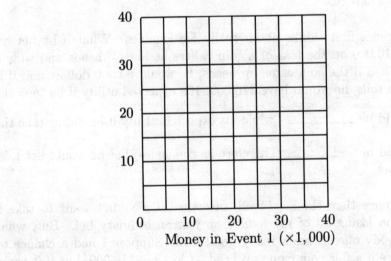

Money in Event 1 ($\times 1,000$)

(e) You can quickly find a third point on this indifference curve. The coin is a fair coin, and Clarence cares whether heads or tails turn up only because that determines his prize. Therefore Clarence will be indifferent between two gambles that are the same except that the assignment of prizes to outcomes are reversed. In this example, Clarence will be indifferent between point B on the graph and a point in which he gets zero if

Event 2 happens and _____ if Event 1 happens. Find this point on the Figure above and label it C.

(f) Another gamble that is on the same indifference curve for Clarence as not gambling at all is the gamble where he loses $5,000 if heads turn up and where he wins _____ dollars if tails turn up. (Hint: To solve this problem, put the utility of not betting on the left side of an equation and on the right side of the equation, put the utility of having $10,000 - $5,000$ in Event 1 and $10,000 + x$ in Event 2. Then solve the resulting equation for x.) On the axes above, plot this point and label it *D*. Now sketch in the entire indifference curve through the points that you have labeled.

12.5 (0) Hjalmer Ingqvist's son-in-law, Earl, has not worked out very well. It turns out that Earl likes to gamble. His preferences over contingent commodity bundles are represented by the expected utility function

$$u(c_1, c_2, \pi_1, \pi_2) = \pi_1 c_1^2 + \pi_2 c_2^2.$$

(a) Just the other day, some of the boys were down at Skoog's tavern when Earl stopped in. They got to talking about just how bad a bet they could get him to take. At the time, Earl had $100. Kenny Olson shuffled a deck of cards and offered to bet Earl $20 that Earl would not cut a spade from the deck. Assuming that Earl believed that Kenny wouldn't cheat, the probability that Earl would win the bet was 1/4 and the probability that Earl would lose the bet was 3/4. If he won the bet, Earl would have

_____ dollars and if he lost the bet, he would have _____ dollars.

Earl's expected utility if he took the bet would be _____ and his

expected utility if he did not take the bet would be _____ Therefore he refused the bet.

(b) Just when they started to think Earl might have changed his ways, Kenny offered to make the same bet with Earl except that they would bet $100 instead of $20. What is Earl's expected utility if he takes that

bet? _____ Would Earl be willing to take this bet?_____

_____.

(c) Let Event 1 be the event that a card drawn from a fair deck of cards is a spade. Let Event 2 be the event that the card is not a spade. Earl's preferences between income contingent on Event 1, c_1, and income contingent

on Event 2, c_2, can be represented by the equation _____ Use blue ink on the graph below to sketch Earl's indifference curve passing through the point $(100, 100)$.

Money in Event 2

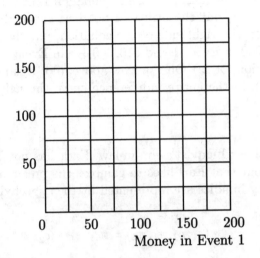

Money in Event 1

(d) On the same graph, let us draw Hjalmer's son-in-law Earl's indifference curves between contingent commodities where the probabilities are different. Suppose that a card is drawn from a fair deck of cards. Let Event 1 be the event that the card is black. Let event 2 be the event that the card drawn is red. Suppose each event has probability 1/2. Then Earl's preferences between income contingent on Event 1 and income contingent on Event 2 are represented by the formula _____ On the graph, use red ink to show two of Earl's indifference curves, including the one that passes through $(100, 100)$.

12.6 (1) Sidewalk Sam makes his living selling sunglasses at the boardwalk in Atlantic City. If the sun shines Sam makes $30, and if it rains Sam only makes $10. For simplicity, we will suppose that there are only two kinds of days, sunny ones and rainy ones.

(a) One of the casinos in Atlantic City has a new gimmick. They are accepting bets on whether or not it will be sunny or rainy the next day. The casino sells dated "rain coupons" for $1 each. If it rains the next day, the casino will give you $2 for every rain coupon you bought on the previous day. If it doesn't rain, your rain coupon is worthless. In the graph below, mark Sam's "endowment" of contingent consumption if he makes no bets with the casino, and label it E.

C_r

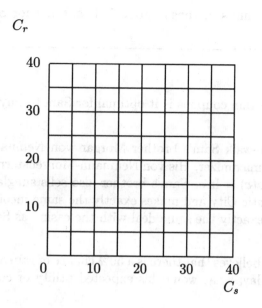

(b) On the same graph, mark the combination of consumption contingent on rain and consumption contingent on sun that he could achieve by buying 10 rain coupons from the casino. Label it *A*.

(c) On the same graph, use blue ink to draw the budget line representing all of the other patterns of consumption that Sam can achieve by buying rain coupons. (Assume that he can buy fractional coupons, but not negative amounts of them.) What is the slope of Sam's budget line at points above and to the left of his initial endowment?_____.

(d) Suppose that the casino also sells sunshine coupons. These tickets also cost $1. With these tickets, the casino gives you $2 if it doesn't rain and nothing if it does. On the graph above, use red ink to sketch in the budget line of contingent consumption bundles that Sam can achieve by buying sunshine tickets.

(e) If the price of a dollar's worth of consumption when it rains is set equal to 1, what is the price of a dollar's worth of consumption if it shines?_____.

12.7 (0) Sidewalk Sam, from the previous problem, has the utility function for consumption in the two states of nature:

$$u(c_s, c_r, \pi) = c_s^{1-\pi} c_r^{\pi},$$

where c_s is the dollar value of his consumption if it shines, c_r is the dollar value of his consumption if it rains, and π is the probability that it will rain. The probability that it will rain is $\pi = .5$.

(a) How many units of consumption is it optimal for Sam to consume conditional on rain?_____.

(b) How many rain coupons is it optimal for Sam to buy?_____.

12.8 (0) Sidewalk Sam's brother Morgan von Neumanstern is an expected utility maximizer. His von Neumann-Morgenstern utility function for wealth is $u(c) = \ln c$. Sam's brother also sells sunglasses on another beach in Atlantic City and makes exactly the same income as Sam does. He can make exactly the same deal with the casino as Sam can.

(a) If Morgan believes that there is a 50% chance of rain and a 50% chance of sun every day, what would his expected utility of consuming (c_s, c_r) be?_____.

(b) How does Morgan's utility function compare to Sam's? Is one a monotonic transformation of the other?_____

_____.

(c) What will Morgan's optimal pattern of consumption be? Answer: Morgan will consume _____ on the sunny days and _____ on the rainy days. How does this compare to Sam's consumption?_____

_____.

12.9 (0) Billy John Pigskin of Mule Shoe, Texas, has a von Neumann-Morgenstern utility function of the form $u(c) = \sqrt{c}$. Billy John also weighs about 300 pounds and can outrun jackrabbits and pizza delivery trucks. Billy John is beginning his senior year of college football. If he is not seriously injured, he will receive a $1,000,000 contract for playing professional football. If an injury ends his football career, he will receive a $10,000 contract as a refuse removal facilitator in his home town. There is a 10% chance that Billy John will be injured badly enough to end his career.

(a) What is Billy John's expected utility?_____

_____.

(b) If Billy John pays $p for an insurance policy that would give him
$1,000,000 if he suffered a career-ending injury while in college, then he
would be sure to have an income of $1,000,000 − p no matter what happened to him. Write an equation that can be solved to find the largest
price that Billy John would be willing to pay for such an insurance policy.

_____.

(c) Solve this equation for *p*._____.

12.10 (1) You have $200 and are thinking about betting on the Big
Game next Saturday. Your team, the Golden Boars, are scheduled to
play their traditional rivals the Robber Barons. It appears that the going
odds are 2 to 1 against the Golden Boars. That is to say if you want to
bet $10 on the Boars you can find someone who will agree to pay you $20
if the Boars win in return for your promise to pay him $10 if the Robber
Barons win. Similarly if you want to bet $10 on the Robber Barons, you
can find someone who will pay you $10 if the Robber Barons win, in return
for your promise to pay him $20 if the Robber Barons lose. Suppose that
you are able to make as large a bet as you like, either on the Boars or on
the Robber Barons so long as your gambling losses do not exceed $200.
(To avoid tedium, let us ignore the possibility of ties.)

(a) If you do not bet at all, you will have $200 whether or not the Boars
win. If you bet $50 on the Boars, then after all gambling obligations are

settled, you will have a total of _____ dollars if the Boars win and

_____ dollars if they lose. On the graph below, use blue ink to draw a
line that represents all of the combinations of "money if the Boars win"
and "money if the Robber Barons win" that you could have by betting
from your initial $200 at these odds.

Money if the Boars lose

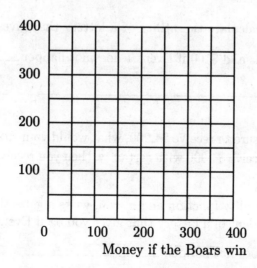

Money if the Boars win

(b) Label the point on this graph where you would be if you did not bet at all with an *E*.

(c) After careful thought you decide to bet $50 on the Boars. Label the point you have chosen on the graph with a *C*. Suppose that after you have made this bet, it is announced that the star Robber Baron quarterback suffered a sprained thumb during a tough economics midterm examination and will miss the game. The market odds shift from 2 to 1 against the Boars to "even money" or 1 to 1. That is, you can now bet on either team and the amount you would win if you bet on the winning team is the same as the amount that you would lose if you bet on the losing team. You cannot cancel your original bet, but you can make new bets at the new odds. Suppose that you keep your first bet, but you now also bet $50 on the Robber Barons at the new odds. If the Boars win, then after you collect your winnings from one bet and your losses from the other,

how much money will you have left? _____ If the Robber Barons win, how much money will you have left after collecting your winnings and paying off your losses?_____.

(d) Use red ink to draw a line on the diagram you made above, showing the combinations of "money if the Boars win" and "money if the Robber Barons win" that you could arrange for yourself by adding possible bets at the new odds to the bet you made before the news of the quarterback's misfortune. On this graph, label the point *D* that you reached by making the two bets discussed above.

12.11 (2) The *certainty equivalent* of a lottery is the amount of money you would have to be given with certainty to be just as well-off with that lottery. Suppose that your von Neumann-Morgenstern utility function over lotteries that give you an amount x if Event 1 happens and y if Event 1 does not happen is $U(x, y, \pi) = \pi\sqrt{x} + (1-\pi)\sqrt{y}$, where π is the probability that Event 1 happens and $1 - \pi$ is the probability that Event 1 does not happen.

(a) If $\pi = .5$, calculate the utility of a lottery that gives you $10,000 if Event 1 happens and $100 if Event 1 does not happen._____

_____.

(b) If you were sure to receive $4,900, what would your utility be? _____ (Hint: If you receive $4,900 with certainty, then you receive $4,900 in both events.)

(c) Given this utility function and $\pi = .5$, write a general formula for the certainty equivalent of a lottery that gives you $$x$ if Event 1 happens and

$$y$ if Event 1 does not happen._____.

(d) Calculate the certainty equivalent of receiving $10,000 if Event 1 happens and $100 if Event 1 does not happen._____.

12.12 (0) Dan Partridge is a risk averter who tries to maximize the expected value of $\sqrt{c}$, where c is his wealth. Dan has $50,000 in safe assets and he also owns a house that is located in an area where there are lots of forest fires. If his house burns down, the remains of his house and the lot it is built on would be worth only $40,000, giving him a total wealth of $90,000. If his home doesn't burn, it will be worth $200,000 and his total wealth will be $250,000. The probability that his home will burn down is .01.

(a) Calculate his expected utility if he doesn't buy fire insurance._____

_____.

(b) Calculate the certainty equivalent of the lottery he faces if he doesn't buy fire insurance._____.

(c) Suppose that he can buy insurance at a price of $1 per $100 of insurance. For example if he buys $100,000 worth of insurance, he will pay $1,000 to the company no matter what happens, but if his house burns he will also receive $100,000 from the company. If Dan buys $160,000 worth of insurance he will be fully insured in the sense that no matter

what happens his after-tax wealth will be_____.

(d) Therefore if he buys full insurance, the certainty equivalent of his

wealth is _____ , and his expected utility is_____.

12.13 (0) Portia has been waiting a long time for her ship to come in and has concluded that there is a 25% chance that it will arrive today. If it does come in today, she will receive $1,600. If it does not come in today, it will never come and her wealth will be zero. Portia has a von Neumann-Morgenstern utility such that she wants to maximize the expected value of $\sqrt{c}$, where c is total income. What is the minimum price at which she

will sell the rights to her ship?_____.

Risky Assets

Introduction. Here you will solve the problems of consumers who wish to divide their wealth optimally between a risky asset and a safe asset. The expected rate of return on a portfolio is just a weighted average of the rate of return on the safe asset and the expected rate of return on the risky asset, where the weights are the fractions of the consumer's wealth held in each. The standard deviation of the portfolio return is just the standard deviation of the return on the risky asset times the fraction of the consumer's wealth held in the risky asset. Sometimes you will look at the problem of a consumer who has preferences over the expected return and the risk of her portfolio and who faces a budget constraint. Since a consumer can always put all of her wealth in the safe asset, one point on this budget constraint will be the combination of the safe rate of return and no risk (zero standard deviation). Now as the consumer puts x percent of her wealth into the risky asset, she gains on that amount the difference between the expected rate of return for the risky asset and the rate of return on the safe asset. But she also absorbs some risk. So the slope of the budget line will be the difference between the two returns divided by the standard deviation of the portfolio that has x percent of the consumer's wealth invested in the risky asset. You can then apply the usual indifference curve–budget line analysis to find the consumer's optimal choice of risk and expected return given her preferences. (Remember that if "standard deviation" is plotted on the horizontal axis and if less risk is preferred to more, the better bundles will lie to the northwest.) You will also be asked to apply the result from the Capital Asset Pricing Model that the expected rate of return on any asset is equal to the sum of the risk-free rate of return plus the risk adjustment. Remember too that the expected rate of return on an asset is its expected change in price divided by its current price.

13.1 (3) Ms. Lynch has a choice of two assets: The first is a risk-free asset that offers a rate of return of r_f, and the second is a risky asset (a china shop that caters to large mammals) that has an expected rate of return of r_m and a standard deviation of σ_m.

(a) If x is the percent of wealth Ms. Lynch invests in the risky asset, what is the equation for the expected rate of return on the portfolio?

_____ What is the equation for the standard deviation

of the portfolio?_____.

(b) By solving the second equation above for x and substituting the result into the first equation, derive an expression for the rate of return on the portfolio in terms of the portfolio's riskiness._____.

(c) Suppose that Ms. Lynch can borrow money at the interest rate r_f and invest it in the risky asset. If $r_m = 20$, $r_f = 10$, and $\sigma_m = 10$, what will be Ms. Lynch's expected return if she borrows an amount equal to 100% of her initial wealth and invests it in the risky asset? (Hint: This is just like investing 200% of her wealth in the risky asset.)_____

_____.

(d) Suppose that Ms. Lynch can borrow or lend at the risk-free rate. If r_f is 10%, r_m is 20%, and σ_m is 10%, what is the formula for the "budget line" Ms. Lynch faces? _____ Plot this budget line in the graph below.

Expected return

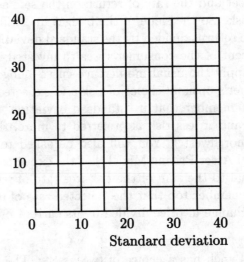

Standard deviation

(e) Which of the following risky assets would Ms. Lynch prefer to her present risky asset, assuming she can only invest in one risky asset at a time and that she can invest a fraction of her wealth in whichever risky asset she chooses? Write the word "better," "worse," or "same" after each of the assets.

Asset A with $r_a = 17\%$ and $\sigma_a = 5\%$._____.

Asset B with $r_b = 30\%$ and $\sigma_b = 25\%$._____.

Asset C with $r_c = 11\%$ and $\sigma_c = 1\%$._____.

Asset D with $r_d = 25\%$ and $\sigma_d = 14\%$._____.

(f) Suppose Ms. Lynch's utility function has the form $u(r_x, \sigma_x) = r_x - 2\sigma_x$. How much of her portfolio will she invest in the original risky asset? (You might want to graph a few of Ms. Lynch's indifference curves before answering, e.g., graph the combinations of r_x and σ_x that imply

$u(r_x, \sigma_x) = 0, 1, \ldots$, etc). _____.

13.2 (3) Fenner Smith is contemplating dividing his portfolio between two assets, a risky asset that has an expected return of 30% and a standard deviation of 10%, and a safe asset that has an expected return of 10% and a standard deviation of 0%.

(a) If Mr. Smith invests x percent of his wealth in the risky asset, what will be his expected return? _____.

(b) If Mr. Smith invests x percent of his wealth in the risky asset, what will be the standard deviation of his wealth? _____.

(c) Solve the above two equations for the expected return on Mr. Smith's wealth as a function of the standard deviation he accepts. _____

_____.

(d) Plot this "budget line" on the graph below.

Expected return

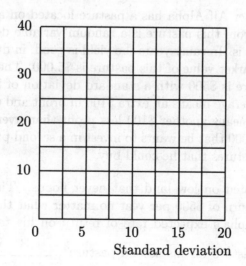

Standard deviation

(e) If Mr. Smith's utility function is $u(r_x, \sigma_x) = \min\{r_x, 30 - 2\sigma_x\}$, then Mr. Smith's optimal value of r_x is _____ , and his optimal value of σ_x is _____ (Hint: You will need to solve two equations in two unknowns. One of the equations is the budget constraint.)

(f) Plot Mr. Smith's optimal choice and an indifference curve through it in the graph.

(g) What fraction of his wealth should Mr. Smith invest in the risky asset?

_____

_____ .

13.3 (2)   Assuming that the Capital Asset Pricing Model is valid, complete the following table. In this table p_0 is the current price of asset i and Ep_1 is the expected price of asset i next period.

r_f	r_m	r_i	β_i	p_0	Ep_1
10	20	10		100	
10	20		1.5		125
10		20	2	200	
0	30		2/3	40	48
10	22		0	80	

13.4 (2)   Farmer Alf Alpha has a pasture located on a sandy hill. The return to him from this pasture is a random variable depending on how much rain there is. In rainy years the yield is good, in dry years the yield is poor. The market value of this pasture is $5,000. The expected return from this pasture is $500 with a standard deviation of $100. Every inch of rain above average means an extra $100 in profit and every inch of rain below average means another $100 less profit than average. Farmer Alf has another $5,000 that he wants to invest in a second pasture. There are two possible pastures that he could buy.

(a) One is located on low land that never floods. This pasture yields an expected return of $500 per year no matter what the weather is like. What is Alf Alpha's expected rate of return on his *total* investment if he buys this pasture for his second pasture? _____ What is the standard deviation of his rate of return in this case?_____ .

(b) Another pasture that he could buy is located on the very edge of the river. This gives very good yields in dry years but in wet years it floods. This pasture also costs $5,000. The expected return from this pasture is $500 and the standard deviation is $100. Every inch of rain *below* average means an extra $100 in profit and every inch of rain above average means another $100 less profit than average. If Alf buys this pasture and keeps his original pasture on the sandy hill, what is his expected rate of return

on his total investment? _____ What is the standard deviation of

the rate of return on his total investment in this case?_____.

(c) If Alf is a risk averter, which of these two pastures should he

buy and why?_____

_____.

(b) Another pasture plan the could buy, is located on the very edge of the river. This gives very good yields in dry years but in wet years it floods. This pasture also costs $6,000. The expected return from this pasture is $500 and the standard deviation is $700. Every year he certain average income an extra $100 in profit and every such year above average means another $100 less profit, else average. If A ... and this pasture ex his offered pasture on fluctuates, but' want is his expected rate of return

on his total investment? _____ What is the standard deviation of

the rate of return on his total investment in this case? _____

(c) If A were a risk averter, which of these, two pastures should he

buy and why _____

Consumer's Surplus

Introduction. In this chapter you will study ways to measure a consumer's valuation of a good given the consumer's demand curve for it. The basic logic is as follows: The height of the demand curve measures how much the consumer is willing to pay for the last unit of the good purchased—the willingness to pay for the marginal unit. Therefore the sum of the willingnesses-to-pay for each unit gives us the total willingness to pay for the consumption of the good.

In geometric terms, the total willingness to pay to consume some amount of the good is just the area under the demand curve up to that amount. This area is called **gross consumer's surplus** or **total benefit** of the consumption of the good. If the consumer has to pay some amount in order to purchase the good, then we must subtract this expenditure in order to calculate the **(net) consumer's surplus**.

When the utility function takes the quasilinear form, $u(x) + m$, the area under the demand curve measures $u(x)$, and the area under the demand curve minus the expenditure on the other good measures $u(x) + m$. Thus in this case, consumer's surplus serves as an exact measure of utility, and the change in consumer's surplus is a monetary measure of a change in utility.

If the utility function has a different form, consumer's surplus will not be an exact measure of utility, but it will often be a good approximation. However, if we want more exact measures, we can use the ideas of the **compensating variation** and the **equivalent variation.**

Recall that the compensating variation is the amount of extra income that the consumer would need at the *new* prices to be as well off as she was facing the old prices; the equivalent variation is the amount of money that it would be necessary to take away from the consumer at the old prices to make her as well off as she would be, facing the new prices. Although different in general, the change in consumer's surplus and the compensating and equivalent variations will be the same if preferences are quasilinear.

In this chapter you will practice

- Calculating consumer's surplus and the change in consumer's surplus

- Calculating compensating and equivalent variations

Example: Suppose that the inverse demand curve is given by $P(q) = 100 - 10q$ and that the consumer currently has 5 units of the good. How much money would you have to pay him to compensate him for reducing his consumption of the good to zero?

Answer: The inverse demand curve has a height of 100 when $q = 0$ and a height of 50 when $q = 5$. The area under the demand curve is a trapezoid with a base of 5 and heights of 100 and 50. We can calculate the area of this trapezoid by applying the formula

$$\text{Area of a trapezoid} \;=\; \text{base} \;\times\; \frac{1}{2}(\text{height}_1 + \text{height}_2).$$

In this case we have $A = 5 \times \frac{1}{2}(100 + 50) = \$375$.

Example: Suppose now that the consumer is purchasing the 5 units at a price of $50 per unit. If you require him to reduce his purchases to zero, how much money would be necessary to compensate him?

In this case, we saw above that his gross benefits decline by $375. On the other hand, he has to spend $5 \times 50 = \$250$ less. The decline in *net* surplus is therefore $125.

Example: Suppose that a consumer has a utility function $u(x_1, x_2) = x_1 + x_2$. Initially the consumer face prices $(1, 2)$ and has income 10. If the prices change to $(4, 2)$, calculate the compensating and equivalent variations.

Answer: Since the two goods are perfect substitutes, the consumer will initially consume the bundle $(10, 0)$ and get a utility of 10. After the prices change, she will consume the bundle $(0, 5)$ and get a utility of 5. After the price change she would need $20 to get a utility of 10; therefore the compensating variation is $20 - 10 = 10$. Before the price change, she would need an income of 5 to get a utility of 5. Therefore the equivalent variation is $10 - 5 = 5$.

14.1 (0) Sir Plus consumes mead, and his demand function for tankards of mead is given by $D(p) = 100 - p$, where p is the price of mead in shillings.

(a) If the price of mead is 50 shillings per tankard, how many tankards of mead will he consume?_____.

(b) How much gross consumer's surplus does he get from this consumption?_____.

(c) How much money does he spend on mead?_____.

(d) What is his net consumer's surplus from mead consumption?_____

_____.

14.2 (0) Here is the table of reservation prices for apartment taken from chapter 1:

Person	=	A	B	C	D	E	F	G	H
Price	=	40	25	30	35	10	18	15	5

(a) If the equilibrium rent for an apartment turns out to be $20, which consumers will get apartments?_____.

(b) If the equilibrium rent for an apartment turns out to be $20, what is the consumer's (net) surplus generated in this market for person A? _____ For person B?_____.

(c) If the equilibrium rent is $20, what is the total net consumers' surplus generated in the market?_____.

(d) If the equilibrium rent is $20, what is the total gross consumers' surplus in the market?_____.

(e) If the rent declines to $19, how much does the gross surplus increase?

_____

(f) If the rent declines to $19, how much does the net surplus increase?

_____

Calculus **14.3 (0)** Quasimodo consumes earplugs and other things. His utility function for earplugs x and money to spend on other goods y is given by

$$u(x, y) = 100x - \frac{x^2}{2} + y.$$

(a) What kind of utility function does Quasimodo have?_____

_____.

(b) What is his inverse demand curve for earplugs?_____.

(c) If the price of earplugs is 50, how many earplugs will he consume?

_____.

(d) If the price of earplugs is 80, how many earplugs will he consume?

_____.

(e) Suppose that Quasimodo has $4,000 in total to spend a month. What is his total utility for earplugs and money to spend on other things if the price of earplugs is 50?_____.

(f) What is his total utility for earplugs and other things if the price of earplugs is 80?_____.

(g) Utility decreases by _____ when the price changes from 50 to 80.

(h) What is the change in (net) consumer's surplus when the price changes from 50 to 80?_____.

14.4 (2) In the graph below, you see a representation of Sarah Gamp's indifference curves between cucumbers and other goods. Suppose that the reference price of cucumbers and the reference price of "other goods" are both 1.

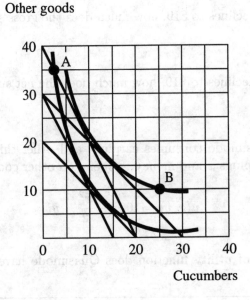

(a) What is the minimum amount of money that Sarah would need in order to purchase a bundle that is indifferent to *A*?_____.

(b) What is the minimum amount of money that Sarah would need in order to purchase a bundle that is indifferent to *B*?_____.

(c) Suppose that the reference price for cucumbers is 2 and the reference price for other goods is 1. How much money does she need in order to purchase a bundle that is indifferent to bundle *A*?_____.

(d) What is the minimum amount of money that Sarah would need to purchase a bundle that is indifferent to *B* using these new prices?_____.

(e) No matter what prices Sarah faces, the amount of money she needs to purchase a bundle indifferent to A must be (higher, lower) than the amount she needs to purchase a bundle indifferent to B._____.

14.5 (2) Bernice's preferences can be represented by $u(x,y) = min\{x,y\}$, where x is pairs of earrings and y is dollars to spend on other things. She faces prices $(p_x, p_y) = (2,1)$ and her income is 12.

(a) Draw in pencil on the graph below some of Bernice's indifference curves and her budget constraint. Her optimal bundle is _____ pairs of earrings and _____ dollars to spend on other things.

Dollars for other things

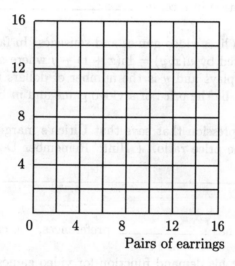

Pairs of earrings

(b) The price of a pair of earrings rises to $3 and Bernice's income stays the same. Using blue ink, draw her new budget constraint on the graph above.

Her new optimal bundle is _____ pairs of earrings and _____ dollars to spend on other things.

(c) What bundle would Bernice choose if she faced the original prices and had just enough income to reach the new indifference curve? _____ Draw with red ink the budget line that passes through this bundle at the original prices. How much income would Bernice need at the original prices to have this (red) budget line?_____.

(d) The maximum amount that Bernice would pay to avoid the price increase is _____ This is the (compensating, equivalent) variation in income._____.

(e) What bundle would Bernice choose if she faced the new prices and had just enough income to reach her original indifference curve? _____ Draw with black ink the budget line that passes through this bundle at the new prices. How much income would Bernice have with this budget?

_____.

(f) In order to be as well off as she was with her original bundle, Bernice's original income would have to rise by _____ This is the (compensating, equivalent) variation in income._____.

Calculus **14.6 (0)** Ulrich likes video games and sausages. In fact, his preferences can be represented by $u(x, y) = \ln(x + 1) + y$ where x is the number of video games he plays and y is the number of dollars that he spends on sausages. Let p_x be the price of a video game and m be his income.

(a) Write an expression that says that Ulrich's marginal rate of substitution equals the price ratio. (Hint: Remember Donald Fribble from Chapter 6?)_____.

(b) Since Ulrich has _____ preferences, you can solve this equation alone to get his demand function for video games, which is _____ _____ His demand function for the dollars to spend on sausages is

_____.

(c) Video games cost $.25 and Ulrich's income is $10. Then Ulrich demands _____ video games and _____ dollars' worth of sausages.

His utility from this bundle is _____ (Round off to two decimal places.)

(d) If we took away all of Ulrich's video games, how much money would he need to have to spend on sausages to be just as well off as before?

_____.

(e) Now an amusement tax of \$.25 is put on video games and is passed on in full to consumers. With the tax in place, Ulrich demands _____ video game and _____ dollars' worth of sausages. His utility from this bundle is _____ (Round off to two decimal places.)

(f) Now if we took away all of Ulrich's video games, how much money would he have to have to spend on sausages to be just as well off as with the bundle he purchased after the tax was in place? _____.

(g) What is the change in Ulrich's consumer surplus due to the tax? _____ How much money did the government collect from Ulrich by means of the tax? _____.

Calculus **14.7 (1)** Lolita, an intelligent and charming Holstein cow, consumes only two goods, cow feed (made of ground corn and oats) and hay. Her preferences are represented by the utility function $U(x, y) = x - x^2/2 + y$, where x is her consumption of cow feed and y is her consumption of hay. Lolita has been instructed in the mysteries of budgets and optimization and always maximizes her utility subject to her budget constraint. Lolita has an income of \$$m$ that she is allowed to spend as she wishes on cow feed and hay. The price of hay is always \$1, and the price of cow feed will be denoted by p, where $0 < p \le 1$.

(a) Write Lolita's inverse demand function for cow feed. (Hint: Lolita's utility function is quasilinear. When y is the numeraire and the price of x is p, the inverse demand function for someone with quasilinear utility $f(x) + y$ is found by simply setting $p = f'(x)$.) _____.

(b) If the price of cow feed is p and her income is m, how much hay does Lolita choose? (Hint: The money that she doesn't spend on feed is used to buy hay.) _____.

(c) Plug these numbers into her utility function to find out the utility level that she enjoys at this price and this income. _____.

(d) Suppose that Lolita's daily income is \$3 and that the price of feed is \$.50. What bundle does she buy? _____ What bundle would she buy if the price of cow feed rose to \$1? _____.

(e) How much money would Lolita be willing to pay to avoid having the price of cow feed rise to $1? _____ This amount is known as the _____ variation.

(f) Suppose that the price of cow feed rose to $1. How much extra money would you have to pay Lolita to make her as well off as she was at the old prices? _____ This amount is known as the _____ variation. Which is bigger, the compensating or the equivalent variation, or are they the same?_____.

(g) At the price $.50 and income $3, how much (net) consumer's surplus is Lolita getting?_____.

14.8 (2) F. Flintstone has quasilinear preferences and his inverse demand function for Brontosaurus Burgers is $P(b) = 30 - 2b$. Mr. Flintstone is currently consuming 10 burgers at a price of 10 dollars.

(a) How much money would he be willing to pay to have this amount rather than no burgers at all? _____ What is his level of (net) consumer's surplus?_____.

(b) The town of Bedrock, the only supplier of Brontosaurus Burgers, decides to raise the price from $10 a burger to $14 a burger. What is Mr. Flintstone's change in consumer's surplus?_____

_____

_____.

14.9 (1) Karl Kapitalist is willing to produce $p/2 - 20$ chairs at every price, $p > 40$. At prices below 40, he will produce nothing. If the price of chairs is $100, Karl will produce _____ chairs. At this price, how much is his producer's surplus?_____.

14.10 (2) Ms. Q. Moto loves to ring the church bells for up to 10 hours a day. Where m is expenditure on other goods, and x is hours of bell ringing, her utility is: $u(m, x) = m + 3x$ for $x \leq 10$. If $x > 10$, she develops painful blisters and is worse off than if she didn't ring the bells. Her income is equal to $100 and the sexton allows her to ring the bell for 10 hours.

(a) Due to complaints from the villagers, the sexton has decided to restrict Ms. Moto to 5 hours of bell ringing per day. This is bad news for Ms. Moto. In fact she regards it as just as bad as losing _____ dollars of income.

(b) The sexton relents and offers to let her ring the bells as much as she likes so long as she pays $2 per hour for the privilege. How much ringing does she do now? _____ This tax on her activities is as bad as a loss of how much income?_____.

(c) The villagers continue to complain. The sexton raises the price of bell ringing to $4 an hour. How much ringing does she do now? _____ _____ This tax, as compared to the situation in which she could ring the bells for free is as bad as a loss of how much income?_____.

Market Demand

Introduction. Some problems in this chapter will ask you to construct the market demand curve from individual demand curves. The market demand at any given price is simply the sum of the individual demands at that price. The key thing to remember in going from individual demands to the market demand is to *add quantities*. Graphically, you sum the individual demands horizontally to get the market demand. The market demand curve will have a kink in it whenever the market price is high enough that some individual demand becomes zero.

Sometimes you will need to find a consumer's reservation price for a good. Recall that the reservation price is the price that makes the consumer indifferent between having the good at that price and not having the good at all. Mathematically, the reservation price p^* satisfies $u(0, m) = u(1, m - p^*)$, where m is income and the quantity of the other good is measured in dollars.

Finally, some of the problems ask you to calculate price and/or income elasticities of demand. These problems are especially easy if you know a little calculus. If the demand function is $D(p)$, and you want to calculate the price elasticity of demand when the price is p, you only need to calculate $dD(p)/dp$ and multiply it by p/q.

15.0 Warm Up Exercise. (Calculating elasticities.) Here are some drills on price elasticities. For each demand function, find an expression for the price elasticity of demand. The answer will typically be a function of the price, p. As an example, consider the linear demand curve, $D(p) = 30 - 6p$. Then $dD(p)/dp = -6$ and $p/q = p/(30 - 6p)$, so the price elasticity of demand is $-6p/(30 - 6p)$.

(a) $D(p) = 60 - p$._____.

(b) $D(p) = a - bp$._____.

(c) $D(p) = 40p^{-2}$._____.

(d) $D(p) = Ap^{-b}$._____.

(e) $D(p) = (p + 3)^{-2}$._____.

(f) $D(p) = (p + a)^{-b}$._____.

15.1 (0) In Gas Pump, South Dakota, there are two kinds of consumers, Buick owners and Dodge owners. Every Buick owner has a demand function for gasoline $D_B(p) = 20 - 5p$ for $p \leq 4$ and $D_B(p) = 0$ if $p > 4$. Every Dodge owner has a demand function $D_D(p) = 15 - 3p$ for $p \leq 5$ and $D_D(p) = 0$ for $p > 5$. (Quantities are measured in gallons per week and price is measured in dollars.) Suppose that Gas Pump has 150 consumers, 100 Buick owners, and 50 Dodge owners.

(a) If the price is \$3, what is the total amount demanded by each individual Buick Owner? _____   And by each individual Dodge owner?

_____.

(b) What is the total amount demanded by all Buick owners? _____

What is the total amount demanded by all Dodge owners?_____.

(c) What is the total amount demanded by all consumers in Gas Pump at a price of 3?_____.

(d) On the graph below, use blue ink to draw the demand curve representing the total demand by Buick owners. Use black ink to draw the demand curve representing total demand by Dodge owners. Use red ink to draw the market demand curve for the whole town.

(e) At what prices does the market demand curve have kinks?_____

_____.

(f) When the price of gasoline is \$1 per gallon, how much does weekly demand fall when price rises by 10 cents?_____.

(g) When the price of gasoline is \$4.50 per gallon, how much does weekly demand fall when price rises by 10 cents?_____.

(h) When the price of gasoline is \$10 per gallon, how much does weekly demand fall when price rises by 10 cents?_____.

Dollars per gallon

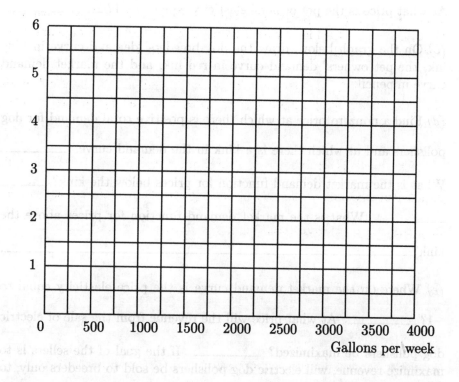

Gallons per week

15.2 (0) For each of the following demand curves, compute the inverse demand curve.

(a) $D(p) = \max\{10 - 2p, 0\}$. _____ .

(b) $D(p) = 100/\sqrt{p}$. _____ .

(c) $\ln D(p) = 10 - 4p$. _____ .

(d) $\ln D(p) = \ln 20 - 2\ln p$. _____ .

15.3 (0) The demand function of dog breeders for electric dog polishers is $q_b = max\{200 - p, 0\}$, and the demand function of pet owners for electric dog polishers is $q_o = max\{90 - 4p, 0\}$.

(a) At price p, what is the price elasticity of dog breeders' demand for electric dog polishers? _____ What is the price elasticity of pet owners' demand? _____ .

(b) At what price is the dog breeders' elasticity equal to −1? _____

At what price is the pet owners' elasticity equal to −1?_____ .

(c) On the graph below, draw the dog breeders' demand curve in blue ink, the pet owners' demand curve in red ink, and the market demand curve in pencil.

(d) Find a nonzero price at which there is positive total demand for dog polishers and at which there is a kink in the demand curve. _____ What is the market demand function for prices below the kink? _____

_____ What is the market demand function for prices above the kink?_____ .

(e) Where on the market demand curve is the price elasticity equal to −1? _____ At what price will the revenue from the sale of electric dog polishers be maximized? _____ If the goal of the sellers is to maximize revenue, will electric dog polishers be sold to breeders only, to pet owners only, or to both?_____ .

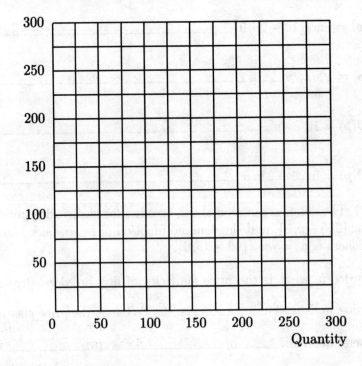

Calculus **15.4 (0)** The demand for kitty litter, in pounds, is $\ln D(p) = 1000 - p + \ln m$, where p is the price of kitty litter and m is income.

(a) What is the price elasticity of demand for kitty litter when $p = 2$ and $m = 500$? _____ When $p = 3$ and $m = 500$? _____ When $p = 4$ and $m = 1500$? _____.

(b) What is the income elasticity of demand for kitty litter when $p = 2$ and $m = 500$? _____ When $p = 2$ and $m = 1,000$? _____ When $p = 3$ and $m = 1,500$? _____.

(c) What is the price elasticity of demand when price is p and income is m? _____ The income elasticity of demand? _____.

Calculus **15.5 (0)** The demand function for drangles is $q(p) = (p+1)^{-2}$.

(a) What is the price elasticity of demand at price p? _____.

(b) At what price is the price elasticity of demand for drangles equal to minus one? _____.

(c) Write an expression for total revenue from the sale of drangles as a function of their price. _____ Use calculus to find the revenue maximizing price. Don't forget to check the second order condition. _____.

(d) Suppose that the demand function for drangles takes the more general form $q(p) = (p+a)^{-b}$ where $a > 0$ and $b > 1$. Calculate an expression for the price elasticity of demand at price p. _____ At what price is the price elasticity of demand equal to -1? _____.

15.6 (0) Ken's utility function is $u_K(x_1, x_2) = x_1 + x_2$ and Barbie's utility function is $u_B(x_1, x_2) = (x_1 + 1)(x_2 + 1)$. A person can buy 1 unit of good 1 or 0 units of good 1. It is impossible for anybody to buy fractional units or to buy more than 1 unit. Either person can buy any quantity of good 2 that he or she can afford at a price of $1 per unit.

(a) Where m is Barbie's wealth and p_1 is the price of good 1, write an equation that can be solved to find Barbie's reservation price for good 1.

_____ What is Barbie's reservation price for good 1?

_____ What is Ken's reservation price for good 1?_____.

(b) If Ken and Barbie each have a wealth of 3, plot the market demand curve for good 1.

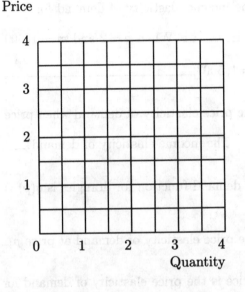

15.7 (0) The demand function for yo-yos is $D(p, M) = 4 - 2p + \frac{1}{100}M$, where p is the price of yo-yos and M is income. If M is 100 and p is 1,

(a) What is the income elasticity of demand for yo-yos?_____.

(b) What is the price elasticity of demand for yo-yos?_____.

15.8 (0) If the demand function for zarfs is $P = 10 - Q$.

(a) At what price will total revenue realized from their sale be at a maximum?_____.

(b) How many zarfs will be sold at that price?_____.

15.9 (0) The demand function for football tickets for a typical game at a large midwestern university is $D(p) = 200,000 - 10,000p$. The university has a clever and avaricious athletic director who sets his ticket prices so as to maximize revenue. The university's football stadium holds 100,000 spectators.

(a) Write down the inverse demand function._____.

(b) Write expressions for total revenue _____ and marginal revenue _____ as a function of the number of tickets sold.

(c) On the graph below, use blue ink to draw the inverse demand function and use red ink to draw the marginal revenue function. On your graph, also draw a vertical blue line representing the capacity of the stadium.

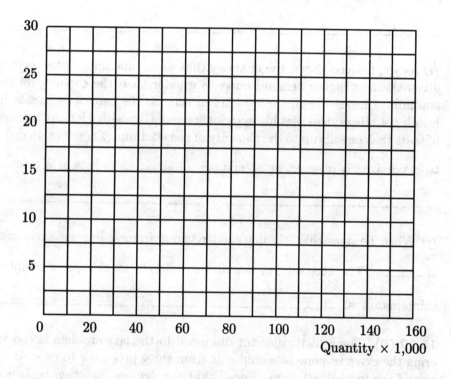

Price

Quantity × 1,000

(d) What price will generate the maximum revenue? _____ What quantity will be sold at this price?_____.

(e) At this quantity, what is marginal revenue?_____ At this quantity, what is the price elasticity of demand?_____ Will the stadium be full?_____.

(f) A series of winning seasons caused the demand curve for football tickets to shift upward. The new demand function is $q(p) = 300,000 - 10,000p$. What is the new inverse demand function?_____

_____ .

(g) Write an expression for marginal revenue as a function of output.

MR(q)=_____ Use red ink to draw the new demand function and use black ink to draw the new marginal revenue function.

(h) Ignoring stadium capacity, what price would generate maximum revenue? _____ What quantity would be sold at this price?_____

_____ .

(i) As you noticed above, the quantity that would maximize total revenue given the new higher demand curve is greater than the capacity of the stadium. Clever though the athletic director is, he cannot sell seats he hasn't got. He notices that his marginal revenue is positive for any number of seats that he sells up to the capacity of the stadium. Therefore, in order to maximize his revenue, he should sell _____ tickets at a price of

_____ .

(j) When he does this, his marginal revenue from selling an extra seat is _____ The elasticity of demand for tickets at this price quantity combination is_____ .

15.10 (0) The athletic director discussed in the last problem is considering the extra revenue he would gain from three proposals to expand the size of the football stadium. Recall that the demand function he is now facing is given by $q(p) = 300,000 - 10,000p$.

(a) How much could the athletic director increase the total revenue per game from ticket sales if he added 1,000 new seats to the stadium's capacity and adjusted the ticket price to maximize his revenue?_____ .

(b) How much could he increase the revenue per game by adding 50,000 new seats? _____ 60,000 new seats? (Hint: The athletic director still wants to maximize revenue.)_____ .

(c) A zealous alumnus offers to build as large a stadium as the athletic director would like and donate it to the university. There is only one hitch. The athletic director must price his tickets so as to keep the stadium full. If the athletic director wants to maximize his revenue from ticket sales,

how large a stadium should he choose?_____.

Equilibrium

Introduction. Supply and demand problems are bread and butter for economists. In the problems below, you will typically want to solve for equilibrium prices and quantities by writing an equation that sets supply equal to demand. Where the price received by suppliers is the same as the price paid by demanders, one writes supply and demand as functions of the same price variable, p, and solves for the price that equalizes supply and demand. But if, as happens with taxes and subsidies, suppliers face different prices from demanders, it is a good idea to denote these two prices by separate variables, p_s and p_d. Then one can solve for equilibrium by solving a system of two equations in the two unknowns p_s and p_d. The two equations are the equation that sets supply equal to demand and the equation that relates the price paid by demanders to the net price received by suppliers.

Example: The demand function for commodity x is $q = 1,000 - 10p_d$, where p_d is the price paid by consumers. The supply function for x is $q = 100 + 20p_s$, where p_s is the price received by suppliers. For each unit sold, the government collects a tax equal to half of the price paid by consumers. Let us find the equilibrium prices and quantities. In equilibrium, supply must equal demand, so that $1,000 - 10p_d = 100 + 20p_s$. Since the government collects a tax equal to half of the price paid by consumers, it must be that the sellers only get half of the price paid by consumers, so it must be that $p_s = p_d/2$. Now we have two equations in the two unknowns, p_s and p_d. Substitute the expression $p_d/2$ for p_s in the first equation, and you have $1,000 - 10p_d = 100 + 10p_d$. Solve this equation to find $p_d = 45$. Then $p_s = 22.5$ and $q = 550$.

16.1 (0) The demand for yak butter is given by $120 - 4p_d$ and the supply is $2p_s - 30$, where p_d is the price paid by demanders and p_s is the price received by suppliers, measured in dollars per hundred pounds. Quantities demanded and supplied are measured in hundred-pound units.

(a) On the axes below, draw the demand curve (with blue ink) and the supply curve (with red ink) for yak butter.

Price

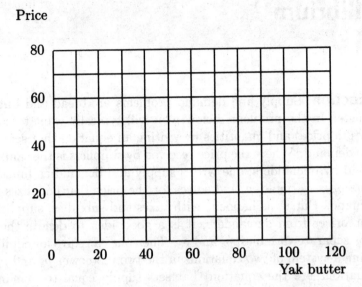

(b) Write down the equation that you would solve to find the equilibrium price._____.

(c) What is the equilibrium price of yak butter? _____   What is the equilibrium quantity? _____   Locate the equilibrium price and quantity on the graph, and label them p_1 and q_1.

(d) A terrible drought strikes the central Ohio steppes, traditional homeland of the yaks. The supply schedule shifts to $2p_s - 60$. The demand schedule remains as before. Draw the new supply schedule. Write down the equation that you would solve to find the new equilibrium price of yak butter._____.

(e) The new equilibrium price is _____ and the quantity is _____ Locate the new equilibrium price and quantity on the graph and label them p_2 and q_2.

(f) The government decides to relieve stricken yak butter consumers and producers by paying a subsidy of $5 per hundred pounds of yak butter to producers. If p_d is the price paid by demanders for yak butter, what is the total amount received by producers for each unit they produce?_____

_____   When the price paid by consumers is p_d, how much yak butter is produced?_____.

(g) Write down an equation that can be solved for the equilibrium price paid by consumers, given the subsidy program. _____
What are the equilibrium price paid by consumers and the equilibrium quantity of yak butter now?_____.

(h) Suppose the government had paid the subsidy to consumers rather than producers. What would be the equilibrium net price paid by consumers? _____ The equilibrium quantity would be_____.

16.2 (0) Here are the supply and demand equations for throstles, where p is the price in dollars:

$$D(p) = 40 - p$$

$$S(p) = 10 + p.$$

On the axes below, draw the demand and supply curves for throstles, using blue ink.

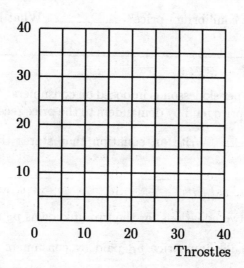

Price

Throstles

(a) The equilibrium price of throstles is _____ and the equilibrium quantity is_____.

(b) Suppose that the government decides to restrict the industry to selling only 20 throstles. At what price would 20 throstles be demanded? _____
How many throstles would suppliers supply at that price? _____ At what price would the suppliers supply only 20 units?_____.

(c) The government wants to make sure that only 20 throstles are bought, but it doesn't want the firms in the industry to receive more than the minimum price that it would take to have them supply 20 throstles. One way to do this is for the government to issue 20 ration coupons. Then in order to buy a throstle, a consumer would need to present a ration coupon along with the necessary amount of money to pay for the good. If the ration coupons were freely bought and sold on the open market, what would be the equilibrium price of these coupons?_____.

(d) On the graph above, shade in the area that represents the deadweight loss from restricting the supply of throstles to 20. How much is this expressed in dollars? (Hint: What is the formula for the area of a triangle?)

_____.

16.3 (0) The demand curve for ski lessons is given by $D(p_D) = 100 - 2p_D$ and the supply curve is given by $S(p_S) = 3p_S$.

(a) What is the equilibrium price? _____ What is the equilibrium

quantity?_____.

(b) A tax of \$10 per ski lesson is imposed on consumers. Write an equation that relates the price paid by demanders to the price received by suppliers.

_____ Write an equation that states that supply equals

demand._____.

(c) Solve these two equations for the two unknowns p_S and p_D. With the

\$10 tax, the equilibrium price p_D paid by consumers would be _____

per lesson. The total number of lessons given would be_____.

(d) A senator from a mountainous state suggests that although ski lesson consumers are rich and deserve to be taxed, ski instructors are poor and deserve a subsidy. He proposes a \$6 subsidy on production while maintaining the \$10 tax on consumption of ski lessons. Would this policy have any different effects for suppliers or for demanders than a tax of \$4 per

lesson?_____.

16.4 (0) The demand curve for salted codfish is $D(P) = 200 - 5P$ and the supply curve $S(P) = 5P$.

(a) On the graph below, use blue ink to draw the demand curve and the supply curve. The equilibrium market price is _____ and the equilibrium quantity sold is_____.

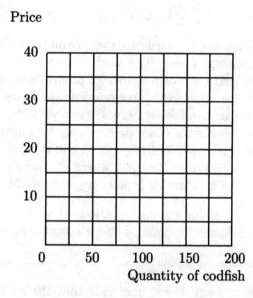

Price

(b) A quantity tax of $2 per unit sold is placed on salted codfish. Use red ink to draw the new supply curve, where the price on the vertical axis remains the price per unit paid by demanders. The new equilibrium

price paid by the demanders will be _____ and the new price received

by the suppliers will be _____ The equilibrium quantity sold will be

_____.

(c) The deadweight loss due to this tax will be _____ On your graph, shade in the area that represents the deadweight loss.

16.5 (0) The demand function for merino ewes is $D(P) = 100/P$, and the supply function is $S(P) = P$.

(a) What is the equilibrium price?_____.

(b) What is the equilibrium quantity?_____.

(c) An ad valorem tax of 300% is imposed on merino ewes so that the price paid by demanders is four times the price received by suppliers. What is the equilibrium price paid by the demanders for merino ewes now?

_____ What is the equilibrium price received by the suppliers for

merino ewes? _____ What is the equilibrium quantity?_____.

16.6 (0) Schrecklich and LaMerde are two justifiably obscure nineteenth-century impressionist painters. The world's total stock of paintings by Schrecklich is 100, and the world's stock of paintings by LaMerde is 150. The two painters are regarded by connoisseurs as being very similar in style. Therefore the demand for either painter's work depends both on its own price and the price of the other painter's work. The demand function for Schrecklichs is $D_S(P) = 200 - 4P_S - 2P_L$, and the demand function for LaMerdes is $D_L(P) = 200 - 3P_L - P_S$, where P_S and P_L are respectively the price in dollars of a Schrecklich painting and a LaMerde painting.

(a) Write down two simultaneous equations that state the equilibrium condition that the demand for each painter's work equals supply.

_____.

(b) Solving these two equations, one finds that the equilibrium price of

Schrecklichs is _____ and the equilibrium price of LaMerdes is_____.

(c) On the diagram below, draw a line that represents all combinations of prices for Schrecklichs and LaMerdes such that the supply of Schrecklichs equals the demand for Schrecklichs. Draw a second line that represents those price combinations at which the demand for LaMerdes equals the supply of LaMerdes. Label the unique price combination at which both markets clear with the letter E.

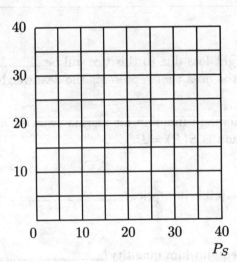

P_L

40

30

20

10

0   10   20   30   40

P_S

(d) A fire in a bowling alley in Hamtramck, Michigan, destroyed one of the world's largest collections of works by Schrecklich. The fire destroyed a total of 10 Schrecklichs. After the fire, the equilibrium price of Schrecklichs was _____ and the equilibrium price of LaMerdes was_____.

(e) On the diagram you drew above, use red ink to draw a line that shows the locus of price combinations at which the demand for Schrecklichs equals the supply of Schrecklichs after the fire. On your diagram, label the new equilibrium combination of prices E'.

16.7 (0) The price elasticity of demand for oatmeal is constant and equal to -1. When the price of oatmeal is \$10 per unit, the total amount demanded is 6,000 units.

(a) Write an equation for the demand function. _____
Graph this demand function below with blue ink. (Hint: If the demand curve has a constant price elasticity equal to ϵ, then $D(p) = ap^\epsilon$ for some constant a. You have to use the data of the problem to solve for the constants a and ϵ that apply in this particular case.)

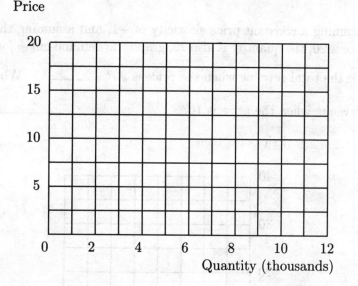

(b) If the supply is perfectly inelastic at 5,000 units, what is the equilibrium price? _____ Show the supply curve on your graph and label the equilibrium with an E.

(c) Suppose that the demand curve shifts outward by 10%. Write down the new equation for the demand function. _____ Suppose that the supply curve remains vertical but shifts to the right by 5%. Solve for the new equilibrium price _____ and quantity_____.

(d) By what percentage approximately did the equilibrium price rise?

_____ Use red ink to draw the new demand curve and the new supply curve on your graph.

(e) Suppose that in the above problem the demand curve shifts outward by $x\%$ and the supply curve shifts right by $y\%$. By approximately what

percentage will the equilibrium price rise?_____.

16.8 (0) An economic historian* reports that econometric studies indicate for the pre–Civil War period, 1820–1860, the price elasticity of demand for cotton from the American South was approximately -1. Due to the rapid expansion of the British textile industry, the demand curve for American cotton is estimated to have shifted outward by about 5% per year during this entire period.

(a) If during this period, cotton production in the United States grew by 3% per year, what (approximately) must be the rate of change of the

price of cotton during this period?_____.

(b) Assuming a constant price elasticity of -1, and assuming that when the price is 20, the quantity is also 20, graph the demand curve for cotton.

What is the total revenue when the price is 20? _____ What is the

total revenue when the price is 10?_____.

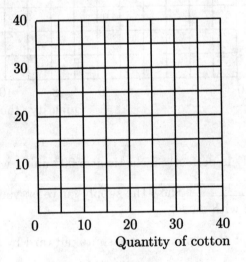

Price of cotton

Quantity of cotton

---

* Gavin Wright, *The Political Economy of the Cotton South*, W. W. Norton, 1978.

(c) If the change in the quantity of cotton supplied by the United States is to be interpreted as a movement along an upward-sloping long-run supply curve, what would the elasticity of supply have to be? (Hint: From 1820

to 1860 quantity rose by about 3% per year and price rose by _____ % per year. [See your earlier answer.] If the quantity change is a movement along the long-run supply curve, then the long-run price elasticity must

be what?)_____.

(d) The American Civil War, beginning in 1861, had a devastating effect on cotton production in the South. Production fell by about 50% and remained at that level throughout the war. What would you predict

would be the effect on the price of cotton?_____

_____.

(e) What would be the effect on total revenue of cotton farmers in

the South?_____

_____.

(f) The expansion of the British textile industry ended in the 1860s, and for the remainder of the nineteenth century, the demand curve for American cotton remained approximately unchanged. By about 1900, the South approximately regained its prewar output level. What do you think

happened to cotton prices then?_____.

16.9 (0) The number of bottles of chardonnay demanded per year is $1,000,000 - 60,000P$, where P is the price per bottle (in U.S. dollars). The number of bottles supplied is $40,000P$.

(a) What is the equilibrium price? _____ What is the equilibrium

quantity?_____.

(b) Suppose that the government introduces a new tax such that the wine maker must pay a tax of $5 per bottle for every bottle that he

produces. What is the new equilibrium price paid by consumers? _____

_____ What is the new price received by suppliers? _____ What is

the new equilibrium quantity?_____.

16.10 (0) The inverse demand function for bananas is $P_d = 18 - 3Q_d$ and the inverse supply function is $P_s = 6 + Q_s$, where prices are measured in cents.

(a) If there are no taxes or subsidies, what is the equilibrium quantity?

_____ What is the equilibrium market price?_____.

(b) If a subsidy of 2 cents per pound is paid to banana growers, then in equilibrium it still must be that the quantity demanded equals the quantity supplied, but now the price received by sellers is 2 cents higher than the price paid by consumers. What is the new equilibrium quantity?

_____ What is the new equilibrium price received by suppliers?

_____ What is the new equilibrium price paid by demanders?

_____.

(c) Express the change in price as a percentage of the original price.

_____ If the cross-elasticity of demand between bananas and apples is +.5, what will happen to the quantity of apples demanded as a consequence of the banana subsidy, if the price of apples stays constant?

(State your answer in terms of percentage change.)_____.

16.11 (1) King Kanuta rules a small tropical island, Nutting Atoll, whose primary crop is coconuts. If the price of coconuts is P, then King Kanuta's subjects will demand $D(P) = 1,200 - 100P$ coconuts per week for their own use. The number of coconuts that will be supplied per week by the island's coconut growers is $S(p) = 100P$.

(a) The equilibrium price of coconuts will be _____ and the equilibrium quantity supplied will be_____.

(b) One day, King Kanuta decided to tax his subjects in order to collect coconuts for the Royal Larder. The king required that every subject who consumed a coconut would have to pay a coconut to the king as a tax. Thus, if a subject wanted 5 coconuts for himself, he would have to purchase 10 coconuts and give 5 to the king. When the price that is received by the sellers is p_S, how much does it cost one of the king's subjects to get an extra coconut for himself?_____.

(c) When the price paid to suppliers is p_S, how many coconuts will the king's subjects demand for their own consumption? (Hint: Express p_D in terms of p_S and substitute into the demand function.)_____

_____.

(d) Since the king consumes a coconut for every coconut consumed by the subjects, the total amount demanded by the king and his subjects is twice the amount demanded by the subjects. Therefore, when the price received by suppliers is p_S, the total number of coconuts demanded per

week by Kanuta and his subjects is_____.

(e) Solve for the equilibrium value of p_S_____ , the equilibrium total

number of coconuts produced_____ , and the equilibrium total number

of coconuts consumed by Kanuta's subjects._____.

(f) King Kanuta's subjects resented paying the extra coconuts to the king, and whispers of revolution spread through the palace. Worried by the hostile atmosphere, the king changed the coconut tax. Now, the shopkeepers who sold the coconuts would be responsible for paying the tax. For every coconut sold to a consumer, the shopkeeper would have

to pay one coconut to the king. This plan resulted in _____

coconuts being sold to the consumers. The shopkeepers got _____ per coconut after paying their tax to the king, and the consumers paid a

price of _____ per coconut.

Technology

Introduction. In this chapter you work with production functions, relating output of a firm to the inputs it uses. This theory will look familiar to you, because it closely parallels the theory of utility functions. In utility theory, an *indifference curve* is a locus of commodity bundles, all of which give a consumer the same utility. In production theory, an *isoquant* is a locus of input combinations, all of which give the same output. In consumer theory, you found that the slope of an indifference curve at the bundle (x_1, x_2) is the ratio of marginal utilities, $MU_1(x_1, x_2)/MU_2(x_1, x_2)$. In production theory, the slope of an isoquant at the input combination (x_1, x_2) is the ratio of the marginal products, $MP_1(x_1, x_2)/MP_2(x_1, x_2)$. Most of the functions that we gave as examples of utility functions can also be used as examples of production functions.

There is one important difference between production functions and utility functions. Remember that utility functions were only "unique up to monotonic transformations." In contrast, two different production functions that are monotonic transformations of each other describe different technologies.

Example: If the utility function $U(x_1, x_2) = x_1 + x_2$ represents a person's preferences, then so would the utility function $U^*(x_1, x_2) = (x_1 + x_2)^2$. A person who had the utility function $U^*(x_1, x_2)$ would have the same indifference curves as a person with the utility function $U(x_1, x_2)$ and would make the same choices from every budget. But suppose that one firm has the production function $f(x_1, x_2) = x_1 + x_2$, and another has the production function $f^*(x_1, x_2) = (x_1 + x_2)^2$. It is true that the two firms would have the same isoquants, but they certainly do not have the same technology. If both firms have the input combination $(x_1, x_2) = (1, 1)$, then the first firm will have an output of 2 and the second firm will have an output of 4.

Now we investigate "returns to scale." Here we are concerned with the change in output if the amount of every input is multiplied by a number $t > 1$. If multiplying inputs by t multiplies output by more than t, then there are increasing returns to scale. If output is multiplied by exactly t, there are constant returns to scale. If output is multiplied by less than t, then there are decreasing returns to scale.

Example: Consider the production function, $f(x_1, x_2) = x_1^{1/2} x_2^{3/4}$. If we multiply the amount of each input by t, then output will be $f(tx_1, tx_2) = (tx_1)^{1/2}(tx_2)^{3/4}$. To compare $f(tx_1, tx_2)$ to $f(x_1, x_2)$, factor out the expressions involving t from the last equation. You get $f(tx_1, tx_2) = t^{5/4} x_1^{1/2} x_2^{3/4} = t^{5/4} f(x_1, x_2)$. Therefore when you multiply the amounts of all inputs by t, you multiply the amount of output by $t^{5/4}$. This means there are *increasing* returns to scale.

Example: Let the production function be $f(x_1, x_2) = \min\{x_1, x_2\}$. Then

$$f(tx_1, tx_2) = \min\{tx_1, tx_2\} = \min t\{x_1, x_2\} = t\min\{x_1, x_2\} = tf(x_1, x_2).$$

Therefore when all inputs are multiplied by t, output is also multiplied by t. It follows that this production function has *constant* returns to scale.

You will also be asked to determine whether the marginal product of each single factor of production increases or decreases as you increase the amount of that factor without changing the amount of other factors. Those of you who know calculus will recognize that the marginal product of a factor is the first derivative of output with respect to the amount of that factor. Therefore the marginal product of a factor will decrease, increase, or stay constant as the amount of the factor increases depending on whether the *second* derivative of the production function with respect to the amount of that factor is negative, positive, or zero.

Example: Consider the production function $f(x_1, x_2) = x_1^{1/2} x_2^{3/4}$. The marginal product of factor 1 is $\frac{1}{2}x_1^{-1/2}x_2^{3/4}$. This is a decreasing function of x_1, as you can verify by taking the derivative of the marginal product with respect to x_1. Similarly, you can show that the marginal product of x_2 decreases as x_2 increases.

17.0 Warm Up Exercise. The first part of this exercise is to calculate marginal products and technical rates of substitution for several frequently encountered production functions. As an example, consider the production function $f(x_1, x_2) = 2x_1 + \sqrt{x_2}$. The marginal product of x_1 is the derivative of $f(x_1, x_2)$ with respect to x_1, holding x_2 fixed. This is just 2. The marginal product of x_2 is the derivative of $f(x_1, x_2)$ with respect to x_2, holding x_1 fixed, which in this case is $\frac{1}{2\sqrt{x_2}}$. The TRS is $-MP_1/MP_2 = -4\sqrt{x_2}$. Those of you who do not know calculus should fill in this table from the answers in the back. The table will be a useful reference for later problems.

Marginal Products and Technical Rates of Substitution

$f(x_1, x_2)$	$MP_1(x_1, x_2)$	$MP_2(x_1, x_2)$	$TRS(x_1, x_2)$
$x_1 + 2x_2$			
$ax_1 + bx_2$			
$50x_1x_2$			
$x_1^{1/4}x_2^{3/4}$	$\frac{1}{4}x_1^{-3/4}x_2^{3/4}$		
$Cx_1^a x_2^b$	$Cax_1^{a-1}x_2^b$		
$(x_1 + 2)(x_2 + 1)$	$x_2 + 1$		
$(x_1 + a)(x_2 + b)$			
$ax_1 + b\sqrt{x_2}$			
$x_1^a + x_2^a$			
$(x_1^a + x_2^a)^b$	$bax_1^{a-1}(x_1^a + x_2^a)^{b-1}$	$bax_2^{a-1}(x_1^a + x_2^a)^{b-1}$	

Returns to Scale and Changes in Marginal Products

For each production function in the table below, put an I, C, or D in the first column if the production function has increasing, constant, or decreasing returns to scale. Put an I, C, or D in the second (third) column, depending on whether the marginal product of factor 1 (factor 2) is increasing, constant, or decreasing, as the amount of that factor alone is varied.

$f(x_1, x_2)$	Scale	MP_1	MP_2
$x_1 + 2x_2$			
$\sqrt{x_1 + 2x_2}$			
$.2x_1 x_2^2$			
$x_1^{1/4} x_2^{3/4}$			
$x_1 + \sqrt{x_2}$			
$(x_1 + 1)^{.5}(x_2)^{.5}$			
$\left(x_1^{1/3} + x_2^{1/3}\right)^3$			

17.1 (0) Prunella raises peaches. Where L is the number of units of labor she uses and T is the number of units of land she uses, her output is $f(L, T) = L^{\frac{1}{2}} T^{\frac{1}{2}}$ bushels of peaches.

(a) On the graph below, plot some input combinations that give her an output of 4 bushels. Sketch a production isoquant that runs through these points. The points on the isoquant that gives her an output of 4 bushels all satisfy the equation $T = $_____.

T

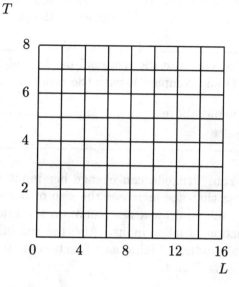

(b) This production function exhibits (constant, increasing, decreasing) returns to scale._____.

(c) In the short run, Prunella cannot vary the amount of land she uses. On the graph below, use blue ink to draw a curve showing Prunella's output as a function of labor input if she has 1 unit of land. Locate the points on your graph at which the amount of labor is 0, 1, 4, 9, and 16 and label them. The slope of this curve is known as the marginal _____

of _____ Is this curve getting steeper or flatter as the amount

of labor increase?_____.

Output

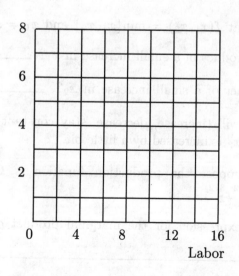

Labor

(d) Assuming she has 1 unit of land, how much extra output does she get from adding an extra unit of labor when she previously used 1 unit

of labor? _____ 4 units of labor? _____ If you know calculus, compute the marginal product of labor at the input combination $(1, 1)$ and compare it with the result from the unit increase

in labor output found above._____

_____.

(e) In the long run, Prunella can change her input of land as well as of labor. Suppose that she increases the size of her orchard to 4 units of land. Use red ink to draw a new curve on the graph above showing output as a function of labor input. Also use red ink to draw a curve showing marginal product of labor as a function of labor input when the amount of land is fixed at 4.

17.2 (0) Suppose x_1 and x_2 are used in fixed proportions and $f(x_1, x_2) = \min\{x_1, x_2\}$.

(a) Suppose that $x_1 < x_2$. The marginal product for x_1 is _____ and

(increases, remains constant, decreases)_____ for small

increases in x_1. For x_2 the marginal product is _____ , and (increases,

remains constant, decreases)_____ for small increases in

x_2. The technical rate of substitution between x_2 and x_1 is _____

_____ This technology demonstrates (increasing, constant, decreasing)

_____ returns to scale.

(b) Suppose that $f(x_1, x_2) = \min\{x_1, x_2\}$ and $x_1 = x_2 = 20$. What is

the marginal product of a small increase in x_1? _____ What is the

marginal product of a small increase in x_2? _____ The marginal

product of x_1 will (increase, decrease, stay constant)_____ if the amount of x_2 is increased by a little bit.

Calculus **17.3 (0)** Suppose the production function is Cobb-Douglas and $f(x_1, x_2) = x_1^{1/2} x_2^{3/2}$.

(a) Write an expression for the marginal product of x_1 at the point

(x_1, x_2)._____.

(b) The marginal product of x_1 (increases, decreases, remains constant) _____ for small increases in x_1, holding x_2 fixed.

(c) The marginal product of factor 2 is _____ , and it (increases, remains constant, decreases)_____ for small increases in x_2.

(d) An increase in the amount of x_2 (increases, leaves unchanged, decreases) _____ the marginal product of x_1.

(e) The technical rate of substitution between x_2 and x_1 is_____.

(f) Does this technology have diminishing technical rate of substitution?

_____.

(g) This technology demonstrates (increasing, constant, decreasing) _____ returns to scale.

17.4 (0) The production function for fragles is $f(K, L) = L/2 + \sqrt{K}$, where L is the amount of labor used and K the amount of capital used.

(a) There are (constant, increasing, decreasing)_____ returns to scale. The marginal product of labor is _____ (constant, increasing, decreasing).

(b) In the short run, capital is fixed at 4 units. Labor is variable. On the graph below, use blue ink to draw output as a function of labor input in the short run. Use red ink to draw the marginal product of labor as a function of labor input in the short run. The average product of labor is defined as total output divided by the amount of labor input. Use black ink to draw the average product of labor as a function of labor input in the short run.

Fragles

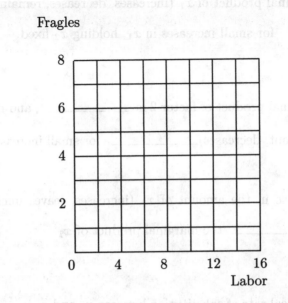

17.5 (0) General Monsters Corporation has two plants for producing juggernauts, one in Flint and one in Inkster. The Flint plant produces according to $f_F(x_1, x_2) = \min\{x_1, 2x_2\}$ and the Inkster plant produces according to $f_I(x_1, x_2) = \min\{2x_1, x_2\}$, where x_1 and x_2 are the inputs.

(a) On the graph below, use blue ink to draw the isoquant for 40 juggernauts at the Flint plant. Use red ink to draw the isoquant for producing 40 juggernauts at the Inkster plant.

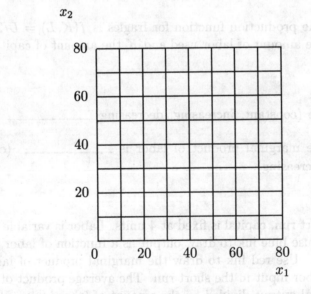

(b) Suppose that the firm wishes to produce 20 juggernauts at each plant. How much of each input will the firm need to produce 20 juggernauts at

the Flint plant? _____ How much of each input will the firm

need to produce 20 juggernauts at the Inkster plant? _____
Label with an *a* on the graph, the point representing the total amount of each of the two inputs that the firm needs to produce a total of 40 juggernauts, 20 at the Flint plant and 20 at the Inkster plant.

(c) Label with a *b* on your graph the point that shows how much of each of the two inputs is needed in total if the firm is to produce 10 juggernauts in the Flint plant and 30 juggernauts in the Inkster plant. Label with a *c* the point that shows how much of each of the two inputs that the firm needs in total if it is to produce 30 juggernauts in the Flint plant and 10 juggernauts in the Inkster plant. Use a black pen to draw the firm's isoquant for producing 40 units of output if it can split production in any manner between the two plants. Is the technology available to this firm

convex?_____.

17.6 (0) You manage a crew of 160 workers who could be assigned to make either of two products. Product A requires 2 workers per unit of output. Product B requires 4 workers per unit of output.

(a) Write an equation to express the combinations of products A and B

that could be produced using exactly 160 workers. _____ On the diagram below, use blue ink to shade in the area depicting the combinations of A and B that could be produced with 160 workers. (Assume that it is also possible for some workers to do nothing at all.)

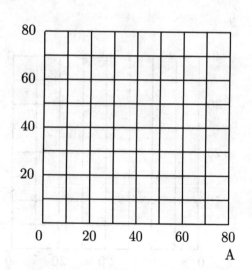

B

(b) Suppose now that every unit of product A that is produced requires the use of 4 shovels as well as 2 workers and that every unit of product B produced requires 2 shovels and 4 workers. On the graph you have just drawn, use red ink to shade in the area depicting combinations of A and B that could be produced with 180 shovels if there were no worries about the labor supply. Write down an equation for the set of combinations of

A and B that require exactly 180 shovels._____.

(c) On the same diagram, use black ink to shade the area that represents possible output combinations when one takes into account both the limited supply of labor and the limited supply of shovels.

(d) On your diagram locate the feasible combination of inputs that use up all of the labor and all of the shovels. If you didn't have the graph,

what equations would you solve to determine this point?_____

_____.

(e) If you have 160 workers and 180 shovels, what is the largest amount of

product A that you could produce? _____ If you produce this amount, you will not use your entire supply of one of the inputs. Which

one? _____ How many will be left unused?_____.

17.7 (0) A firm has the production function $f(x, y) = \min\{2x, x + y\}$. On the graph below, use red ink to sketch a couple of production isoquants for this firm. A second firm has the production function $f(x, y) = x + \min\{x, y\}$. Do either or both of these firms have constant returns to scale?

_____ On the same graph, use black ink to draw a couple of isoquants for the second firm.

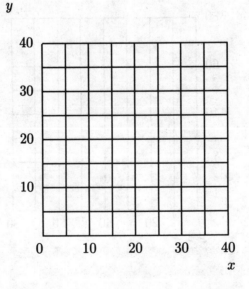

17.8 (0) Suppose the production function has the form

$$f(x_1, x_2, x_3) = A x_1^a x_2^b x_3^c,$$

where $a + b + c > 1$. Prove that there are increasing returns to scale.

_____.

17.9 (0) Suppose that the production function is $f(x_1, x_2) = C x_1^a x_2^b$, where a, b, and C are positive constants.

(a) For what positive values of a, b, and C are there decreasing returns to scale?_____ constant returns to scale? _____

_____ increasing returns to scale?_____.

(b) For what positive values of a, b, and C is there decreasing marginal product for factor 1?_____.

(c) For what positive values of a, b, and C is there diminishing technical rate of substitution?_____.

17.10 (0) Suppose that the production function is $f(x_1, x_2) = (x_1^a + x_2^a)^b$, where a and b are positive constants.

(a) For what positive values of a and b are there decreasing returns to scale?_____ Constant returns to scale? _____ Increasing

returns to scale?_____.

17.11 (0) Suppose that a firm has the production function $f(x_1, x_2) = \sqrt{x_1} + x_2^2$.

(a) The marginal product of factor 1 (increases, decreases, stays constant)

_____ as the amount of factor 1 increases. The marginal product

of factor 2 (increases, decreases, stays constant) _____ as the amount of factor 2 increases.

(b) This production function does not satisfy the definition of increasing returns to scale, constant returns to scale, or decreasing returns to scale.

How can this be? _____

_____ Find a combination of inputs such that doubling the amount of both inputs will more than double the amount

of output. _____ Find a combination of inputs such that doubling the amount of both inputs will less than double output.

_____.

Chapter 18

NAME_____

Profit Maximization

Introduction. A firm in a competitive industry cannot charge more than the market price for its output. If it also must compete for its inputs, then it has to pay the market price for inputs as well. Suppose that a profit-maximizing competitive firm can vary the amount of only one factor and that the marginal product of this factor decreases as its quantity increases. Then the firm will maximize its profits by hiring enough of the variable factor so that the value of its marginal product is equal to the wage. Even if a firm uses several factors, only some of them may be variable in the short run.

Example: A firm has the production function $f(x_1, x_2) = x_1^{1/2} x_2^{1/2}$. Suppose that this firm is using 16 units of factor 2 and is unable to vary this quantity in the short run. In the short run, the only thing that is left for the firm to choose is the amount of factor 1. Let the price of the firm's output be p, and let the price it pays per unit of factor 1 be w_1. We want to find the amount of x_1 that the firm will use and the amount of output it will produce. Since the amount of factor 2 used in the short run must be 16, we have output equal to $f(x_1, 16) = 4x_1^{1/2}$. The marginal product of x_1 is calculated by taking the derivative of output with respect to x_1. This marginal product is equal to $2x_1^{-1/2}$. Setting the value of the marginal product of factor 1 equal to its wage, we have $p2x_1^{-1/2} = w_1$. Now we can solve this for x_1. We find $x_1 = (2p/w_1)^2$. Plugging this into the production function, we see that the firm will choose to produce $4x_1^{1/2} = 8p/w_1$ units of output.

In the long run, a firm is able to vary all of its inputs. Consider the case of a competitive firm that uses two inputs. Then if the firm is maximizing its profits, it must be that the value of the marginal product of each of the two factors is equal to its wage. This gives two equations in the two unknown factor quantities. If there are decreasing returns to scale, these two equations are enough to determine the two factor quantities. If there are constant returns to scale, it turns out that these two equations are only sufficient to determine the *ratio* in which the factors are used.

In the problems on the weak axiom of profit mazimization, you are asked to determine whether the observed behavior of firms is consistent with profit-maximizing behavior. To do this you will need to plot some of the firm's isoprofit lines. An isoprofit line relates all of the input-output combinations that yield the same amount of profit for some given input and output prices. To get the equation for an isoprofit line, just write down an equation for the firm's profits at the given input and output prices. Then solve it for the amount of output produced as a function of the amount of the input chosen. Graphically, you know that a firm's behavior is consistent with profit maximization if its input-output choice in each period lies below the isoprofit lines of the other periods.

18.1 (0) The short-run production function of a competitive firm is given by $f(L) = 6L^{2/3}$, where L is the amount of labor it uses. (For those who do not know calculus—if total output is aL^b, where a and b are constants, and where L is the amount of some factor of production, then the marginal product of L is given by the formula abL^{b-1}.) The cost per unit of labor is $w = 6$ and the price per unit of output is $p = 3$.

(a) Plot a few points on the graph of this firm's production function and sketch the graph of the production function, using blue ink. Use black ink to draw the isoprofit line that passes through the point $(0, 12)$, the isoprofit line that passes through $(0, 8)$, and the isoprofit line that passes through the point $(0, 4)$. What is the slope of each of the isoprofit lines?

_____ How many points on the isoprofit line through

$(0, 12)$ consist of input-output points that are actually possible?_____

_____ Make a squiggly line over the part of the isoprofit line through $(0, 4)$ that consists of outputs that are actually possible.

(b) How many units of labor will the firm hire? _____ How much

output will it produce? _____ If the firm has no other costs, how much

will its total profits be?_____.

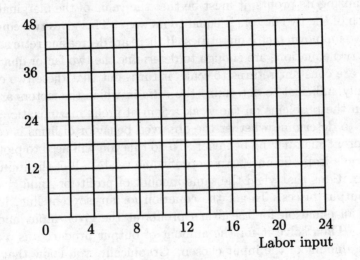

(c) Suppose that the wage of labor falls to 4, and the price of output remains at p. On the graph, use red ink to draw the new isoprofit line for the firm that passes through its old choice of input and output. Will the firm increase its output at the new price?_____ Explain why, referring to your diagram._____

_____.

Calculus **18.2 (0)** A Los Angeles firm uses a single input to produce a recreational commodity according to a production function $f(x) = 4\sqrt{x}$, where x is the number of units of input. The commodity sells for \$100 per unit. The input costs \$50 per unit.

(a) Write down a function that states the firm's profit as a function of the amount of input._____.

(b) What is the profit-maximizing amount of input? _____ of output?

_____ How much profits does it make when it maximizes profits?

_____.

(c) Suppose that the firm is taxed \$20 per unit of its output and the price of its input is subsidized by \$10. What is its new input level?

_____ What is its new output level? _____ How much profit does it make now?_____ (Hint: A good way to solve this is to write an expression for the firm's profit as a function of its input and solve for the profit-maximizing amount of input.)

(d) Suppose that instead of these taxes and subsidies, the firm is taxed at 50% of its profits. Write down its after-tax profits as a function of the amount of input._____ What is the profit-maximizing amount of output? _____ How much profit does it make after taxes?_____.

18.3 (0) Brother Jed takes heathens and reforms them into righteous individuals. There are two inputs needed in this process: heathens (who are widely available) and preaching. The production function has the following form: $r_p = \min\{h, p\}$, where r_p is the number of righteous persons produced, h is the number of heathens who attend Jed's sermons, and p is the number of hours of preaching. For every person converted, Jed receives a payment of s from the grateful convert. Sad to say, heathens do not flock to Jed's sermons of their own accord. Jed must offer heathens a payment of w to attract them to his sermons. Suppose the amount of preaching is fixed at $\bar{p}$ and that Jed is a profit-maximizing prophet.

(a) If $h < \bar{p}$, what is the marginal product of heathens? _____ What is the value of the marginal product of an additional heathen?_____.

(b) If $h > \bar{p}$, what is the marginal product of heathens? _____ What is the value of the marginal product of an additional heathen in this case?

_____.

(c) Sketch the shape of this production function in the graph below. Label the axes, and indicate the amount of the input where $h = \bar{p}$.

(d) If $w < s$, how many heathens will be converted? _____ If $w > s$, how many heathens will be converted?_____.

18.4 (0) Allie's Apples, Inc. purchases apples in bulk and sells two products, boxes of apples and jugs of cider. Allie's has capacity limitations of three kinds: warehouse space, crating facilities, and pressing facilities. A box of apples requires 6 units of warehouse space, 2 units of crating facilities, and no pressing facilities. A jug of cider requires 3 units of warehouse space, 2 units of crating facilities, and 1 unit of pressing facilities. The total amounts available each day are: 1,200 units of warehouse space, 600 units of crating facilities, and 250 units of pressing facilities.

(a) If the only capacity limitations were on warehouse facilities, and if all warehouse space were used for the production of apples, how many boxes of apples could be produced in one day? _____ How many jugs of cider could be produced each day if, instead, all warehouse space were used in the production of cider and there were no other capacity constraints? _____ Draw a blue line in the following graph to represent the warehouse space constraint on production combinations.

(b) Following the same reasoning, draw a red line to represent the constraints on output to limitations on crating capacity. How many boxes of apples could Allie produce if he only had to worry about crating capacity? _____ How many jugs of cider?_____.

(c) Finally draw a black line to represent constraints on output combinations due to limitations on pressing facilities. How many boxes of apples could Allie produce if he only had to worry about the pressing capacity and no other constraints? _____ How many jugs of cider?_____.

(d) Now shade the area that represents feasible combinations of daily production of apples and cider for Allie's Apples.

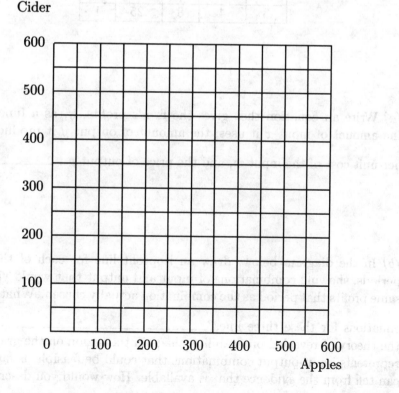

(e) Allie's can sell apples for $5 per box of apples and cider for $2 per jug. Draw a black line to show the combinations of sales of apples and cider that would generate a revenue of $1,000 per day. At the profit-maximizing production plan, Allie's is producing _____ boxes of apples

and _____ jugs of cider. Total revenues are_____.

18.5 (0) A profit-maximizing firm produces one output, y, and uses one input, x, to produce it. The price per unit of the factor is denoted by w and the price of the output is denoted by p. You observe the firm's behavior over three periods and find the following:

Period	y	x	w	p
1	1	1	1	1
2	2.5	3	.5	1
3	4	8	.25	1

(a) Write an equation that gives the firm's profits, π, as a function of the amount of input x it uses, the amount of output y it produces, the per-unit cost of the input w, and the price of output p._____.

(b) In the diagram below, draw an isoprofit line for each of the three periods, showing combinations of input and output that would yield the same profits that period as the combination actually chosen. What are the

equations for these three lines?_____ Using the theory of revealed profitability, shade in the region on the graph that represents input-output combinations that could be feasible as far as one can tell from the evidence that is available. How would you describe this

region in words?_____.

Output

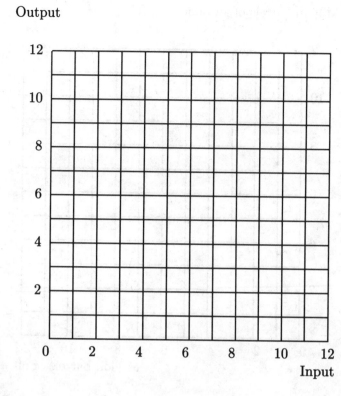

Input

18.6 (0) T-bone Pickens is a corporate raider. This means that he looks for companies that are not maximizing profits, buys them, and then tries to operate them at higher profits. T-bone is examining the financial records of two refineries that he might buy, the Shill Oil Company and the Golf Oil Company. Each of these companies buys oil and produces gasoline. During the time period covered by these records, the price of gasoline fluctuated significantly, while the cost of oil remained constant at $10 a barrel. For simplicity, we assume that oil is the only input to gasoline production.

Shill Oil produced 1 million barrels of gasoline using 1 million barrels of oil when the price of gasoline was $10 a barrel. When the price of gasoline was $20 a barrel, Shill produced 3 million barrels of gasoline using 4 million barrels of oil. Finally, when the price of gasoline was $40 a barrel, Shill used 10 million barrels of oil to produce 5 million barrels of gasoline.

Golf Oil (which is managed by Martin E. Lunch III) did exactly the same when the price of gasoline was $10 and $20, but when the price of gasoline hit $40, Golf produced 3.5 million barrels of gasoline using 8 million barrels of oil.

(a) Using black ink plot Shill Oil's isoprofit lines and choices for the three different periods. Label them 10, 20, and 40. Using red ink draw Golf Oil's isoprofit line and production choice. Label it with a 40 in red ink.

Million barrels of gasoline

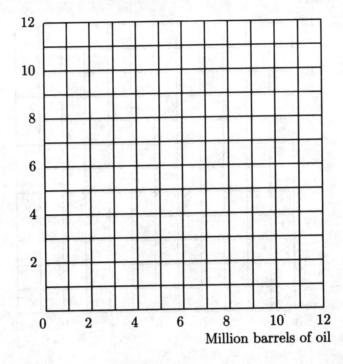

Million barrels of oil

(b) How much profits could Golf Oil have made when the price of gasoline was $40 a barrel if they had chosen to produce the same amount that they did when the price was $20 a barrel? _____ What profits did Golf actually make when the price of gasoline was $40?_____.

(c) Is there any evidence that Shill Oil is not maximizing profits? Explain.

_____.

(d) Is there any evidence that Golf Oil is not maximizing profits? Explain.

_____

_____.

18.7 (0) After carefully studying Shill Oil, T-bone Pickens decides that it has probably been maximizing its profits. But he still is very interested in buying Shill Oil. He wants to use the gasoline they produce to fuel his delivery fleet for his chicken farms, Capon Truckin'. In order to do this Shill Oil would have to be able to produce 5 million barrels of gasoline from 8 million barrels of oil. Mark this point on your graph. Assuming that Shill always maximizes profits, would it be technologically feasible for it to produce this input-output combination? Why or why not?

_____

_____.

18.8 (0) Suppose that firms operate in a competitive market, attempt to maximize profits, and only use one factor of production. Then we know that for any changes in the input and output price, the input choice and the output choice must obey the Weak Axiom of Profit Maximization, $\Delta p \Delta y - \Delta w \Delta x \geq 0$.

Which of the following propositions can be proven by the Weak Axiom of Profit Maximizing Behavior (WAPM)? Respond yes or no, and give a short argument.

(a) If the price of the input does not change, then a decrease in the price of the output will imply that the firm will produce the same amount

or less output._____

_____.

(b) If the price of the output remains constant, then a decrease in the input price will imply that the firm will use the same amount or

more of the input._____

_____.

(c) If both the price of the output and the input increase and the firm

produces less output, then the firm will use more of the input._____

_____.

18.9 (1) Farmer Hoglund has discovered that on his farm, he can get 30 bushels of corn per acre if he applies no fertilizer. When he applies N pounds of fertilizer to an acre of land, the *marginal product* of fertilizer is $1 - N/200$ bushels of corn per pound of fertilizer.

(a) If the price of corn is \$3 a bushel and the price of fertilizer is \$$p$ per pound (where $p < 3$), how many pounds of fertilizer should he use per

acre in order to maximize profits?_____.

(b) (Only for those who remember a bit of easy integral calculus.) Write down a function that states Farmer Hoglund's yield per acre as a function

of the amount of fertilizer he uses._____

(c) Hoglund's neighbor, Skoglund, has better land than Hoglund. In fact, for any amount of fertilizer that he applies, he gets exactly twice as much corn per acre as Hoglund would get with the same amount of fertilizer. How much fertilizer will Skoglund use per acre when the price of corn is \$3 a bushel and the price of fertilizer is \$$p$ a pound? _____ (Hint: Start by writing down Skoglund's marginal product of fertilizer as a function of N.)

(d) When Hoglund and Skoglund are both maximizing profits, will Skoglund's output will be more than twice as much, less than twice as much or exactly twice as much as Hoglund's? Explain._____

_____ .

(e) Explain how someone who looked at Hoglund's and Skoglund's corn yields and their fertilizer inputs but couldn't observe the quality of their land, would get a misleading idea of the productivity of fertilizer._____

_____ .

18.10 (0) A firm has two variable factors and a production function, $f(x_1, x_2) = x_1^{1/2} x_2^{1/4}$. The price of its output is 4. Factor 1 receives a wage of w_1 and factor 2 receives a wage of w_2.

(a) Write an equation that says that the value of the marginal product of factor 1 is equal to the wage of factor 1 _____ and an equation that says that the value of the marginal product of factor 2 is equal to the wage of factor 2._____ Solve two equations in the two unknowns, x_1 and x_2, to give the amounts of factors 1 and 2 that maximize the firm's profits as a function of w_1 and w_2. This gives $x_1 =$_____ and $x_2 =$_____ (Hint: You could use the first equation to solve for x_1 as a function of x_2 and of the factor wages. Then substitute the answer into the second equation and solve for x_2 as a function of the two wage rates. Finally use your solution for x_2 to find the solution for x_1.)

(b) If the wage of factor 1 is 2, and the wage of factor 2 is 1, how many units of factor 1 will the firm demand?_____ How many units of factor 2 will it demand?_____ How much output will it produce?

_____ How much profit will it make?_____ .

18.11 (0) A firm has two variable factors and a production function $f(x_1, x_2) = x_1^{1/2} x_2^{1/2}$. The price of its output is 4, the price of factor 1 is w_1, and the price of factor 2 is w_2.

(a) Write the two equations that say that the value of the marginal product of each factor is equal to its wage. _____

_____ If $w_1 = 2w_2$, these two equations imply that $x_1/x_2 =$_____.

(b) For this production function, is it possible to solve the two marginal productivity equations uniquely for x_1 and x_2?_____.

18.12 (1) A firm has two variable factors and a production function $f(x_1, x_2) = \sqrt{2x_1 + 4x_2}$. On the graph below, draw production isoquants corresponding to an ouput of 3 and to an output of 4.

(a) If the price of the output good is 4, the price of factor 1 is 2 and the price of factor 2 is 3, find the profit-maximizing amount of factor 1,

_____ , the profit-maximizing amount of factor 2_____ , and the

profit-maximizing output_____.

Factor 2

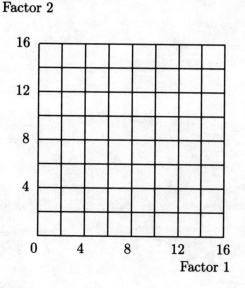

Factor 1

Cost Minimization

Introduction. In the chapter on consumer choice, you studied a consumer who tries to maximize his utility subject to the constraint that he has a fixed amount of money to spend. In this chapter you study the behavior of a firm that is trying to produce a fixed amount of output in the cheapest possible way. In both theories, you look for a point of tangency between a curved line and a straight line. In consumer theory, there is an "indifference curve" and a "budget line." In producer theory, there is a "production isoquant" and an "isocost line." As you recall, in consumer theory, finding a tangency gives you only one of the two equations you need to locate the consumer's chosen point. The second equation you used was the budget equation. In cost-minimization theory, again the tangency condition gives you one equation. This time you don't know in advance how much the producer is spending, instead you are told how much output he wants to produce and must find the cheapest way to produce it. So your second equation is the equation that tells you that the desired amount is being produced.

Example. A firm has the production function $f(x_1, x_2) = (\sqrt{x_1} + 3\sqrt{x_2})^2$. The price of factor 1 is $w_1 = 1$ and the price of factor 2 is $w_2 = 1$. Let us find the cheapest way to produce 16 units of output. We will be looking for a point where the technical rate of substitution equals $-w_1/w_2$. If you calculate the technical rate of substitution (or look it up from the warm up exercise in Chapter 17), you find $TRS(x_1, x_2) = -(1/3)(x_2/x_1)^{1/2}$. Therefore we must have $-(1/3)(x_2/x_1)^{1/2} = -w_1/w_2 = -1$. This equation can be simplified to $x_2 = 9x_1$. So we know that the combination of inputs chosen has to lie somewhere on the line $x_2 = 9x_1$. We are looking for the cheapest way to produce 16 units of output. So the point we are looking for must satisfy the equation $(\sqrt{x_1} + 3\sqrt{x_2})^2 = 16$, or equivalently $\sqrt{x_1} + 3\sqrt{x_2} = 4$. Since $x_2 = 9x_1$, we can substitute for x_2 in the previous equation to get $\sqrt{x_1} + 3\sqrt{9x_1} = 4$. This equation simplifies further to $10\sqrt{x_1} = 4$. Solving this for x_1, we have $x_1 = 16/100$. Then $x_2 = 9x_1 = 144/100$.

The amounts x_1 and x_2 that we solved for in the previous paragraph are known as the *conditional factor demands for factors 1 and 2*, conditional on the wages $w_1 = 1$, $w_2 = 1$, and output $y = 16$. We express this by saying $x_1(1, 1, 16) = 16/100$ and $x_2(1, 1, 16) = 144/100$. Since we know the amount of each factor that will be used to produce 16 units of output and since we know the price of each factor, we can now calculate the cost of producing 16 units. This cost is $c(w_1, w_2, 16) = w_1 x_1(w_1, w_2, 16) + w_2 x_2(w_1, w_2, 16)$. In this instance since $w_1 = w_2 = 1$, we have $c(1, 1, 16) = x_1(1, 1, 16) + x_2(1, 1, 16) = 160/100$.

In consumer theory, you also dealt with cases where the consumer's indifference "curves" were straight lines and with cases where there were kinks in the indifference curves. Then you found that the consumer's choice might occur at a boundary or at a kink. Usually a careful look at the diagram would tell you what is going on. The story with kinks and boundary solutions is almost exactly the same in the case of cost-minimizing firms. You will find some exercises that show how this works.

19.1 (0) Nadine sells user-friendly software. Her firm's production function is: $f(x_1, x_2) = x_1 + 2x_2$, where x_1 is the amount of unskilled labor and x_2 is the amount of skilled labor that she employs.

(a) In the graph below, draw a production isoquant representing input combinations that will produce 20 units of output. Draw another isoquant representing input combinations that will produce 40 units of output.

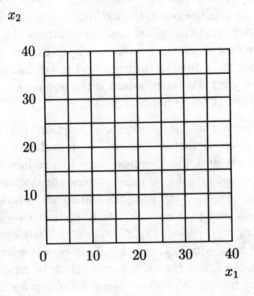

(b) Does this production function exhibit increasing, decreasing, or constant returns to scale?_____.

(c) If Nadine uses only unskilled labor, how much unskilled labor would she need in order to produce y units of output?_____.

(d) If Nadine uses only skilled labor to produce output, how much skilled labor would she need in order to produce y units of output?_____.

(e) If Nadine faces factor prices $(1, 1)$, what is the cheapest way for her to produce 20 units of output? $x_1 = $ _____ , $x_2 = $_____.

(f) If Nadine faces factor prices $(1,3)$, what is the cheapest way for her to produce 20 units of output? $x_1 =$ _____ , $x_2 =$_____.

(g) If Nadine faces factor prices (w_1, w_2), what will be the minimal cost of producing 20 units of output?_____.

(h) If Nadine faces factor prices (w_1, w_2), what will be the minimal cost of producing y units of output?_____.

19.2 (0) The Ontario Brassworks produces brazen effronteries. As you know brass is an alloy of copper and zinc, used in fixed proportions. The production function is given by: $f(x_1, x_2) = \min\{x_1, 2x_2\}$, where x_1 is the amount of copper it uses and x_2 is the amount of zinc that it uses in production.

(a) Illustrate a typical isoquant for this production function in the graph below.

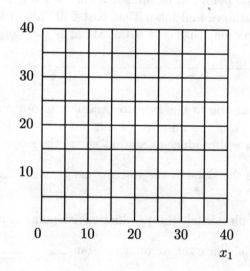

(b) Does this production function exhibit increasing, decreasing, or constant returns to scale?_____.

(c) If the firm wanted to produce 10 effronteries, how much copper would it need? _____ How much zinc would it need?_____.

(d) If the firm faces factor prices $(1, 1)$, what is the cheapest way for it to produce 10 effronteries? How much will this cost?_____

_____

_____.

(e) If the firm faces factor prices (w_1, w_2), what is the cheapest cost to produce 10 effronteries?_____.

(f) If the firm faces factor prices (w_1, w_2), what will be the minimal cost of producing y effronteries?_____.

Calculus   **19.3 (0)** A firm uses labor and machines to produce output according to the production function $f(L, M) = 4L^{1/2}M^{1/2}$, where L is the number of units of labor used and M is the number of machines. The cost of labor is $40 per unit and the cost of using a machine is $10.

(a) On the graph below, draw an isocost line for this firm, showing combinations of machines and labor that cost $400 and another isocost line showing combinations that cost $200. What is the slope of these isocost

lines?_____.

(b) Suppose that the firm wants to produce its output in the cheapest possible way. Find the number of machines it would use per worker. (Hint: The firm will produce at a point where the slope of the production

isoquant equals the slope of the isocost line.)_____.

(c) On the graph, sketch the production isoquant corresponding to an

output of 40. Calculate the amount of labor _____ and the number

of machines _____ that are used to produce 40 units of output in the cheapest possible way, given the above factor prices. Calculate the cost

of producing 40 units at these factor prices. $c(40, 10, 40) =$_____.

(d) How many units of labor _____ and how many machines _____ would the firm use to produce y units in the cheapest possible way? How

much would this cost? _____ (Hint: Notice that there are constant returns to scale.)

Machines

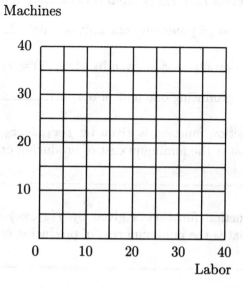

Labor

19.4 (0) Earl sells lemonade in a competitive market on a busy street corner in Philadelphia. His production function is $f(x_1, x_2) = x_1^{1/3} x_2^{1/3}$, where output is measured in gallons, x_1 is the number of pounds of lemons he uses, and x_2 is the number of labor-hours spent squeezing them.

(a) Does Earl have constant returns to scale, decreasing returns to scale, or increasing returns to scale?_____.

(b) Where w_1 is the cost of a pound of lemons and w_2 is the wage rate for lemon-squeezers, the cheapest way for Earl to produce lemonade is to use _____ hours of labor per pound of lemons. (Hint: Set the slope of his isoquant equal to the slope of his isocost line.)

(c) If he is going to produce y units in the cheapest way possible, then the number of pounds of lemons he will use is $x_1(w_1, w_2, y) =$_____ and the number of hours of labor that he will use is $x_2(w_1, w_2, y) =$_____.

_____ (Hint: Use the production function and the equation you found in the last part of the answer to solve for the input quantities.)

(d) The cost to Earl of producing y units at factor prices w_1 and w_2 is $c(w_1, w_2, y) = w_1 x_1(w_1, w_2, y) + w_2 x_2(w_1, w_2, y) =$_____.

19.5 (0) The prices of inputs (x_1, x_2, x_3, x_4) are $(4, 1, 3, 2)$.

(a) If the production function is given by $f(x_1, x_2) = min\{x_1, x_2\}$, what is the minimum cost of producing one unit of output?_____.

(b) If the production function is given by $f(x_3, x_4) = x_3 + x_4$, what is the minimum cost of producing one unit of output?_____.

(c) If the production function is given by $f(x_1, x_2, x_3, x_4) = min\{x_1 + x_2, x_3 + x_4\}$, what is the minimum cost of producing one unit of output?

_____.

(d) If the production function is given by $f(x_1, x_2) = min\{x_1, x_2\} + min\{x_3, x_4\}$, what is the minimum cost of producing one unit of output?

_____.

19.6 (0) Joe Grow, an avid indoor gardener, has found that the number of happy plants, h, depends on the amount of light, l, and water, w. In fact, Joe noticed that plants require twice as much light as water, and any more or less will be wasted. Thus, Joe's production function is as follows: $h = min\{l, 2w\}$.

(a) Suppose Joe is using 1 unit of light, what is the least amount of water he can use and still produce a happy plant?_____.

(b) If Suppose Joe wants to produce 4 happy plants, what are the minimum amounts of light and water required?_____.

(c) Joe's conditional factor demand function for light is $l(w_1, w_2, h) = $ _____ and his conditional factor demand function for water is $w(w_1, w_2, h) = $_____.

(d) If each unit of light costs w_1 and each unit of water costs w_2, Joe's cost function is $c(w_1, w_2, h) = $_____.

19.7 (1) Joe's sister, Flo Grow, is a university administrator. She uses an alternative method of gardening. Flo has found that happy plants only need fertilizer and talk. (*Warning:* Frivolous observations about university administrators' talk being a perfect substitute for fertilizer is in extremely poor taste.) Where f is the number of bags of fertilizer used and t is the number of hours she talks to her plants, the number of happy plants produced is exactly $h = t + 2f$. Suppose fertilizer costs w_f per bag and talk costs w_t per hour.

(a) If Flo uses no fertilizer, how many hours of talk must she devote if she wants one happy plant? _____ If she doesn't talk to her plants at all, how many bags of fertilizer will she need for one happy plant?

_____.

(b) If $w_t < w_f/2$, would it be cheaper for Flo to use fertilizer or talk to raise one happy plant?_____.

(c) Flo's cost function is $c(w_f, w_t, h) =$_____.

(d) Her conditional factor demand for talk is $t(w_f, w_t, h) =$_____ if $w_t < w_f/2$ and _____ if $w_t > w_f/2$.

19.8 (0) Remember T-bone Pickens, the corporate raider? Now he's concerned about his chicken farms, Pickens' Chickens. He feeds his chickens on a mixture of soybeans and corn, depending on the prices of each. According to the data submitted by his managers, when the price of soybeans was $10 a bushel and the price of corn was $10 a bushel, they used 50 bushels of corn and 150 bushels of soybeans for each coop of chickens. When the price of soybeans was $20 a bushel and the price of corn was $10 a bushel, they used 300 bushels of corn and no soybeans per coop of chickens. When the price of corn was $20 a bushel and the price of soybeans was $10 a bushel, they used 250 bushels of soybeans and no corn for each coop of chickens.

(a) Graph these three input combinations and isocost lines in the following diagram.

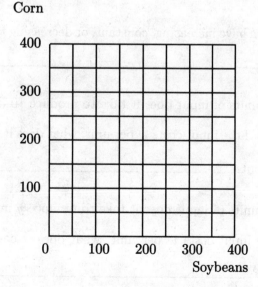

(b) How much money did Pickens' managers spend per coop of chickens when the prices were $(10, 10)$? _____ When the prices were $(10, 20)$? _____ When the prices were $(20, 10)$? _____.

(c) Is there any evidence that Picken's managers were not minimizing costs? Why or why not?

_____.

(d) Pickens wonders whether there are any prices of corn and soybeans at which his managers will use 150 bushels of corn and 50 bushels of soybeans to produce a coop of chickens. How much would this production method cost per coop of chickens if the prices were $p_s = 10$ and $p_c = 10$? _____ if the prices were $p_s = 10$, $p_c = 20$? _____ if the prices were $p_s = 20$, $p_c = 10$? _____.

(e) If Pickens' managers were always minimizing costs, can it be possible to produce a coop of chickens using 150 bushels and 50 bushels of soybeans? _____

_____

_____.

19.9 (0) A genealogical firm called Roots produces its output using only one input. Its production function is $f(x) = \sqrt{x}$.

(a) Does the firm have increasing, constant, or decreasing returns to scale?

_____.

(b) How many units of input does it take to produce 10 units of output? _____ If the input costs w per unit, what does it cost to produce 10 units of output? _____.

(c) How many units of input does it take to produce y units of output? _____ If the input costs w per unit, what does it cost to produce y units of output? _____.

(d) If the input costs w per unit, what is the average cost of producing y units? $AC(w, y) =$_____.

19.10 (0) A university cafeteria produces square meals, using only one input and a rather remarkable production process. We are not allowed to say what that ingredient is, but an authoritative kitchen source says that "fungus is involved." The cafeteria's production function is $f(x) = x^2$, where x is the amount of input and $f(x)$ is the number of square meals produced.

(a) Does the cafeteria have increasing, constant, or decreasing returns to scale?_____.

(b) How many units of input does it take to produce 144 square meals? _____ If the input costs w per unit, what does it cost to produce 144 square meals?_____.

(c) How many units of input does it take to produce y square meals? _____ If the input costs w per unit, what does it cost to produce y square meals?_____.

(d) If the input costs w per unit, what is the average cost of producing y square meals? $AC(w, y) =$_____.

19.11 (0) Irma's Handicrafts produces plastic deer for lawn ornaments. "It's hard work," says Irma, "but anything to make a buck." Her production function is given by: $f(x_1, x_2) = (\min\{x_1, 2x_2\})^{1/2}$, where x_1 is the amount of plastic used, x_2 is the amount of labor used, and $f(x_1, x_2)$ is the number of deer produced.

(a) In the graph below, draw a production isoquant representing input combinations that will produce 4 deer. Draw another production isoquant representing input combinations that will produce 5 deer.

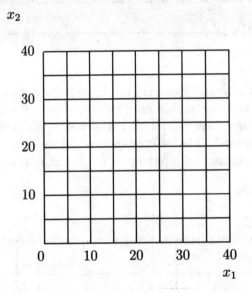

(b) Does this production function exhibit increasing, decreasing, or constant returns to scale?_____.

(c) If Irma faces factor prices $(1, 1)$, what is the cheapest way for her to produce 4 deer? _____ How much does this cost?_____.

(d) At the factor prices $(1, 1)$, what is the cheapest way to produce 5 deer? _____ How much does this cost?_____.

(e) At the factor prices $(1, 1)$, the cost of producing y deer with this technology is $c(1, 1, y) =$_____.

(f) At the factor prices (w_1, w_2), the cost of producing y deer with this technology is $c(w_1, w_2, y) =$_____.

19.12 (0) Al Deardwarf also makes plastic deer for lawn ornaments. Al has found a way to automate the production process completely. He doesn't use any labor—only wood and plastic. Al says he likes the business "because I need the doe." Al's production function is given by $f(x_1, x_2) = (2x_1 + x_2)^{1/2}$, where x_1 is the amount of plastic used, x_2 is the amount of wood used, and $f(x_1, x_2)$ is the number of deer produced.

(a) In the graph below, draw a production isoquant representing input combinations that will produce 4 deer. Draw another production isoquant representing input combinations that will produce 6 deer.

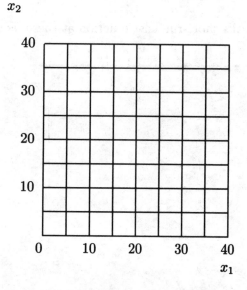

(b) Does this production function exhibit increasing, decreasing, or constant returns to scale?_____.

(c) If Al faces factor prices $(1,1)$, what is the cheapest way for him to produce 4 deer? _____ How much does this cost?_____.

(d) At the factor prices $(1,1)$, what is the cheapest way to produce 6 deer? _____ How much does this cost?_____.

(e) At the factor prices $(1,1)$, the cost of producing y deer with this technology is $c(1,1,y) =$_____.

(f) At the factor prices $(3,1)$, the cost of producing y deer with this technology is $c(3,1,y) =$_____.

19.13 (0) Suppose that Al Deardwarf from the last problem cannot vary the amount of wood that he uses in the short run and is stuck with using 20 units of wood. Suppose that he can change the amount of plastic that he uses, even in the short run.

(a) How much plastic would Al need in order to make 100 deer?_____

_____.

(b) If the cost of plastic is \$1 per unit and the cost of wood is \$1 per unit, how much would it cost Al to make 100 deer?_____.

(c) Write down Al's short-run cost function at these factor prices._____

_____.

Chapter 20

NAME_____

Cost Curves

Introduction. Here you continue to work on cost functions. Total cost can be divided into fixed cost, the part that doesn't change as output changes, and variable cost. To get the average (total) cost, average fixed cost, and average variable cost, just divide the appropriate cost function by y, the level of output. The marginal cost function is the derivative of the total cost function with respect to output—or the rate of increase in cost as output increases, if you don't know calculus.

Remember that the marginal cost curve intersects both the average cost curve and the average variable cost curve at their minimum points. So to find the minimum point on the average cost curve, you simply set marginal cost equal to average cost and similarly for the minimum of average variable cost.

Example: A firm has the total cost function $C(y) = 100 + 10y$. Let us find the equations for its various cost curves. Total fixed costs are 100, so the equation of the average fixed cost curve is $100/y$. Total variable costs are $10y$, so average variable costs are $10y/y = 10$ for all y. Marginal cost is 10 for all y. Average total costs are $(100 + 10y)/y = 10 + 10/y$. Notice that for this firm, average total cost decreases as y increases. Notice also that marginal cost is less than average total cost for all y.

20.1 (0) Mr. Otto Carr, owner of Otto's Autos, sells cars. Otto buys autos for $\$c$ each and has no other costs.

(a) What is his total cost if he sells 10 cars? _____ What if he sells 20 cars? _____ Write down the equation for Otto's total costs assuming he sells y cars: $TC(y) =$_____.

(b) What is Otto's average cost function? $AC(y) =$ _____ For every additional auto Otto sells his costs increase by? _____ Write down Otto's marginal cost function, $MC(y) =$_____.

(c) In the graph below draw Otto's average and marginal cost curves if $c = 20$.

AC, MC

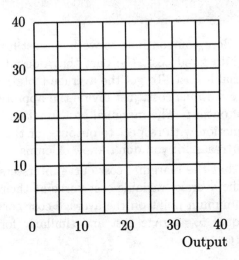

Output

(d) Suppose Otto has to pay $\$b$ a year to produce obnoxious television commercials. Otto's total cost curve is now $TC(y) =$ _____ , his average cost curve is now $AC(y) =$ _____ , and his marginal cost curve is: $MC(y) =$ _____ .

(e) If $b = \$100$, use red ink to draw Otto's average cost curve on the graph above.

20.2 (0) Otto's brother, Dent Carr, is in the auto repair business. Dent recently had little else to do and decided to calculate his cost conditions. He found that the total cost of repairing s cars is $TC(s) = 2s^2 + 10$. But Dent's attention was diverted to other things ... and that's where you come in. Please complete the following:

Dent's Total Variable Costs:_____.

Total Fixed Costs:_____.

Average Variable Costs:_____.

Average Fixed Costs:_____.

Average Total Costs:_____.

Marginal Costs:_____.

20.3 (0) A third brother, Rex Carr, owns a junk yard. Rex can use one of two methods to destroy cars. The first involves purchasing a hydraulic car smasher that costs $200 a year to own and then spending $1 for every car smashed into oblivion; the second method involves purchasing a shovel that will last one year and costs $10 and paying the last Carr brother, Scoop, to bury the cars at a cost of $5 each.

(a) Write down the total cost functions for the two methods, where y is output per year: $TC_1(y) =$ _____ , $TC_2(y) =$ _____.

(b) The first method has an average cost function _____ and a marginal cost function _____ For the second method these costs are

_____ and_____.

(c) If Rex wrecks 40 cars per year, which method should he use? _____

_____ If Rex wrecks 50 cars per year, which method should he use?

_____ What is the smallest number of cars per year for which it would pay him to buy the hydraulic smasher?_____.

20.4 (0) Mary Magnolia wants to open a flower shop, the Petal Pusher, in a new mall. She has her choice of three different floor sizes, 200 square feet, 500 square feet, or 1,000 square feet. The monthly rent will be $1 a square foot. Mary estimates that if she has F square feet of floor space and sells y bouquets a month, her variable costs will be $c_v(y) = y^2/F$ per month.

(a) If she has 200 square feet of floor space, write down her marginal cost function: _____ and her average cost function: _____

_____ At what amount of output is average cost minimized?_____ At this level of output, how much is average cost?_____.

(b) If she has 500 square feet, write down her marginal cost function:

_____ and her average cost function: _____ At what amount of output is average cost minimized? _____ At this level of output, how much is average cost?_____.

(c) If she has 1,000 square feet of floor space, write down her marginal cost function: _____ and her average cost function: _____

_____ At what amount of output is average cost minimized?

_____ At this level of output, how much is average cost?_____.

(d) Use red ink to show Mary's average cost curve and her marginal cost curves if she has 200 square feet. Use blue ink to show her average cost curve and her marginal cost curve if she has 500 square feet. Use black ink to show her average cost curve and her marginal cost curve if she has 1,000 square feet. Label the average cost curves AC and the marginal cost curves MC.

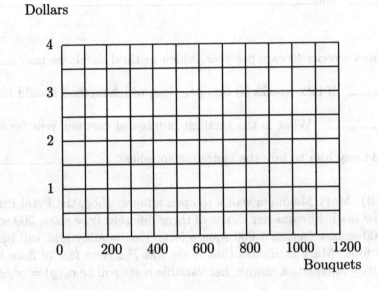

Dollars

(e) Use yellow marker to show Mary's long-run average cost curve and her long-run marginal cost curve in your graph. Label them LRAC and LRMC.

20.5 (0) Touchie MacFeelie publishes comic books. The only inputs he needs are old jokes and cartoonists. His production function is

$$Q = .1J^{\frac{1}{2}}L^{3/4},$$

where J is the number of old jokes used, L the number of hours of cartoonists' labor used as inputs, and Q is the number of comic books produced.

(a) Does this production process exhibit increasing, decreasing, or constant returns to scale? Explain your answer._____

_____.

(b) If the number of old jokes used is 100, write an expression for the marginal product of cartoonists' labor as a function of L. _____
Is the marginal product of labor decreasing or increasing as the amount of labor increases?_____.

20.6 (0) Touchie MacFeelie's irascible business manager, Gander Mac-Grope, announces that old jokes can be purchased for $1 each and that the wage rate of cartoonists' labor is $2.

(a) Suppose that in the short run, Touchie is stuck with exactly 100 old jokes (for which he paid $1 each) but is able to hire as much labor as he wishes. How much labor would he have to hire in order produce Q comic books?_____.

(b) Write down Touchie's short-run total cost as a function of his output

_____.

(c) His short-run marginal cost function is_____.

(d) His short-run average cost function is_____.

Calculus **20.7 (1)** Touchie asks his brother, Sir Francis MacFeelie, to study the long-run picture. Sir Francis, who has carefully studied the appendix to Chapter 19 in your text, prepared the following report.

(a) If all inputs are variable, and if old jokes cost $1 each and cartoonist labor costs $2 per hour, the cheapest way to produce exactly one comic book is to use _____ jokes and _____ hours of labor. (Fractional jokes are certainly allowable.)

(b) This would cost _____ dollars.

(c) Given our production function, the cheapest proportions in which to use jokes and labor are the same no matter how many comic books we print. But when we double the amount of both inputs, the number of comic books produced is multiplied by_____.

20.8 (0) Consider the cost function $c(y) = 4y^2 + 16$.

(a) The average cost function is_____.

(b) The marginal cost function is_____.

(c) The level of output that yields the minimum average cost of production

is_____.

(d) The average variable cost function is_____.

(e) At what level of output does average variable cost equal marginal

cost?_____.

20.9 (0) A competitive firm has a production function of the form: $Y = 2L + 5K$. If $w = \$2$ and $r = \$3$, what will be the minimum cost of

producing 10 units of output?_____.

Chapter 21

Firm Supply

Introduction. The short-run supply curve of a competitive firm is the portion of its short-run marginal cost curve that is upward sloping and lies above its average variable cost curve. The long-run supply curve of a competitive firm is the portion of its short-run marginal cost curve that is upward-sloping and lies above its long-run average cost curve.

Example: A firm has the long-run cost function $c(y) = 2y^2 + 200$ for $y > 0$ and $c(0) = 0$. Let us find its long-run supply curve. The firm's marginal cost when its output is y is $MC(y) = 4y$. If we graph output on the horizontal axis and dollars on the vertical axis, then we find that the long-run marginal cost curve is an upward sloping straight line through the origin with slope 4. The long-run supply curve is the portion of this curve that lies above the long-run average cost curve. When output is y, long-run average costs of this firm are $AC(y) = 2y + 200/y$. This is a U-shaped curve. As y gets close to zero, $AC(y)$ becomes very large because $200/y$ becomes very large. When y is very large, $AC(y)$ becomes very large because $2y$ is very large. When is it true that $AC(y) < MC(y)$? This happens when $2y + 200/y < 4y$. Simplify this inequality to find that $AC(y) < MC(y)$ when $y > 10$. Therefore the long-run supply curve is the piece of the long-run marginal cost curve for which $y > 10$. So the long-run supply curve has the equation $p = 4y$ for $y > 10$. If we want to find quantity supplied as a function of price, we just solve this expression for y as a function of p. Then we have $y = p/4$ whenever $p > 40$.

Suppose that $p < 40$. For example, what if $p = 20$, how much will the firm supply? At a price of 20, if the firm produces where price equals long run marginal cost, it will produce 5=20/4 units of output. When the firm produces only 5 units, its average costs are $2 \times 5 + 200/5 = 50$. Therefore when the price is 20, the best the firm can do if it produces a positive amount is to produce 5 units. But then it will have total costs of $5 \times 50 = 250$ and total revenue of $5 \times 20 = 100$. It will be losing money. It would be better off producing nothing at all. In fact, for any price $p < 40$, the firm will choose to produce zero output.

21.1 (0) Remember Otto's brother, Dent Carr, who is in the auto repair business? Dent found that the total cost of repairing s cars is $c(s) = 2s^2 + 100$.

(a) This implies that Dent's average cost is equal to _____ , average variable cost is equal to _____ , and his marginal cost is equal to _____ On the graph below, plot the above curves, and also plot Dent's supply curve.

Dollars

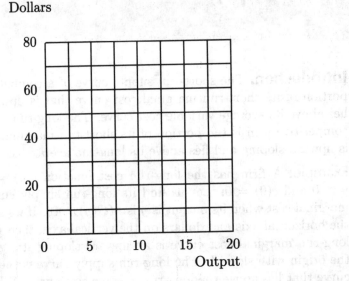

(b) If the market price is $20, how many cars will Dent be willing to repair? _____ If the market price is $40, how many cars will Dent repair?_____.

(c) Suppose the market price is $40 and Dent maximizes his profits. On the above graph, shade in and label the following areas: total costs, total revenue, and total profits.

Calculus **21.2 (0)** A competitive firm has the following short-run cost function: $c(y) = y^3 - 8y^2 + 30y + 5$.

(a) The firm's marginal cost function is $MC(y) =$_____.

(b) The firm's average variable cost function is $AVC(y) =$_____
(Hint: Notice that total variable costs equal $c(y) - c(0)$.)

(c) On the axes below, sketch and label a graph of the marginal cost function and of the average variable cost function.

(d) Average variable cost is falling as output rises if output is less than _____ and rising as output rises if output is greater than_____.

(e) Marginal cost equals average variable cost when output is_____.

(f) The firm will supply zero output if the price is less than_____.

(g) The smallest positive amount that the firm will ever supply at any price is _____ At what price would the firm supply exactly 6 units of output?_____.

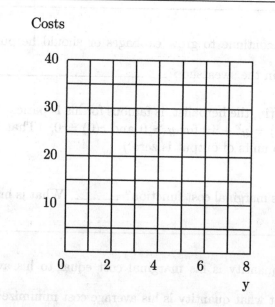

Costs

Mr. McGregor owns a 5-acre cabbage patch. He forces his wife, Flopsy, and his son, Peter, to work in the cabbage patch without wages. Assume for the time being that the land can be used for nothing other than cabbages and that Flopsy and Peter can find no alternative employment. The only input that Mr. McGregor pays for is fertilizer. If he uses x sacks of fertilizer, the amount of cabbages that he gets is $10\sqrt{x}$. Fertilizer costs $1 per sack.

Calculus **21.3 (0)**

(a) What is the total cost of the fertilizer needed to produce 100 cabbages?

_____ What is the total cost of the amount of fertilizer needed to produce y cabbages?_____.

(b) If the only way that Mr. McGregor can vary his output is by varying the amount of fertilizer applied to his cabbage patch, write an expression for his marginal cost, as a function of y. $MC(y) =$_____.

(c) If the price of cabbages is $2 each, how many cabbages will Mr. McGregor produce? _____ How many sacks of fertilizer will he buy?

_____ How much profit will he make?_____.

(d) The price of fertilizer and of cabbages remain as before, but Mr. McGregor learns that he could find summer jobs for Flopsy and Peter in a local sweatshop. Flopsy and Peter would together earn $300 for the summer, which Mr. McGregor could pocket, but they would have no time to work in the cabbage patch. Without their labor, he would get no cabbages. Now what is Mr. McGregor's total cost of producing y cabbages?

_____.

(e) Should he continue to grow cabbages or should he put Flopsy and

Peter to work in the sweatshop?_____.

21.4 (0) Severin, the herbalist, is famous for his hepatica. His total cost function is $c(y) = y^2 + 10$ for $y > 0$ and $c(0) = 0$. (That is, his cost of producing zero units of output is zero.)

(a) What is his marginal cost function? _____ What is his average cost

function?_____.

(b) At what quantity is his marginal cost equal to his average cost?

_____ At what quantity is his average cost minimized?_____.

(c) In a competitive market, what is the lowest price at which he will

supply a positive quantity in long-run equilibrium? _____ How

much would he supply at that price?_____.

21.5 (1) Stanley Ford makes mountains out of molehills. He can do this with almost no effort, so for the purposes of this problem, let us assume that molehills are the only input used in the production of mountains. Suppose mountains are produced at constant returns to scale and that it takes 100 molehills to make 1 mountain. The current market price of molehills is $20 each. A few years ago, Stan bought an "option" that permits him to buy up to 2,000 molehills at $10 each. His option contract explicitly says that he can buy fewer than 2,000 molehills if he wishes, but he can not resell the molehills that he buys under this contract. In order to get governmental permission to produce mountains from molehills, Stanley would have to pay $10,000 for a molehill-masher's license.

(a) The marginal cost of producing a mountain for Stanley is _____ if he produces fewer than 20 mountains. The marginal cost of producing

a mountain is _____ if he produces more than 20 mountains.

(b) On the graph below, show Stanley Ford's marginal cost curve (in blue ink) and his average cost curve (in red ink).

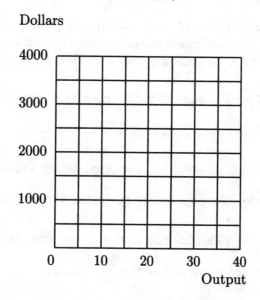

Dollars

(c) If the price of mountains is $1,600, how many mountains will Stanley produce?_____.

(d) The government is considering raising the price of a molehill masher's license to $11,000. Stanley claims that if it does so he will have to go out of business. Is Stanley telling the truth? _____ What is the highest fee for a license that the government could charge without driving him out of business?_____

_____.

(e) Stanley's lawyer, Eliot Sleaze, has discovered a clause in Stanley's option contract that allows him to resell the molehills that he purchased under the option contract at the market price. On the graph above, use a pencil to draw Stanley's new marginal cost curve. If the price of mountains remains $1,600, how many mountains will Stanley produce now?_____.

21.6 (1) Lady Wellesleigh makes silk purses out of sows' ears. She is the only person in the world who knows how to do so. It takes one sow's ear and 1 hour of her labor to make a silk purse. She can buy as many sows' ears as she likes for $1 each. Lady Wellesleigh has no other source of income than her labor. Her utility function is a Cobb-Douglas function $U(c,r) = c^{1/3}r^{2/3}$, where c is the amount of money per day that she has to spend on consumption goods and r is the amount of leisure that she has. Lady Wellesleigh has 24 hours a day that she can devote either to leisure or to working.

(a) Lady Wellesleigh can either make silk purses or she can earn $5 an hour as a seamstress in a sweatshop. If she worked in the sweat shop, how many hours would she work? _____ (Hint: To solve for this amount, write down Lady Wellesleigh's budget constraint and recall how to find the demand function for someone with a Cobb-Douglas utility function.)

(b) If she could earn a wage of $w an hour as a seamstress, how much would she work?_____.

(c) If the price of silk purses is $p, how much money will Lady Wellesleigh earn per purse after she pays for the sows' ears that she uses?_____.

(d) If she can earn $5 an hour as a seamstress, what is the lowest price at which she will make any silk purses?_____.

(e) What is the supply function for silk purses? (Hint: The price of silk purses determines the "wage rate" that Lady W. can earn by making silk purses. This determines the number of hours she will choose to work and hence the supply of silk purses.)_____.

Calculus **21.7 (0)** Remember Earl, who sells lemonade in Philadelphia? You met him in the chapter on cost functions. Earl's production function is $f(x_1, x_2) = x_1^{1/3} x_2^{1/3}$, where x_1 is the number of pounds of lemons he uses and x_2 is the number of hours he spends squeezing them. As you found out, his cost function is $c(w_1, w_2, y) = 2w_1^{1/2} w_2^{1/2} y^{3/2}$, where y is the number of units of lemonade produced.

(a) If lemons cost $1 per pound and the wage rate $1 per hour and the price of lemonade is p, Earl's marginal cost function is $MC(y) = $ _____ _____ and his supply function is $S(p) = $_____ If lemons cost $4 per pound and the wage rate is $9 per hour, his supply function will be

$S(p) = $_____.

(b) In general, Earl's marginal cost depends on the price of lemons and the wage rate. At prices w_1 for lemons and w_2 for labor, his marginal cost when he is producing y units of lemonade is $MC(w_1, w_2, y) = $_____

_____ The amount that Earl will supply depends on the three variables, p, w_1, w_2. As a function of these three variables, Earl's supply is $S(p, w_1, w_2) = $_____.

Calculus **21.8 (0)** As you may recall from the chapter on cost functions, Irma's handicrafts has the production function $f(x_1, x_2) = (\min\{x_1, 2x_2\})^{1/2}$, where x_1 is the amount of plastic used, x_2 is the amount of labor used, and $f(x_1, x_2)$ is the number of lawn ornaments produced. Let w_1 be the price per unit of plastic and w_2 be the wage per unit of labor.

(a) Irma's cost function is $c(w_1, w_2, y) =$_____.

(b) If $w_1 = w_2 = 1$, then Irma's marginal cost of producing y units of output is $MC(y) =$_____ The number of units of output that she would supply at price p is $S(p) =$_____ At these factor prices, her average cost per unit of output would be $AC(y) =$_____.

(c) If the competitive price of the lawn ornaments she sells is $p = 48$, and $w_1 = w_2 = 1$, how many will she produce?_____ How much profit will she make?_____.

(d) More generally, at factor prices w_1 and w_2, her marginal cost is a function $MC(w_1, w_2, y) =$_____ At these factor prices and an output price of p, the number of units she will choose to supply is $S(p, w_1, w_2) =$

_____.

21.9 (0) Jack Benny can get blood from a stone. If he has x stones, the number of pints of blood he can extract from it is $f(x) = 2x^{\frac{1}{3}}$. Stones cost Jack $\$w$ each. Jack can sell each pint of blood for $\$p$.

(a) How many stones does Jack need to extract y pints of blood?_____

_____.

(b) What is the cost of extracting y pints of blood?_____.

(c) What is Jack's supply function when stones cost $8 each? _____

_____ When stones cost $\$w$ each?_____.

(d) If Jack has 19 relatives who can also get blood from a stone in the same way, what is the aggregate supply function for blood when stones cost w each?_____.

21.10 (1) The Miss Manners Refinery in Dry Rock, Oklahoma, converts crude oil into gasoline. It takes 1 barrel of crude oil to produce 1 barrel of gasoline. In addition to the cost of oil there are some other costs involved in refining gasoline. Total costs of producing y barrels of gasoline are described by the cost function $c(y) = y^2/2 + p_o y$, where p_o is the price of a barrel of crude oil.

(a) Express the marginal cost of producing gasoline as a function of p_o

and y._____.

(b) Suppose that the refinery can buy 50 barrels of crude oil for $5 a barrel but must pay $15 a barrel for any more that it buys beyond 50

barrels. The marginal cost curve for gasoline will be _____ up to

50 barrels of gasoline and _____ thereafter.

(c) Plot Miss Manners' supply curve in the diagram below using blue ink.

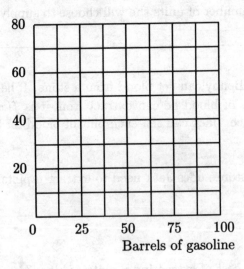

Price of gasoline

Barrels of gasoline

(d) Suppose that Miss Manners faces a horizontal demand curve for gasoline at a price of $30 per barrel. Plot this demand curve on the graph above using red ink. How much gasoline will she supply?_____.

(e) If Miss Manners could no longer get the first 50 barrels of crude for $5, but had to pay $15 a barrel for all crude oil, how would her output change?_____.

(f) Now suppose that an entitlement program is introduced that permits refineries to buy one barrel of oil at $5 for each barrel of oil that they buy for $15. What will Miss Manners' supply curve be now? _____

_____ Assume that it can buy fractions of a barrel in the same manner. Plot this supply curve on the graph above using black ink. If the demand curve is horizontal at $30 a barrel, how much gasoline will Miss Manners supply now?_____.

21.11 (2) Suppose that a farmer's cost of growing y bushels of corn is given by the cost function $c(y) = (y^2/20) + y$.

(a) If the price of corn is $5 a bushel, how much corn will this farmer grow?_____.

(b) What is the farmer's supply curve of corn as a function of the price of corn? $S(p) =$_____.

(c) The government now introduces a Payment in Kind (PIK) program. If the farmer decides to grow y bushels of corn, he will get $(40-y)/2$ bushels from the government stockpiles. Write an expression for the farmer's profits as a function of his output and the market price of corn, taking into account the value of payments in kind received._____

_____.

(d) At the market price p, what will be the farmer's profit-maximizing output of corn? _____ Plot a supply curve for corn in the graph below.

Price

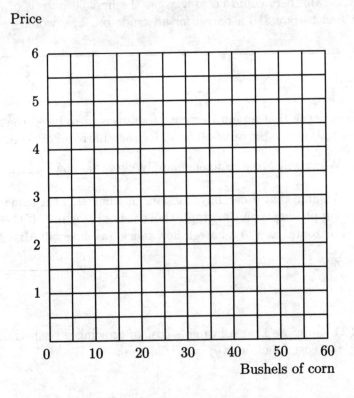

Bushels of corn

(e) If $p = \$2$, how many bushels of corn will he produce? _____ How many bushels will he get from the government stockpiles?_____.

(f) If $p = \$5$, how much corn will he supply? _____ How many bushels of corn will he get from the government stockpiles, assuming he chooses to be in the PIK program?_____.

(g) At any price between $p = \$2$ and $p = \$5$, write a formula for the size of the PIK payment._____

_____.

(h) How much corn will he supply to the market, counting both production and PIK payment, as a function of the market price p?_____

_____.

(i) Use red ink to illustrate the total supply curve of corn (including the corn from the PIK payment) in your graph above.

Industry Supply

Introduction. To find the industry supply of output, just add up the supply of output coming from each individual firm. Remember to add quantities, not prices. The industry supply curve will have a kink in it where the market price becomes low enough that some firm reduces its quantity supplied to zero.

The last three questions of this chapter apply supply and demand analysis to some problems in the economics of illegal activities. In these examples, you will make use of your knowledge of where supply functions come from.

22.0 Warm Up Exercise. Here are some drills for you on finding market supply functions from linear firm supply functions. The trick here is to remember that the market supply function may have kinks in it. For example, if the firm supply functions are $s_1(p) = p$ and $s_2(p) = p - 2$, then the market supply function is: $S(p) = p$ for $p \le 2$, $S(p) = 2p - 2$ for $p > 2$; that is, only the first firm supplies a positive output at prices below \$2, and both firms supply output at prices above \$2. Now try to construct the market supply function in each of the following cases.

(a) $s_1(p) = p, s_2(p) = 2p, s_3(p) = 3p.$ _____.

(b) $s_1(p) = 2p, s_2(p) = p - 1.$ _____.

(c) 200 firms each have a supply function $s_1(p) = 2p - 8$ and 100 firms each have a supply function $s_2(p) = p - 3.$ _____

_____.

(d) $s_1(p) = 3p - 12, s_2(p) = 2p - 8, s_3(p) = p - 4.$ _____.

22.1 (1) Al Deardwarf's cousin, Zwerg, makes plaster garden gnomes. The technology in the garden gnome business is as follows. You need a gnome mold, plaster, and labor. A gnome mold is a piece of equipment that costs \$1,000 and will last exactly one year. After a year, a gnome mold is completely worn out and has no scrap value. With a gnome mold, you can make 500 gnomes per year. For every gnome that you make, you also have to use a total of \$7 worth of plaster and labor. The total amounts of plaster and labor used are variable in the short run. If you want to produce only 100 gnomes a year with a gnome mold, you spend only \$700 a year on plaster and labor, and so on. The number of gnome molds in the industry cannot be changed in the short run. To get a newly built one, you have to special-order it from the gnome-mold factory. The gnome-mold factory only takes orders on January 1 of any given year, and it takes one whole year from the time a gnome mold is ordered until it is delivered on the next January 1. When a gnome mold is installed in your plant, it is stuck there. To move it would destroy it. Gnome molds are useless for anything other than making garden gnomes.

For many years, the demand function facing the garden-gnome industry has been $D(p) = 60,000 - 5,000p$, where $D(p)$ is the total number of garden gnomes sold per year and p is the price. Prices of inputs have been constant for many years and the technology has not changed. Nobody expects any changes in the future, and the industry is in long-run equilibrium. The interest rate is 10%. When you buy a new gnome mold, you have to pay for it when it is delivered. For simplicity of calculations, we will assume that all of the gnomes that you build during the one-year life of the gnome mold are sold at Christmas and that the employees and plaster suppliers are paid only at Christmas for the work they have done during the past year. Also for simplicity of calculations, let us approximate the date of Christmas by December 31.

(a) If you invested \$1,000 in the bank on January 1, how much money could you expect to get out of the bank one year later? _____ If you received delivery of a gnome mold on January 1 and paid for it at that time, by how much would your revenue have to exceed the costs of plaster and labor if it is to be worthwhile to buy the machine? (Remember that the machine will be worn out and worthless at the end of the year.)

_____.

(b) Suppose that you have exactly one newly installed gnome mold in your plant, what is your short-run marginal cost of production if you produce up to 500 gnomes? _____ What is your average *variable* cost for producing up to 500 gnomes? _____ With this equipment, is it possible in the short run to produce more than 500 gnomes?_____.

(c) If you have exactly one newly installed gnome mold, you would produce 500 gnomes if the price of gnomes is above _____ dollars. You would produce no gnomes if the price of gnomes is below _____ dollars. You would be indifferent between producing any number of gnomes between 0 and 500 if the price of gnomes is _____ dollars.

(d) If you could sell as many gnomes as you liked for $10 each and none at a higher price, what rate of return would you make on your $1,000 by investing in a gnome mold? _____ Is this higher than the return from putting your money in the bank? _____ What is the lowest price for gnomes at which investing in a gnome mold gives the same rate of return as you get from the bank? _____ Could the long-run equilibrium price be lower than this?_____.

(e) At the price you found in the last section, how many gnomes would be demanded each year? _____ How many molds would be purchased each year? _____ Is this a long-run equilibrium price?_____.

22.2 (1) We continue our study of the garden-gnome industry. Suppose that initially everything was as described in the previous problem. To the complete surprise of everyone in the industry, on January 1, 1993, the invention of a new kind of plaster was announced. This new plaster made it possible to produce garden gnomes using the same molds, but it reduced the cost of the plaster and labor needed to produce a gnome from $7 to $5 per gnome. Assume that consumers' demand function for gnomes in 1993 was not changed by this news. The announcement came early enough in the day for everybody to change his order for gnome molds to be delivered on January 1, 1994, but of course, the number of molds available to be used in 1993 is already determined from orders made one year ago. The manufacturer of garden gnome molds contracted to sell them for $1,000 a year ago, so he can't change the price he charges on delivery.

(a) In 1993, what will be the equilibrium total output of garden gnomes? _____ What will be the equilibrium price of garden gnomes? _____ Cousin Zwerg bought a gnome mold that was delivered on January 1, 1993, and, as had been agreed, he paid $1,000 for it on that day. On January 1, 1994, when he sold the gnomes he had made during the year and when he paid the workers and the suppliers of plaster, he received a net cash flow of $_____ Did he make more than a 10% rate of return on his investment in the gnome mold?_____ What rate of return did he make?_____.

(b) Zwerg's neighbor, Munchkin, also makes garden gnomes, and he has a gnome mold that is to be delivered on January 1, 1993. On this day, Zwerg, who is looking for a way to invest some more money, is considering buying Munchkin's new mold from Munchkin and installing it in his own

plant. If Munchkin keeps his mold, he will get a net cash flow of $_____

_____ in one year. If the interest rate that Munchkin faces, both for borrowing and lending is 10%, then should he be willing to sell his mold for $1,000? _____ What is the lowest price that he would be willing to

sell it for?_____ If the best rate of return that Zwerg can make on alternative investments of additional funds is 10%, what is the most that

Zwerg would be willing to pay for Munchkin's new mold?_____.

(c) What do you think will happen to the number of garden gnomes ordered for delivery on January 1, 1994? Will it be larger, smaller, or

the same as the number ordered the previous year? _____ After the passage of sufficient time, the industry will reach a new long run

equilibrium. What will be the new equilibrium price of gnomes?_____

_____.

22.3 (1) On January 1, 1993, there were no changes in technology or demand functions from that in our original description of the industry, but the government astonished the garden gnome industry by introducing a tax on the production of garden gnomes. For every garden gnome produced, the manufacturer must pay a $1 tax. The announcement came early enough in the day so that there was time for gnome producers to change their orders of gnome molds for 1994. Of course the gnome molds to be used in 1993 had been already ordered a year ago. Gnome makers had signed contracts promising to pay $1,000 for each gnome that they ordered, and they couldn't back out of these promises.

(a) Recalling from previous problems the number of gnome molds ordered for delivery on January 1, 1993, we see that if gnome makers produce up

to capacity in 1993, they will produce _____ gnomes. Given the demand function, we see that the market price would then have to be

_____.

(b) If you have a garden gnome mold, the marginal cost of producing a

garden gnome, including the tax, is _____ Therefore all gnome molds

(would) (would not) _____ be used up to capacity in 1993.

(c) In 1993, what will be the total output of garden gnomes? _____

What will be the price of garden gnomes? _____ What rate of

return will Deardwarf's cousin Zwerg make on his investment in a garden gnome mold that he ordered a year ago and paid $1,000 for at that time?

_____.

(d) Remember that Zwerg's neighbor, Munchkin, also has a gnome mold that is to be delivered on January 1, 1993. Knowing about the tax makes Munchkin's mold a less attractive investment than it was without the tax, but still Zwerg would buy it if he can get it cheap enough so that he makes a 10% rate of return on his investment. How much should he be

willing to pay for Munchkin's new mold?_____.

(e) What do you think will happen to the number of gnome molds ordered for delivery on January 1, 1994? Will it be larger, smaller, or the same

as the number ordered the previous year?_____.

(f) The tax on garden gnomes was left in place for many years, and nobody expected any further changes in the tax or in demand or supply conditions. After the passage of sufficient time, the industry reached a new long run equilibrium. What was the new equilibrium price of gnomes?

_____.

(g) In the short run, who would end up paying the tax on garden gnomes,

the producers or the consumers? _____ In the long run, did the price of gnomes go up by more, less, or the same amount as the tax per

gnome?_____.

(h) Suppose that early in the morning of January 1, 1993, the government had announced that there would be a $1 tax on garden gnomes, but that the tax would not go into effect until January 1, 1994. Would the producers of garden gnomes necessarily be worse off than if there were

no tax? Why or why not?_____

_____.

(i) Is it reasonable to suppose that the government could introduce "surprise" taxes without making firms suspicious that there will be similar "surprises" in the future? Suppose that the introduction of the tax in January 1993, makes gnome makers suspicious that there will be more taxes introduced in later years. Would this affect equilibrium prices and supplies? How?_____

_____

_____.

22.4 (0) Consider a competitive industry with a large number of firms, all of which have identical cost functions $c(y) = y^2 + 1$ for $y > 0$ and $c(0) = 0$. Suppose that initially the demand curve for this industry is given by $D(p) = 52 - p$. (The output of a firm does not have to be an integer number, but the number of firms does have to be an integer.)

(a) What is the supply curve of an individual firm? $S(p) =$_____ If there are n firms in the industry, what will be the industry supply curve?

_____.

(b) What is the smallest price at which the product can be sold?_____

_____.

(c) What will be the equilibrium number of firms in the industry? (Hint: Take a guess at what the industry price will be and see if it works.)

_____.

(d) What will be the equilibrium price? _____ What will be the

equilibrium output of each firm?_____.

(e) What will be the equilibrium output of the industry?_____.

(f) Now suppose that the demand curve shifts to $D(p) = 52.5 - p$. What will be the equilibrium number of firms? (Hint: Can a new firm enter the

market and make nonnegative profits?)_____

_____

_____.

(g) What will be the equilibrium price? _____

_____ What will be the equilibrium output of each firm? _____

What will be the equilibrium profits of each firm?_____.

(h) Now suppose that the demand curve shifts to $D(p) = 53 - p$. What

will be the equilibrium number of firms? _____ What will be the

equilibrium price?_____.

(i) What will be the equilibrium output of each firm? _____ What

will be the equilibrium profits of each firm?_____.

22.5 (3) In 1990, the town of Ham Harbor had a more-or-less free market in taxi services. Any respectable firm could provide taxi service as long as the drivers and cabs satisfied certain safety standards.

Let us suppose that the constant marginal cost per trip of a taxi ride is $5, and that the average taxi has a capacity of 20 trips per day. Let the demand function for taxi rides be given by $D(p) = 1,200 - 20p$, where demand is measured in rides per day, and price is measured in dollars. Assume that the industry is perfectly competitive.

(a) What is the competitive equilibrium price per ride? (Hint: In competitive equilibrium, price must equal marginal cost.) _____ What

is the equilibrium number of rides per day? _____ How many taxi

cabs will there be in equilibrium?_____.

(b) In 1990 the city council of Ham Harbor created a taxicab licensing board and issued a license to each of the existing cabs. The board stated that it would continue to adjust the taxi cab fares so that the demand for rides equals the supply of rides, but no new licenses will be issued in the future. In 1995 costs had not changed, but the demand curve for taxi cab rides had become $D(p) = 1,220 - 20p$. What was the equilibrium price

of a ride in 1995?_____.

(c) What was the profit per ride in 1995, neglecting any costs associated

with acquiring a taxicab license? _____ What was the profit per taxicab

license per day? _____ If the taxi operated every day, what was the

profit per taxicab license per year?_____.

(d) If the interest rate was 10% and costs, demand, and the number of licenses were expected to remain constant forever, what would be the

market price of a taxicab license?_____.

(e) Suppose that the commission decided in 1995 to issue enough new licenses to reduce the taxicab price per ride to $5. How many more

licenses would this take?_____.

(f) Assuming that demand in Ham Harbor is not going to grow any more, how much would a taxicab license be worth at this new fare?_____

_____.

(g) How much money would each current taxicab owner be willing to pay to prevent any new licenses from being issued? _____ What is the total amount that all taxicab owners together would be willing to pay to prevent any new licences from ever being issued? _____ The total amount that consumers would be willing to pay to have another taxicab license issued would be (more than), (less than), (the same as) _____ this amount.

22.6 (2) In this problem, we will determine the equilibrium pattern of agricultural land use surrounding a city. Think of the city as being located in the middle of a large featureless plain. The price of wheat at the market at the center of town is $10 a bushel, and it only costs $5 a bushel to grow wheat. However, it costs 10 cents a mile to transport a bushel of wheat to the center of town.

(a) If a farm is located t miles from the center of town, write down a formula for its profit per bushel of wheat transported to market._____

_____.

(b) Suppose you can grow 1,000 bushels on an acre of land. How much will an acre of land located t miles from the market rent for?_____

_____.

(c) How far away from the market do you have to be for land to be worth zero?_____.

22.7 (1) Consider an industry with three firms. Suppose the firms have the following supply functions: $S_1(p) = p$, $S_2(p) = p - 5$, and $S_3(p) = 2p$ respectively. On the graph below plot each of the three supply curves and the resulting industry supply curve.

Price

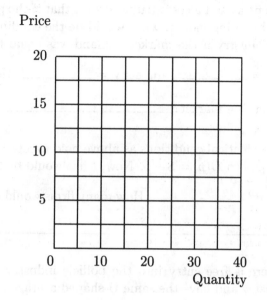

Quantity

(a) If the market demand curve has the form, $D(p) = 15$ what is the resulting market price? _____ Output? _____ What is the output level for firm 1 at this price? _____ Firm 2? _____ Firm 3?

_____.

22.8 (0) Suppose all firms in a given industry have the same supply curve given by $S_i(p) = p/2$. Plot and label the four industry supply curves generated by these firms if there are 1, 2, 3, or 4 firms operating in the industry.

Price

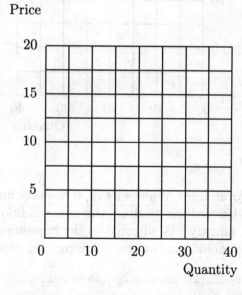

Quantity

(a) If all of the firms had a cost structure such that if the price was below $3 they would be losing money, what would be the equilibrium price and output in the industry if the market demand was equal to $D(p) = 3.5$?

Answer: price = _____ , quantity = _____ How many firms

would exist in such a market?_____.

(b) What if the identical conditions as above hold except that the market demand was equal to $D(p) = 8 - p$. Now, what would be the equilibrium

price and output? _____ How many firms would operate in such

a market?_____.

22.9 (0) There is free entry into the pollicle industry. Anybody can enter this industry and have the same U-shaped average cost curve as all of the other firms in the industry.

(a) On the diagram below, draw a representative firm's average and marginal cost curves using blue ink. Also, indicate the long-run equilibrium level of the market price.

Price

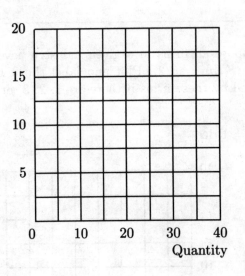

(b) Suppose the government imposes a tax, t, on every unit of output sold by the industry. Use red ink to draw the new conditions on the above graph. After the industry has adjusted to the imposition of the tax, the competitive model would predict the following: the market price would

(increase/decrease) _____ by amount _____ , there would be

(more/the same/fewer) _____ firms operating in the industry, and the output level for each firm operating in the industry would _____

_____ (increase/stay the same/decrease).

(c) What if the government imposes a tax, l, on every *firm* in the industry. Draw the new cost conditions on the above graph using black ink. After the industry has adjusted to the imposition of the tax the competitive model would predict the following: the market price would (increase/decrease) _____ , there would be (more/the same/fewer)

_____ firms operating in the industry, and the output level for each

firm operating in the industry would _____ (increase/stay the same/decrease).

22.10 (0) In many communities, a restaurant that sells alcoholic beverages is required to have a license. Suppose that the number of licenses is limited and that they may be easily transferred to other restaurant owners. Suppose that the conditions of this industry closely approximate perfect competition. If the average restaurant's revenue is $100,000 a year, and if a liquor license can be leased for a year for $85,000 from an existing restaurant, what is the average variable cost in the industry?

_____

22.11 (2) In order to protect the wild populations of cockatoos, the Australian authorities have outlawed the export of these large parrots. An illegal market in cockatoos has developed. The cost of capturing an Australian cockatoo and shipping him to the United States is about $40 per bird. Smuggled parrots are drugged and shipped in suitcases. This is extremely traumatic for the birds and about 50% of the cockatoos shipped die in transit. Each smuggled cockatoo has a 10% chance of being discovered, in which case the bird is confiscated and a fine of $500 is charged. Confiscated cockatoos that are alive are returned to the wild. Confiscated cockatoos that are found dead are donated to university cafeterias.*

(a) The probability that a smuggled parrot will reach the buyer alive

and unconfiscated is _____ Therefore when the price of smuggled parrots is p, what is the expected gross revenue to a parrot-smuggler from

shipping a parrot?_____.

_____

* The story behind this problem is based on actual fact, but the numbers we use are just made up for illustration. It would be very interesting to have some good estimates of the actual demand functions and cost functions.

(b) What is the expected cost, including expected fines and the cost of capturing and shipping, per parrot._____.

(c) The supply schedule for smuggled parrots will be a horizontal line at the market price, _____ (Hint: At what price does a parrot-smuggler just break even?)

(d) The demand function for smuggled cockatoos in the United States is $D(p) = 7,200 - 20p$ per year. How many smuggled cockatoos will be sold in the United States per year at the equilibrium price? _____ How many cockatoos must be caught in Australia in order that this number of live birds reaches U.S. buyers?_____.

(e) Suppose that instead of returning live confiscated cockatoos to the wild, the customs authorities sold them in the American market. The profits from smuggling a cockatoo do not change from this policy change. Since the supply curve is horizontal, it must be that the equilibrium price of smuggled cockatoos will have to be the same as the equilibrium price when the confiscated cockatoos were returned to nature. How many live cockatoos will be sold in the United States in equilibrium? _____ How many cockatoos will be permanently removed from the Australian wild?_____.

(f) Suppose that the trade in cockatoos is legalized. Suppose that it costs about $40 to capture and ship a cockatoo to the United States in a comfortable cage and that the number of deaths in transit by this method is negligible. What would be the equilibrium price of cockatoos in the United States? _____ How many cockatoos would be sold in the United States? _____ How many cockatoos would have to be caught in Australia for the U.S. market?_____.

22.12 (0) The horn of the rhinoceros is prized in Japan and China for its alleged aphrodisiac properties. This has proved to be most unfortunate for the rhinoceroses of East Africa. Although it is illegal to kill rhinoceroses in the game parks of Kenya, the rhinoceros population of these parks has been almost totally depleted by poachers. The price of rhinoceros horns in recent years has risen so high that a poacher can earn half a year's wages by simply killing one rhinoceros. Such high rewards for poaching have made laws against poaching almost impossible to enforce in East Africa. There are also large game parks with rhinoceros populations in South Africa. Since South Africa is much more of a police state than Kenya, game wardens have been able to prevent poaching almost completely.

Therefore the rhinoceros population of South Africa has prospered. In a recent program from the television series *Nova*, a South African game warden explained that some rhinoceroses even have to be "harvested" in order to prevent overpopulation of rhinoceroses. "What then," asked the interviewer, "do you do with the horns from the animals that are harvested or that die of natural causes?" The South African game warden proudly explained that since international trade in rhinoceros horns was illegal, South Africa did not contribute to international crime by selling these horns. Instead the horns were either destroyed or stored in a warehouse.

(a) Suppose that all of the rhinoceros horns produced in South Africa are destroyed. Label the axes below and draw world supply and demand curves for rhinoceros horns with blue ink. Label the equilibrium price and quantity.

(b) If South Africa were to sell its rhinoceros horns on the world market, which of the curves in your diagram would shift and in what direction?

_____ Use red ink to illustrate the shifted curve or curves. If South Africa were to do this, would world consumption of rhinoceros horns be increased or decreased? _____ Would

the world price of rhinoceros horns be increased or decreased? _____

_____ Would the amount of rhinoceros poaching be increased or

decreased?_____.

22.13 (1) The sale of rhinoceros horns is not prohibited because of concern about the wicked pleasures of aphrodisiac imbibers, but because the supply activity is bad for rhinoceroses. Similarly, the Australian reason for restricting the exportation of cockatoos to the United States is not because having a cockatoo is bad for you. Indeed it is legal for Australians to have cockatoos as pets. The motive for the restriction is simply to protect the wild populations from being overexploited. In the case of other commodities, it appears that society has no particular interest in restricting the supply activities but wishes to restrict consumption. A good example is illicit drugs. The growing of marijuana, for example, is a simple pastoral activity, which in itself is no more harmful than growing sweet corn or brussels sprouts. It is the consumption of marijuana to which society objects.

Suppose that there is a constant marginal cost of $5 per ounce for growing marijuana and delivering it to buyers. But whenever the marijuana authorities find marijuana growing or in the hands of dealers, they seize the marijuana and fine the supplier. Suppose that the probability that marijuana is seized is .3 and that the fine if you are caught is $10 per ounce.

(a) If the "street price" is p per ounce, what is the expected revenue net of fines to a dealer from selling an ounce of marijuana? _____

What then would be the equilibrium price of marijuana?_____.

(b) Suppose that the demand function for marijuana has the equation $Q = A - Bp$. If all confiscated marijuana is destroyed, what will be the equilibrium consumption of marijuana? _____ Suppose that confiscated marijuana is not destroyed but sold on the open market.

What will be the equilibrium consumption of marijuana?_____.

(c) The price of marijuana will (increase, decrease, stay the same)?_____

_____.

(d) If there were increasing rather than constant marginal cost in marijuana production, do you think that consumption would be greater if confiscated marijuana were sold than if it were destroyed? Explain._____

_____

_____.

Monopoly

Introduction. The profit-maximizing output of a monopolist is found by solving for the output at which marginal revenue is equal to marginal cost. Having solved for this output, you find the monopolist's price by plugging the profit-maximizing output into the demand function. In general, the marginal revenue function can be found by taking the derivative of the total revenue function with respect to the quantity. But in the special case of linear demand, it is easy to find the marginal revenue curve graphically. With a linear inverse demand curve, $p(y) = a - by$, the marginal revenue curve always takes the form $MR(y) = a - 2by$.

23.1 (0) Professor Bong has just written the first textbook in Punk Economics. It is called *Up Your Isoquant*. Market research suggests that the demand curve for this book will be $Q = 2,000 - 100P$, where P is its price. It will cost \$1,000 to set the book in type. This setup cost is necessary before any copies can be printed. In addition to the setup cost, there is a marginal cost of \$4 per book for every book printed.

(a) The total revenue function for Professor Bong's book is $R(Q) =$_____

_____.

(b) The total cost function for producing Professor Bong's book is $C(Q) =$

_____.

(c) The marginal revenue function is $MR(Q) =$_____ and the marginal cost function is $MC(Q) =$_____ The profit-maximizing quantity of books for professor Bong to sell is $Q^* =$_____.

23.2 (0) Peter Morgan sells pigeon pies from a pushcart in Central Park. Morgan is the only supplier of this delicacy in Central Park. His costs are zero due to the abundant supplies of raw materials available in the park.

(a) When he first started his business, the inverse demand curve for pigeon pies was $p(y) = 100 - y$, where the price is measured in cents and y measures the number of pies sold. Use black ink to plot this curve in the graph below. On the same graph, use red ink to plot the marginal revenue curve.

Cents

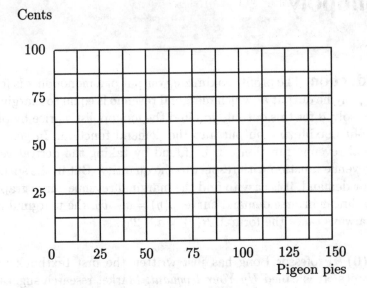

Pigeon pies

(b) What level of output will maximize Peter's profits? _____ What

price will Peter charge per pie?_____.

(c) After Peter had been in business for several months, he noticed that the demand curve had shifted to $p(y) = 75 - y/2$. Use blue ink to plot this curve in the graph above. Plot the new marginal revenue curve on the same graph with black ink.

(d) What is his profit-maximizing output at this new price? _____

What is the new profit-maximizing price?_____.

23.3 (0) Suppose that the demand function for Japanese cars in the United States is such that annual sales of cars (in thousands of cars) will be $250 - 2P$, where P is the price of Japanese cars in thousands of dollars.

(a) If the supply schedule is horizontal at a price of $5,000 what will be the equilibrium number of Japanese cars sold in the United States?

_____ thousand. How much money will Americans spend in total on

Japanese cars? _____ billion dollars.

(b) Suppose that in response to pressure from American car manufacturers, the United States imposes an import duty on Japanese cars in such a way that for every car exported to the United States the Japanese manufacturers must pay a tax to the U.S. government of $2,000. How many

Japanese automobiles will now be sold in the United States? _____

thousand. At what price will they be sold? _____ thousand dollars.

(c) How much revenue will the U.S. government collect with this tariff?

_____ million dollars.

(d) On the graph below, the price paid by American consumers is measured on the vertical axis. Use blue ink to show the demand and supply schedules before the import duty is imposed. After the import duty is imposed, the supply schedule shifts and the demand schedule stays as before. Use red ink to draw the new supply schedule.

Price (thousands)

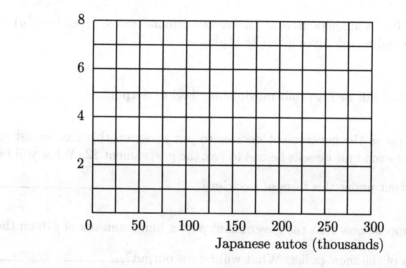

Japanese autos (thousands)

(e) Suppose that instead of imposing an import duty, the U.S. government persuades the Japanese government to impose "voluntary export restrictions" on their exports of cars to the United States. Suppose that the Japanese agree to restrain their exports by requiring that every car exported to the United States must have an export license. Suppose further that the Japanese government agrees to issue only 236,000 export licenses and sells these licenses to the Japanese firms. If the Japanese firms know the American demand curve and if they know that only 236,000 Japanese cars will be sold in America, what price will they be able to charge in America for their cars? _____ thousand dollars.

(f) How much will a Japanese firm be willing to pay the Japanese government for an export license? _____ thousand dollars. (Hint: Think about what it costs to produce a car and how much it can be sold for if you have an export license.)

(g) How much will be the Japanese government's total revenue from the sale of export licenses? _____ million dollars.

(h) How much money will Americans spend on Japanese cars? _____ billion dollars.

(i) Why might the Japanese "voluntarily" submit to export controls?

_____

_____

_____.

23.4 (0) A monopolist has an inverse demand curve given by $p(y) = 12 - y$ and a cost curve given by $c(y) = y^2$.

(a) What will be his profit-maximizing level of output?_____.

(b) Suppose the government decides to put a tax on this monopolist so that for each unit he sells he has to pay the government \$2. What will be his output under this form of taxation?_____.

(c) Suppose now that the government puts a lump sum tax of \$10 on the profits of the monopolist. What will be his output?_____.

23.5 (1) In Gomorrah, New Jersey, there is only one newspaper, the *Daily Calumny*. The demand for the paper depends on the price and the amount of scandal reported. The demand function is $Q = 15S^{1/2}P^{-3}$, where Q is the number of issues sold per day, S is the number of column inches of scandal reported in the paper, and P is the price. Scandals are not a scarce commodity in Gomorrah. However, it takes resources to write, edit, and print stories of scandal. The cost of reporting S units of scandal is \$10S. These costs are independent of the number of papers sold. In addition it costs money to print and deliver the paper. These cost \$.10 per copy and the cost per unit is independent of the amount of scandal reported in the paper. Therefore the total cost of printing Q copies of the paper with S column inches of scandal is \$10$S + .10Q$.

(a) Calculate the price elasticity of demand for the *Daily Calumny*.

_____ Does the price elasticity depend on the amount of scandal

reported? _____ Is the price elasticity constant over all prices?_____

_____.

(b) Remember that $MR = P(1 + \frac{1}{\epsilon})$. To maximize profits, the *Daily Calumny* will set marginal revenue equal to marginal cost. Solve for the profit-maximizing price for the *Calumny* to charge per newspaper. _____

_____ When the newspaper charges this price, the difference between the price and the marginal cost of printing and delivering each newspaper

is_____.

(c) If the *Daily Calumny* charges the profit-maximizing price and prints 100 column inches of scandal, how many copies would it sell? (Round to the nearest integer.) _____ Write a general expression for the number of copies sold as a function of S, $Q(S) =$_____

_____.

(d) Assuming that the paper charges the profit-maximizing price, write an expression for profits as a function of Q and S. _____

_____ Using the solution for $Q(S)$ that you found in the last section, substitute $Q(S)$ for Q to write an expression for profits as a function of S alone._____.

(e) If the *Daily Calumny* charges its profit-maximizing price, and prints the profit-maximizing amount of scandal, how many column inches of scandal should it print. _____ How many copies are sold

_____ and what is the amount of profit for the *Daily Calumny* if it maximizes its profits?_____.

23.6 (0) In the graph below, use black ink to draw the inverse demand curve, $p_1(y) = 200 - y$.

(a) If the monopolist has zero costs, where on this curve will it choose to operate?_____.

(b) Now draw another demand curve that passes through the profit-maximizing point and is flatter than the original demand curve. Use a red pen to mark the part of this new demand curve on which the monopolist would choose to operate. (Hint: Remember the idea of revealed preference?)

(c) The monopolist would have (larger, smaller) profits at the new demand curve than he had at the original demand curve._____.

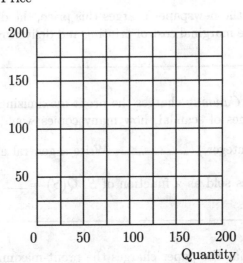

Monopoly Behavior

Introduction. In this chapter you will find some problems about price discrimination. Remember that a price discriminator wants the *marginal revenue* in each market to be equal to the marginal cost of production. Since he produces all of his output in one place, his marginal cost of production is the same for both markets and depends on his *total* output. The trick for solving these problems is to write marginal revenue in each market as a function of quantity sold in that market and to write marginal cost as a function of the sum of quantities sold in the two markets. The profit-maximizing conditions then become two equations that you can solve for the two unknown quantities sold in the two markets. Of course, if marginal cost is constant, your job is even easier, since all you have to do is find the quantities in each market for which marginal revenue equals the constant marginal cost.

Example: A monopolist sells in two markets. The inverse demand curve in market 1 is $p_1 = 200 - q_1$. The inverse demand curve in market 2 is $p_2 = 300 - q_2$. The firm's total cost function is $C(q_1 + q_2) = (q_1 + q_2)^2$. The firm is able to price discriminate between the two markets. Let us find the prices that he will charge in each market. In market 1, the firm's marginal revenue is $200 - 2q_1$. In market 2, marginal revenue is $300 - 2q_2$. The firm's marginal costs are $2(q_1 + q_2)$. To maximize its profits, the firm sets marginal revenue in each market equal to marginal cost. This gives us the two equations, $200 - 2q_1 = 2(q_1 + q_2)$, and $300 - 2q_2 = 2(q_1 + q_2)$. Solving these two equations in two unknowns for q_1 and q_2, we find $q_1 = 16.67$ and $q_2 = 66.67$. We can find the price charged in each market by plugging these quantities into the demand functions. The price charged in market 1 will be 183.33. The price charged in market 2 will be 233.33.

24.1 (0) Ferdinand Sludge has just written a disgusting new book, *Orgy in the Piggery*. His publisher, Graw McSwill, estimates that the demand for this book in the United States is $Q_1 = 50,000 - 2,000P_1$, where P_1 is the price in America measured in U.S. dollars. The demand for Sludge's opus in England is $Q_2 = 10,000 - 500P_2$, where P_2 is its price in England measured in U. S. dollars. His publisher has a cost function $C(Q) = \$50,000 + \$2Q$, where Q is the total number of copies of *Orgy* that it produces.

(a) If McSwill must charge the same price in both countries, how many

copies should it sell _____ and what price should it charge _____

to maximize its profits, and how much will those profits be?_____

_____

(b) If McSwill can charge a different price in each country, and wants to maximize profits, how many copies should it sell in the United States?

_____ What price should it charge in the United States? _____

_____ How many copies should it sell in England? _____ What

price should it charge in England?. _____ How much will its total

profits be?_____.

24.2 (0) A monopoly faces an inverse demand curve, $p(y) = 100 - 2y$, and has constant marginal costs of 20.

(a) What is its profit-maximizing level of output? _____

(b) What is its profit-maximizing price?_____.

(c) What is the socially optimal price for this firm?_____.

(d) What is the socially optimal level of output for this firm?_____.

(e) What is the deadweight loss due to the monopolistic behavior of this

firm?_____.

(f) Suppose this monopolist could operate as a perfectly discriminating monopolist and sell each unit of output at the highest price it would fetch.

The deadweight loss in this case would be_____.

Calculus **24.3 (1)** Banana Computer Company sells Banana computers both in the domestic and foreign markets. Because of differences in the power supplies, a Banana purchased in one market can not be used in the other market. The demand and marginal revenue curves associated with the two markets are as follows:

$$P_d = 20,000 - 20Q \quad P_f = 25,000 - 50Q$$
$$MR_d = 20,000 - 40Q \quad MR_f = 25,000 - 100Q.$$

Banana's production process exhibits constant returns to scale and it takes $1,000,000 to produce 100 computers.

(a) Banana's long-run average cost function is $AC(Q) =$_____ and

its long-run marginal cost function is $MC(Q) =$_____ (Hint: If there are constant returns to scale, does long-run average cost change as output changes?) Draw the average and marginal cost curves on the graph.

(b) Draw the demand curve for the domestic market in black ink and the marginal revenue curve for the domestic market in pencil. Draw the demand curve for the foreign market in red ink and the marginal revenue curve for the foreign market in blue ink.

Dollars (1,000s)

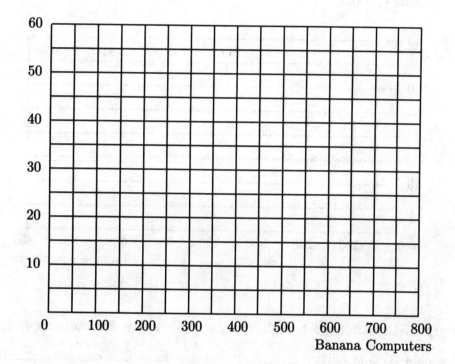

Banana Computers

(c) If Banana is maximizing its profits, it will sell _____ computers in the domestic market at _____ dollars each and _____ computers in the foreign market at _____ dollars each. What are Banana's total profits?_____.

(d) At the profit-maximizing price and quantity, what is the price elasticity of demand in the domestic market? _____ What is the price elasticity of demand in the foreign market? _____ Is demand more or less elastic in the market where the higher price is charged?_____

_____

(e) Suppose that somebody figures out a wiring trick that allows a Banana computer built for either market to be costlessly converted to work in the other. (Ignore transportation costs.) On the graph below, draw the new inverse demand curve (with blue ink) and marginal revenue curve (with black ink) facing Banana.

Dollars (1,000s)

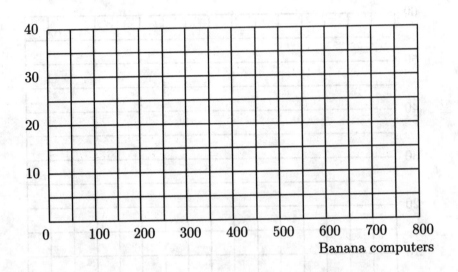

Banana computers

(f) Given that costs haven't changed, how many Banana computers should Banana sell? _____ What price will it charge? _____

_____ How will Banana's profits change now that it can no longer

practice price discrimination?_____.

24.4 (0) A monopolist has a cost function given by $c(y) = y^2$ and faces a demand curve given by $P(y) = 120 - y$.

(a) What is his profit-maximizing level of output? _____ What price

will the monopolist charge?_____.

(b) If you put a lump sum tax of $100 on this monopolist, what would

his output be?_____.

(c) If you wanted to choose a price ceiling for this monopolist so as to maximize consumer plus producer surplus, what price ceiling should you

choose?_____.

(d) How much output will the monopolist produce at this price ceiling?

_____.

(e) Suppose that you put a specific tax on the monopolist of $20 per unit output. What would his profit-maximizing level of output be?_____.

24.5 (1) The Grand Theater is a movie house in a medium-size college town. This theater shows unusual films and treats early arriving moviegoers to live organ music and Bugs Bunny cartoons. If the theater is open, the owners have to pay a fixed nightly amount of $500 for films, ushers, and so on, regardless of how many people come to the movie. For simplicity, assume that if the theater is closed, its costs are zero. The nightly demand for Grand Theater movies by students is $Q_S = 220 - 40P_S$, where Q_S is the number of movie tickets demanded by students at price P_S. The nightly demand for nonstudent moviegoers is $Q_N = 140 - 20P_N$.

(a) If the Grand Theater charges a single price, P_T, to everybody, then at prices between 0 and $5.50, the aggregate demand function for movie tickets is $Q_T(P_T) =$ _____ Over this range of prices, the inverse demand function is then $P_T(Q_T) =$ _____.

(b) What is the profit-maximizing number of tickets for the Grand Theater to sell if it charges one price to everybody? _____ At what price would this number of tickets be sold? _____ How much profits would the Grand make? _____ How many tickets would be sold to students? _____ To nonstudents? _____.

(c) Suppose that the cashier can accurately separate the students from the nonstudents at the door by making students show their school ID cards. Students cannot resell their tickets and nonstudents do not have access to student ID cards. Then the Grand can increase its profits by charging students and nonstudents different prices. What price will be charged to students? _____ How many student tickets will be sold? _____ What price will be charged to nonstudents? _____ How many nonstudent tickets will be sold? _____ How much profit will the Grand Theater make?_____.

(d) If you know calculus, see if you can do this part. Suppose that the Grand Theater can hold only 150 people and that the manager wants to maximize profits by charging separate prices to students and nonstudents. If the capacity of the theater is 150 seats and Q_S tickets are sold to students, what is the maximum number of tickets that can be sold to nonstudents? $Q_N =$ _____ Write an expression for the price of *nonstudent* tickets as a function of the number of *student* tickets sold. (Hint: First find the inverse nonstudent demand function.)

_____ Write an expression for Grand Theater profits as a function of the number of Q_S only. (Hint: Make substitutions using your previous answers.) _____

_____ How many student tickets should the Grand sell to maximize profits? _____ What price is charged to students?

_____ How many nonstudent tickets are sold? _____ What price is charged to nonstudents? _____ How much profit does the Grand make under this arrangement?_____.

24.6 (2) The *Mall Street Journal* is considering offering a new service which will send news articles to readers by email. Their market research indicates that there are two types of potential users, impecunious undergraduates studying microeconomics and high-level executives. Let x be the number of articles that a user requests per year. The executives have an inverse demand function $P_E(x) = 100 - x$ and the undergraduates have an inverse demand function $P_U(x) = 80 - x$. (Prices are measured in cents.) The *Journal* has a zero marginal cost of sending articles via email. Please draw these demand functions in the graph below and label them.

Price (1,000s)

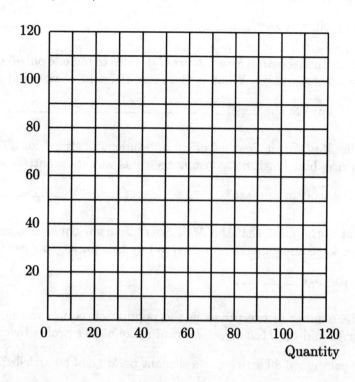

(a) Suppose that the *Journal* can identify which of the users are undergraduates and which are executives. It decides to offer a plan where users can buy a fixed number of articles per year for a fixed price per year.

If it wants to maximize total profits it will offer _____ articles to the

executives and _____ articles per year to the students.

(b) It will charge _____ per year to the executives and _____ per year to the students.

(c) Suppose that the *Journal* cannot identify which users are executives and which are undergraduates. In this case it simply offers two packages, and lets the users self select the one that is optimal for them. Suppose that it offers two packages: one that allows up to 80 articles per year the other that allows up to 100 articles per year. What's the highest price that

the undergraduates will pay for the 80-article subscription?_____.

(d) What (gross) consumer surplus would the executives get if they con-

sumed 80 articles per year?_____.

(e) What is the the maximum price that the *Journal* can charge for 100 articles per year if it offers 80 a year at the highest price the undergraduates are willing to pay?_____.

(f) Suppose that the *Mall Street Journal* decides to include only 60 articles in the student package. What is the most it could charge and still get student to buy this package?_____.

(g) If the *Mall Street Journal* offers a "student package" of 60 articles at this price, how much *net* consumer surplus would executives get from buying the student package?_____.

(h) What is the most that the *Mall Street Journal* could charge for 100 article package and expect executives to buy this package rather than the student package_____.

(i) If the number of executives in the population equals the number of students, would the *Mall Street Journal* make higher profits by offering a student package of 80 articles or a student package of 60 articles?_____.

24.7 (2) Bill Barriers, CEO of MightySoft software, is contemplating a new marketing strategy: bundling their best-selling wordprocessor and their spreadsheet together and selling the pair of software products for one price.

From the viewpoint of the company, bundling software and selling it at a discounted price has two effects on sales: 1) revenues go up due to to additional sales of the bundle; and 2) revenues go down since there is less of a demand for the individual components of the bundle.

The profitability of bundling depends on which of these two effects dominates. Suppose that MightySoft sells the wordprocessor for $200 and the spreadsheet for $250. A marketing survey of 100 people who purchased either of these packages in the last year turned up the following facts:

1) 20 people bought both.
2) 40 people bought only the wordprocessor. They would be willing to spend up to $120 more for the spreadsheet.
3) 40 people bought only the spreadsheet. They would be willing to spend up to $100 more for the wordprocessor.

In answering the following questions you may assume the following:

1) New purchasers of MightySoft products will have the same characteristics as this group.
2) There is a zero marginal cost to producing extra copies of either software package.
3) There is a zero marginal cost to creating a bundle.

(a) Let us assume that MightySoft also offers the products separately as well as bundled. In order to determine how to price the bundle, Bill Barriers asks himself the following questions. In order to sell the bundle to the wordprocessor purchasers, the price would have to be less than

_____ .

(b) In order to sell to the spreadsheet users, the price would have to be less than_____ .

(c) What would MightySoft's profits be on a group of 100 users if it priced the bundle at $320?_____

_____ .

(d) What would MightySoft's profits be on a group of 100 users if it priced the bundle at $350?_____

_____

_____

_____

(e) If MightySoft offers the bundle, what price should it set?_____

_____ .

(f) What would profits be without offering the bundle?_____

_____ .

(g) What would be the profits with the bundle?_____ .

(h) Is it more profitable to bundle or not bundle?_____ .

(i) Suppose that MightySoft worries about the reliability of their market survey and decides that they believe that without bundling t of the 100 people will buy both products, and $(100-t)/2$ will buy the wordprocessor only and $(100-t)/2$ will buy the spreadsheet only. Calculate profits as a function of t if there is no bundling._____

(j) What are profits with the bundle?_____.

(k) At what values of t would it be unprofitable to offer the bundle?_____

_____

_____

_____.

(l) This analysis so far has been concerned only with customers who would purchase at least one of the programs at the original set of prices. Is there any additional source of demand for the bundle? What does this say about the calculations we have made about the prof-

itability of bundling?_____

_____

_____

_____.

24.8 (0) Col. Tom Barker is about to open his newest amusement park, Elvis World. Elvis World features a number of exciting attractions: you can ride the rapids in the Blue Suede Chutes, climb the Jailhouse Rock and eat dinner in the Heartburn Hotel. Col. Tom figures that Elvis World will attract 1,000 people per day, and each person will take $x = 50 - 50p$ rides, where p is the price of a ride. Everyone who visits Elvis World is pretty much the same and negative rides are not allowed. The marginal cost of a ride is essentially zero.

(a) What is each person's inverse demand function for rides?_____

_____.

(b) If Col. Tom sets the price to maximize profit, how many rides will be

taken per day by a typical visitor?_____.

(c) What will the price of a ride be?_____.

(d) What will Col. Tom's profits be per person?_____.

(e) What is the Pareto efficient price of a ride?_____.

(f) If Col. Tom charged the Pareto efficient price for a ride, how many rides would be purchased?_____.

(g) How much consumers' surplus would be generated at this price and quantity?_____.

(h) If Col. Tom decided to use a two-part tariff, he would set an admission fee of _____ and charge a price per ride of_____.

24.9 (1) The city of String Valley is squeezed between two mountains and is 36 miles long, running from north to south, and only about 1 block wide. Within the town, the population has a uniform density of 100 people per mile. Because of the rocky terrain, nobody lives outside the city limits on either the north or the south edge of town. Because of strict zoning regulations, the city has only three bowling alleys. One of these is located at the city limits on the north edge of town, one of them is located at the city limits on the south edge of town, and one is located at the exact center of town. Travel costs including time and gasoline are $1 per mile. All of the citizens of the town have the same preferences. They are willing to bowl once a week if the cost of bowling including travel costs and the price charged by the bowling alley does not exceed $15.

(a) Consider one of the bowling alleys at either edge of town. If it charges $10 for a night of bowling, how far will a citizen of String Valley be willing to travel to bowl there?_____ . How many customers would this bowling alley have per week if it charged $10 per night of bowling?

_____.

(b) Write a formula for the number of customers that a bowling alley at the edge of town will have if it charges $p per night of bowling._____

_____.

(c) Write a formula for this bowling alley's inverse demand function

_____.

(d) Suppose that the bowling alleys at the end of town have a marginal cost of $3 per customer and set their prices to maximize profits. (For the time being assume that these bowling alleys faces no competition from the other bowling alleys in town.) How many customers will they have?

_____ What price will they charge?_____ How far away from the

edge of town does their most distant customer live?_____.

(e) Now consider the bowling alley in the center of town. If it charges a price of $p, how many customers will it have per week?_____.

(f) If the bowling alley in the center of town also has marginal costs of $3 per customer and maximizes its profits, what price will it charge? _____ How many customers will it have per week?_____ How far away from the center of town will its most distant customers live?

_____.

(g) Suppose that the city relaxes its zoning restrictions on where the bowling alleys can locate, but continues to issue operating licenses to only 3 bowling alleys. Both of the bowling alleys at the end of town are about to lose their leases and can locate anywhere in town that they like at about the same cost. The bowling alley in the center of town is committed to stay where it is. Would either of the alleys at the edge of town improve its profits by locating next to the existing bowling alley in the center of town?_____ What would be a profit-maximizing location for each of these two bowling alleys?_____

_____.

Factor Markets

Introduction. In this chapter you will examine the factor demand decision of a monopolist. If a firm is a monopolist in some industry, it will produce less output than if the industry were competitively organized. Therefore it will in general want to use less inputs than does a competitive firm. The value marginal product is just the value of the extra output produced by hiring an extra unit of the factor. The ordinary logic of competitive profit maximization implies that a competitive firm will hire a factor up until the point where the **value marginal product** equals the price of the factor.

The **marginal revenue product** is the extra revenue produced by hiring an extra unit of a factor. For a competitive firm, the marginal revenue product is the same as the value of the marginal product, but they differ for monopolist. A monopolist has to take account of the fact that increasing his production will force the price down, so the marginal revenue product of an extra unit of a factor will be *less* than the value marginal product.

Another thing we study in this chapters is **monopsony**, which is the case of a market dominated by a single buyer of some good. The case of monopsony is very similar to the case of a monopoly: The monopsonist hires less of a factor than a similar competitive firm because the monopsony recognizes that the price it has to pay for the factor depends on how much it buys.

Finally, we consider an interesting example of factor supply, in which a monopolist produces a good that is used by another monopolist.

Example: Suppose a monopolist faces a demand curve for output of the form $p(y) = 100 - 2y$. The production function takes the simple form $y = 2x$, and the factor costs $4 per unit. How much of the factor of production will the monopolist want to employ? How much of the factor would a competitive industry employ if all the firms in the industry had the same production function?

Answer: The monopolist will employ the factor up to the point where the marginal revenue product equals the price of the factor. Revenue as a function of output is $R(y) = p(y)y = (100 - 2y)y$. To find revenue as a function of the input, we substitute $y = 2x$ to find

$$R(x) = (100 - 4x)2x = (200 - 8x)x.$$

The marginal revenue product function will have the form $MRP_x = 200 - 16x$. Setting marginal revenue product equal to factor price gives us the equation

$$200 - 16x = 4.$$

Solving this equation gives us $x^* = 12.25$.

If the industry were competitive, then the industry would employ the factor up to the point where the value of the marginal product was equal to 4. This gives us the equation

$$p2 = 4,$$

so $p^* = 2$. How much output would be demanded at this price? We plug this into the demand function to get the equation $2 = 100 - 2y$, which implies $y^* = 49$. Since the production function is $y = 2x$, we can solve for $x^* = y^*/2 = 24.5$.

25.1 (0) Gargantuan Enterprises has a monopoly in the production of antimacassars. Its factory is located in the town of Pantagruel. There is no other industry in Pantagruel, and the labor supply equation there is $W = 10 + .1L$, where W is the daily wage and L is the number of person-days of work performed. Antimacassars are produced with a production function, $Q = 10L$, where L is daily labor supply and Q is daily output. The demand curve for antimacassars is $P = 41 - \frac{Q}{1,000}$, where P is the price and Q is the number of sales per day.

(a) Find the profit-maximizing output for Gargantuan. (Hint: Use the production function to find the labor input requirements for any level of output. Make substitutions so you can write the firm's total costs as a function of its output and then its profit as a function of output. Solve for the profit–maximizing output.)_____.

(b) How much labor does it use? _____ What is the wage rate that

it pays?_____.

(c) What is the price of antimacassars? _____ How much profit is

made?_____.

25.2 (0) The residents of Seltzer Springs, Michigan, consume bottles of mineral water according to the demand function $D(p) = 1,000 - p$. Here $D(p)$ is the demand per year for bottles of mineral water if the price per bottle is p.

The sole distributor of mineral water in Seltzer Springs, Bubble Up, purchases mineral water at c per bottle from their supplier Perry Air. Perry Air is the only supplier of mineral water in the area and behaves as a profit-maximizing monopolist. For simplicity we suppose that it has zero costs of production.

(a) What is the equilibrium price charged by the distributor Bubble Up?

_____.

(b) What is the equilibrium quantity sold by Bubble Up?_____

_____.

(c) What is the equilibrium price charged by the producer Perry Air?

_____.

(d) What is the equilibrium quantity sold by Perry Air?_____.

(e) What are the profits of Bubble Up?_____.

(f) What are the profits of Perry Air?_____.

(g) How much consumer's surplus is generated in this market?_____

_____.

(h) Suppose that this situation is expected to persist forever and that the interest rate is expected to be constant at 10% per year. What is the minimum lump sum payment that Perry Air would need to pay to Bubble

Up to buy out their operation?_____.

(i) Suppose that they do this. What will be the new price and quantity

for mineral water?_____.

(j) What are the profits of the new merged firm?_____.

(k) What is the total amount of consumers' surplus generated? How does

this compare to the previous level of consumers' surplus?_____

_____.

Calculus **25.3 (0)** Upper Peninsula Underground Recordings (UPUR) has a monopoly on the recordings of the famous rock group Moosecake. Moosecake's music is only provided on digital tape, and blank digital tapes cost them c per tape. There are no other manufacturing or distribution costs. Let $p(x)$ be the inverse demand function for Moosecake's music as a function of x, the number of tapes sold.

(a) What is the first-order condition for profit maximization? For future reference, let x^* be the profit-maximizing amount produced and p^* be the price at which it sells. (In this part, assume that tapes cannot be copied.)

_____.

Now a new kind of consumer digital tape recorder becomes widely available that allows the user to make 1 and only 1 copy of a prerecorded digital tape. The copies are a perfect substitute in consumption value for the original prerecorded tape, and there are no barriers to their use or sale. However, everyone can see the difference between the copies and the orginals and recognizes that the copies cannot be used to make further copies. Blank tapes cost the consumers c per tape, the same price the monopolist pays.

(b) All Moosecake fans take advantage of the opportunity to make a single copy of the tape and sell it on the secondary market. How is the price of an original tape related to the price of a copy? Derive the inverse demand curve for original tapes facing UPUR. (Hint: There are two sources of demand for a new tape: the pleasure of listening to it, and the profits from

selling a copy.)_____

_____

_____

(c) Write an expression for UPUR's profits if it produces x tapes._____

_____.

(d) Let x^{**} be the profit-maximizing level of production by UPUR. How does it compare to the former profit-maximizing level of production?

_____.

(e) How does the price of a *copy* of a Moosecake tape compare to the

price determined in Part *(a)*?_____.

(f) If p^{**} is the price of a copy of a Moosecake tape, how much will a *new*

Moosecake tape sell for?_____

Oligopoly

Introduction. In this chapter you will solve problems for firm and industry outcomes when the firms engage in Cournot competition, Stackelberg competition, and other sorts of oligopoly behavior. In Cournot competition, each firm chooses its own output to maximize its profits given the output that it expects the other firm to produce. The industry price depends on the industry output, say, $q_A + q_B$, where A and B are the firms. To maximize profits, firm A sets its marginal revenue (which depends on the output of firm A and the expected output of firm B since the expected industry price depends on the sum of these outputs) equal to its marginal cost. Solving this equation for firm A's output as a function of firm B's expected output gives you one reaction function; analogous steps give you firm B's reaction function. Solve these two equations simultaneously to get the Cournot equilibrium outputs of the two firms.

Example: In Heifer's Breath, Wisconsin, there are two bakers, Anderson and Carlson. Anderson's bread tastes just like Carlson's—nobody can tell the difference. Anderson has constant marginal costs of $1 per loaf of bread. Carlson has constant marginal costs of $2 per loaf. Fixed costs are zero for both of them. The inverse demand function for bread in Heifer's Breath is $p(q) = 6 - .01q$, where q is the total number of loaves sold per day.

Let us find Anderson's Cournot reaction function. If Carlson bakes q_C loaves, then if Anderson bakes q_A loaves, total output will be $q_A + q_C$ and price will be $6 - .01(q_A + q_C)$. For Anderson, the total cost of producing q_A units of bread is just q_A, so his profits are

$$pq_A - q_A = (6 - .01q_A - .01q_C)q_A - q_A$$
$$= 6q_A - .01q_A^2 - .01q_Cq_A - q_A.$$

Therefore if Carlson is going to bake q_C units, then Anderson will choose q_A to maximize $6q_A - .01q_A^2 - .01q_Cq_A - q_A$. This expression is maximized when $6 - .02q_A - .01q_C = 1$. (You can find this out either by setting A's marginal revenue equal to his marginal cost or directly by setting the derivative of profits with respect to q_A equal to zero.) Anderson's reaction function, $R_A(q_C)$ tells us Anderson's best output if he knows that Carlson is going to bake q_C. We solve from the previous equation to find $R_A(q_C) = (5 - .01q_C)/.02 = 250 - .5q_C$.

We can find Carlson's reaction function in the same way. If Carlson knows that Anderson is going to produce q_A units, then Carlson's profits will be $p(q_A + q_C) - 2q_C = (6 - .01q_A - .01q_C)q_C - 2q_C = 6q_C - .01q_Aq_C - .01q_C^2 - 2q_C$. Carlson's profits will be maximized if he chooses q_C to satisfy the equation $6 - .01q_A - .02q_C = 2$. Therefore Carlson's reaction function is $R_C(q_A) = (4 - .01q_A)/.02 = 200 - .5q_A$.

Let us denote the Cournot equilibrium quantities by $\bar{q}_A$ and $\bar{q}_C$. The Cournot equilibrium conditions are that $\bar{q}_A = R_A(\bar{q}_C)$ and $\bar{q}_C = R_C(\bar{q}_A)$. Solving these two equations in two unknowns we find that $\bar{q}_A = 200$ and $\bar{q}_C = 100$. Now we can also solve for the Cournot equilibrium price and for the profits of each baker. The Cournot equilibrium price is $6 - .01(200 + 100) = \$3$. Then in Cournot equilibrium, Anderson makes a profit of \$2 on each of 200 loaves and Carlson makes \$1 on each of 100 loaves.

In Stackelberg competition, the follower's profit-maximizing output choice depends on the amount of output that he expects the leader to produce. His reaction function, $R_F(q_L)$, is constructed in the same way as for a Cournot competitor. The leader knows the reaction function of the follower and gets to choose her own output, q_L, first. So the leader knows that the industry price depends on the *sum* of her own output and the follower's output, that is, on $q_L + R_F(q_L)$. Since the industry price can be expressed as a function of q_L only, so can the leader's marginal revenue. So once you get the follower's reaction function and substitute it into the inverse demand function, you can write down an expression that depends on just q_L and that says marginal revenue equals marginal cost for the leader. You can solve this expression for the leader's Stackelberg output and plug in to the follower's reaction function to get the follower's Stackelberg output.

Example: Suppose that one of the bakers of Heifer's Breath plays the role of Stackelberg leader. Perhaps this is because Carlson always gets up an hour earlier than Anderson and has his bread in the oven before Anderson gets started. If Anderson always finds out how much bread Carlson has in his oven and if Carlson knows that Anderson knows this, then Carlson can act like a Stackelberg leader. Carlson knows that Anderson's reaction function is $R_A(q_C) = 250 - .5q_C$. Therefore Carlson knows that if he bakes q_C loaves of bread, then the total amount of bread that will be baked in Heifer's Breath will be $q_C + R_A(q_C) = q_C + 250 - .5q_C = 250 + .5q_C$. Since Carlson's production decision determines total production and hence the price of bread, we can write Carlson's profit simply as a function of his own output. Carlson will choose the quantity that maximizes this profit. If Carlson bakes q_C loaves, the price will be $p = 6 - .01(250 + .5q_C) = 3.5 - .005q_C$. Then Carlson's profits will be $pq_C - 2q_C = (3.5 - .005q_C)q_C - 2q_C = 1.5q_C - .005q_C^2$. His profits are maximized when $q_C = 150$. (Find this either by setting marginal revenue equal to marginal cost or directly by setting the derivative of profits to zero and solving for q_C.) If Carlson produces 150 loaves, then Anderson will produce $250 - .5 \times 150 = 175$ loaves. The price of bread will be $6 - .01(175 + 150) = 2.75$. Carlson will now make \$.75 per loaf on each of 150 loaves and Anderson will make \$1.75 on each of 175 loaves.

26.1 (0) Carl and Simon are two rival pumpkin growers who sell their pumpkins at the Farmers' Market in Lake Witchisit, Minnesota. They are the only sellers of pumpkins at the market, where the demand function for pumpkins is $q = 3,200 - 1,600p$. The total number of pumpkins sold at the market is $q = q_C + q_S$, where q_C is the number that Carl sells and q_S is the number that Simon sells. The cost of producing pumpkins for either farmer is $.50 per pumpkin no matter how many pumpkins he produces.

(a) The inverse demand function for pumpkins at the Farmers' Market is

$p = a - b(q_C + q_S)$, where $a =$ _____ and $b =$ _____ The

marginal cost of producing a pumpkin for either farmer is_____.

(b) Every spring, each of the farmers decides how many pumpkins to grow. They both know the local demand function and they each know how many pumpkins were sold by the other farmer last year. In fact, each farmer assumes that the other farmer will sell the same number this year as he sold last year. So, for example, if Simon sold 400 pumpkins last year, Carl believes that Simon will sell 400 pumpkins again this year. If Simon sold 400 pumpkins last year, what does Carl think the price of

pumpkins will be if Carl sells 1,200 pumpkins this year? _____ If Simon sold q_S^{t-1} pumpkins in year $t-1$, then in the spring of year t, Carl thinks that if he, Carl, sells q_C^t pumpkins this year, the price of pumpkins

this year will be_____.

(c) If Simon sold 400 pumpkins last year, Carl believes that if he sells q_C^t pumpkins this year then the inverse demand function that he faces is $p = 2 - 400/1,600 - q_C^t/1,600 = 1.75 - q_C^t/1,600$. Therefore if Simon sold 400 pumpkins last year, Carl's marginal revenue this year will be $1.75 - q_C^t/800$. More generally, if Simon sold q_S^{t-1} pumpkins last year, then Carl believes that if he, himself, sells q_C^t pumpkins this year, his

marginal revenue this year will be_____.

(d) Carl believes that Simon will never change the amount of pumpkins that he produces from the amount q_S^{t-1} that he sold last year. Therefore Carl plants enough pumpkins this year so that he can sell the amount that maximizes his profits this year. To maximize this profit, he chooses the output this year that sets his marginal revenue this year equal to his marginal cost. This means that to find Carl's output this year when Simon's output last year was q_S^{t-1}, Carl solves the following equation.

_____.

(e) Carl's Cournot reaction function, $R_C^t(q_S^{t-1})$, is a function that tells us what Carl's profit-maximizing output this year would be as a function of Simon's output last year. Use the equation you wrote in the last answer

to find Carl's reaction function, $R_C^t(q_S^{t-1}) =$ _____ (Hint: This is a linear expression of the form $a - bq_S^{t-1}$. You have to find the constants a and b.)

(f) Suppose that Simon makes his decisions in the same way that Carl does. Notice that the problem is completely symmetric in the roles played by Carl and Simon. Therefore without even calculating it, we can guess that Simon's reaction function is $R_S^t(q_C^{t-1}) = $ _____ (Of course, if you don't like to guess, you could work this out by following similar steps to the ones you used to find Carl's reaction function.)

(g) Suppose that in year 1, Carl produced 200 pumpkins and Simon produced 1,000 pumpkins. In year 2, how many would Carl produce?

_____ How many would Simon produce? _____ In year 3, how many would Carl produce? _____ How many would Simon produce? _____ Use a calculator or pen and paper to work out several more terms in this series. To what level of output does Carl's output appear to be converging?_____ How about Simon's?_____.

(h) Write down two simultaneous equations that could be solved to find outputs q_S and q_C such that, if Carl is producing q_C and Simon is producing q_S, then they will both want to produce the same amount in the next period. (Hint: Use the reaction functions.)_____

_____.

(i) Solve the two equations you wrote down in the last part for an equilibrium output for each farmer. Each farmer, in Cournot equilibrium, produces _____ units of output. The total amount of pumpkins brought to the Farmers' market in Lake Witchisit is _____ The price of pumpkins in that market is _____ How much profit does each farmer make?

_____.

26.2 (0) Suppose that the pumpkin market in Lake Witchisit is as we described it in the last problem except for one detail. Every spring, the snow thaws off of Carl's pumpkin field a week before it thaws off of Simon's. Therefore Carl can plant his pumpkins one week earlier than Simon can. Now Simon lives just down the road from Carl, and he can tell by looking at Carl's fields how many pumpkins Carl planted and how many Carl will harvest in the fall. (Suppose also that Carl will sell every pumpkin that he produces.) Therefore instead of assuming that Carl will sell the same amount of pumpkins that he did last year, Simon sees how many Carl is actually going to sell this year. Simon has this information before he makes his own decision about how many to plant.

(a) If Carl plants enough pumpkins to yield q_C^t this year, then Simon knows that the profit maximizing amount to produce this year is $q_S^t =$ Hint: Remember the reaction functions you found in the last problem.

_____

(b) When Carl plants his pumpkins, he understands how Simon will make his decision. Therefore Carl knows that the amount that Simon will produce this year will be determined by the amount that Carl produces. In particular, if Carl's output is q_C^t , then Simon will produce and sell

_____ and the total output of the two producers will be _____

_____ Therefore Carl knows that if his own output is q_C, the

price of pumpkins in the market will be_____.

(c) In the last part of the problem, you found how the price of pumpkins this year in the Farmers' Market is related to the number of pumpkins that Carl produces this year. Now write an expression for Carl's total

revenue in year t as a function of his own output, q_C^t. _____

_____ Write an expression for Carl's marginal revenue in year t as a

function of q_C^t._____.

(d) Find the profit-maximizing output for Carl. _____ Find the

profit-maximizing output for Simon. _____ Find the equilibrium

price of pumpkins in the Lake Witchisit Farmers' Market. _____

How much profit does Carl make? _____ How much profit does

Simon make? _____ An equilibrium of the type we discuss here is

known as a _____ equilibrium.

(e) If he wanted to, it would be possible for Carl to delay his planting until the same time that Simon planted so that neither of them would know the other's plans for this year when he planted. Would it be in Carl's interest to do this? Explain. (Hint: What are Carl's profits in the equilibrium above? How do they compare with his profits

in Cournot equilibrium?)_____

_____

26.3 (0) Suppose that Carl and Simon sign a marketing agreement. They decide to determine their total output jointly and to each produce the same number of pumpkins. To maximize their joint profits, how many pumpkins should they produce in total? _____ How much does each one of them produce? _____ How much profits does each one of them make?_____.

26.4 (0) The inverse market demand curve for bean sprouts is given by $P(Y) = 100 - 2Y$, and the total cost function for any firm in the industry is given by $TC(y) = 4y$.

(a) The marginal cost for any firm in the industry is equal to _____ The change in price for a one-unit increase in output is equal to_____

_____.

(b) If the bean-sprout industry were perfectly competitive, the industry output would be _____ , and the industry price would be_____.

(c) Suppose that two Cournot firms operate in the market. The reaction function for Firm 1 would be _____ (Reminder: Unlike the example in your textbook, the marginal cost is not zero here.) The reaction function of Firm 2 will be _____ If the firms were operating at the Cournot equilibrium point, industry output would be _____ , each firm would produce _____ , and the market price would be_____.

(d) For the Cournot case, draw the two reaction curves and indicate the equilibrium point on the graph below.

y_2

(e) If the two firms decided to collude, industry output would be _____

and the market price would equal_____.

(f) Suppose both of the colluding firms are producing equal amounts of output. If one of the colluding firms assumes that the other firm would not react to a change in industry output, what would happen to a firm's own

profits if it increased its output by one unit? _____

(g) Suppose one firm acts as a Stackleberg leader and the other firm behaves as a follower. The maximization problem for the leader can be

written as:_____.
    Solving this problem results in the leader producing an output of

_____ and the follower producing _____ This implies an industry

output of _____ and price of_____.

26.5 (0) Grinch is the sole owner of a mineral water spring that costlessly burbles forth as much mineral water as Grinch cares to bottle. It costs Grinch \$2 per gallon to bottle this water. The inverse demand curve for Grinch's mineral water is $p = \$20 - .20q$, where p is the price per gallon and q is the number of gallons sold.

(a) Write down an expression for profits as a function of q, $\Pi(q) = $ _____

_____ Find the profit-maximizing choice of q for Grinch._____.

(b) What price does Grinch get per gallon of mineral water if he produces the profit-maximizing quantity? _____ How much profit does he make?_____.

(c) Suppose, now, that Grinch's neighbor, Grubb finds a mineral spring that produces mineral water that is just as good as Grinch's water, but that it costs Grubb $6 a bottle to get his water out of the ground and bottle it. Total market demand for mineral water remains as before. Suppose that Grinch and Grubb each believe that the other's quantity decision is independent of his own. What is the Cournot equilibrium output for Grubb?_____ What is the price in the Cournot equilibrium?

_____.

26.6 (1) Albatross Airlines has a monopoly on air travel between Peoria and Dubuque. If Albatross makes one trip in each direction per day, the demand schedule for round trips is $q = 160 - 2p$, where q is the number of passengers per day. (Assume that nobody makes one-way trips.) There is an "overhead" fixed cost of $2,000 per day that is necessary to fly the airplane regardless of the number of passengers. In addition, there is a marginal cost of $10 per passenger. Thus, total daily costs are $2,000+10q$ if the plane flies at all.

(a) On the graph below, sketch and label the marginal revenue curve, and the average and marginal cost curves.

AC, MR, MC

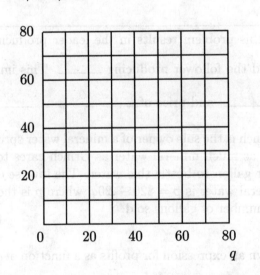

(b) Calculate the profit-maximizing price and quantity and total daily profits for Albatross Airlines. $p =$_____ , $q =$_____ , $\pi =$_____

_____.

(c) If the interest rate is 10% per year, how much would someone be willing to pay to own Albatross Airlines' monopoly on the Dubuque-Peoria route. (Assuming that demand and cost conditions remain unchanged forever.)

_____.

(d) If another firm with the same costs as Albatross Airlines were to enter the Dubuque-Peoria market and if the industry then became a Cournot duopoly, would the new entrant make a profit?_____

_____.

(e) Suppose that the throbbing night life in Peoria and Dubuque becomes widely known and in consequence the population of both places doubles. As a result, the demand for airplane trips between the two places doubles to become $q = 320 - 4p$. Suppose that the original airplane had a capacity of 80 passengers. If AA must stick with this single plane and if no other airline enters the market, what price should it charge to maximize its output and how much profit would it make? $p =$_____ , $\pi =$_____

_____.

(f) Let us assume that the overhead costs per plane are constant regardless of the number of planes. If AA added a second plane with the same costs and capacity as the first plane, what price would it charge _____ , how many tickets would it sell? _____ How much would its profits be?

_____ If AA could prevent entry by another competitor, would it choose to add a second plane?_____.

(g) Suppose that AA stuck with one plane and another firm entered the market with a plane of its own. If the second firm has the same cost function as the first and if the two firms act as Cournot oligopolists, what will be the price, _____ , quantities, _____ , and profits?

_____.

26.7 (0) Alex and Anna are the only sellers of kangaroos in Sydney, Australia. Anna chooses her profit-maximizing number of kangaroos to sell, q_1, based on the number of kangaroos that she expects Alex to sell. Alex knows how Anna will react and chooses the number of kangaroos that she herself will sell, q_2, after taking this information into account. The inverse demand function for kangaroos is $P(q_1 + q_2) = 2,000 - 2(q_1 + q_2)$. It costs $400 to raise a kangaroo to sell.

(a) Alex and Anna are Stackelberg competitors. _____ is the leader and _____ is the follower.

(b) If Anna expects Alex to sell q_2 kangaroos, what will her own marginal revenue be if she herself sells q_1 kangaroos?_____.

(c) What is Anna's reaction function, $R(q_2)$?_____.

(d) Now if Alex sells q_2 kangaroos, what is the total number of kangaroos that will be sold? _____ What will be the market price as a function of q_2 only?_____.

(e) What is Alex's marginal revenue as a function of q_2 only? _____ _____ How many kangaroos will Alex sell? _____ How many kangaroos will Anna sell? _____ What will the industry price be?_____.

26.8 (0) Consider an industry with the following structure. There are 50 firms that behave in a competitive manner and have identical cost functions given by $c(y) = y^2/2$. There is one monopolist that has 0 marginal costs. The demand curve for the product is given by

$$D(p) = 1,000 - 50p.$$

(a) What is the supply curve of one of the competitive firms? _____ The total supply from the competitive sector at price p is $S(p) =$_____

_____.

(b) If the monopolist sets a price p, the amount that he can sell is $D_m(p) =$

_____.

(c) The monopolist's profit-maximizing output is $y_m =$ _____ What

is the monopolist's profit-maximizing price?_____.

(d) How much output will the competitive sector provide at this price?

_____ What will be the total amount of output sold in this

industry?_____.

26.9 (0) Consider a market with one large firm and many small firms.
The supply curve of the small firms taken together is:

$$S(p) = 100 + p.$$

The demand curve for the product is:

$$D(p) = 200 - p.$$

The cost function for the one large firm is:

$$c(y) = 25y.$$

(a) Suppose that the large firm is forced to operate at a zero level of

output. What will be the equilibrium price? _____ What will be the

equilibrium quantity?_____.

(b) Suppose now that the large firm attempts to exploit its market power
and set a profit-maximizing price. In order to model this we assume
that customers always go first to the competitive firms and buy as much
as they are able to and then go to the monopolist. In this situation,

the equilibrium price will be _____ The quantity supplied by the

monopolist will be _____ and the equilibrium quantity supplied by the

competitive firms will be_____.

(c) What will be the large firm's profits?_____.

(d) Finally suppose that the large firm could force the competitive firms
out of the business and behave as a real monopolist. What will be the

equilibrium price? _____ What will be the equilibrium quantity?

_____ What will be the large firm's profits?_____.

Calculus   **26.10 (2)** In a remote area of the American Midwest before the railroads arrived, cast iron cookstoves were much desired, but people lived far apart, roads were poor, and heavy stoves were expensive to transport. Stoves could be shipped by river boat to the town of Bouncing Springs, Missouri. Ben Kinmore was the only stove dealer in Bouncing Springs. He could buy as many stoves as he wished for $20 each, delivered to his store. The only farmers who traded in Bouncing Springs lived along a road that ran east and west through town. Along that road, there was one farm every mile and the cost of hauling a stove was $1 per mile. There were no other stove dealers on the road in either direction. The owners of every farm along the road had a reservation price of $120 for a cast iron cookstove. That is, any of them would be willing to pay up to $120 to have a stove rather than to not have one. Nobody had use for more than one stove. Ben Kinmore charged a base price of $p for stoves and added to the price the cost of delivery. For example, if the base price of stoves was $40 and you lived 45 miles west of Bouncing Springs, you would have to pay $85 to get a stove, $40 base price plus a hauling charge of $45. Since the reservation price of every farmer was $120, it follows that if the base price were $40, any farmer who lived within 80 miles of Bouncing Springs would be willing to pay $40 plus the price of delivery to have a cookstove. Therefore at a base price of $40, Ben could sell 80 cookstoves to the farmers living west of him. Similarly, if his base price is $40, he could sell 80 cookstoves to the farmers living within 80 miles to his east, for a total of 160 cookstoves.

(a) If Ben set a base price of $p for cookstoves where $p < 120$, and if he charged $1 a mile for delivering them, what would be the total number of

cookstoves he could sell? _____ (Remember to count the ones he could sell to his east as well as to his west.) Assume that Ben has no other costs than buying the stoves and delivering them. Then Ben would make a profit of $p - 20$ per stove. Write Ben's total profit as a function of

the base price, $p, that he charges:_____.

(b) Ben's profit-maximizing base price is _____ (Hint: You just wrote profits as a function of prices. Now differentiate this expression for profits with respect to p.) Ben's most distant customer would be

located at a distance of _____ miles from him. Ben would sell _____

cookstoves and make a total profit of_____.

(c) Suppose that instead of setting a single base price and making all buyers pay for the cost of transportation, Ben offers free delivery of cookstoves. He sets a price $p and promises to deliver for free to any farmer who lives within $p - 20$ miles of him. (He won't deliver to anyone who lives further than that, because it then costs him more than $p to buy a stove and deliver it.) If he is going to price in this way,

how high should he set p? _____ How many cookstoves would

Ben deliver?_____ How much would his total revenue be? _____

_____ How much would his total costs be, including the cost of deliveries and the cost of buying the stoves? _____ (Hint: What is the average distance that he has to haul a cookstove?) How much

profit would he make? _____ Can you explain why it is more profitable for Ben to use this pricing scheme where he pays the cost of delivery himself rather than the scheme where the farmers pay for

their own deliveries?_____

_____

_____

_____.

Calculus **26.11 (2)** Perhaps you wondered what Ben Kinmore, who lives off in the woods quietly collecting his monopoly profits, is doing in this chapter on oligopoly. Well, unfortunately for Ben, before he got around to selling any stoves, the railroad built a track to the town of Deep Furrow, just 40 miles down the road, west of Bouncing Springs. The storekeeper in Deep Furrow, Huey Sunshine, was also able to get cookstoves delivered by train to his store for $20 each. Huey and Ben were the only stove dealers on the road. Let us concentrate our attention on how they would compete for the customers who lived between them. We can do this, because Ben can charge different base prices for the cookstoves he ships east and the cookstoves he ships west. So can Huey.

Suppose that Ben sets a base price, p_B, for stoves he sends west and adds a charge of $1 per mile for delivery. Suppose that Huey sets a base price, p_H, for stoves he sends east and adds a charge of $1 per mile for delivery. Farmers who live between Ben and Huey would buy from the seller who is willing to deliver most cheaply to them (so long as the delivered price does not exceed $120). If Ben's base price is p_B and Huey's base price is p_H, somebody who lives x miles west of Ben would have to pay a total of $p_B + x$ to have a stove delivered from Ben and $p_H + (40 - x)$ to have a stove delivered by Huey.

(a) If Ben's base price is p_B and Huey's is p_H, write down an equation that could be solved for the distance x^* to the west of Bouncing Springs that Ben's market extends. _____ If Ben's base price

is p_B and Huey's is p_H, then Ben will sell _____ cookstoves

and Huey will sell _____ cookstoves.

(b) Recalling that Ben makes a profit of $p_B - 20$ on every cookstove that he sells, Ben's profits can be expressed as the following function of p_B and p_H._____.

(c) If Ben thinks that Huey's price will stay at p_H, no matter what price Ben chooses, what choice of p_B would maximize Ben's profits? _____

_____ (Hint: Set the derivative of Ben's profits with respect to his price equal to zero.) Suppose that Huey thinks that Ben's price will stay at p_B, no matter what price Huey chooses, what choice of p_H would maximize Huey's profits? _____ (Hint: Use the symmetry of the problem and the answer to the last question.)

(d) Can you find a base price for Ben and a base price for Huey such that each is a profit-maximizing choice given what the other guy is doing? (Hint: Find prices p_B and p_H that simultaneously solve the last two equations.) _____ How many cookstoves does Ben sell to farmers living west of him? _____ How much profits does he make on these sales?_____.

(e) Suppose that Ben and Huey decided to compete for the customers who live between them by price discriminating. Suppose that Ben offers to deliver a stove to a farmer who lives x miles west of him for a price equal to the maximum of Ben's total cost of delivering a stove to that farmer and Huey's total cost of delivering to the same farmer less 1 penny. Suppose that Huey offers to deliver a stove to a farmer who lives x miles west of Ben for a price equal to the maximum of Huey's own total cost of delivering to this farmer and Ben's total cost of delivering to him less a penny. For example, if a farmer lives 10 miles west of Ben, Ben's total cost of delivering to him is $30, $20 to get the stove and $10 for hauling it 10 miles west. Huey's total cost of delivering it to him is $50, $20 to get the stove and $30 to haul it 30 miles east. Ben will charge the maximum of his own cost, which is $30, and Huey's cost less a penny, which is $49.99.

The maximum of these two numbers is _____ . Huey will charge the maximum of his own total cost of delivering to this farmer, which is $50, and Ben's cost less a penny, which is $29.99. Therefore Huey will charge

_____ to deliver to this farmer. This farmer will buy from _____ whose price to him is cheaper by one penny. When the two merchants have this pricing policy, all farmers who live within _____ miles of

Ben will buy from Ben and all farmers who live within _____ miles of Huey will buy from Huey. A farmer who lives x miles west of Ben and buys from Ben must pay _____ dollars to have a cookstove delivered to him. A farmer who lives x miles east of Huey and buys from

Huey must pay _____ for delivery of a stove. On the graph below, use blue ink to graph the cost to Ben of delivering to a farmer who lives x miles west of him. Use red ink to graph the total cost to Huey of delivering a cookstove to a farmer who lives x miles west of Ben. Use pencil to mark the lowest price available to a farmer as a function of how far west he lives from Ben.

Dollars

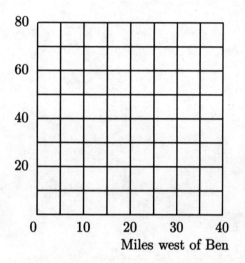

Miles west of Ben

(f) With the pricing policies you just graphed, which farmers get stoves delivered most cheaply, those who live closest to the merchants or those

who live midway between them? _____
On the graph you made, shade in the area representing each merchant's

profits. How much profits does each merchant make? _____ If Ben and Huey are pricing in this way, is there any way for either of them to increase his profits by changing the price he charges to some farmers?

_____.

...nd buys from Ben must pay _____ dollars to have it look delivered to him. A farmer who lives _____ miles east of Huey and buys from

Huey must pay _____ for delivery. ...

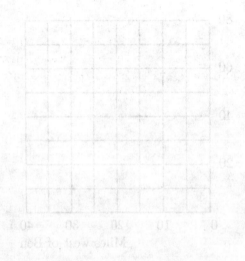

Midwest of Ben

(7) With the pricing policies you just described, which farmers get stores delivered most cheaply, those who live closer to the two stores or those

who live midway between them? _____

On the graph you might sketch in the area representing the merchant's profits. How much profit does each one chart make? _____ If Ben and Huey are pricing in this way, is there any way for either of them to increase his profit by changing the price he charges to some farmers

Game Theory

Introduction. In this introduction we offer three examples of two-person games. The first game has a dominant strategy equilibrium. The second has a Nash equilibrium in pure strategies that is not a dominant strategy equilibrium. The third has no pure strategy Nash equilibrium, but it does have a mixed strategy equilibrium.

Example: Albert and Victoria are roommates. Each of them prefers a clean room to a dirty room, but neither likes to clean the room. If both clean the room, they each get a payoff of 5. If one cleans and the other doesn't clean the room, the person who does the cleaning has a utility of 0, and the person who doesn't clean the room has a utility of 8. If neither cleans the room, the room stays a mess and each has a utility of 1. The payoffs from the strategies "Clean" and "Don't Clean" are shown in the box below.

Clean Room–Dirty Room

		Victoria	
		Clean	Don't Clean
Albert	Clean	5, 5	0, 8
	Don't Clean	8, 0	1, 1

In this game, notice that if Victoria chooses to clean, then Albert will be better off not cleaning than he would be if he chose to clean. Likewise if Victoria chooses not to clean, Albert is better off not cleaning than cleaning. Therefore "Don't Clean" is a dominant strategy for Albert. Similar reasoning shows that no matter what Albert chooses to do, Victoria is better off if she chooses "Don't Clean." Therefore the outcome where both roommates choose "Don't Clean" is a dominant strategy equilibrium. It is interesting to notice that this is true, even though both persons would be better off if they both chose the strategy "Clean."

Example: This game is set in the South Pacific in 1943. Admiral Imamura must transport Japanese troops from the port of Rabaul in New Britain, across the Bismarck Sea to New Guinea. The Japanese fleet could either travel north of New Britain, where it is likely to be foggy, or south of New Britain, where the weather is likely to be clear. U.S. Admiral Kenney hopes to bomb the troop ships. Kenney has to choose whether to concentrate his reconnaissance aircraft on the Northern or the Southern route. Once he finds the convoy, he can bomb it until its arrival in New Guinea. Kenney's staff has estimated the number of days of bombing time for each of the outcomes. The payoffs to Kenney and Imamura from each outcome are shown in the box below. The game is modeled as a "zero-sum game." For each outcome, Imamura's payoff is the negative of Kenney's payoff.

The Battle of the Bismarck Sea

		Imamura	
		North	South
Kenney	North	2, −2	2, −2
	South	1, −1	3, −3

This game does not have a dominant strategy equilibrium, since there is no dominant strategy for Kenney. His best choice depends on what Imamura does. The only Nash equilibrium for this game is where Imamura chooses the northern route and Kenney concentrates his search on the northern route. To check this, notice that if Imamura goes North, then Kenney gets an expected two days of bombing if he (Kenney) chooses North and only one day if he (Kenney) chooses South. Furthermore, if Kenney concentrates on the north, Imamura is indifferent between going north or south, since he can be expected to be bombed for two days either way. Therefore if both choose "North," then neither has an incentive to act differently. You can verify that for any other combination of choices, one admiral or the other would want to change. As things actually worked out, Imamura chose the Northern route and Kenney concentrated his search on the North. After about a day's search the Americans found the Japanese fleet and inflicted heavy damage on it.*

Some two-player games do not have a "Nash equilibrium in pure strategies." But every two-player game of the kind we look at has a Nash equilibrium in mixed strategies. If a player is indifferent between two strategies, then he is also willing to choose randomly between them. Sometimes this is just what is needed to give an equilibrium.

Example: A soccer player has been awarded a free kick. The only player allowed to defend against his kick is the opposing team's goalie. The kicker has two possible strategies. He can try to kick the ball into the right side of the goal or he can try to kick the ball into the left side of the

---

* This example is discussed in Luce and Raiffa's *Games and Decisions*, John Wiley, 1957 or Dover, 1989. We recommend this book to anyone interested in reading more about game theory.

goal. There is not time for the goalie to determine where the ball is going before he must commit himself by jumping either to the left or to the right side of the net. Let us suppose that if the goalie guesses correctly where the kicker is going to kick, then the goalie always stops the ball. The kicker has a very accurate shot to the right side of the net, but is not so good at shooting left. If he kicks to the right side of the net and the goalie jumps left, the kicker will always score. But the kicker kicks to the left side of the net and the goalie jumps to the right, then the kicker will score only half of the time. This story leads us to the following payoff matrix, where if the kicker makes the goal, the kicker gets a payoff of 1 and the goalie a payoff of 0 and if the kicker does not make the goal, the goalie gets a payoff of 1 and the kicker a payoff of 0.

The Free Kick

		Kicker	
		Kick Left	Kick Right
Goalie	Jump Left	1, 0	0, 1
	Jump Right	.5, .5	1, 0

This game has no Nash equilibrium in pure strategies. There is no combination of actions taken with certainty such that each is making the best response to the other's action. The goalie always wants to be where the kicker is kicking and the kicker always wants to kick where the goalie isn't. What we can find is a pair of equilibrium mixed strategies.

In this mixed strategy equilibrium each player's strategy is chosen at random. The kicker will be willing to choose a random strategy only if the expected payoff is the same from kicking to either side. The payoffs from kicking to the right and to the left depend on what the goalie is doing. Let π_G be the probability that the goalie will jump left and $1 - \pi_G$ be the probability that he will jump right. The kicker realizes that if he kicks to the right, he will score when the goalie goes left and he will not score when the goalie goes right. The expected payoff to the kicker if he kicks to the right is therefore just π_G. If the kicker kicks to the left, then the only way that he can score is if the goalie jumps right. This happens with probability $1 - \pi_G$. Even then he will only score half the time. So the expected payoff to the kicker from kicking left is $.5(1 - \pi_G)$. These two expected payoffs are equalized when $\pi_G = .5(1 - \pi_G)$. If we solve this equation, we find $\pi_G = 1/3$. This has to be the probability that the goalie goes left in a mixed strategy equilibrium.

Now let us find the probability that the kicker kicks left in a mixed strategy equilibrium. In equilibrium, the kicker's probability π_K of kicking left must be such that the goalie gets the same expected payoff from jumping left as from jumping right. The expected payoff to the goalie is the probability that the kicker does *not* score. If the goalie jumps left, then the kicker will not score if he kicks left and will score if he kicks right, so the expected payoff to the goalie from going left is π_K. If the goalie jumps right, then with probability $(1 - \pi_K)$, the kicker will kick right and the goalie will stop the ball. When the kicker is kicking to the undefended left side of the net, he only makes it half the time, so if the goalie jumps right, the probability that the kicker kicks left and makes the kick is only $.5\pi_K$. Therefore the expected payoff to the goalie from jumping right is $(1 - \pi_K) + .5\pi_K = 1 - .5\pi_K$. Equalizing the payoff to the goalie from jumping left or jumping right requires $\pi_K = 1 - .5\pi_K$. Solving this equation we find that in the equilibrium mixed strategy, $\pi_K = 2/3$.

27.1 (0) Perhaps you have wondered what it could mean that "the meek shall inherit the earth." While we don't claim this is always the case, here is an example where it is true. In a famous experiment, two psychologists* put two pigs—a little one and a big one—into a pen that had a lever at one end and a trough at the other end. When the lever was pressed, a serving of pigfeed would appear in a trough at the other end of the pen. If the little pig would press the lever, then the big pig would eat all of the pigfeed and keep the little pig from getting any. If the big pig pressed the lever, there would be time for the little pig to get some of the pigfeed before the big pig was able to run to the trough and push him away.

Let us represent this situation by a game, in which each pig has two possible strategies. One strategy is Press the Lever. The other strategy is Wait at the Trough. If both pigs wait at the trough, neither gets any feed. If both pigs press the lever, the big pig gets all of the feed and the little pig gets a poke in the ribs. If the little pig presses the lever and the big pig waits at the trough, the big pig gets all of the feed and the little pig has to watch in frustration. If the big pig presses the lever and the little pig waits at the trough, then the little pig is able to eat 2/3 of the feed before the big pig is able to push him away. The payoffs are as follows. (These numbers are just made up, but their relative sizes are consistent with the payoffs in the Baldwin-Meese experiment.)

Big Pig–Little Pig

		Big Pig	
		Press	Wait
Little Pig	Press	−1, 10	−1, 10
	Wait	6, 4	0, 0

---

* Baldwin and Meese (1979), *Animal Behavior*, "Social Behavior in Pigs Studied by Means of Operant Conditioning."

(a) Is there a dominant strategy for the little pig?_____ Is there

a dominant strategy for the big pig?_____.

(b) Find a Nash equilibrium for this game. Does the game have more

than one Nash equilibrium?_____

_____ (Incidentally, while Baldwin and Meese
did not interpret this experiment as a game, the result they observed was
the result that would be predicted by Nash equilibrium.)

(c) Which pig gets more feed in Nash equilibrium?_____.

27.2 (0) Consider the following game matrix.

A Game Matrix

		Player B	
		Left	Right
Player A	Top	a, b	c, d
	Bottom	e, f	g, h

(a) If (top, left) is a dominant strategy equilibrium, then we know that

$a >$_____ , $b >$_____ , _____ $> g$, and _____ $> h$.

(b) If (top, left) is a Nash equilibrium, then which of the above inequalities

must be satisfied?_____.

(c) If (top, left) is a dominant strategy equilibrium must it be a

Nash equilibrium? Why?_____

_____.

27.3 (1) This problem is based on an example developed by the biologist
John Maynard Smith to illustrate the uses of game theory in the theory
of evolution. Males of a certain species frequently come into conflict with
other males over the opportunity to mate with females. If a male runs
into a situation of conflict, he has two alternative "strategies." A male
can play "Hawk" in which case he will fight the other male until he either

wins or is badly hurt. Or he can play "Dove," in which case he makes a display of bravery but retreats if his opponent starts to fight. If an animal plays Hawk and meets another male who is playing Hawk, they both are seriously injured in battle. If he is playing Hawk and meets an animal who is playing Dove, the Hawk gets to mate with the female and the Dove slinks off to celibate contemplation. If an animal is playing Dove and meets another Dove, they both strut around for a while. Eventually the female either chooses one of them or gets bored and wanders off. The expected payoffs to each of two males in a single encounter depend on which strategy each adopts. These payoffs are depicted in the box below.

The Hawk-Dove Game

		Animal B	
		Hawk	Dove
Animal A	Hawk	−5, −5	10, 0
	Dove	0, 10	4, 4

(a) Now while wandering through the forest, a male will encounter many conflict situations of this type. Suppose that he cannot tell in advance whether another animal that he meets will behave like a Hawk or like a Dove. The payoff to adopting either strategy oneself depends on the proportion of the other guys that are Hawks and the proportion that are Doves. For example, suppose all of the other males in the forest act like Doves. Any male that acted like a Hawk would find that his rival always retreated and would therefore enjoy a payoff of _____ on every encounter. If a male acted like a Dove when all other males acted like Doves, he would receive an average payoff of_____.

(b) If strategies that are more profitable tend to be chosen over strategies that are less profitable, explain why there cannot be an equilibrium in which all males act like Doves._____

_____.

(c) If all the other males acted like Hawks, then a male who adopted the Hawk strategy would be sure to encounter another Hawk and would get a payoff of _____ If instead, this male adopted the Dove strategy, he would again be sure to encounter a Hawk, but his payoff would be_____.

(d) Explain why there could not be an equilibrium where all of the animals acted like Hawks._____

_____.

(e) Since there is not an equilibrium in which everybody chooses the same strategy, we might ask whether there might be an equilibrium in which some fraction of the males chose the Hawk strategy and the rest chose the Dove strategy. Suppose that the fraction of a large male population that chooses the Hawk strategy is p. Then if one acts like a Hawk, the fraction of one's encounters in which he meets another Hawk is about p and the fraction of one's encounters in which he meets a Dove is about $1 - p$. Therefore the average payoff to being a Hawk when the fraction of Hawks in the population is p, must be $p \times (-5) + (1 - p) \times 10 = 10 - 15p$. Similarly, if one acts like a Dove, the probability of meeting a Hawk is about p and the probability of meeting another Dove is about $(1 - p)$. Therefore the average payoff to being a Dove when the proportion of

Hawks in the population is p will be_____.

(f) Write an equation that states that when the proportion of the population that acts like Hawks is p, the payoff to Hawks is the same as the

payoffs to Doves._____.

(g) Solve this equation for the value of p such that at this value Hawks

do exactly as well as Doves. This requires that $p =$_____.

(h) On the axes below, use blue ink to graph the average payoff to the strategy Dove when the proportion of the male population who are Hawks is p. Use red ink to graph the average payoff to the strategy, Hawk, when the proportion of the male population who are Hawks is p. Label the equilibrium proportion in your diagram by E.

Payoff

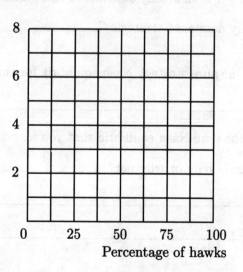

Percentage of hawks

(i) If the proportion of Hawks is slightly greater than E, which strategy does better? _____ If the proportion of Hawks is slightly less than E, which strategy does better? _____ If the more profitable strategy tends to be adopted more frequently in future plays, then if the strategy proportions are out of equilibrium, will changes tend to move the proportions back toward equilibrium or further away from equilibrium?

_____.

27.4 (1) Evangeline and Gabriel met at a freshman mixer. They want desperately to meet each other again, but they forgot to exchange names or phone numbers when they met the first time. There are two possible strategies available for each of them. These are Go to the Big Party or Stay Home and Study. They will surely meet if they both go to the party, and they will surely not otherwise. The payoff to meeting is 1,000 for each of them. The payoff to not meeting is zero for both of them. The payoffs are described by the matrix below.

Close Encounters of the Second Kind

		Gabriel	
		Go to Party	Stay Home
Evangeline	Go to Party	1000, 1000	0, 0
	Stay Home	0, 0	0, 0

(a) A strategy is said to be a weakly dominant strategy for a player if the payoff from using this strategy is *at least as high* as the payoff from using any other strategy. Is there any outcome in this game where both players are using weakly dominant strategies?_____

(b) Find all of the pure-strategy Nash equilibria for this game._____

_____.

(c) Do any of the pure Nash equilibria that you found seem more reasonable than others? Why or why not?_____

_____

_____.

(d) Let us change the game a little bit. Evangeline and Gabriel are still desperate to find each other. But now there are two parties that they might go to. There is a little party at which they would be sure to meet if they both went there and a huge party at which they might never see each other. The expected payoff to each of them is 1,000 if they both go to the little party. Since there is only a 50-50 chance that they would find each other at the huge party, the expected payoff to each of them is only 500. If they go to different parties, the payoff to both of them is zero. The payoff matrix for this game is:

More Close Encounters

		Gabriel	
		Little Party	Big Party
Evangeline	Little Party	1000, 1000	0, 0
	Big Party	0, 0	500, 500

(e) Does this game have a dominant strategy equilibrium?_____ What are the two Nash equilibria in pure strategies?_____

_____.

(f) One of the Nash equilibria is Pareto superior to the other. Suppose that each person thought that there was some slight chance that the other would go to the little party. Would that be enough to convince them both to attend the little party?_____ Can you think of any reason why the Pareto superior equilibrium might emerge if both players understand the game matrix, if both know that the other understands it, and each knows that the other knows that he or she understands the game matrix?_____

_____.

27.5 (1) This is a famous game, known to game theorists as "The Battle of the Sexes." The story goes like this. Two people, let us call them Michelle and Roger, although they greatly enjoy each other's company, have very different tastes in entertainment. Roger's tastes run to ladies' mud wrestling, while Michelle prefers Italian opera. They are planning their entertainment activities for next Saturday night. For each of them, there are two possible actions, go to the wrestling match or go to the opera. Roger would be happiest if both of them went to see mud wrestling.

His second choice would be for both of them to go to the opera. Michelle would prefer if both went to the opera. Her second choice would be that they both went to see the mud wrestling. They both think that the worst outcome would be that they didn't agree on where to go. If this happened, they would both stay home and sulk.

Battle of the Sexes

		Michelle	
		Wrestling	Opera
Roger	Wrestling	2, 1	0, 0
	Opera	0, 0	1, 2

(a) Is the sum of the payoffs to Michelle and Roger constant over all outcomes?_____ (If so, this is called a "zero-sum game." Otherwise it is called a "nonzero sum game.") Does this game have a dominant strategy equilibrium?_____.

(b) Find two Nash equilibria in pure strategies for this game._____

_____

(c) Find a Nash equilibrium in mixed strategies._____

_____

_____.

27.6 (1) This is another famous two-person game, known to game theorists as "Chicken." Two teenagers in souped-up cars drive toward each other at great speed. The first one to swerve out of the road is "chicken." The best thing that can happen to you is that the other guy swerves and you don't. Then you are the hero and the other guy is the chicken. If you both swerve, you are both chickens. If neither swerves, you both end up in the hospital. A payoff matrix for a chicken-type game is the following.

Chicken

		Leroy	
		Swerve	Don't Swerve
Joe Bob	Swerve	1, 1	1, 2
	Don't Swerve	2, 1	0, 0

(a) Does this game have a dominant strategy?_____ What are the

two Nash equilibria in pure strategies?_____

_____.

(b) Find a Nash equilibrium in mixed strategies for this game._____

_____.

27.7 (0) I propose the following game: I flip a coin, and while it is in the air, you call either heads or tails. If you call the coin correctly, you get to keep the coin. Suppose that you know that the coin always comes up heads. What is the best strategy for you to pursue?_____.

(a) Suppose that the coin is unbalanced and comes up heads 80% of the

time and tails 20% of the time. Now what is your best strategy?_____

_____.

(b) What if the coin comes up heads 50% of the time and tails 50% of

the time? What is your best strategy?_____

_____.

(c) Now, suppose that I am able to choose the type of coin that I will toss (where a coin's type is the probability that it comes up heads), and that you will know my choice. What type of coin should I choose to minimize

my losses?_____.

(d) What is the Nash mixed strategy equilibrium for this game? (It may help to recognize that a lot of symmetry exists in the game.)_____

_____.

27.8 (0) Ned and Ruth love to play "Hide and Seek." It is a simple game, but it continues to amuse. It goes like this. Ruth hides upstairs or downstairs. Ned can look upstairs or downstairs but not in both places. If he finds Ruth, Ned gets one scoop of ice cream and Ruth gets none. If he does not find Ruth, Ruth gets one scoop of ice cream and Ned gets none. Fill in the payoffs in the matrix below.

Hide and Seek

		Ruth	
		Upstairs	Downstairs
Ned	Upstairs		
	Downstairs		

(a) Is this a zero-sum game? _____ What are the Nash equilibria in pure strategies?_____.

(b) Find a Nash equilibrium in mixed strategies for this game?_____

_____.

(c) After years of playing this game, Ned and Ruth thought of a way to liven it up a little. Now if Ned finds Ruth upstairs, he gets two scoops of ice cream, but if he finds her downstairs, he gets one scoop. If Ned finds Ruth, she gets no ice cream, but if he doesn't find her, she gets one scoop. Fill in the payoffs in the graph below.

Advanced Hide and Seek

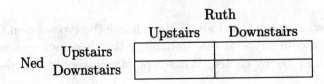

		Ruth	
		Upstairs	Downstairs
Ned	Upstairs		
	Downstairs		

(d) Are there any Nash equilibria in pure strategies? _____ What mixed

strategy equilibrium can you find? _____

_____ If both use equilibrium strategies,

what fraction of the time will Ned find Ruth?_____.

27.9 (1) Let's have another look at the soccer example that was discussed in the introduction to this section. But this time, we will generalize the payoff matrix just a little bit. Suppose the payoff matrix is as follows.

The Free Kick

		Kicker	
		Kick Left	Kick Right
Goalie	Jump Left	1, 0	0, 1
	Jump Right	1-p, p	1, 0

Now the probability that the kicker will score if he kicks to the left and the goalie jumps to the right is p. We will want to see how the equilibrium probabilities change as p changes.

(a) If the goalie jumps left with probability π_G, then if the kicker kicks

right, his probability of scoring is_____.

(b) If the goalie jumps left with probability π_G, then if the kicker kicks

left, his probability of scoring is_____.

(c) Find the probability π_G that makes kicking left and kicking right lead to the same probability of scoring for the kicker. (Your answer will be a

function of p.)_____.

(d) If the kicker kicks left with probability π_K, then if the goalie jumps

left, the probability that the kicker will *not* score is_____.

(e) If the kicker kicks left with probability π_K, then if the goalie jumps

right, the probability that the kicker will *not* score is_____

_____.

(f) Find the probability π_K that makes the payoff to the goalie equal from jumping left or jumping right._____.

(g) The variable p tells us how good the kicker is at kicking the ball into the left side of the goal when it is undefended. As p increases, does the equilibrium probability that the kicker kicks to the left increase or decrease?_____ Explain why this happens in a way that even a TV sports announcer might understand._____

_____

_____.

27.10 (0) Maynard's Cross is a trendy bistro that specializes in carpaccio and other uncooked substances. Most people who come to Maynard's come to see and be seen by other people of the kind who come to Maynard's. There is, however, a hard core of 10 customers per evening who come for the carpaccio and don't care how many other people come. The number of additional customers who appear at Maynard's depends on how many people they expect to see. In particular, if people expect that the number of customers at Maynard's in an evening will be X, then the number of people who actually come to Maynard's is $Y = 10 + .8X$. In equilibrium, it must be true that the number of people who actually attend the restaurant is equal to the number who are expected to attend.

(a) What two simultaneous equations must you solve to find the equilibrium attendance at Maynard's?_____.

(b) What is the equilibrium nightly attendance?_____.

(c) On the following axes, draw the lines that represent each of the two equations you mentioned in Part (a). Label the equilibrium attendance level.

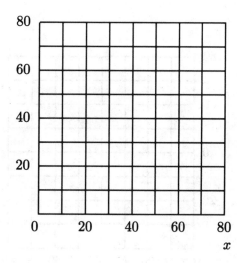

(d) Suppose that one additional carpaccio enthusiast moves to the area. Like the other 10, he eats at Maynard's every night no matter how many others eat there. Write down the new equations determining attendance at Maynard's and solve for the new equilibrium number of customers.

_____.

(e) Use a different color ink to draw a new line representing the equation that changed. How many additional customers did the new steady

customer attract (besides himself)?_____.

(f) Suppose that everyone bases expectations about tonight's attendance on last night's attendance and that last night's attendance is public knowledge. Then $X_t = Y_{t-1}$, where X_t is expected attendance on day t and Y_{t-1} is actual attendance on day $t-1$. At any time t, $Y_t = 10 + .8X_t$. Suppose that on the first night that Maynard's is open, attendance is 20.

What will be attendance on the second night?_____.

(g) What will be the attendance on the third night?_____.

(h) Attendance will tend toward some limiting value. What is it?_____.

27.11 (0) Yogi's Bar and Grill is frequented by unsociable types who hate crowds. If Yogi's regular customers expect that the crowd at Yogi's will be X, then the number of people who show up at Yogi's, Y, will be the larger of the two numbers, $120 - 2X$ and 0. Thus $Y = \max\{120 - 2X, 0\}$.

(a) Solve for the equilibrium attendance at Yogi's. Draw a diagram depicting this equilibrium on the axes below.

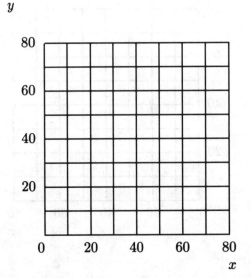

(b) Suppose that people expect the number of customers on any given night to be the same as the number on the previous night. Suppose that 50 customers show up at Yogi's on the first day of business. How many

will show up on the second day? _____ The third day? _____ The

fourth day? _____ The fifth day? _____ The ninety-ninth day?

_____ The hundredth day?_____.

(c) What would you say is wrong with this model if at least some of Yogi's customers have memory spans of more than a day or two?

_____

_____

_____

27.12 (2) Economic ideas and equilibrium analysis have many fascinating applications in biology. Popular discussions of natural selection and biological fitness often take it for granted that animal traits are selected for the benefit of the species. Modern thinking in biology emphasizes that individuals (or strictly speaking, genes) are the unit of selection. A mutant gene that induces an animal to behave in such a way as to help the species at the expense of the individuals that carry that gene will soon be eliminated, no matter how beneficial that behavior is to the species.

A good illustration is a paper in the *Journal of Theoretical Biology*, 1979, by H. J. Brockmann, A. Grafen, and R. Dawkins, called "Evolutionarily Stable Nesting Strategy in a Digger Wasp." They maintain that natural selection results in behavioral strategies that maximize an individual animal's expected rate of reproduction over the course of its lifetime. According to the authors, "Time is the currency which an animal spends."

Females of the digger wasp *Sphex ichneumoneus* nest in underground burrows. Some of these wasps dig their own burrows. After she has dug her burrow, a wasp goes out to the fields and hunts katydids. These she stores in her burrow to be used as food for her offspring when they hatch. When she has accumulated several katydids, she lays a single egg in the burrow, closes off the food chamber, and starts the process over again. But digging burrows and catching katydids is time-consuming. An alternative strategy for a female wasp is to sneak into somebody else's burrow while she is out hunting katydids. This happens frequently in digger wasp colonies. A wasp will enter a burrow that has been dug by another wasp and partially stocked with katydids. The invader will start catching katydids, herself, to add to the stock. When the founder and the invader finally meet, they fight. The loser of the fight goes away and never comes back. The winner gets to lay her egg in the nest.

Since some wasps dig their own burrows and some invade burrows begun by others, it is likely that we are observing a biological equilibrium in which each strategy is as effective a way for a wasp to use its time for producing offspring as the other. If one strategy were more effective than the other, then we would expect that a gene that led wasps to behave in the more effective way would prosper at the expense of genes that led them to behave in a less effective way.

Suppose the average nesting episode takes 5 days for a wasp that digs its own burrow and tries to stock it with katydids. Suppose that the average nesting episode takes only 4 days for invaders. Suppose that when they meet, half the time the founder of the nest wins the fight and half the time the invader wins. Let D be the number of wasps that dig their own burrows and let I be the number of wasps that invade the burrows of others. The fraction of the digging wasps that are invaded will be about $\frac{5}{4}\frac{I}{D}$. (Assume for the time being that $\frac{5}{4}\frac{I}{D} < 1$.) Half of the diggers who are invaded will win their fight and get to keep their burrows. The fraction of digging wasps who lose their burrows to other wasps is then $\frac{1}{2}\frac{5}{4}\frac{I}{D} = \frac{5}{8}\frac{I}{D}$. Assume also that all the wasps who are not invaded by other wasps will successfully stock their burrows and lay their eggs.

(a) Then the fraction of the digging wasps who do not lose their burrows

is just_____.

Therefore over a period of 40 days, a wasp who dug her own burrow every time would have 8 nesting episodes. Her expected number of

successes would be_____.

(b) In 40 days, a wasp who chose to invade every time she had a chance would have time for 10 invasions. Assuming that she is successful half the

time on average, her expected number of successes would be_____.

Write an equation that expresses the condition that wasps who always dig their own burrows do exactly as well as wasps who always invade burrows dug by others._____.

(c) The equation you have just written should contain the expression $\frac{I}{D}$. Solve for the numerical value of $\frac{I}{D}$ that just equates the expected number of successes for diggers and invaders. The answer is_____.

(d) But there is a problem here: the equilibrium we found doesn't appear to be stable. On the axes below, use blue ink to graph the expected number of successes in a 40-day period for wasps that dig their own burrows every time where the number of successes is a function of $\frac{I}{D}$. Use black ink to graph the expected number of successes in a 40-day period for invaders. Notice that this number is the same for all values of $\frac{I}{D}$. Label the point where these two lines cross and notice that this is equilibrium. Just to the right of the crossing, where $\frac{I}{D}$ is just a little bit bigger than the equilibrium value, which line is higher, the blue or the black? _____ At this level of $\frac{I}{D}$, which is the more effective strategy for any individual wasp? _____ Suppose that if one strategy is more effective than the other, the proportion of wasps adopting the more effective one increases. If, after being in equilibrium, the population got joggled just a little to the right of equilibrium, would the proportions of diggers and invaders return toward equilibrium or move further away?_____.

(e) The authors noticed this likely instability and cast around for possible changes in the model that would lead to stability. They observed that an invading wasp does help to stock the burrow with katydids. This may save the founder some time. If founders win their battles often enough and get enough help with katydids from invaders, it might be that the expected number of eggs that a founder gets to lay is an increasing rather

than a decreasing function of the number of invaders. On the axes below, show an equilibrium in which digging one's own burrow is an increasingly effective strategy as $\frac{I}{D}$ increases and in which the payoff to invading is constant over all ratios of $\frac{I}{D}$. Is this equilibrium stable?_____.

Exchange

Introduction. The *Edgeworth box* is a thing of beauty. An amazing amount of information is displayed with a few lines, points and curves. In fact one can use an Edgeworth box to tell just about everything there is to say about the case of two traders dealing in two commodities. Economists know that the real world has more than two people and more than two commodities. But it turns out that the insights gained from this model extend nicely to the case of many traders and many commodities. So for the purpose of introducing the subject of exchange equilibrium, the Edgeworth box is exactly the right tool. We will start you out with an example of two gardeners engaged in trade.

Example: Alice and Byron consume two goods, camelias and dahlias. Alice has 16 camelias and 4 dahlias. Byron has 8 camelias and 8 dahlias. They consume no other goods, and they trade only with each other. To describe the possible allocations of flowers, we first draw a box whose width is the total number of camelias and whose height is the total number of dahlias that Alice and Byron have between them. The width of the box is therefore $16 + 8 = 24$ and the height of the box is $4 + 8 = 12$.

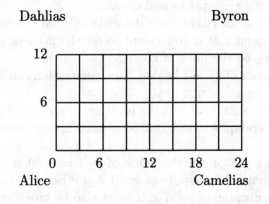

Any feasible allocation of flowers between Alice and Byron is fully described by a single point in the box. Consider, for example, the allocation where Alice gets the bundle $(15, 9)$ and Byron gets the bundle $(9, 3)$. This allocation is represented by the point $A = (15, 9)$ in the Edgeworth box. The distance 15 from A to the left side of the box is the number of camelias for Alice and the distance 9 from A to the bottom of the box is the number of dahlias for Alice. This point also determines Byron's consumption of camelias and dahlias. The distance 9 from A to the right side of the box is the total number of camelias consumed by Byron, and the distance from A to the top of the box is the number of dahlias consumed by Byron. Since the width of the box is the total supply of camelias and the height of the box is the total supply of dahlias, these conventions ensure that any point in the box represents a feasible allocation of the total supply of camelias and dahlias.

It is useful to mark the initial allocation on the Edgeworth box. In this case, the initial allocation is represented by the point $E = (16, 4)$. Now suppose that Alice's utility function is $U(c, d) = c + 2d$ and Byron's utility funtion is $U(c, d) = cd$. Alice's indifference curves will be straight lines with slope $-1/2$. The indifference curve that passes through her initial endowment, for example, will be a line that runs from the point $(24, 0)$ to the point $(0, 12)$. Since Byron has Cobb-Douglas utility, his indifference curves will be rectangular hyperbolas, but since quantities for Byron are measured from the upper right corner of the box, these indifference curves will be flipped over as in the diagram.

The *Pareto set* or *contract curve* is the set of points where Alice's indifference curves are tangent to Byron's. There will be tangency if the slopes are the same. The slope of Alice's indifference curve at any point is $-1/2$. The slope of Byron's indifference curve depends on his consumption of the two goods. When Byron is consuming the bundle (c_B, d_B), the slope of his indifference curve is equal to his marginal rate of substitution, which is $-d_B/c_B$. Therefore Alice's and Byron's indifference curves will nuzzle up in a nice tangency whenever $-d_B/c_B = -1/2$. So the Pareto set in this example is just the diagonal of the Edgeworth box.

Some problems ask you to find a competitive equilibrium. For an economy with two goods, the following procedure is often a good way a to calculate equilibrium prices and quantities.

- Since demand for either good depends only on the ratio of prices of good 1 to good 2, it is convenient to set the price of good 1 equal to 1 and let p_2 be the price of good 2.
- With the price of good 1 held at 1, calculate each consumer's demand for good 2 as a function of p_2.
- Write an equation that sets the total amount of good 2 demanded by all consumers equal to the total of all participants' initial endowments of good 2 .
- Solve this equation for the value of p_2 that makes the demand for good 2 equal to the supply of good 2. (When the supply of good 2 equals the demand of good 2, it must also be true that the supply of good 1 equals the demand for good 1.)
- Plug this price into the demand functions to determine quantities.

Example: Frank's utility function is $U(x_1, x_2) = x_1 x_2$ and Maggie's is $U(x_1, x_2) = \min\{x_1, x_2\}$. Frank's initial endowment is 0 units of good 1 and 10 units of good 2. Maggie's initial endowment is 20 units of good 1 and 5 units of good 2. Let us find a competitive equilibrium for Maggie and Frank.

Set $p_1 = 1$ and find Frank's and Maggie's demand functions for good 2 as a function of p_2. Using the techniques learned in Chapter 6, we find that Frank's demand function for good 2 is $m/2p_2$, where m is his income. Since Frank's initial endowment is 0 units of good 1 and 10 units of good 2, his income is $10p_2$. Therefore Frank's demand for good 2 is $10p_2/2p_2 = 5$. Since goods 1 and 2 are perfect complements for Maggie, she will choose to consume where $x_1 = x_2$. This fact, together with her budget constraint implies that Maggie's demand function for good 2 is

$m/(1 + p_2)$. Since her endowment is 20 units of good 1 and 5 units of good 2, her income is $20 + 5p_2$. Therefore at price p_2, Maggie's demand is $(20 + 5p_2)/(1 + p_2)$. Frank's demand plus Maggie's demand for good 2 adds up to $5 + (20 + 5p_2)/(1 + p_2)$. The total supply of good 2 is Frank's 10 unit endowment plus Maggie's 5 unit endowment, which adds to 15 units. Therefore demand equals supply when

$$5 + \frac{(20 + 5p_2)}{(1 + p_2)} = 15.$$

Solving this equation, one finds that the equilibrium price is $p_2 = 2$. At the equilibrium price, Frank will demand 5 units of good 2 and Maggie will demand 10 units of good 2.

28.1 (0) Morris Zapp and Philip Swallow consume wine and books. Morris has an initial endowment of 60 books and 10 bottles of wine. Philip has an initial endowment of 20 books and 30 bottles of wine. They have no other assets and make no trades with anyone other than each other. For Morris, a book and a bottle of wine are perfect substitutes. His utility function is $U(b, w) = b + w$, where b is the number of books he consumes and w is the number of bottles of wine he consumes. Philip's preferences are more subtle and convex. He has a Cobb-Douglas utility function, $U(b, w) = bw$. In the Edgeworth box below, Morris's consumption is measured from the lower left, and Philip's is measured from the upper right corner of the box.

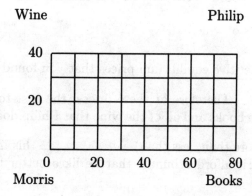

(a) On this diagram, mark the initial endowment and label it E. Use red ink to draw Morris Zapp's indifference curve that passes through his initial endowment. Use blue ink to draw in Philip Swallow's indifference curve that passes through his initial endowment. (Remember that quantities for Philip are measured from the upper right corner, so his indifference curves are "Phlipped over.")

(b) At any Pareto optimum, where both people consume some of each good, it must be that their marginal rates of substitution are equal. No matter what he consumes, Morris's marginal rate of substitution is equal

to _____ When Philip consumes the bundle, (b_P, w_P), his MRS is

_____ Therefore every Pareto optimal allocation where both

consume positive amounts of both goods satisfies the equation _____

_____ Use black ink on the diagram above to draw the locus of Pareto optimal allocations.

(c) At a competitive equilibrium, it will have to be that Morris consumes some books and some wine. But in order for him to do so, it must be that

the ratio of the price of wine to the price of books is _____ Therefore we know that if we make books the *numeraire*, then the price of wine in

competitive equilibrium must be_____.

(d) At the equilibrium prices you found in the last part of the question,

what is the value of Philip Swallow's initial endowment?_____   At

these prices, Philip will choose to consume _____ books and _____ bottles of wine. If Morris Zapp consumes all of the books and all of the

wine that Philip doesn't consume, he will consume _____ books and

_____ bottles of wine.

(e) At the competitive equilibrium prices that you found above, Morris's

income is _____ Therefore at these prices, the cost to Morris of consuming all of the books and all of the wine that Philip doesn't consume is

(the same as, more than, less than) _____ his income. At these prices, can Morris afford a bundle that he likes better than the bundle

$(55, 15)$?_____

(f) Suppose that an economy consisted of 1,000 people just like Morris and 1,000 people just like Philip. Each of the Morris types has the same endowment and the same tastes as Morris. Each of the Philip types has the same endowment and tastes as Philip. Would the prices that you found to be equilibrium prices for Morris and Philip still be competitive

equilibrium prices?_____   If each of the Morris types and each of the Philip types behaved in the same way as Morris and Philip did above,

would supply equal demand for both wine and books?_____.

28.2 (0) Consider a small exchange economy with two consumers, Astrid and Birger, and two commodities, herring and cheese. Astrid's initial endowment is 4 units of herring and 1 unit of cheese. Birger's initial endowment has no herring and 7 units of cheese. Astrid's utility function is $U(H_A, C_A) = H_A C_A$. Birger is a more inflexible person. His utility function is $U(H_B, C_B) = \min\{H_B, C_B\}$. (Here H_A and C_A are the amounts of herring and cheese for Astrid, and H_B and C_B are amounts of herring and cheese for Birger.)

(a) Draw an Edgeworth box, showing the initial allocation and sketching in a few indifference curves. Measure Astrid's consumption from the lower left and Birger's from the upper right. In your Edgeworth box, draw two different indifference curves for each person, using blue ink for Astrid's and red ink for Birger's.

(b) Use black ink to show the locus of Pareto optimal allocations. (Hint: Since Birger is kinky, calculus won't help much here. But notice that because of the rigidity of the proportions in which he demands the two goods, it would be inefficient to give Birger a positive amount of either good if he had less than that amount of the other good. What does that tell you about where the Pareto efficient locus has

to be?)_____

_____.

28.3 (0) Dean Foster Z. Interface and Professor J. Fetid Nightsoil exchange bromides and platitudes. Dean Interface's utility function is

$$U_I(B_I, P_I) = B_I + 2\sqrt{P_I}.$$

Professor Nightsoil's utility function is

$$U_N(B_N, P_N) = B_N + 4\sqrt{P_N}.$$

Dean Interface's initial endowment is 8 bromides and 12 platitudes. Professor Nightsoil's initial endowment is 8 bromides and 4 platitudes.

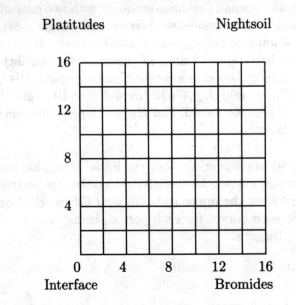

Platitudes   Nightsoil

Interface   Bromides

(a) If Dean Interface consumes P_I platitudes and B_I bromides, his marginal rate of substitution will be _____ If Professor Nightsoil consumes P_N platitudes and B_N bromides, his marginal rate of substitution will be_____.

(b) On the contract curve, Dean Interface's marginal rate of substitution equals Professor Nightsoil's. Write an equation that states this condition.

_____ This equation is especially simple because each person's marginal rate of substitution depends only on his consumption of platitudes and not on his consumption of bromides.

(c) From this equation we see that $P_I/P_N =$ _____ at all points on the contract curve. This gives us one equation in the two unknowns P_I and P_N.

(d) But we also know that along the contract curve it must be that $P_I + P_N =$_____ , since the total consumption of platitudes must equal the total endowment of platitudes.

(e) Solving these two equations in two unknowns, we find that everywhere on the contract curve, P_I and P_N are constant and equal to _____

and_____.

(f) In the Edgeworth box, label the initial endowment with the letter *E*. Dean Interface has thick gray penciled indifference curves. Professor Nightsoil has red indifference curves. Draw a few of these in the Edgeworth box you made. Use blue ink to show the locus of Pareto optimal points. The contract curve is a (vertical, horizontal, diagonal) _____

_____ line in the Edgeworth box.

(g) Find the competitive equilibrium prices and quantities. You know what the prices have to be at competitive equilibrium because you know what the marginal rates of substitution have to be at every Pareto optimum. _____.

28.4 (0) A little exchange economy contains just two consumers, named Ken and Barbie, and two commodities, quiche and wine. Ken's initial endowment is 3 units of quiche and 2 units of wine. Barbie's initial endowment is 1 unit of quiche and 6 units of wine. Ken and Barbie have identical utility functions. We write Ken's utility function as, $U(Q_K, W_K) = Q_K W_K$ and Barbie's utility function as $U(Q_B, W_B) = Q_B W_B$, where Q_K and W_K are the amounts of quiche and wine for Ken and Q_B and W_B are amounts of quiche and wine for Barbie.

(a) Draw an Edgeworth box below, to illustrate this situation. Put quiche on the horizontal axis and wine on the vertical axis. Measure goods for Ken from the lower left corner of the box and goods for Barbie from the upper right corner of the box. (Be sure that you make the length of the box equal to the total supply of quiche and the height equal to the total supply of wine.) Locate the initial allocation in your box, and label it W. On the sides of the box, label the quantities of quiche and wine for each of the two consumers in the initial endowment.

(b) Use blue ink to draw an indifference curve for Ken that shows allocations in which his utility is 6. Use red ink to draw an indifference curve for Barbie that shows allocations in which her utility is 6.

(c) At any Pareto optimal allocation where both consume some of each good, Ken's marginal rate of substitution between quiche and wine must equal Barbie's. Write an equation that states this condition in terms of the consumptions of each good by each person._____.

(d) On your graph, show the locus of points that are Pareto efficient. (Hint: If two people must each consume two goods in the same proportions as each other, and if together they must consume twice as much wine as quiche, what must those proportions be?)

(e) In this example, at any Pareto efficient allocation, where both persons consume both goods, the slope of Ken's indifference curve will be _____

_____ Therefore, since we know that competitive equilibrium must be Pareto efficient, we know that at a competitive equilibrium, $p_Q/p_W =$

_____.

(f) What must be Ken's consumption bundle in competitive equilibrium?

_____ How about Barbie's consumption bundle? _____

_____ (Hint: You found competitive equilibrium prices above. You know Ken's initial endowment and you know the equilibrium prices. In equilibrium Ken's income will be the value of his endowment at competitive prices. Knowing his income and the prices, you can compute his demand in competitive equilibrium. Having solved for Ken's consumption and knowing that total consumption by Ken and Barbie equals the sum of their endowments, it should be easy to find Barbie's consumption.)

(g) On the Edgeworth box for Ken and Barbie, draw in the competitive equilibrium allocation and draw Ken's competitive budget line (with black ink).

28.5 (0) Linus Straight's utility function is $U(a, b) = a + 2b$, where a is his consumption of apples and b is his consumption of bananas. Lucy Kink's utility function is $U(a, b) = \min\{a, 2b\}$. Lucy initially has 12 apples and no bananas. Linus initially has 12 bananas and no apples. In the Edgeworth box below, goods for Lucy are measured from the upper right corner of the box and goods for Linus are measured from the lower left corner. Label the initial endowment point on the graph with the letter E. Draw two of Lucy's indifference curves in red ink and two of Linus's indifference curves in blue ink. Use black ink to draw a line through all of the Pareto optimal allocations.

Bananas   Lucy

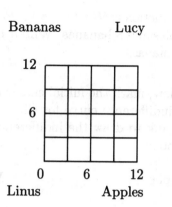

0   6   12

Linus   Apples

(a) In this economy, in competitive equilibrium, the ratio of the price of

apples to the price of bananas must be_____.

(b) Let a_S be Linus's consumption of apples and let b_S be his consumption
of bananas. At competititive equilibrium, Linus's consumption will have

to satisfy the budget constraint, a_s+_____ $b_S =$_____ This gives us
one equation in two unknowns. To find a second equation, consider Lucy's
consumption. In competitive equilibrium, total consumption of apples
equals the total supply of apples and total consumption of bananas equals
the total supply of bananas. Therefore Lucy will consume $12 - a_s$ apples

and _____ $-b_s$ bananas. At a competitive equilibrium, Lucy will be
consuming at one of her kink points. The kinks occur at bundles where

Lucy consumes _____ apples for every banana that she consumes.

Therefore we know that $\frac{12-a_s}{12-b_s} =$_____.

(c) You can solve the two equations that you found above to find the
quantities of apples and bananas consumed in competitive equilibrium

by Linus and Lucy. Linus will consume _____ units of apples and

_____ units of bananas. Lucy will consume _____ units of apples
and 3 units of bananas.

28.6 (0) Consider a pure exchange economy with two consumers and
two goods. At some given Pareto efficient allocation it is known that both
consumers are consuming both goods and that consumer A has a marginal
rate of substitution between the two goods of 2. What is consumer B's

marginal rate of substitution between these two goods?_____.

28.7 (0) Charlotte loves apples and hates bananas. Her utility function
is $U(a, b) = a - \frac{1}{4}b^2$, where a is the number of apples she consumes and
b is the number of bananas she consumes. Wilbur likes both apples and

bananas. His utility function is $U(a, b) = a + 2\sqrt{b}$. Charlotte has an initial endowment of no apples and 8 bananas. Wilbur has an initial endowment of 16 apples and 8 bananas.

(a) On the graph below, mark the initial endowment and label it E. Use red ink to draw the indifference curve for Charlotte that passes through this point. Use blue ink to draw the indifference curve for Wilbur that passes through this point.

Apples   Wilbur

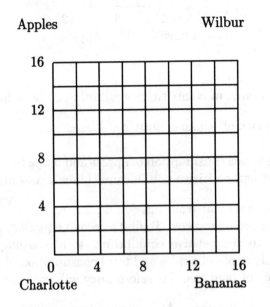

0   4   8   12   16

Charlotte   Bananas

(b) If Charlotte hates bananas and Wilbur likes them, how many bananas can Charlotte be consuming at a Pareto optimal allocation?_____ On the graph above, use black ink to mark the locus of Pareto optimal allocations of apples and bananas between Charlotte and Wilbur.

(c) We know that a competitive equilibrium allocation must be Pareto optimal and the total consumption of each good must equal the total supply, so we know that at a competitive equilibrium, Wilbur must be consuming _____ bananas. If Wilbur is consuming this number of bananas, his marginal utility for bananas will be _____ and his marginal utility of apples will be _____ If apples are the *numeraire*, then the only price of bananas at which he will want to consume exactly 16 bananas is _____ In competitive equilibrium, for the Charlotte-Wilbur economy, Wilbur will consume _____ bananas and _____ apples and Charlotte will consume _____ bananas and _____ apples.

28.8 (0)   Mutt and Jeff have 8 cups of milk and 8 cups of juice to divide between themselves. Each has the same utility function given by $u(m, j) = \max\{m, j\}$, where m is the amount of milk and j is the amount of juice that each has. That is, each of them cares only about the larger of the two amounts of liquid that he has and is indifferent to the liquid of which he has the smaller amount.

(a) Sketch an Edgeworth box for Mutt and Jeff. Use blue ink to show a couple of indifference curves for each. Use red ink to show the locus of Pareto optimal allocations. (Hint: Look for boundary solutions.)

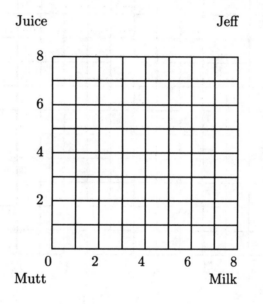

28.9 (1)   Remember Tommy Twit from Chapter 3. Tommy is happiest when he has 8 cookies and 4 glasses of milk per day and his indifference curves are concentric circles centered around (8,4). Tommy's mother, Mrs. Twit, has strong views on nutrition. She believes that too much of anything is as bad as too little. She believes that the perfect diet for Tommy would be 7 glasses of milk and 2 cookies per day. In her view, a diet is healthier the smaller is the sum of the absolute values of the differences between the amounts of each food consumed and the ideal amounts. For example, if Tommy eats 6 cookies and drinks 6 glasses of milk, Mrs. Twit believes that he has 4 too many cookies and 1 too few glasses of milk, so the sum of the absolute values of the differences from her ideal amounts is 5. On the axes below, use blue ink to draw the locus of combinations that Mrs. Twit thinks are exactly as good for Tommy as $(6, 6)$. Also, use red ink to draw the locus of combinations that she thinks is just as good as $(8, 4)$. On the same graph, use red ink to draw an indifference "curve" representing the locus of combinations that Tommy likes just as well as 7 cookies and 8 glasses of milk.

Milk

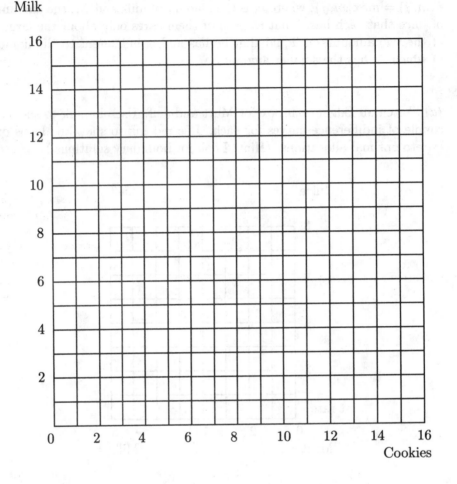

(a) On the graph, shade in the area consisting of combinations of cookies and milk that both Tommy and his mother agree are better than 7 cookies and 8 glasses of milk, where "better" for Mrs. Twit means she thinks it is healthier, and where "better" for Tommy means he likes it better.

(b) Use black ink to sketch the locus of "Pareto optimal" bundles of cookies and milk for Tommy. In this situation, a bundle is Pareto optimal if any bundle that Tommy prefers to this bundle is a bundle that Mrs. Twit thinks is worse for him. The locus of Pareto optimal points that you just drew should consist of two line segments. These run from the point

(8,4) to the point _____ and from that point to the point_____.

28.10 (2) This problem combines equilibrium analysis with some of the things you learned in the chapter on intertemporal choice. It concerns the economics of saving and the life cycle on an imaginary planet where life is short and simple. In advanced courses in macroeconomics, you would study more complicated versions of this model that build in more earthly realism. For the present, this simple model gives you a good idea of how the analysis must go.

On the planet Drongo there is just one commodity, cake, and two time periods. There are two kinds of creatures, "old" and "young." Old creatures have an income of I units of cake in period 1 and no income in period 2. Young creatures have no income in period 1 and an income of I^* units of cake in period 2. There are N_1 old creatures and N_2 young creatures. The consumption bundles of interest to creatures are pairs (c_1, c_2), where c_1 is cake in period 1 and c_2 is cake in period 2. All creatures, old and young, have identical utility functions, representing preferences over cake in the two periods. This utility function is $U(c_1, c_2) = c_1^a c_2^{1-a}$, where a is a number such that $0 \leq a \leq 1$.

(a) If current cake is taken to be the *numeraire*, (that is, its price is set at 1), write an expression for the present value of a consumption bundle (c_1, c_2). _____ Write down the present value of income for old creatures _____ and for young creatures_____ The budget line for any creature is determined by the condition that the present value of its consumption bundle equals the present value of its income. Write down this budget equation for old creatures: _____

_____ and for young creatures:_____.

(b) If the interest rate is r, write down an expression for an old creature's demand for cake in period 1 _____ and in period 2 _____

_____ Write an expression for a young creature's demand for cake in period 1 _____ and in period 2_____ (Hint: If its budget line is $p_1 c_1 + p_2 c_2 = W$ and its utility function is of the form proposed above, then a creature's demand function for good 1 is $c_1 = aW/p$ and demand for good 2 is $c_2 = (1-a)W/p$.) If the interest rate is zero, how much cake would a young creature choose in period 1?

_____ For what value of a would it choose the same amount in each period if the interest rate is zero?_____ If $a = .55$, what would r have to be in order that young creatures would want to consume the same amount in each period_____.

(c) The total supply of cake in period 1 equals the total cake earnings of all old creatures, since young creatures earn no cake in this period. There are N_1 old creatures and each earns I units of cake, so this total is $N_1 I$. Similarly, the total supply of cake in period 2 equals the total amount earned by young creatures. This amount is_____.

(d) At the equilibrium interest rate, the total demand of creatures for period-1 cake must equal total supply of period-1 cake, and similarly the demand for period-2 cake must equal supply. If the interest rate is r, then the demand for period 1 cake by each old creature is _____ and the demand for period-1 cake by each young creature is _____ Since there are N_1 old creatures and N_2 young creatures, the total demand for period-1 cake at interest rate r is_____.

(e) Using the results of the last section, write an equation that sets the demand for period-1 cake equal to the supply. _____

_____ Write a general expression for the equilibrium value of r, given N_1, N_2, I, and I^*. _____ Solve this equation for the special case when $N_1 = N_2$ and $I = I^*$ and $a = 11/21$._____.

(f) In the special case at the end of the last section, show that the interest rate that equalizes supply and demand for period-1 cake will also equalize supply and demand for period-2 cake. (This illustrates Walras' law.)_____

_____

_____.

Production

Introduction. In this section we explore economywide production possibility sets. We pay special attention to the principle of comparative advantage. The principle is simply that efficiency suggests that people should specialize according to their *relative* abilities in different activities rather than absolute abilities.

Example: For simplicity, let us imagine an island with only two people on it, both of them farmers. They do not trade with the outside world. Farmer A has 100 acres and is able to grow two crops, wheat and hay. Each acre of his land that he plants to wheat will give him 50 bushels of wheat. Each acre of his land that he plants to hay will give him 2 tons of hay. Farmer B also has 100 acres, but his land is not so good. Each acre of his land yields only 20 bushels of wheat and only 1 ton of hay. Notice that, although farmer A's land is better for *both* wheat and hay, farmer B's land has *comparative* advantage in the production of hay. This is true because the ratio of tons of hay to bushels of wheat per acre 2/50=.04 for Farmer A and 1/20=.05 for Farmer B. Farmer A, on the other hand, has comparative advantage in the production of wheat, since the ratio of bushels of wheat to tons of hay is 50/2=25 for Farmer A and 20/1=20 for Farmer B. The efficient way to arrange production is to have Farmer A "specialize" in wheat and farmer B "specialize" in hay. If Farmer A devotes all of his land to wheat and Farmer B devotes all of his land to hay, then total wheat production will be 5,000 bushels and total hay production will be 100 tons. Suppose that they decide to produce only 4,000 bushels of wheat. Given that they are going to produce 4,000 bushels of wheat, the most hay they can possibly produce together will be obtained if Farmer A devotes 80 acres to wheat and 20 acres to hay while Farmer B devotes all of his land to hay. Suppose that they decide to produce 6,000 bushels of wheat. Then they will get the most hay possible given that they are producing 6,000 bushels of wheat if Farmer A puts all of his land into wheat and Farmer B puts 50 acres into wheat and the remaining 50 acres into hay.

29.1 (0) Tip and Spot finally got into college. Tip can write term papers at the rate of 10 pages per hour and solve workbook problems at the rate of 3 per hour. Spot can write term papers at the rate of 6 pages per hour and solve workbook problems at the rate of 2 per hour. Which of these two has comparative advantage in solving workbook problems?

Problems

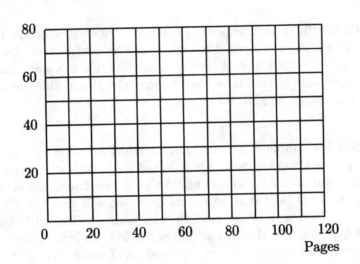

(a) Tip and Spot each work 6 hours a day. They decide to work together and to produce a combination of term papers and workbook problems that lies on their joint production possibility frontier. On the above graph plot their joint production possibility frontier. If they produce less than

60 pages of term papers, then _____ will write all of the term papers.

If they produce more than _____ pages of term papers, then _____

will continue to specialize in writing term papers and _____ will also write some term papers.

29.2 (0) Robinson Crusoe has decided that he will spend exactly 8 hours a day gathering food. He can either spend this time gathering coconuts or catching fish. He can catch 1 fish per hour and he can gather 2 coconuts per hour. On the graph above, show Robinson's production possibility frontier between fish and coconuts per day. Write an equation for the line

segment that is Robinson's production possibility frontier._____

_____.

Coconuts

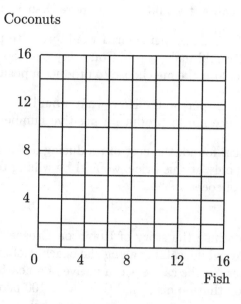

(a) Robinson's utility function is $U(F,C) = FC$, where F is his daily fish consumption and C is his daily coconut consumption. On the graph above, sketch the indifference curve that gives Robinson a utility of 4, and also sketch the indifference curve that gives him a utility of 8. How

many fish will Robinson choose to catch per day?_____ How many

coconuts will he collect? _____ (Hint: Robinson will choose a bundle that maximizes his utility subject to the constraint that the bundle lies in his production possibility set. But for this technology, his production possibility set looks just like a budget set.)

(b) Suppose Robinson is not isolated on an island in the Pacific, but is retired and lives next to a grocery store where he can buy either fish or coconuts. If fish cost $1 per fish, how much would coconuts have to cost in order that he would choose to consume twice as many coconuts as

fish? _____ Suppose that a social planner decided that he wanted Robinson to consume 4 fish and 8 coconuts per day. He could do this by setting the price of fish equal to $1, the price of coconuts equal to

_____ and giving Robinson a daily income of $_____ .

(c) Back on his island, Robinson has little else to do, so he pretends that he is running a competitive firm that produces fish and coconuts. He wonders, "What would the price have to be to make me do just what I am actually doing? Let's assume that fish are the *numeraire* and have a price of $1. And let's pretend that I have access to a competitive labor market where I can hire as much labor as I want at some given wage. There is a constant returns to scale technology. An hour's labor produces one fish

or 2 coconuts. At wages above $_____ per hour, I wouldn't produce any fish at all, because it would cost me more than $1 to produce a fish.

At wages below $_____ per hour, I would want to produce infinitely many fish since I would make a profit on every one. So the only possible wage rate that would make me choose to produce a positive finite amount

of fish is $_____ per hour. Now what would the price of coconuts have to be to induce me to produce a positive number of coconuts. At

the wage rate I just found, the cost of producing a coconut is _____ At this price and only at this price, would I be willing to produce a finite positive number of coconuts."

29.3 (0) We continue the story of Robinson Crusoe from the previous problem. One day, while walking along the beach, Robinson Crusoe saw a canoe in the water. In the canoe was a native of a nearby island. The native told Robinson that on his island there were 100 people and that they all lived on fish and coconuts. The native said that on his island, it takes two hours to catch a fish and 1 hour to find a coconut. The native said that there was a competitive economy on his island and that fish were the *numeraire*. The price of coconuts on the neighboring island must have been

_____ The native offered to trade with Crusoe at these prices. "I will trade you either fish for coconuts or coconuts for fish at the exchange rate

of _____ coconuts for a fish," said he. "But you will have to give me 1 fish as payment for rowing over to your island." Would Robinson gain

by trading with him?_____ If so, would he buy fish and sell coconuts or

*vice versa?*_____

_____.

(a) Several days later, Robinson saw another canoe in the water on the other side of his island. In this canoe was a native who came from a different island. The native reported that on his island, one could catch only 1 fish for every 4 hours of fishing and that it takes 1 hour to find a coconut. This island also had a competitive economy. The native offered to trade with Robinson at the same exchange rate that prevailed on his own island, but said that he would have to have 2 fish in return for rowing between the islands. If Robinson decides to trade with this

island, he choose to produce only _____ and would get his _____

_____ from the other island. On the graph below, use black ink to draw Robinson's production possibility frontier if he doesn't trade and use blue ink to show the bundles he can afford if he chooses to trade and specializes appropriately. Remember to take away 2 fish to pay the trader.

Coconuts

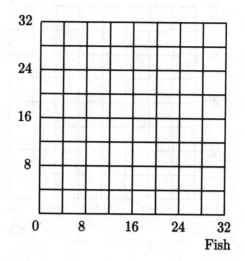

(b) Write an equation for Crusoe's "budget line" if he specializes appropriately and trades with the second trader. If he does this, what bundle

will he choose to consume?_____ Does he like this bundle

better than the bundle he would have if he didn't trade?_____.

29.4 (0) The Isle of Veritas has made it illegal to trade with the outside world. Only two commodities are consumed on this island, milk and wheat. On the north side of the island are 40 farms. Each of these farms can produce any combination of non-negative amounts of milk and wheat that satisfies the equation $m = 60 - 6w$. On the south side of the island are 60 farms. Each of these farms can produce any combination of non-negative amounts of milk and wheat that satisfies the equation $m = 40 - 2w$. The economy is in competitive equilibrium and 1 unit of wheat exchanges for 4 units of milk.

(a) On the diagram below, use black ink to draw the production possibility set for a typical farmer from the *north* side of the island. Given the equilibrium prices, will this farmer specialize in milk, specialize in wheat,

or produce both goods? _____ Use blue ink to draw the budget that he faces in his role as a consumer if he makes the optimal choice of what to produce.

Milk

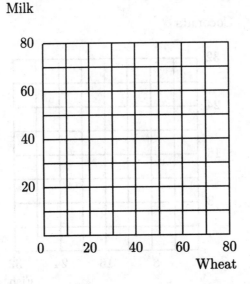

(b) On the diagram below, use black ink to draw the production possibility set for a typical farmer from the *south* side of the island. Given the equilibrium prices, will this farmer specialize in milk, specialize in wheat,

or produce both goods? _____ Use blue ink to draw the budget that he faces in his role as a consumer if he makes the optimal choice of what to produce.

Milk

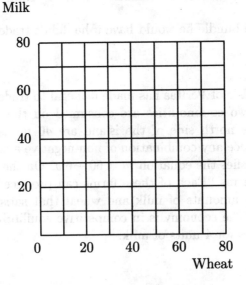

(c) Suppose that peaceful Viking traders discover Veritas and offer to exchange either wheat for milk or milk for wheat at an exchange rate of 1 unit of wheat for 3 units of milk. If the Isle of Veritas allows free trade with the Vikings, then this will be the new price ratio on the island. At

this price ratio, would either type of farmer change his output?_____.

(d) On the first of the two graphs above, use red ink to draw the budget for northern farmers if free trade is allowed and the farmers make the right choice of what to produce. On the second of the two graphs, use red ink to draw the budget for southern farmers if free trade is allowed and the farmers make the right choice of what to produce.

(e) The council of elders of Veritas will meet to vote on whether to accept the Viking offer. The elders from the north end of the island get 40 votes and the elders from the south end get 60 votes. Assuming that everyone votes in the selfish interest of his end of the island,

how will the northerners vote?_____ How will the southern-

ers vote?_____ How is it that you can make a definite answer to the last two questions without knowing anything about the farmers's

consumption preferences?_____

_____.

(f) Suppose that instead of offering to make exchanges at the rate of 1 unit of wheat for 3 units of milk, the Vikings had offered to trade at the price of 1 unit of wheat for 1 unit of milk and *vice versa*. Would either type

of farmer change his output? _____

_____ Use pencil to sketch the budget line for each kind of farmer at these prices if he makes the right production decision. How will

the northerners vote now?_____ How will the southerners vote

now?_____ Explain why it is that your answer to one of the last two questions has to be "it depends."

_____.

29.5 (0) Recall our friends the Mungoans of Chapter 2. They have a strange two-currency system consisting of Blue Money and Red Money. Originally, there were two prices for everything, a blue-money price and a red-money price. The blue-money prices are 1 bcu per unit of ambrosia and 1 bcu per unit of bubble gum. The red-money prices are 2 rcu's per unit of ambrosia and 4 rcu's per unit of bubble gum.

(a) Harold has a blue income of 9 and a red income of 24. If it has to pay in *both* currencies for any purchase, draw its budget set in the graph below. (Hint: You answered this question a few months ago.)

Bubble gum

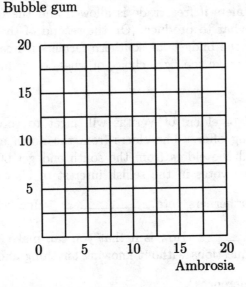

Ambrosia

(b) The Free Choice party campaigns on a platform that Mungoans should be allowed to purchase goods at *either* the blue-money price or the red-money price, whichever they prefer. We want to construct Harold's budget set if this reform is instituted. To begin with, how much bubble gum could Harold consume if it spent all of its blue money and its red money

on bubble gum?_____.

(c) How much ambrosia could it consume if it spent all of its blue money

and all of its red money on ambrosia?_____.

(d) If Harold were spending all of its money of both colors on bubble gum and it decided to purchase a little bit of ambrosia, which currency would

it use?_____.

(e) How much ambrosia could it buy before it ran out of that color money?

_____.

(f) What would be the slope of this budget line before it ran out of that

kind of money?_____.

(g) If Harold were spending all of its money of both colors on ambrosia and it decided to purchase a little bit of bubble gum, which currency

would it use?_____.

(h) How much bubble gum could it buy before it ran out of that color money?_____.

(i) What would be the slope of this budget line before it ran out of that kind of money?_____.

(j) Use your answers to the above questions to draw Harold's budget set in the above graph if it could purchase bubble gum and ambrosia using either currency.

Welfare

Introduction. Here you will look at various ways of determining social preferences. You will check to see which of the Arrow axioms for aggregating individual preferences are satisfied by these welfare relations. You will also try to find optimal allocations for some given social welfare functions. The method for solving these last problems is analogous to solving for a consumer's optimal bundle given preferences and a budget constraint. Two hints. Remember that for a Pareto optimal allocation inside the Edgeworth box, the consumers' marginal rates of substitution will be equal. Also, in a "fair allocation", neither consumer prefers the other consumer's bundle to his own.

Example: A social planner has decided that she wants to allocate income between 2 people so as to maximize $\sqrt{Y_1} + \sqrt{Y_2}$ where Y_i is the amount of income that person i gets. Suppose that the planner has a fixed amount of money to allocate and that she can enforce any income distribution such that $Y_1 + Y_2 = W$, where W is some fixed amount. This planner would have ordinary convex indifference curves between Y_1 and Y_2 and a "budget constraint" where the "price" of income for each person is 1. Therefore the planner would set her marginal rate of substitution between income for the two people equal to the relative price which is 1. When you solve this, you will find that she sets $Y_1 = Y_2 = W/2$. Suppose instead that it is "more expensive" for the planner to give money to person 1 than to person 2. (Perhaps person 1 is forgetful and loses money, or perhaps person 1 is frequently robbed.) For example, suppose that the planner's budget is $2Y_1 + Y_2 = W$. Then the planner maximizes $\sqrt{Y_1} + \sqrt{Y_2}$ subject to $2Y_1 + Y_2 = W$. Setting her MRS equal to the price ratio, we find that $\frac{\sqrt{Y_2}}{\sqrt{Y_1}} = 2$. So $Y_2 = 4Y_1$. Therefore the planner makes $Y_1 = W/5$ and $Y_2 = 4W/5$.

30.1 (2) One possible method of determining a social preference relation is the *Borda count*, also known as rank-order voting. Each voter is asked to rank all of the alternatives. If there are 10 alternatives, you give your first choice a 1, your second choice a 2, and so on. The voters' scores for each alternative are then added over all voters. The total score for an alternative is called its Borda count. For any two alternatives, x and y, if the Borda count of x is smaller than or the same as the Borda count for y, then x is "socially at least as good as" y. Suppose that there are a finite number of alternatives to choose from and that every individual has complete, reflexive, and transitive preferences. For the time being, let us also suppose that individuals are never indifferent between any two different alternatives but always prefer one to the other.

(a) Is the social preference ordering defined in this way complete?_____

_____ Reflexive?_____ Transitive?_____.

(b) If everyone prefers x to y, will the Borda count rank x as socially preferred to y? Explain your answer._____

_____

_____.

(c) Suppose that there are two voters and three candidates, x, y, and
z. Suppose that Voter 1 ranks the candidates, x first, z second, and y
third. Suppose that Voter 2 ranks the candidates, y first, x second, and
z third. What is the Borda count for x?_____ For y?_____ For

z?_____ Now suppose that it is discovered that candidate z once
lifted a beagle by the ears. Voter 1, who has rather large ears himself,
is appalled and changes his ranking to x first, y second, z third. Voter
2, who picks up his own children by the ears, is favorably impressed and
changes his ranking to y first, z second, x third. Now what is the Borda

count for x?_____ For y?_____ For z?_____.

(d) Does the social preference relation defined by the Borda count have
the property that social preferences between x and y depend only on
how people rank x versus y and not on how they rank other alter-

natives? Explain._____

_____

_____.

30.2 (2) Suppose the utility possibility frontier for two individuals is
given by $U_A + 2U_B = 200$. On the graph below, plot the utility frontier.

U_B

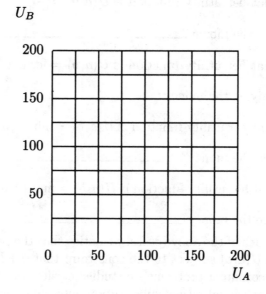

U_A

(a) In order to maximize a "Nietzschean social welfare function," $W(U_A, U_B) = \max\{U_A, U_B\}$, on the utility possibility frontier shown above, one would set U_A equal to _____ and U_B equal to _____.

(b) If instead we use a Rawlsian criterion, $W(U_A, U_B) = \min\{U_A, U_B\}$, then the social welfare function is maximized on the above utility possibility frontier where U_A equals _____ and U_B equals_____.

(c) Suppose that social welfare is given by $W(U_A, U_B) = U_A^{1/2} U_B^{1/2}$. In this case, with the above utility possibility frontier, social welfare is maximized where U_A equals _____ and U_B is _____ (Hint: You might want to think about the similarities between this maximization problem and the consumer's maximization problem with a Cobb-Douglas utility function.)

(d) Show the three social maxima on the above graph. Use black ink to draw a Nietzschean isowelfare line through the Nietzschean maximum. Use red ink to draw a Rawlsian isowelfare line through the Rawlsian maximum. Use blue ink to draw a Cobb-Douglas isowelfare line through the Cobb-Douglas maximum.

30.3 (2) A parent has two children named A and B and she loves both of them equally. She has a total of \$1,000 to give to them.

(a) The parent's utility function is $U(a, b) = \sqrt{a} + \sqrt{b}$, where a is the amount of money she gives to A and b is the amount of money she gives to B. How will she choose to divide the money?_____.

(b) Suppose that her utility function is $U(a,b) = -\frac{1}{a} - \frac{1}{b}$. How will she choose to divide the money?_____.

(c) Suppose that her utility function is $U(a,b) = \log a + \log b$. How will she choose to divide the money?_____.

(d) Suppose that her utility function is $U(a,b) = \min\{a,b\}$. How will she choose to divide the money?_____.

(e) Suppose that her utility function is $U(a,b) = \max\{a,b\}$. How will she choose to divide the money?_____.

(Hint: In each of the above cases, we notice that the parent's problem is to maximize $U(a,b)$ subject to the constraint that $a + b = 1,000$. This is just like the consumer problems we studied earlier. It must be that the parent sets her marginal rate of substitution between a and b equal to one since it costs the same to give money to each child.)

(f) Suppose that her utility function is $U(a,b) = a^2 + b^2$. How will she choose to divide the money between her children? Explain why she doesn't set her marginal rate of substitution equal to

1 in this case._____

_____.

30.4 (2) In the previous problem, suppose that A is a much more efficient shopper than B so that A is able to get twice as much consumption goods as B can for every dollar that he spends. Let a be the amount of consumption goods that A gets and b the amount that B gets. We will measure consumption goods so that one unit of consumption goods costs \$1 for A and \$2 for B. Thus the parent's budget constraint is $a + 2b = 1,000$.

(a) If the mother's utility function is $U(a,b) = a + b$, which child will get more money?_____ Which child will consume more goods?_____.

(b) If the mother's utility function is $U(a,b) = a \times b$, which child will get more money?_____ Which child will get to consume more?_____.

(c) If the mother's utility function is $U(a,b) = -\frac{1}{a} - \frac{1}{b}$, which child will get more money?_____ Which child will get to consume more?_____.

(d) If the mother's utility function is $U(a, b) = \max\{a, b\}$, which child will get more money?_____ Which child will get to consume more?

_____.

(e) If the mother's utility function is $U(a, b) = \min\{a, b\}$, which child will get more money?_____ Which child will get to consume more?

_____.

Calculus **30.5 (1)** Norton and Ralph have a utility possibility frontier that is given by the following equation, $U_R + U_N^2 = 100$ (where R and N signify Ralph and Norton respectively).

(a) If we set Norton's utility to zero, what is the highest possible utility Ralph can achieve? _____ If we set Ralph's utility to zero, what is the best Norton can do?_____.

(b) Plot the utility possibility frontier on the graph below.

Ralph's utility

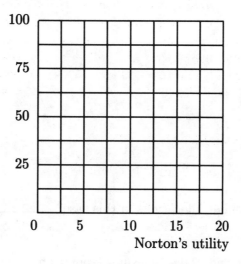

Norton's utility

(c) Derive an equation for the slope of the above utility possibility curve.

_____.

(d) Both Ralph and Norton believe that the ideal allocation is given by maximizing an appropriate social welfare function. Ralph thinks that $U_R = 75$, $U_N = 5$ is the best distribution of welfare, and presents the maximization solution to a weighted-sum-of-the-utilities social welfare function that confirms this observation. What was Ralph's social welfare function? (Hint: What is the slope of Ralph's social welfare function?)

_____.

(e) Norton, on the other hand, believes that $U_R = 19$, $U_N = 9$ is the best distribution. What is the social welfare function Norton presents?

_____.

30.6 (2) Roger and Gordon have identical utility functions, $U(x, y) = x^2 + y^2$. There are 10 units of x and 10 units of y to be divided between them. Roger has blue indifference curves. Gordon has red ones.

(a) Draw an Edgeworth box showing some of their indifference curves and mark the Pareto optimal allocations with black ink. (Hint: Notice that the indifference curves are nonconvex.)

(b) What are the fair allocations in this case?_____.

30.7 (2) Paul and David consume apples and oranges. Paul's utility function is $U_P(A_P, O_P) = 2A_P + O_P$ and David's utility function is $U_D(A_D, O_D) = A_D + 2O_D$, where A_P and A_D are apple consumption for Paul and David and O_P and O_D are orange consumption for Paul and David. There are a total of 12 apples and 12 oranges to divide between Paul and David. Paul has blue indifference curves. David has red ones. Draw an Edgeworth box showing some of their indifference curves. Mark the Pareto optimal allocations on your graph.

(a) Write one inequality that says that Paul likes his own bundle as well as he likes David's and write another inequality that says that David likes his own bundle as well as he likes Paul's._____

_____.

(b) Use the fact that at feasible allocations, $A_P + A_D = 12$ and $O_P + O_D = 12$ to eliminate A_D and O_D from the first of these equations. Write the resulting inequality involving only the variables A_P and O_P. Now in your Edgeworth box, use blue ink to shade in all of the allocations such that

Paul prefers his own allocation to David's._____.

(c) Use a procedure similar to that you used above to find the allocations where David prefers his own bundle to Paul's. Describe these points with

an inequality and shade them in on your diagram with red ink._____

_____.

(d) On your Edgeworth box, mark the fair allocations.

30.8 (3) Romeo loves Juliet and Juliet loves Romeo. Besides love, they consume only one good, spaghetti. Romeo likes spaghetti, but he also likes Juliet to be happy and he knows that spaghetti makes her happy. Juliet likes spaghetti, but she also likes Romeo to be happy and she knows that spaghetti makes Romeo happy. Romeo's utility function is $U_R(S_R, S_J) = S_R^a S_J^{1-a}$ and Juliet's utility function is $U_J(S_J, S_R) = S_J^a S_R^{1-a}$, where S_J and S_R are the amount of spaghetti for Romeo and the amount of spaghetti for Juliet respectively. There is a total of 24 units of spaghetti to be divided between Romeo and Juliet.

(a) Suppose that $a = 2/3$. If Romeo got to allocate the 24 units of spaghetti exactly as he wanted to, how much would he give himself?

_____ How much would he give Juliet?_____ (Hint: Notice that this problem is formally just like the choice problem for a consumer with a Cobb-Douglas utility function choosing between two goods with a budget constraint. What is the budget constraint?)

(b) If Juliet got to allocate the spaghetti exactly as she wanted to, how much would she take for herself? _____ How much would she give Romeo?_____.

(c) What are the Pareto optimal allocations? (Hint: An allocation will not be Pareto optimal if both persons' utility will be increased by a gift from one to the other.)_____

_____.

(d) When we had to allocate two goods between two people, we drew an Edgeworth box with indifference curves in it. When we have just one good to allocate between two people, all we need is an "Edgeworth line" and instead of indifference curves, we will just have indifference dots. Draw an Edgeworth line below. Let the distance from left to right denote spaghetti for Romeo and the distance from right to left denote spaghetti for Juliet.

(e) On the Edgeworth line you drew above, show Romeo's favorite point and Juliet's favorite point.

(f) Suppose that $a = 1/3$. If Romeo got to allocate the spaghetti, how much would he choose for himself? _____ If Juliet got to allocate the spaghetti, how much would she choose for herself? _____ Label the "Edgeworth line" below, showing the two people's favorite points and the locus of Pareto optimal points.

(g) When $a = 1/3$, at the Pareto optimal allocations what do Romeo and Juliet disagree about?_____

_____

_____

_____.

30.9 (2) Hatfield and McCoy hate each other but love corn whiskey. Because they hate for each other to be happy, each wants the other to have less whiskey. Hatfield's utility function is $U_H(W_H, W_M) = W_H - W_M^2$ and McCoy's utility function is $U_M(W_M, W_H) = W_M - W_H^2$, where W_M is McCoy's daily whiskey consumption and W_H is Hatfield's daily whiskey consumption (both measured in quarts). There are 4 quarts of whiskey to be allocated.

(a) If McCoy got to allocate all of the whiskey, how would he allocate it?

_____ If Hatfield got to allocate all of the whiskey, how

would he allocate it?_____.

(b) If each of them gets 2 quarts of whiskey, what will the utility of each

of them be?_____ If a bear spilled 2 quarts of their whiskey and they divided the remaining 2 quarts equally between them, what would

the utility of each of them be?_____ If it is possible to throw away some of the whiskey, is it Pareto optimal for them each to consume 2 quarts of

whiskey?_____.

(c) If it is possible to throw away some whiskey and they must consume

equal amounts of whiskey, how much should they throw away?_____

_____.

Externalities

Introduction. When there are externalities, the outcome from independently chosen actions is typically not Pareto efficient. In these exercises, you explore the consequences of alternative mechanisms and institutional arrangements for dealing with externalities.

Example: A large factory pumps its waste into a nearby lake. The lake is also used for recreation by 1,000 people. Let X be the amount of waste that the firm pumps into the lake. Let Y_i be the number of hours per day that person i spends swimming and boating in the lake, and let C_i be the number of dollars that person i spends on consumption goods. If the firm pumps X units of waste into the lake, its profits will be $1,200X - 100X^2$. Consumers have identical utility functions, $U(Y_i, C_i, X) = C_i + 9Y_i - Y_i^2 - XY_i$, and identical incomes. Suppose that there are no restrictions on pumping waste into the lake and there is no charge to consumers for using the lake. Also, suppose that the factory and the consumers make their decisions independently. The factory will maximize its profits by choosing $X = 6$. (Set the derivative of profits with respect to X equal to zero.) When $X = 6$, each consumer maximizes utility by choosing $Y_i = 1.5$. (Set the derivative of utility with respect to Y_i equal to zero.) Notice from the utility functions that when each person is spending 1.5 hours a day in the lake, she will be willing to pay 1.5 dollars to reduce X by 1 unit. Since there are 1,000 people, the total amount that people will be willing to pay to reduce the amount of waste by 1 unit is $1,500. If the amount of waste is reduced from 6 to 5 units, the factory's profits will fall from $3,600 to $3,500. Evidently the consumers could afford to bribe the factory to reduce its waste production by 1 unit.

31.1 (2) The picturesque village of Horsehead, Massachusetts, lies on a bay that is inhabited by the delectable crustacean, *homarus americanus*, also known as the lobster. The town council of Horsehead issues permits to trap lobsters and is trying to determine how many permits to issue. The economics of the situation is this:

1. It costs $2,000 dollars a month to operate a lobster boat.

2. If there are x boats operating in Horsehead Bay, the total revenue from the lobster catch per month will be $f(x) = \$1,000(10x - x^2)$.

(a) In the graph below, plot the curves for average product, $AP(x) = f(x)/x$, and the marginal product, $MP(x) = 10,000 - 2,000x$. In the same graph, plot the line indicating the cost of operating a boat.

AP, MP

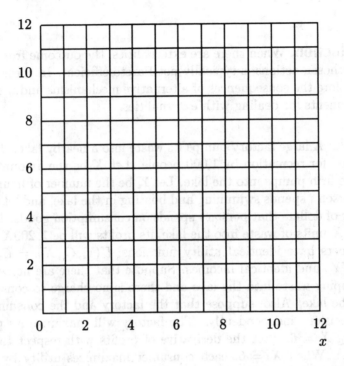

(b) If the permits are free of charge, how many boats will trap lobsters in Horsehead, Massachusetts? (Hint: How many boats must enter before there are zero profits?)_____.

(c) What number of boats maximizes total profits?_____

_____.

(d) If Horsehead, Massachusetts, wants to restrict the number of boats to the number that maximizes total profits, how much should it charge per month for a lobstering permit? (Hint: With a license fee of F thousand dollars per month, the marginal cost of operating a boat for a month would be $(2 + F)$ thousand dollars per month.)_____.

31.2 (2) Suppose that a honey farm is located next to an apple orchard and each acts as a competitive firm. Let the amount of apples produced be measured by A and the amount of honey produced be measured by H. The cost functions of the two firms are: $c_H(H) = H^2/100$ and $c_A(A) = A^2/100 - H$. The price of honey is \$2 and the price of apples is \$3.

(a) If the firms each operate independently, the equilibrium amount of honey produced will be _____ and the equilibrium amount of apples produced will be _____.

(b) Suppose that the honey and apple firms merged. What would be the profit-maximizing output of honey for the combined firm? _____

What would be the profit-maximizing amount of apples?_____.

(c) What is the socially efficient output of honey? _____ If the firms stayed separate, how much would honey production have to be subsidized to induce an efficient supply?_____.

31.3 (2) In El Carburetor, California, population 1,001, there is not much to do except to drive your car around town. Everybody in town is just like everybody else. While everybody likes to drive, everybody complains about the congestion, noise, and pollution caused by traffic. A typical resident's utility function is $U(m, d, h) = m + 16d - d^2 - 6h/1,000$, where m is the resident's daily consumption of Big Macs, d is the number of hours per day that he, himself, drives and h is the total amount of driving (measured in person-hours per day) done by all other residents of El Carburetor. The price of Big Macs is \$1 each. Every person in El Carburetor has an income of \$40 per day. To keep calculations simple, suppose it costs nothing to drive a car.

(a) If an individual believes that the amount of driving he does won't affect the amount that others drive, how many hours per day will he choose to drive? _____ (Hint: What value of d maximizes $U(m, d, h)$?)

(b) If everybody chooses his best d, then what is the total amount h of driving by other persons?_____.

(c) What will be the utility of each resident?_____.

(d) If everybody drives 6 hours a day, what will be the utility level of a typical resident of El Carburetor?_____.

(e) Suppose that the residents decided to pass a law restricting the total number of hours that anyone is allowed to drive. How much driving should everyone be allowed if the objective is to maximize the utility of the typical resident? (Hint: Rewrite the utility function, substituting $1,000d$ for h, and maximize with respect to d.)_____.

(f) The same objective could be achieved with a tax on driving. How much would the tax have to be per hour of driving? (Hint: This price would have to equal an individual's marginal rate of substitution between

driving and Big Macs when he is driving the "right" amount.)_____.

31.4 (3) Tom and Jerry are roommates. They spend a total of 80 hours a week together in their room. Tom likes loud music, even when he sleeps. His utility function is $U_T(C_T, M) = C_T + M$, where C_T is the number of cookies he eats per week and M is the number of hours of loud music per week that is played while he is in their room. Jerry hates all kinds of music. His utility function is $U(C_J, M) = C_J - M^2/12$. Every week, Tom and Jerry *each* get two dozen chocolate chip cookies sent from home. They have no other source of cookies. We can describe this situation with a box that looks like an Edgeworth box. The box has cookies on the horizontal axis and hours of music on the vertical axis. Since cookies are private goods, the number of cookies that Tom consumes per week plus the number that Jerry consumes per week must equal 48. But music in their room is a public good. Each must consume the same number of hours of music, whether he likes it or not. In the box, let the height of a point represent the total number of hours of music played in their room per week. Let the distance of the point from the left side of the box be "cookies for Tom" and the distance of the point from the right side of the box be "cookies for Jerry."

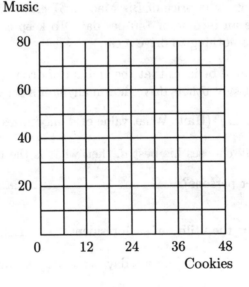

Music

(a) Suppose the dorm's policy is that you must have your roommate's permission to play music. The *initial endowment* in this case denotes the situation if Tom and Jerry make no deals. There would be no music, and each person would consume 2 dozen cookies a week. Mark this initial endowment on the box above with the label A. Use red ink to sketch the indifference curve for Tom that passes through this point, and use blue ink to sketch the indifference curve for Jerry that passes through

this point. [Hint: When you draw Jerry's indifference curve, remember two things: (1) He hates music, so he prefers lower points on the graph to higher ones. (2) Cookies for Jerry are measured from the right side of the box, so he prefers points that are toward the left side of the box to points that are toward the right.] Use blue ink to shade in the points representing situations that would make both roommates better off than they are at point A.

(b) Suppose, alternatively, that the dorm's policy is "rock-n-roll is good for the soul." You don't need your roommate's permission to play music. Then the *initial endowment* is one in which Tom plays music for all of the 80 hours per week that they are in the room together and where each consumes 2 dozen cookies per week. Mark this endowment point in the box above and label it B. Use red ink to sketch the indifference curve for Tom that passes through this point, and use blue ink to sketch the indifference curve for Jerry that passes through this point. Given the available resources, can *both* Tom and Jerry be made better off than they are at point B?_____.

Calculus **31.5 (0)** A clothing store and a jewelry store are located side by side in a small shopping mall. The number of customers who come to the shopping mall intending to shop at either store depends on the amount of money that the store spends on advertising per day. Each store also attracts some customers who came to shop at the neighboring store. If the clothing store spends $\$x_C$ per day on advertising, and the jeweler spends $\$x_J$ on advertising per day, then the total profits per day of the clothing store are $\Pi_C(x_C, x_J) = (60 + x_J)x_C - 2x_C^2$, and the total profits per day of the jewelry are $\Pi_J(x_C, x_J) = (105 + x_C)x_J - 2x_J^2$. (In each case, these are profits net of *all* costs, including advertising.)

(a) If each store believes that the other store's amount of advertising is independent of its own advertising expenditure, then we can find the equilibrium amount of advertising for each store by solving two equations in two unknowns. One of these equations says that the derivative of the clothing store's profits with respect to its own advertising is zero. The other equation requires that the derivative of the jeweler's profits with respect to its own advertising is zero. These two equations are written

as _____ . The equilibrium amounts of ad-

vertising are _____ and _____ . Profits of the clothing store

would be _____ and profits of the jeweler would be_____.

(b) The extra profit that the jeweler would get from an extra dollar's worth of advertising by the clothing store is approximately equal to the derivative of the jeweler's profits with respect to the clothing store's advertising expenditure. When the two stores are doing the equilibrium

amount of advertising that you calculated above, a dollar's worth of advertising by the clothing store would give the jeweler an extra profit of

about _____ and an extra dollar's worth of advertising by the jeweler

would give the clothing store an extra profit of about_____.

(c) Suppose that the owner of the clothing store knows the profit functions of both stores. She reasons to herself as follows. Suppose that I can decide how much advertising I will do before the jeweler decides what he is going to do. When I tell him what I am doing, he will have to adjust his behavior accordingly. I can calculate his reaction function to my choice of x_C, by setting the derivative of his profits with respect to his own advertising equal to zero and solving for his amount of advertising as a function of

my own advertising. When I do this, I find that $x_J =$_____ . If I substitute this value of x_J into my profit function and then choose x_C

to maximize my own profits, I will choose $x_C =$_____ and he will

choose $x_J =$_____ . In this case my profits will be _____

and his profits will be_____.

(d) Suppose that the clothing store and the jewelry store have the same profit functions as before but are owned by a single firm that chooses the amounts of advertising so as to maximize the sum of the two stores'

profits. The single firm would choose $x_C =$_____ and $x_J =$_____

_____ . Without calculating actual profits, can you determine whether total profits will be higher, lower, or the same as total profits would be

when they made their decisions independently? _____

_____ . How much would the total profits be?_____.

31.6 (2) The cottagers on the shores of Lake Invidious are an unsavory bunch. There are 100 of them, and they live in a circle around the lake. Each cottager has two neighbors, one on his right and one on his left. There is only one commodity, and they all consume it on their front lawns in full view of their two neighbors. Each cottager likes to consume the commodity but is very envious of consumption by the neighbor on his left. Curiously, nobody cares what the neighbor on his right is doing. In fact every consumer has a utility function $U(c, l) = c - l^2$, where c is his own consumption and l is consumption by his neighbor on the left. Suppose that each consumer owns 1 unit of the consumption good and consumes it.

(a) Calculate his utility level._____.

(b) Suppose that each consumer consumes only 3/4 of a unit. Will all individuals be better off or worse off?_____.

(c) What is the best possible consumption if all are to consume the same amount?_____.

(d) Suppose that everybody around the lake is consuming 1 unit. Can any two people make themselves both better off either by redistributing consumption between them or by throwing something away?_____.

(e) How about a group of three people?_____.

(f) How large is the smallest group that could cooperate to benefit all its members?_____.

31.7 (0) Jim and Tammy are partners in Business and in Life. As is all too common in this imperfect world, each has a little habit that annoys the other. Jim's habit, we will call activity X, and Tammy's habit, activity Y. Let x be the amount of activity X that Jim pursues and y be the amount of activity Y that Tammy pursues. Due to a series of unfortunate reverses, Jim and Tammy have a total of only \$1,000,000 a year to spend. Jim's utility function is $U_J = c_J + 500 \ln x - 10y$, where c_J is the money he spends per year on goods other than his habit, x is the number of units of activity X that he consumes per year, and y is the number of units of activity Y that Tammy consumes per year. Tammy's utility function is $U_T = c_T + 500 \ln y - 10x$, where c_T is the amount of money she spends on goods other than activity Y, y is the number of units of activity Y that she consumes, and x is the number of units of activity X that Jim consumes. Activity X costs \$20 per unit. Activity Y costs \$100 per unit.

(a) Suppose that Jim has a right to half their joint income and Tammy has a right to the other half. Suppose further that they make no bargains with each other about how much activities X and Y they will consume.

How much of activity X will Jim choose to consume?_____ How

much of activity Y will Tammy consume?_____.

(b) Because Jim and Tammy have quasilinear utility functions, their utility possibility frontier includes a straight line segment. Furthermore, this segment can be found by maximizing the sum of their utilities. Notice that

$$U_J(c_J, x, y) + U_T(c_T, x, y)$$
$$= c_J + 500 \ln x - 20y + c_T + 500 \ln y - 10x$$
$$= c_J + c_T + 500 \ln x - 10x + 500 \ln y - 10y.$$

But we know from the family budget constraint that $c_J + c_T = 1,000,000 - 20x - 100y$. Therefore we can write

$$U_J(c_J, x, y) + U_T(c_T, x, y) = 1,000,000 - 20x - 100y + 500\ln x - 10x +$$
$$500\ln y - 10y$$
$$= 1,000,000 + 500\ln x + 500\ln y - 30x - 110y.$$

Let us now choose x and y so as to maximize $U_J(c_J, x, y) + U_T(c_T, x, y)$. Setting the partial derivatives with respect to x and y equal to zero, we

find the maximum where $x =$ _____ and $y =$ _____ . If we plug these numbers into the equation $U_J(c_J, x, y) + U_T(c_T, x, y) = 1,000,000 + 500\ln x + 500\ln y - 30x - 110y$, we find that the utility possibility frontier

is described by the equation $U_J + U_C =$ _____.
(You need a calculator or a log table to find this answer.) Along this frontier, the total expenditure on the annoying habits X and Y by Jim

and Tammy is _____ . The rest of the $1,000,000 is spent on c_J and c_T. Each possible way of dividing this expenditure corresponds to a different point on the utility possibility frontier. The slope of the utility

possibility frontier constructed in this way is_____.

31.8 (0) An airport is located next to a large tract of land owned by a housing developer. The developer would like to build houses on this land, but noise from the airport reduces the value of the land. The more planes that fly, the lower is the amount of profits that the developer makes. Let X be the number of planes that fly per day and let Y be the number of houses that the developer builds. The airport's total profits are $48X - X^2$, and the developer's total profits are $60Y - Y^2 - XY$. Let us consider the outcome under various assumptions about institutional rules and about bargaining between the airport and the developer.

(a) "Free to Choose with No Bargaining": Suppose that no bargains can be struck between the airport and the developer and that each can decide on its own level of activity. No matter how many houses the developer builds, the number of planes per day that maximizes profits for the airport

is _____ . Given that the airport is landing this number of planes, the

number of houses that maximizes the developer's profits is _____ . Total

profits of the airport will be _____ and total profits of the developer

will be _____ . The sum of their profits will be_____.

(b) "Strict Prohibition": Suppose that a local ordinance makes it illegal to land planes at the airport because they impose an externality on the

developer. Then no planes will fly. The developer will build _____

houses and will have total profits of_____.

(c) "Lawyer's Paradise": Suppose that a law is passed that makes the airport liable for all damages to the developer's property values. Since the developer's profits are $60Y - Y^2 - XY$ and his profits would be $60Y - Y^2$ if no planes were flown, the total amount of damages awarded to the developer will be XY. Therefore if the airport flies X planes and the developer builds Y houses, then the airport's profits after it has paid damages will be $48X - X^2 - XY$. The developer's profits including the amount he receives in payment of damages will be $60Y - Y^2 - XY + XY = 60Y - Y^2$. To maximize his net profits, the developer will choose to build

_____ houses no matter how many planes are flown. To maximize its

profits, net of damages, the airport will choose to land _____ planes.

Total profits of the developer will be _____ and total profits of the

airport will be _____ The sum of their profits will be_____.

Calculus **31.9 (1)** This problem concerns the airport and the developer from the previous problem.

(a) "The Conglomerate": Suppose that a single firm bought the developer's land and the airport and managed both to maximize joint profits.

Total profits, expressed as a function of X and Y would be _____

_____ . Total profits are maximized when $X =$_____

and $Y =$_____ . Total profits are then equal to_____.

(b) "Dealing": Suppose that the airport and the developer remain independent. If the original situation was one of "free to choose," could the developer increase his net profits by bribing the airport to cut back one flight per day if the developer has to pay for all of the airport's lost

profits?_____ The developer decides to get the airport to reduce its flights by paying for all lost profits coming from the reduction of flights. To maximize its own net profits, how many flights per day should it pay

the airport to eliminate?_____.

Chapter 32

Law

Introduction. These problems are based on the survey of law and economics found in your text. We hope that you will be pleased to see that the techniques you learned in earlier chapters can provide useful insights into issues that arise in law.

32.1 (2) Madame Norrell makes her living in Florida by stealing gold buttons from designer jackets in expensive boutiques. She can sell each button to a fence for $10. The maximum number of buttons she can steal in a day is 50. Florida has a law against button theft. There is a fine of F dollars if someone is caught stealing any number of buttons. The police catch about 10 percent of all button thieves and these must pay the fine and forfeit any buttons they have stolen.

(a) Suppose that the only thing that Madame Norrell cares about is her expected profits. What is the smallest fine that will discourage Madame

Norrell from stealing buttons?_____.

(b) Due to an oversupply of buttons, Madame Norrell's fence announces that he will no longer pay her a flat price for buttons. If Madame Norrell delivers x buttons, she will be paid $5 \ln x$. (Assume that Madame Norrell will take at least 1 button if she takes any at all.) Initially Madame Norrell has $100, and the fine if she is caught stealing x buttons is $3 per button. However, she only has to pay the fine if she is caught, in which case all her buttons are confiscated and she collects zero from the fence. How many buttons will Madame Norrell try to take, assuming she

maximizes her expected profit?_____.

(c) What does the fine per button have to be to induce Madame Norrell

to limit herself to taking 10 buttons?_____.

(d) Now assume that Madame Norrell is an expected utility maximizer. With probability .10, she is caught with x buttons and pays a fine of $3x$. With probability .90, she gets away with x buttons, which she can sell for $10 each. She cares about the expected utility of her wealth, with von Neumann-Morgenstern utility function $\ln x$. Initially her wealth is $100.

How many buttons will she take?_____.

32.2 (2) Jim Levson rides his bike through the forest with reckless abandon, while Dick Stout likes to hike in the woods. Let s be the speed in miles per hour that James rides and w the speed with which Dick walks.

Jim's utility depends on how fast he rides and how many dollars he has, while Dick's utility depends on how fast he walks and how much money he has.

$$U_{Jim} = 6\sqrt{s} - s + m$$
$$U_{Dick} = 4\sqrt{w} - w + m.$$

(a) How fast will Dick walk?_____   How fast will Jim

ride?_____.

(b) Alas, since Jim and Dick are both moving in the same forest, there is some chance that Jim will run into Dick. Suppose that the expected cost to Dick of such an accident depends on the speed that each moves: $c(s, w) = \frac{s^2}{16} + \frac{w^2}{2}$. (Assume that Jim is fitter than Dick and will incur negligable costs in an accident.) If Dick has to pay the entire cost of an

accident, how fast will he walk?_____   How fast will Jim

ride?_____.

(c) Suppose that Jim now has full liability and must pay any costs that

he imposes on Dick. How fast will Dick walk?_____   How

fast will Jim ride?_____.

(d) What are the socially optimal speeds for Jim and Dick to move? Dick

should walk _____ and Jim should ride_____

_____.

32.3 (2) Derri Bottled Water of Christchurch, New Zealand, sells bottled water from "the bottom of the world." Due to a number of fortuitous circumstances, Derri has a monopoly on bottled water in the South Island. The demand for bottled water in the South Island is $p(x) = 10 - x/200$, and the cost of producing x bottles of water is $c(x) = x^2/200$. Here the price is measured in New Zealand dollars and the quantity is measured in $1,000$ cases per month.

(a) Draw the demand curve, the marginal revenue curve, and the marginal

cost curve in the graph below. The profit-maximizing quantity is _____

cases of water, and the profit maximizing price is _____ dollars per
case.

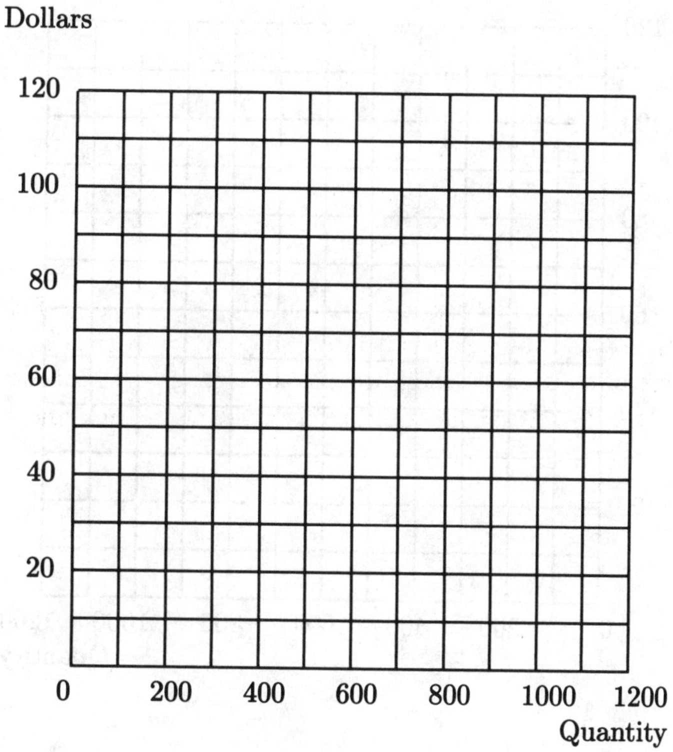

Dollars

(b) The New Zealand antitrust authorities now bring action against Derri waters for monopolizing the bottled water industry. They announce that during the coming year they will confiscate 50 percent of Derri's profits. Part of these confiscated profits will be used to distribute rebates to the consumers of bottled water. In particular, each purchaser of bottled water will receive $2 per case from the government. How does this rebate

influence the demand for bottled water? _____ What is

the equation for the new inverse demand curve?_____.

(c) Solve for the new levels of output and price. Draw the marginal revenue curve, marginal cost curve, and inverse demand curve in the following graph.

Dollars

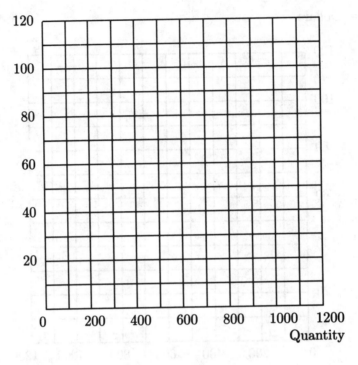

Information Technology

33.1 (2) Bill Barriers, the president of MightySoft software company is about to introduce a new computer operating system called DoorKnobs. Because it is easier to swap files with people who have the same operating system, the amount people are willing to pay to have DoorKnobs on their computers is greater the larger they believe DoorKnobs' market share to be.

The *perceived market share* for DoorKnobs is the fraction of all computers that the public *believes* is using DoorKnobs. When the price of DoorKnobs is p, then its *actual market share* is the fraction of all computer owners that would be willing to pay at least $\$p$ to have DoorKnobs installed on their computers. Market researchers have discovered that if DoorKnobs' perceived market share is s and the price of DoorKnobs is $\$p$, then its actual market share will be x, where x is related to the price p and perceived market share s by the formula

$$p = 256s(1 - x). \tag{1}$$

In the short run, MightySoft can influence the perceived market share of DoorKnobs by publicity, advertising, giving liquor and gifts to friendly journalists, and giving away copies in conspicuous ways. In the long run, the truth will emerge, and DoorKnobs' perceived market share s must equal its actual market share x.

(a) If the perceived market share is s, then the demand curve for DoorKnobs is given by Equation 1. On the graph below, draw the demand curve relating price to actual market share in the case in which DoorKnobs' perceived market share is $s = 1/2$. Label this curve $s = 1/2$.

(b) On the demand curve that you just drew with $s = 1/2$, mark a red dot on the point at which the actual market share of DoorKnobs is $1/2$. (This is the point on the demand curve directly above $x = 1/2$.) What is the price at which half of the computer owners actually want to buy DoorKnobs, given that everybody believes that half of all computer owners want to buy DoorKnobs?_____.

(c) On the same graph, draw and label a separate demand curve for the case where DoorKnobs' perceived market share s takes on each of the following values: $s =1/8, 1/4, 3/4, 7/8, 1$.

Willingness to Pay

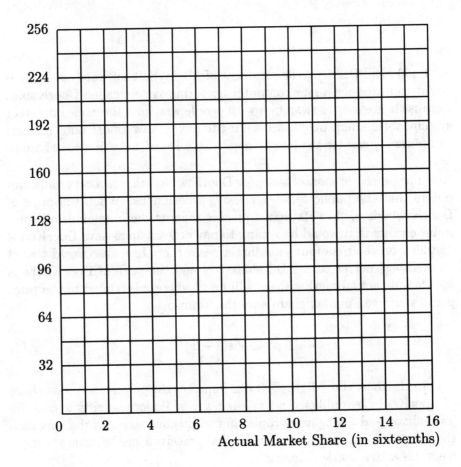

Actual Market Share (in sixteenths)

(d) On the demand curve for a perceived market share of $s = 1/4$, put a red dot on the point at which the actual market share of DoorKnobs is 1/4. (This is the point on this demand curve directly above $x = 1/4$.) If the perceived market share of DoorKnobs is 1/4, at what price is the

actual market share of DoorKnobs also 1/4?_____.

(e) Just as you did for $s = 1/2$ and $s = 1/4$, make red marks on the demand curves corresponding to $s = 1/8$, 3/4, 7/8, and 1, showing the price at which the actual market share is s, given that the perceived market share is s.

(f) Let us now draw the long-run demand curve for DoorKnobs, where we assume that computer owners' perceived market shares s are the same as the actual market shares x. If this is the case, it must be that $s = x$, so the demand curve is given by $p = 256x(1 - x)$. On the graph above, plot a few points on this curve and sketch in an approximation of the curve. [Hint: Notice that the curve you draw must go through all the red points that you have already plotted.]

(g) Suppose that MightySoft sets a price of \$48 for DoorKnobs and sticks with that price. There are 3 different perceived market shares such that the fraction of consumers who would actually want to buy DoorKnobs for \$48 is equal to the perceived market share. One such perceived market share is 0. What are the other two possibilities?_____.

(h) Suppose that by using its advertising and media influence, MightySoft can temporarily set its perceived market share at any number between 0 and 1. If DoorKnobs' perceived market share is x and if MightySoft charges a price $p = 256x(1 - x)$, the actual market fraction will also be x and the earlier perceptions will be reinforced and maintained. Assuming that MightySoft chooses a perceived market share x and a price that makes the actual market share equal to the perceived market share, what market share x should MightySoft choose in order to maximize its revenue and what price should it charge in order to maintain this market share? [Hint: Revenue is $px = 256x^2(1 - x)$.] Use calculus and show

your work._____

_____

_____.

33.2 (1) Suppose that demand for DoorKnobs is as given in the previous problem, and assume that the perceived market share in any period is equal to the actual market share in the previous period. Then where x_t is the actual market share in period t, the equation $p = 256x_{t-1}(1 - x_t)$ is satisfied. Rearranging this equation, we find that $x_t = 1 - (p/256x_{t-1})$ whenever $p/256x_{t-1} \leq 1$. If $p/256x_{t-1} \leq 0$, then $x_t = 0$. With this formula, if we know actual market share for any time period, we can calculate market share for the next period.

Let us assume that DoorKnobs sets the price at $p = \$32$ and never changes this price. (To answer the following questions, you will find a calculator useful.)

(a) If the actual market share in the first period was $1/2$, find the actual

market share in the second period_____ the third period_____ .

Write down the actual market shares for the next few periods_____

_____ . Do they seem to be approaching a limit? If so, what?_____.

(b) Notice that when price is held constant at p, if DoorKnobs' market share converges to a constant $\bar{x}$, it must be that $\bar{x} = 1 - (p/256\bar{x})$. Solve this equation for $\bar{x}$ in the case where $p = \$32$. What do you make of the

fact that there are two solutions?_____

_____

_____.

33.3 (2) The management at Hammermesh Software is thinking about developing a new family-oriented computer game, called *Lust for Labor Economics*. Hammermesh estimates that if the price of the game is p, the number of units demanded will be $q = 10,000 - 100p$. Hammermesh estimates that the total cost of developing this software will be $100,000. To simplify our calculations, let us assume that the marginal cost of distribution is zero, so that if Hammermesh Software develops *Lust for Labor Economics*, its only costs will be $100,000, no matter how many units it sells.

Unfortunately for Hammermesh, software pirates will also be able to copy and sell copies of *Lust for Labor Economics* without having to bear the costs of development. Again for simplicity of calculation, let us assume that the software pirates have zero production costs. The government, however, does try to enforce rules against unauthorized copying of software. If the government catches someone selling copied software, it makes them pay a fine of F and it also confiscates all the revenue that the seller received for his sales. The probability $\pi(x)$ that the government catches a software pirate is an increasing function of the number of copies the pirate sells. The expected profit of a software pirate who sells x copies of *Lust for Labor Economics* is

$$V(x) = px - \pi(x)(px + F).$$

(a) If there were no competition from software pirates, and Hammermesh set the price to maximize its revenue, what price would it choose and how many copies would it sell?_____ Would it be profitable for Hammermesh to develop this software, and if so, how much profit would it make?_____.

(b) What is the lowest price that Hammermesh could charge and still recover its development costs of $100,000? Hint: To solve for this price, solve the quadratic equation $p(10,000 - 100p) = 100,000$._____.

(c) Each software pirate chooses to sell a number of copies x^* that maximizes his profits, taking p as fixed. The first order calculus condition for profit maximization is $V'(x^*) = 0$, which implies that $\frac{p}{px^*+F} =$_____.

(d) If there is free entry into the software piracy business, it must be that

$\frac{p}{px^*+F} =$_____.

(e) Using your answers to the previous two questions, solve for x^* in terms of $\pi(x^*)$ and $\pi'(x^*)$. $x^* =$_____.

(f) Suppose that the probability that a pirate is caught is given by the function $\pi(x) = \frac{1}{1+e^{-.05x}}$ (where e is the mathematical constant, 2.7183, known as the exponential). Show that

$$\frac{\pi(x)(1-\pi(x))}{\pi'(x)} = \frac{1}{.05} = 20.$$

_____

_____.

(g) Use your answer to the previous two questions to solve for the profit maximizing number of copies for any pirate to make, $x^* =$ _____ . The probability that a pirate who is making this number of copies gets caught is therefore $\pi(x^*) =$_____.

(h) If the fine for pirates who are caught is $\$F$, what is the lowest price at which software pirates will not lose money by selling copies of *Lust for Labor Economics*? Hint: A pirate who chooses to make x^* copies will have expected profits of $V(x^*) = px^* - \pi(x^*)(px^* + F)$. Solve this equation for $V(x^*) = 0$._____.

(i) What is the lowest fine that would be sufficient to allow Hammermesh Software to charge its revenue-maximizing price without having software pirates compete down the price?_____.

(j) What is the lowest fine for software pirates that would be sufficient to allow Hammermesh Software to be able to charge a price high enough to recover its development costs?_____.

33.4 (2) Professor Kremepuff has written a new, highly simplified economics text, *Microeconomics for the Muddleheaded*, which will be published by East Frisian Press. The first edition of this book will be in print for two years, at which time it will be replaced by a new edition. East Frisian Press has already made all its fixed cost investments in the book, and must pay a constant marginal cost of $\$c$ for each copy that it sells.

Let p_1 be the price charged for new copies sold in the first year of publication and let p_2 be the price charged for new copies sold in the second year of publication. The publisher and the students who buy the book are aware that there will be an active market for used copies of *Microeconomics for the Muddleheaded* one year after publication, and that used copies of the first edition will have zero resale value, two years after publication. At the end of the first year of publication, students can resell their used textbooks to bookstores for 40% of the second-year price p_2.

The net cost to a student of buying the book in the first year, using it for class, and reselling it at the end of the year is $p_1 - 0.4p_2$. The number of copies demanded in the first year of publication is given by a demand function, $q_1 = D_1(p_1 - 0.4p_2)$.

Some of the students who use the book in the first year of publication will want to keep their copies for future reference and some will damage their books so that they cannot be resold. The cost of keeping one's old copy or of damaging it is the resale price $0.4p_2$. The number of books that are either damaged or kept for reference is given by a "keepers" demand function, $D^k(0.4p_2)$. It follows that the number of used copies available at the end of the first year will be $D_1(p_1 - 0.4p_2) - D^k(0.4p_2)$.

Students who buy *Microeconomics for the Muddleheaded* in the second year of publication will not be able to resell their used copies, since a new edition will then be available. These students can, however, buy either a new copy or a used copy of the book. For simplicity of calculations, let us assume that students are indifferent between buying a new copy or a used copy and that used copies cost the same as new copies in the book store. (The results would be the same if students preferred new to used copies, but bookstores priced used copies so that students were indifferent between buying new and used copies.) The total number of copies, new and used, that are purchased in the second year of publication is $q_2 = D_2(p_2)$.

(a) Write an expression for the number of new copies that East Frisian Press can sell in the second year after publication if it sets prices p_1 in

year 1 and p_2 in year 2._____.

(b) Write an expression for the total number of new copies of *Microeconomics for the Muddleheaded* that East Frisian can sell over two years at

prices p_1 and p_2 in years 1 and 2._____

_____.

(c) Would the total number of copies sold over two years increase, decrease, or remain constant if p_1 were increased and p_2 remained constant?

_____.

(d) Write an expression for the total revenue that East Frisian Press will

receive over the next two years if it sets prices p_1 and p_2. _____

_____

_____.

(e) To maximize its total profits over the next two years, East Frisian must maximize the difference between its total revenue and its variable costs. Show that this difference can be written as

$$(p_1 - p_2)D_1(p_1 - .4p_2) + (p_2 - c)\left[D_2(p_2) + D^k(.4p_2)\right].$$

_____

_____.

(f) Suppose that East Frisian has decided that it must charge the same price for the first edition in both years that it is sold. Thus it must set $p = p_1 = p_2$. Write an expression for East Frisian's revenue net of variable

costs over the next two years as a function of p. _____

_____.

33.5 (2) Suppose that East Frisian Press, discussed in the previous problem, has a constant marginal cost of $c = \$10$ for each copy of *Microeconomics for the Muddleheaded* that it sells and let the demand functions be:

$$D_1(p_1 - 0.4p_2) = 100(90 - p_1 + 0.4p_2)$$
$$D_2(p_2) = 100(90 - p_2).$$

The number of books that people either damage or keep for reference after the first year is

$$D^k(0.4p_2) = 100(90 - 0.8p_2).$$

(This assumption is consistent with the assumption that everyone's willingness to pay for keeping the book is half as great as her willingness to pay to have the book while she is taking the course.) Assume that East Frisian Press is determined to charge the same price in both years, so that $p_1 = p_2 = p$.

(a) If East Frisian Press charges the same price p for *Microeconomics for the Muddleheaded* in the first and second years, show that the total sales of new copies over the two years are equal to

$$18,000 - 180p.$$

_____

_____.

(b) Write an expression for East Frisian's total revenue, net of variable

costs, over the first two years as a function of the price p._____

_____.

(c) Solve for the price p that maximizes its total revenue net of variable costs over the first two years: _____ . At this price, the net cost to students in the first year of buying the text and reselling it is_____.

The total number of copies sold in the first year will be _____ . The total number of copies that are resold as used books is_____.
The total number of copies purchased by students in the second year will be _____ . (Remember students in the second year know that they cannot resell the book, so they have to pay the full price p for using it.) The total number of new copies purchased by students in the second year will be _____ . Total revenue net of variable costs over the two years will be_____.

33.6 (2) East Frisian Press is trying to decide whether it would be profitable to produce a new edition of *Microeconomics for the Muddleheaded* after one year rather than after two years. If it produces a new edition after one year, it will destroy the used book market and all copies that are purchased will be new copies. In this case, the number of new copies that will be demanded in each of the two years will be $100(90-p)$, where p is the price charged. The variable cost of each copy sold remains $10.

(a) Write an expression for the total number of copies sold over the course of two years if the price is p in each year _____ . Also, write an expression for total revenue net of variable costs as a function of p._____

_____.

(b) Find the price that maximizes total revenue net of variable costs.

_____.

(c) The total number of new books sold in the first year would be _____ and the total number of books sold in the second year would be

_____.

(d) East Frisian's total revenue net of variable costs, if it markets a new edition after one year, will be_____.

(e) Would it be more profitable for East Frisian Press to produce a new edition after one year or after two years?_____ . Which would be better for students? (Hint: The answer is not the same for all students.)_____

_____

_____.

33.7 (3) Suppose that East Frisian Press publishes a new edition only after two years and that demands and costs are as in the previous problems. Suppose that it sets two different prices p_1 and p_2 in the two periods.

(a) Write an expression for the total number of new copies sold at prices p_1 and p_2 and show that this number depends on p_2 but not on p_1.

_____.

(b) Show that at prices p_1 and p_2. the difference between revenues and variable costs is equal to

$$100\left(90p_1 + 108p_2 + 1.4p_1p_2 - p_1^2 - 2.2p_2^2 - 1,800\right).$$

_____

_____.

(c) Calculate the prices p_1 and p_2 that maximize the difference between total revenue and variable costs and hence maximize profits. _____

_____.

(d) If East Frisian Press chooses its profit-maximizing p_1 and p_2, compare the cost of using *Microeconomics for the Muddleheaded* for a student who buys the book when it is first published and resells it at the end of the first year with the cost for a student who buys the book at the beginning of the second year and then discards it._____

_____.

Chapter 34

Public Goods

Introduction. In previous chapters we studied selfish consumers consuming private goods. A unit of private goods consumed by one person can not be simultaneously consumed by another. If you eat a ham sandwich, I cannot eat the same ham sandwich. (Of course we can both eat ham sandwiches, but we must eat different ones.) Public goods are a different matter. They can be jointly consumed. You and I can both enjoy looking at a beautiful garden or watching fireworks at the same time. The conditions for efficient allocation of public goods are different from those for private goods. With private goods, efficiency demands that if you and I both consume ham sandwiches and bananas, then our marginal rates of substitution must be equal. If our tastes differ, however, we may consume different amounts of the two private goods.

If you and I live in the same town, then when the local fireworks show is held, there will be the same amount of fireworks for each of us. Efficiency does not require that my marginal rate of substitution between fireworks and ham sandwiches equals yours. Instead, efficiency requires that the *sum* of the amount that viewers are willing to pay for a marginal increase in the amount of fireworks equals the marginal cost of fireworks. This means that the sum of the absolute values of viewers' marginal rates of substitution between fireworks and private goods must equal the marginal cost of public goods in terms of private goods.

Example: A quiet midwestern town has 5,000 people, all of whom are interested only in private consumption and in the quality of the city streets. The utility function of person i is $U(X_i, G) = X_i + A_i G - B_i G^2$, where X_i is the amount of money that person i has to spend on private goods and G is the amount of money that the town spends on fixing its streets. To find the Pareto optimal amount of money for this town to spend on fixing its streets, we must set the sum of the absolute values of marginal rates of substitution between public and private goods equal to the relative prices of public and private goods. In this example we measure both goods in dollar values, so the price ratio is 1. The absolute value of person i's marginal rate of substitution between public goods and private goods is the ratio of the marginal utility of public goods to the marginal utility of private goods. The marginal utility of private goods is 1 and the marginal utility of public goods for person i is $A_i - B_i G$. Therefore the absolute value of person i's MRS is $A_i - B_i G$ and the sum of absolute values of marginal rates of substitution is $\sum_i (A_i - B_i G) = \sum_i A_i - (\sum B_i)G$. Therefore Pareto efficiency requires that $\sum_i A_i - (\sum_i B_i)G = 1$. Solving this for G, we have $G = (\sum_i A_i - 1)/\sum_i B_i$.

34.1 (0) Muskrat, Ontario, has 1,000 people. Citizens of Muskrat consume only one private good, Labatt's ale. There is one public good, the town skating rink. Although they may differ in other respects, inhabitants have the same utility function. This function is $U(X_i, G) = X_i - 100/G$, where X_i is the number of bottles of Labatt's consumed by citizen i and G is the size of the town skating rink, measured in square meters. The price of Labatt's ale is \$1 per bottle and the price of the skating rink is \$10 per square meter. Everyone who lives in Muskrat has an income of \$1,000 per year.

(a) Write down an expression for the absolute value of the marginal rate of substitution between skating rink and Labatt's ale for a typical citizen.

_____ What is the marginal cost of an extra square meter of skating

rink (measured in terms of Labatt's ale)?_____.

(b) Since there are 1,000 people in town, all with the same marginal rate of substitution, you should now be able to write an equation that states the condition that the sum of absolute values of marginal rates of substitution equals marginal cost. Write this equation and solve it for the

Pareto efficient amount of G._____.

(c) Suppose that everyone in town pays an equal share of the cost of the skating rink. Total expenditure by the town on its skating rink will be \$10G. Then the tax bill paid by an individual citizen to pay for the skating rink is \$10G/1,000 = \$$G$/100. Every year the citizens of Muskrat vote on how big the skating rink should be. Citizens realize that they will have to pay their share of the cost of the skating rink. Knowing this, a citizen realizes that if the size of the skating rink is G, then the amount

of Labatt's ale that he will be able to afford is_____.

(d) Therefore we can write a voter's budget constraint as $X_i + G/100 = 1,000$. In order to decide how big a skating rink to vote for, a voter simply solves for the combination of X_i and G that maximizes his utility subject to his budget constraint and votes for that amount of G. How much G is

that in our example?_____.

(e) If the town supplies a skating rink that is the size demanded by the voters will it be larger than, smaller than, or the same size as the Pareto

optimal rink?_____.

(f) Suppose that the Ontario cultural commission decides to promote Canadian culture by subsidizing local skating rinks. The provincial government will pay 50% of the cost of skating rinks in all towns. The costs of this subsidy will be shared by all citizens of the province of Ontario. There are hundreds of towns like Muskrat in Ontario. It is true that to pay for this subsidy, taxes paid to the provincial government will have to be increased. But there are hundreds of towns from which this tax is collected, so that the effect of an increase in expenditures in Muskrat on the taxes its citizens have to pay to the state can be safely neglected. Now, approximately how large a skating rink would citizens of Muskrat vote

for? _____ (Hint: Rewrite the budget constraint for individuals observing that local taxes will be only half as large as before and the cost of increasing the size of the rink only half as much as before. Then solve for the utility maximizing combination.)

(g) Does this subsidy promote economic efficiency?_____.

34.2 (0) Ten people have dinner together at an expensive restaurant and agree that the total bill will be divided equally among them.

(a) What is the additional cost to any one of them of ordering an appetizer

that costs $20?_____.

(b) Explain why this may be an inefficient system._____

_____.

34.3 (0) Cowflop, Wisconsin, has 1,000 people. Every year they have a fireworks show on the Fourth of July. The citizens are interested in only two things—drinking milk and watching fireworks. Fireworks cost 1 gallon of milk per unit. People in Cowflop are all pretty much the same. In fact, they have identical utility functions. The utility function of each citizen i is $U_i(x_i, g) = x_i + \sqrt{g}/20$, where x_i is the number of gallons of milk per year consumed by citizen i and g is the number of units of fireworks exploded in the town's Fourth of July extravaganza. (Private use of fireworks is outlawed.)

(a) Solve for the absolute value of each citizen's marginal rate of substi-

tution between fireworks and milk._____.

(b) Find the Pareto optimal amount of fireworks for Cowflop._____.

34.4 (0) Bob and Ray are two hungry economics majors who are sharing an apartment for the year. In a flea market they spot a 25-year-old sofa that would look great in their living room.

Bob's utility function is $u_B(S, M_B) = (1 + S)M_B$, and Ray's utility function is $u_R(S, M_R) = (2+S)M_R$. In these expressions M_B and M_R are the amounts of money that Bob and Ray have to spend on other goods, $S = 1$ if they get the sofa, and $S = 0$ if they don't get the sofa. Bob has W_B dollars to spend, and Ray has W_R dollars.

(a) What is Bob's reservation price for the sofa?_____

_____.

(b) What is Ray's reservation price for the sofa?_____

_____.

(c) If Bob has a total of $W_B = \$100$ and Ray has a total of $W_R = \$75$ to spend on sofas and other stuff, they could buy the sofa and have a Pareto improvement over not buying it so long as the cost of the sofa is

no greater than_____.

34.5 (0) Bonnie and Clyde are business partners. Whenever they work, they have to work together. Their only source of income is profit from their partnership. Their total profits per year are $50H$, where H is the number of hours that they work per year. Since they must work together, they both must work the same number of hours, so the variable "hours of labor" is like a public "bad" for the two person community consisting of Bonnie and Clyde. Bonnie's utility function is $U_B(C_B, H) = C_B - .02H^2$ and Clyde's utility function is $U_C(C_C, H) = C_C - .005H^2$, where C_B and C_C are the annual amounts of money spent on consumption for Bonnie and for Clyde.

(a) If the number of hours that they both work is H, what is the ratio of Bonnie's marginal utility of hours of work to her marginal utility of

private goods?_____   What is the ratio of Clyde's marginal utility

of hours of work to his marginal utility of private goods?_____.

(b) If Bonnie and Clyde are both working H hours, then the total amount of money that would be needed to compensate them both for having to work an extra hour is the sum of what is needed to compensate Bonnie and the amount that is needed to compensate Clyde. This amount is approximately equal to the sum of the absolute values of their marginal rates of substitution between work and money. Write an expression for

this amount as a function of H_____   How much extra money will

they make if they work an extra hour?_____.

(c) Write an equation that can be solved for the Pareto optimal number

of hours for Bonnie and Clyde to work._____.

Find the Pareto optimal H. _____   (Hint: Notice that this model is formally the same as a model with one public good H and one private good, income.)

34.6 (0) Lucy and Melvin share an apartment. They spend some of their income on private goods like food and clothing that they consume separately and some of their income on public goods like the refrigerator, the household heating, and the rent, which they share. Lucy's utility function is $2X_L + G$ and Melvin's utility function is $X_M G$, where X_L and X_M are the amounts of money spent on private goods for Lucy and for Melvin and where G is the amount of money that they spend on public goods. Lucy and Melvin have a total of \$8,000 per year between them to spend on private goods for each of them and on public goods.

(a) What is the absolute value of Lucy's marginal rate of substitution between public and private goods?_____ What is the absolute value of Melvin's?_____.

(b) Write an equation that expresses the condition for provision of the Pareto efficient quantity of the public good._____.

(c) Suppose that Melvin and Lucy each spend \$2,000 on private goods for themselves and they spend the remaining \$4,000 on public goods. Is this a Pareto efficient outcome?_____.

(d) Give an example of another Pareto optimal outcome in which Melvin gets more than \$2,000 and Lucy gets less than \$2,000 worth of private goods._____.
    Give an example of another Pareto optimum in which Lucy gets more than \$2,000._____.

(e) Describe the set of Pareto optimal allocations._____

_____.

(f) The Pareto optima that treat Lucy better and Melvin worse will have (more of, less of, the same amount of) public good as the Pareto optimum that treats them equally._____.

34.7 (0) This problem is set in a fanciful location, but it deals with a very practical issue that concerns residents of this earth. The question is, "In a Democracy, when can we expect that a majority of citizens will favor having the government supply pure private goods publicly?" This problem also deals with the efficiency issues raised by public provision of private goods. We leave it to you to see whether you can think of important examples of publicly supplied private goods in modern Western economies.

On the planet Jumpo there are two goods, aerobics lessons and bread. The citizens all have Cobb-Douglas utility functions of the form $U_i(A_i, B_i) = A_i^{1/2} B_i^{1/2}$, where A_i and B_i are i's consumptions of aerobics lessons and bread. Although tastes are all the same, there are two different income groups, the rich and the poor. Each rich creature on Jumpo has an income of 100 fondas and every poor creature has an income of 50 fondas (the currency unit on Jumpo). There are two million poor creatures and one million rich creatures on Jumpo. Bread is sold in the usual way, but aerobics lessons are provided by the state despite the fact that they are private goods. The state gives the same amount of aerobics lessons to every creature on Jumpo. The price of bread is 1 fonda per loaf. The cost to the state of aerobics lessons is 2 fondas per lesson. This cost of the state-provided lessons is paid for by taxes collected from the citizens of Jumpo. The government has no other expenses than providing aerobics lessons and collects no more or less taxes than the amount needed to pay for them. Jumpo is a democracy, and the amount of aerobics to be supplied will be determined by majority vote.

(a) Suppose that the cost of the aerobics lessons provided by the state is paid for by making every creature on Jumpo pay an equal amount of taxes. On planets, such as Jumpo, where every creature has exactly one head, such a tax is known as a "head tax." If every citizen of Jumpo gets 20 lessons, how much will be total government expenditures on lessons?

_____ How much taxes will every citizen have to pay?

_____ If 20 lessons are given, how much will a rich creature

have left to spend on bread after it has paid its taxes?_____ How much will a poor creature have left to spend on bread after it has

paid its taxes?_____.

(b) More generally, when everybody pays the same amount of taxes, if x lessons are provided by the government to each creature, the total cost to

the government is _____ times x and the taxes that one creature

has to pay is _____ times x.

(c) Since aerobics lessons are going to be publicly provided with everybody getting the same amount and nobody able to get more lessons from another source, each creature faces a choice problem that is formally the same as that faced by a consumer, i, who is trying to maximize a Cobb-Douglas utility function subject to the budget constraint $2A + B = I$, where I is its income. Explain why this

is the case._____

_____.

(d) Suppose that the aerobics lessons are paid for by a head tax and all lessons are provided by the government in equal amounts to everyone.

How many lessons would the rich people prefer to have supplied?._____

How many would the poor people prefer to have supplied?_____
(Hint: In each case you just have to solve for the Cobb-Douglas demand with an appropriate budget.)

(e) If the outcome is determined by majority rule, how many aerobics

lessons will be provided? _____ How much bread will the rich get?

_____ How much bread will the poor get?_____.

(f) Suppose that aerobics lessons are "privatized," so that no lessons are supplied publicly and no taxes are collected. Every creature is allowed to buy as many lessons as it likes and as much bread as it likes. Suppose that the price of bread stays at 1 fonda per unit and the price of lessons stays at 2 fondas per unit. How many aerobics lessons will the rich get?

_____ How many will the poor get?_____ How much bread will

the rich get?_____ How much bread will the poor get?_____.

(g) Suppose that aerobics lessons remain publicly supplied but are paid for by a proportional income tax. The tax rate is set so that tax revenue pays for the lessons. If A aerobics lessons are offered to each creature on Jumpo, the tax bill for a rich person will be $3A$ fondas and the tax bill for a poor person will be $1.5A$ fondas. If A lessons are given to each creature, show that total tax revenue collected will be the total cost of

A lessons._____

_____

_____.

(h) With the proportional income tax scheme discussed above, what budget constraint would a rich person consider in deciding how many aerobics

lessons to vote for?_____ What is the relevant budget con-

straint for a poor creature?_____ With these tax rates, how

many aerobics lessons per creature would the rich favor?_____ How

many would the poor favor?_____ What quantity of aerobics lessons

per capita would be chosen under majority rule?_____ How much bread would the rich get?_____ How much bread would the poor get?

_____.

(i) Calculate the utility of a rich creature under a head tax._____

Under privatization._____ Under a proportional income tax._____

_____ (Hint: In each case, solve for the consumption of bread and the consumption of aerobics lessons that a rich person gets, and plug these into the utility function.) Now calculate the utility of each poor

creature under the head tax._____ Privatization_____ Under

the proportional income tax. _____ (Express these utilities as square roots rather than calculating out the roots.)

(j) Is privatization Pareto superior to the head tax?_____ Is a

proportional income tax Pareto superior to the head tax? _____ Is

privatization Pareto superior to the proportional income tax? _____

Explain the last two answers._____

_____.

Information

Introduction. The economics of information and incentives is a relatively new branch of microeconomics, in which much intriguing work is going on. This chapter ishows you a sample of problems these problems and the way that economists think about them.

35.1 (0) There are two types of electric pencil-sharpener producers. "High-quality" manufacturers produce very good sharpeners that consumers value at $14. "Low-quality" manufacturers produce less good ones that are valued at $8. At the time of purchase, customers cannot distinguish between a high-quality product and a low-quality product; nor can they identify the manufacturer. However, they can determine the quality of the product after purchase. The consumers are risk neutral; if they have probability q of getting a high-quality product and $1 - q$ of getting a low-quality product, then they value this prospect at $14q + 8(1 - q)$. Each type of manufacturer can manufacture the product at a constant unit cost of $11.50. All manufacturers behave competitively.

(a) Suppose that the sale of low-quality electric pencil-sharpeners is illegal, so that the only items allowed to appear on the market are of high quality. What will be the equilibrium price?_____.

(b) Suppose that there were no high-quality sellers. How many low-quality sharpeners would you expect to be sold in equilibrium?_____

_____

_____

(c) Could there be an equilibrium in which equal (positive) quantities of the two types of pencil sharpeners appear in the market?_____

_____

_____

(d) Now we change our assumptions about the technology. Suppose that each producer can *choose* to manufacture either a high-quality or a low-quality pencil-sharpener, with a unit cost of $11.50 for the former and $11 for the latter, what would we expect to happen in equilibrium?_____

_____

_____

_____.

_(e)_ Assuming that each producer is able to make the production choice described in the last question, what good would it do if the government banned production of low-quality electric pencil-sharpeners?_____

_____

_____

_____.

35.2 (0) In West Bend, Indiana, there are exactly two kinds of workers. One kind has a (constant) marginal product worth $10 and the other kind has a (constant) marginal product worth $15. There are equal numbers of workers of each kind. A firm cannot directly tell the difference between the two kinds of workers. Even after it has hired them, it won't be able to monitor their work closely enough to determine which workers are of which type.

_(a)_ If the labor market is competitive, workers will be paid the average value of their marginal product. This amount is_____.

_(b)_ Suppose that the local community college offers a microeconomics course in night school, taught by Professor M. De Sade. The high-productivity workers think that taking this course is just as bad as a $3 wage cut, and the low-productivity workers think it is just as bad as a $6 wage cut. The firm can observe whether or not an individual takes the microeconomics course. Suppose that the high-productivity workers all choose to take the microeconomics course and the low productivity workers all choose not to. The competitive wage for people who take the microeconomics course will be _____ and the wage for people who don't take the microeconomics course will be_____.

_(c)_ If there is a separating equilibrium, with high-productivity workers taking the course and low-productivity workers not taking it, then the net benefits from taking the microeconomics course will be _____ for the high-productivity workers and _____ for the low-productivity workers. Therefore there (will be, won't be)_____ a separating equilibrium of this type.

(d) Suppose that Professor De Sade is called off to Washington, to lecture wayward Congressmen on the economics of family values. His replacement is Professor Morton Kremepuff. Kremepuff prides himself on his ability to make economics "as easy as political science and as fun as the scaps on TV". Professor Kremepuff's claims are exaggerated, but at least students like him better than De Sade. High-productivity workers think that taking Kremepuff's course is as bad as a $1 wage cut, and low-productivity workers think that taking Kremepuff's course is as bad as a $4 wage cut. If the high-productivity workers all choose to take the microeconomics course and the low productivity workers all choose not to, the competitive

wage for people who take the microeconomics course will be _____ and the wage for people who don't take the microeconomics course will be

_____.

(e) If there is a separating equilibrium with high-productivity workers taking the course and low productivity workers not taking it, then the net

benefits from taking Kremepuff's microeconomics course will be _____

for the high-productivity workers and _____ for the low-productivity

workers. Therefore there (will be, won't be)_____ a separating equilibrium of this type.

35.3 (1) In Enigma, Ohio, there are two kinds of workers, Klutzes whose labor is worth $1,000 per month and and Kandos, whose labor is worth $2,500 per month. Enigma has exactly twice as many klutzes as kandos. Klutzes look just like Kandos and are accomplished liars. If you ask, they will claim to be Kandos. Kandos always tell the truth. Monitoring individual work accomplishments is too expensive to be worthwhile. In the old days, there was no way to distinguish the two types of labor, so everyone was paid the same wage. If labor markets were competitive,

what was this wage?_____.

(a) A professor who loves to talk offered to give a free lecture, once a month on macroeconomics and personal hygiene to the employees of one small firm. These lectures had no effect on productivity, but both Klutzes and Kandos found them to be excruciatingly dull. To a Klutz, each hour's lecture is as bad as losing $100. To a Kando, each hour's lecture is as bad as losing $50. Suppose that the firm gave each of its employees a pay raise of $55 a month but insisted that they attend the professor's lectures. What would happen to

the firm's labor force?_____

_____ What

would happen to the average productivity of the firm's employees?_____

_____

_(b)_ Other firms noticed that those who had listened to the professor's lectures were more productive than those who had not. So they tried to bid them away from their original employer. Since all those who agreed to listen to the original lecture series were Kandos, their wage was bid up

to_____.

_(c)_ After observing the "effect of his lectures on labor productivity," the professor decided to expand his efforts. He found a huge auditorium where he could lecture to all the laborers in Enigma who would listen to him. If employers believed that listening to the professors' lectures improved productivity by the improvement in productivity in the first small firm and offered bonuses for attending the lectures accordingly, who would

attend the lectures?_____ Having observed this outcome, how much of a wage premium would firms pay for those who had attended the

professor's lectures?_____.

_(d)_ The professor was disappointed by the results of his big lecture and decided that if he gave more lectures per month, his pupils might "learn more". So he decided to give a course of lectures for 20 hours a month. Would there now be an equilibrium in which the Kandos all took his course and none of the Klutzes took it and where those who took the course were paid according to their

true productivity?_____

_____

_____

_____

_____

_(e)_ What is the smallest number of hours the professor could lecture and

still maintain a separating equilibrium?_____.

35.4 (1) Old MacDonald produces hay. He has a single employee, Jack. If Jack works for x hours he can produce x bales of hay. Each bale of hay sells for \$1. The cost to Jack of working x hours is $c(x) = x^2/10$.

_(a)_ What is the efficient number of bales of hay for Jack to cut?_____.

(b) If the most that Jack could earn elsewhere is zero, how much would MacDonald have to pay him to get him to work the efficient amount?

_____.

(c) What is MacDonald's net profit?_____.

(d) Suppose that Jack would receive $1 for passing out leaflets, an activity that involves no effort whatsoever. How much would he have to receive from MacDonald for cutting the efficient number of bales of hay?_____

_____.

(e) Suppose now that the opportunity for passing out leaflets is no longer available, but that MacDonald decides to rent his hayfield out to Jack for a flat fee. How much would he rent it for?_____.

35.5 (0) In Rustbucket, Michigan, there are 200 people who want to sell their used cars. Everybody knows that 100 of these cars are "lemons" and 100 of these cars are "good." The problem is that nobody except the original owners know which are which. Owners of lemons will be happy to get rid of their cars for any price greater than $200. Owners of good used cars will be willing to sell them for any price greater than $1,500, but will keep them if they can't get $1,500. There are a large number of buyers who would be willing to pay $2,500 for a good used car, but would pay only $300 for a lemon. When these buyers are not sure of the quality of the car they buy, they are willing to pay the expected value of the car, given the knowledge they have.

(a) If all 200 used cars in Rustbucket were for sale, how much would buyers be willing to pay for a used car?_____ Would owners of good used cars be willing to sell their used cars at this price?_____ Would there be an equilibrium in which all used cars are sold?_____ Describe the equilibrium that would take place in Rustbucket._____

_____.

(b) Suppose that instead of there being 100 cars of each kind, everyone in town is aware that there are 120 good cars and 80 lemons. How much would buyers be willing to pay for a used car?_____ Would owners of good used cars be willing to sell their used cars at this price?_____

Would there be an equilibrium in which all used cars are sold?_____

Would there be an equilibrium in which only the lemons were sold?

_____ Describe the possible equilibrium or equilibria that would

take place in Rustbucket._____

_____.

35.6 (1) Each year, 1,000 citizens of New Crankshaft, Pennsylvania, sell their used cars and buy new cars. The original owners of the old cars have no place to keep a second car and must sell them. These used cars vary a great deal in quality. Their original owners know exactly what is good and what is bad about their cars, but potential buyers can't tell them apart by looking at them. Lamentably, though they are in other respects model citizens, the used-car owners in New Crankshaft have no scruples about lying about their old jalopies. Each car has a value, V, which a buyer who knew all about its qualities would be willing to pay. There is a very large number of potential buyers, any one of which would be willing to pay V for a car of value V.

The distribution of values of used cars on the market is quite simply described. In any year, for any V between 0 and \$2,000, the number of used cars available for sale that are worth less than V, is $V/2$. Potential used-car buyers are all risk-neutral. That is if they don't know the value of a car for certain, they value it at its expected value, given the information they have.

Rod's Garage in New Crankshaft will test out any used car and find its true value V. Rod's Garage is known to be perfectly accurate and perfectly honest in its appraisals. The only problem is that getting an accurate appraisal costs \$200. People with terrible cars are not going to want to pay \$200 to have Rod tell the world how bad their cars are. But people with very good cars will be willing to pay Rod the \$200 to get their cars appraised, so they can sell them for their true values.

Let's try to figure our exactly how the equilibrium works, which cars get appraised, and what the unappraised cars sell for.

(a) If nobody had their car appraised, what would the market price for used cars in North Crankshaft be and what would be the total revenue

received by used-car owners for their cars?_____

_____.

(b) If all the cars that are worth more than X are appraised and all the cars that are worth less than X are sold without appraisal, what will the market price of unappraised used cars be? (Hint: What is the expected value of a random draw from the set of cars worth less than

X?)_____.

(c) If all the cars that are worth more than X are appraised and all the cars that are worth less than X are sold without appraisal, then if your car is worth X, how much money would you have left if you

had it appraised and then sold it for its true value?_____ How much money would you get if you sold it without having it appraised?

_____.

(d) In equilibrium, there will be a car of marginal quality such that all cars better than this car will be appraised and all cars worse than this car will be sold without being appraised. The owner of this car will be just indifferent between selling his car unappraised and having it appraised.

What will be the value of this marginal car?_____

_____.

(e) In equilibrium, how many cars will be sold unappraised and what

will they sell for?_____

_____.

(f) In equilibrium, what will be the total net revenue of all owners of used

cars, after Rod's Garage has been paid for its appraisals?_____

_____.

35.7 (2) In Pot Hole, Georgia, 1,000 people want to sell their used cars. These cars vary in quality. Original owners know exactly what their cars are worth. All used cars look the same to potential buyers until they have bought them; then they find out the truth. For any number X between 0 and 2,000, the number of cars of quality lower than X is $X/2$. If a car is of quality X, its original owner will be willing to sell it for any price greater than X. If a buyer knew that a car was of quality X, she would be willing to pay $X + 500$ for it. When buyers are not sure of the quality of a car, they are willing to pay its expected value, given their knowledge of the distribution of qualities on the market.

(a) Suppose that everybody knows that all the used cars in Pot Hole are

for sale. What would used cars sell for? _____ Would every used

car owner be willing to sell at this price? _____ Which used cars

would appear on the market?_____.

(b) Let X^* be some number between 0 and 2,000 and suppose that all cars of quality lower than X^* are sold, but original owners keep all cars of quality higher than X^*. What would buyers be willing to pay for a used

car? _____ At this price, which used cars would be for sale?

_____.

(c) Write an equation for the equilibrium value of X^*, at which the price that buyers are willing to pay is exactly enough to induce all cars of quality

less than X^* into the market. _____ Solve this equation for

the equilibrium value of X^*._____.

Introduction

This section contains short multiple-choice quizzes based on the workbook problems in each chapter. Typically the questions are slight variations on the workbook problems, so that if you have worked and understood the corresponding workbook problem, the quiz question will be pretty easy.

But there is more ... instructors who have adopted *Microeconomic Workouts* for their course can get a free copy of a neat computer program called the *Norton TestMaker*, that will generate new versions of these questions with different numerical values but the same internal logic. This can be used to make additional problems for students to practice on or make short quizzes to be taken in class.

With these quizzes and *Norton TestMaker* it is possible to assign and give credit for homework, even with very large classes. Grading is quick and reliable because the quizzes are multiple-choice and can be graded electronically. We have found it convenient to use these quizzes in the following way. On alternate weeks, students are asked to turn in "homework exercises" in the form of machine-gradeable sheet on which they mark the correct answers to the quizzes for the week's lessons. In the alternate weeks when homework exercises are not due, we have a short in-class quiz. In class, students are given newly generated versions of the week's quizzes which the instructor has created using TestMaker. Students who have done their homework and worked through the week's quizzes in here will find it easy to do well on this quiz.

Budget Constraint

2.1 In Problem 2.1, if you have an income of 12 to spend, if commodity 1 costs $2 per unit, and if commodity 2 costs $6 per unit, then the equation for your budget line can be written as

(a) $x_1/2 + x_2/6 = 12$.

(b) $(x_1 + x_2)/(8) = 12$.

(c) $x_1 + 3x_2 = 6$.

(d) $3x_1 + 7x_2 = 13$.

(e) $8(x_1 + x_2) = 12$

2.2 In Problem 2.3, if you could exactly afford either 6 units of x and 14 units of y, or 10 units of x and 6 units of y, then if you spent all of your income on y, how many units of y could you buy?

(a) 26

(b) 18

(c) 34

(d) 16

(e) None of the other options are correct.

2.3 In Problem 2.4, Murphy used to consume 100 units of x and 50 units of y when the price of x was 2 and the price of y was 4. If the price of x rose to 5 and the price of y rose to 8, how much would Murphy's income have to rise so that he could still afford his original bundle?

(a) 700

(b) 500

(c) 350

(d) 1050

(e) None of the other options are correct.

2.4 In Problem 2.7, Edmund must pay \$6 each for punk rock video casettes. If Edmund is paid \$48 per sack for accepting garbage and if his relatives send him an allowance of \$384, then his budget line is described by the equation:

(a) $6V = 48G$.

(b) $6V + 48G = 384$.

(c) $6V - 48G = 384$.

(d) $6V = 384 - G$.

(e) None of the other options are correct.

2.5 In Problem 2.10, if in the same amount of time that it takes her to read 40 pages of economics and 30 pages of sociology, Martha could read 30 pages of economics and 50 pages of sociology, then which of these equations describes combinations of pages of economics, E, and sociology, S, that she could read in the time it takes to read 40 pages of economics and 30 pages of sociology?

(a) $E + S = 70$

(b) $E/2 + S = 50$

(c) $2E + S = 110$

(d) $E + S = 80$

(e) All of the above.

2.6 In Problem 2.11, ads in the boring business magazine are read by 300 lawyers and 1000 M.B.As. Ads in the consumer publication are read by 250 lawyers and 300 M.B.A.'s. If Harry had \$3000 to spend on advertising, if the price of ads in the boring business magazine were 600 and the price of ads in the consumer magazine were 300, then the combinations of recent M.B.A's and lawyers with hot tubs whom he could reach with his advertising budget would be represented by the integer values along a line segment that runs between the two points

(a) (2500,3000) and (1500,5000) .

(b) (3000,3500) and (1500,6000) .

(c) (0,3000) and (1500,0).

(d) (3000,0) and (0,6000).

(e) (2000,0) and (0,5000).

2.7 In the economy of Mungo, discussed in Problem 2.12, there is a third creature called Ike. Ike has a red income of 40 and a blue income of 10. (Recall that blue prices are 1 bcu (blue currency unit) per unit of ambrosia and 1 bcu per unit of bubble gum. Red prices are 2 rcus (red currency units) per unit of ambrosia and 6 rcus per unit of bubble gum. You have to pay twice for what you buy, once in red currency, once in blue currency.) If Ike spends all of its blue income, but not all of its red income, then it must be that

(a) it consumes at least 5 units of bubble gum.

(b) it consumes at least 5 units of ambrosia.

(c) it consumes exactly twice as much bubblegum as ambrosia.

(d) it consumes at least 15 units of bubble gum.

(e) it consumes equal amounts of ambrosia and bubble gum.

Preferences

3.1 In Problem 3.1, Charlie's indifference curves have the equation $x_B = \text{constant}/x_A$, where larger constants correspond to better indifference curves. Charlie strictly prefers the bundle (7,15) to the following bundle

(a) (15,7).

(b) (8,14).

(c) (11,11).

(d) all three of these bundles.

(e) none of these bundles.

3.2 In Problem 3.2, Ambrose has indifference curves with the equation $x_2 = \text{constant} - 4x_1^{1/2}$, where larger constants correspond to higher indifference curves. If good 1 is drawn on the horizontal axis and good 2 on the vertical axis, what is the slope of Ambrose's indifference curve when his consumption bundle is (1,6)?

(a) −1/6

(b) −6/1

(c) −2

(d) −7

(e) −1

3.3 In Problem 3.8, Nancy Lerner is taking a course from Professor Goodheart who will count only her best midterm grade and from Professor Stern who will count only her worst midterm grade. In one of her classes, Nancy has scores of 50 on her first midterm and 30 on her second midterm. When the first midterm score is measured on the horizontal axis and her second midterm score on the vertical, her indifference curve has a slope of zero at the point (50,30). Therefore it must be that

(a) this class could be Professor Goodheart's but couldn't be Professor Stern's.

(b) this class could be Professor Stern's but couldn't be Professor Good-heart's.

(c) this class couldn't be either Goodheart's or Stern's.

(d) this class could be either Goodheart's or Stern's.

3.4 In Problem 3.9, if we graph Mary Granola's indifference curves with avocados on the horizontal axis and grapefruits on the vertical axis, then whenever she has more grapefruits than avocados, the slope of her indifference curve is -2. Whenever she has more avocados than grapefruits, the slope is $-1/2$. Mary would be indifferent between a bundle with 24 avocados and 36 grapefruits and another bundle that has 34 avocados and

(a) 28 grapefruits.

(b) 32 grapefruits.

(c) 22 grapefruits.

(d) 25 grapefruits.

(e) 26.50 grapefruits.

3.5 In Problem 3.12, recall that Tommy Twit's mother measures the departure of any bundle from her favorite bundle for Tommy by the sum of the absolute values of the differences. Her favorite bundle for Tommy is (2,7)–that is, 2 cookies and 7 glasses of milk. Tommy's mother's indifference curve that passes through the point $(c, m) = (3, 6)$ also passes through

(a) (4,5).

(b) the points (2,5), (4,7), and (3,8).

(c) (2,7).

(d) the points (3, 7), (2, 6), and (2, 8).

(e) None of the other options are correct.

3.6 In Problem 3.1, Charlie's indifference curves have the equation $x_B = \text{constant}/x_A$, where larger constants correspond to better indifference curves. Charlie strictly prefers the bundle (9,19) to the following bundle:

(a) (19,9).

(b) (10,18).

(c) (15,17).

(d) more than one of these options are correct.

(e) none of the above are correct.

Utility

4.1 In Problem 4.1, Charlie has the utility function $U(x_A, x_B) = x_A x_B$. His indifference curve passing through 10 apples and 30 bananas will also pass through the point where he consumes 2 apples and

(a) 25 bananas.

(b) 50 bananas.

(c) 152 bananas.

(d) 158 bananas.

(e) 150 bananas.

4.2 In Problem 4.1, Charlie's utility function is $U(A, B) = AB$ where A and B are the numbers of apples and bananas, respectively, that he consumes. When Charlie is consuming 20 apples and 100 bananas, then if we put apples on the horizontal axis and bananas on the vertical axis, the slope of his indifference curve at his current consumption is

(a) −20.

(b) −5.

(c) −10.

(d) −1/5.

(e) −1/10.

4.3 In Problem 4.2, Ambrose has the utility function $U(x_1, x_2) = 4x_1^{1/2} + x_2$. If Ambrose were initially consuming 81 units of nuts and 14 units of berries, then what is the largest number of berries that he would be willing to give up in return for an additional 40 units of nuts.

(a) 11

(b) 25

(c) 8

(d) 4

(e) 2

4.4 Joe Bob, from Problem 4.12 has a cousin Jonas who consume goods 1 and 2. Jonas thinks that 2 units of good 1 is always a perfect substitute for 3 units of good 2. Which of the following utility functions is the only one that would NOT represent Jonas's preferences?

(a) $U(x_1, x_2) = 3x_1 + 2x_2 + 1000.$

(b) $U(x_1, x_2) = 9x_1^2 + 12x_1x_2 + 4x_2^2.$

(c) $U(x_1, x_2) = \min 3x_1, 2x_2.$

(d) $U(x_1, x_2) = 30x_1 + 20x_2 - 10,000.$

(e) More than one of the above does NOT represent Jonas's preferences.

4.5 In Problem 4.7, Harry Mazzola has the utility function $U(x_1, x_2) = \min\{x_1 + 2x_2, 2x_1 + x_2\}$. He has \$40 to spend on corn chips and french fries, if the price of corn chips is 5 dollar(s) per unit and the price of french fries is 5 dollars per unit, then Harry will

(a) definitely spend all of his income on corn chips.

(b) definitely spend all of his income on french fries.

(c) consume at least as much corn chips as french fries, but might consume both.

(d) consume at least as much french fries as corn chips, but might consume both.

(e) consume equal amounts of french fries and corn chips.

4.6 Phil Rupp's sister Ethel has the utility function $U(x, y) = \min\{2x + y, 3y\}$. Where x is measured on the horizontal axis and y on the vertical axis, her indifference curves

(a) consist of a vertical line segment and a horizontal line segment which meet in a kink along the line $y = 2x$.

(b) consist of a vertical line segment and a horizontal line segment which meet in a kink along the line $x = 2y$.

(c) consist of a horizontal line segment and a negatively sloped line segment which meet in a kink along the line $x = y$.

(d) consist of a positively sloped line segment and a negatively sloped line segment which meet along the line $x = y$.

(e) consist of a horizontal line segment and a positively sloped line segment which meet in a kink along the line $x = 2y$.

Choice

5.1 In Problem 5.1, Charlie has a utility function $U(x_A, x_B) = x_A x_B$, the price of apples is 1 and the price of bananas is 2. If Charlie's income were 240, how many units of bananas would he consume if he chooses the bundle that maximizes his utility subject to his budget constraint?

(a) 60

(b) 30

(c) 120

(d) 12

(e) 180

5.2 In Problem 5.1, if Charlie's income were 40, the price of apples were 5 and the price of bananas were 6, how many apples would there be in the best bundle that Charlie could afford?

(a) 8

(b) 15

(c) 10

(d) 11

(e) 4

5.3 In Problem 5.2, Clara's utility function is $U(X, Y) = (X + 2)(Y + 1)$. If Clara's marginal rate of substitution is -2 and she is consuming 10 units of Good X, how many units of good Y is she consuming?

(a) 2

(b) 24

(c) 12

(d) 23

(e) 5

5.4 In Problem 5.3, Ambrose's utility function is $U(x_1, x_2) = 4x_1^{1/2} + x_2$. If the price of nuts is 1, the price of berries is 4, and his income is 72, how many units of nuts will Ambrose choose.

(a) 2

(b) 64

(c) 128

(d) 67

(e) 32

5.5 Ambrose's utility function is $4x_1^{1/2} + x_2$. If the price of nuts is 1, the price of berries is 4, and his income is 100, how many units of berries will Ambrose choose?

(a) 65

(b) 9

(c) 18

(d) 8

(e) 12

5.6 In Problem 5.6, Elmer's utility function is $U(x, y) = \min\{x, y^2\}$. If the price of x is 15, the price of y is 10, and Elmer chooses to consume 7 units of y, what must Elmer's income be?

(a) 1610

(b) 175

(c) 905

(d) 805

(e) There is not enough information to tell.

NAME_____

Demand

6.1 In Problem 6.1, if Charlie's utility function were $X_A^4 X_B$, if apples cost 90 cents each and bananas cost 10 cents each, Charlie's budget line would be tangent to one of his indifference curves whenever the following equation is satisfied:

(a) $4X_B = 9X_A$.

(b) $X_B = X_A$.

(c) $X_A = 4X_B$.

(d) $X_B = 4X_A$.

(e) $90X_A + 10X_B = M$.

6.2 In Problem 6.1, if Charlie's utility function were $X_A^4 X_B$, if the price of apples were p_A, the price of bananas were p_B, and his income were m, then Charlie's demand for apples would be

(a) $m/(2p_A)$.

(b) $0.25p_A m$.

(c) $m/(p_A + p_B)$.

(d) $0.80m/p_A$.

(e) $1.25p_B m/p_A$.

6.3 Ambrose's brother Bartholomew has a utility function $U(x_1, x_2) = 24x_1^{1/2} + x_2$. His income is 51, the price of good 1 (nuts) is 4 and the price of good 2 (berries) is 1. How many units of nuts will Bartholomew demand?

(a) 19

(b) 5

(c) 7

(d) 9

(e) 16

6.4 Ambrose's brother Bartholomew has a utility function $U(x_1, x_2) = 8x_1^{1/2} + x_2$. His income is 23, the price of nuts is 2 and the price of berries is 1. How many units of berries will Bartholomew demand?

(a) 15

(b) 4

(c) 30

(d) 10

(e) There is not enough information to determine the answer.

6.5 In Problem 6.6, recall that Miss Muffet insists on consuming 2 units of whey per unit of curds. If the price of curds is 3 and the price of whey is 6, then if Miss Muffett's income is m, her demand for curds will be

(a) $m/3$.

(b) $6m/3$.

(c) $3C + 6W = m$.

(d) $3m$.

(e) $m/15$.

6.6 In Problem 6.8, recall that Casper's utility function is $3x + y$, where x is his consumption of cocoa and y is his consumption of cheese. If the total cost of x units of cocoa is x^2, if the price of cheese is 8, and Casper's income is $174, how many units of cocoa will he consume?

(a) 9

(b) 12

(c) 23

(d) 11

(e) 24

6.7 In Problem 6.13, where x is whips and y is leather jackets, if Kinko's utility function were $U(x, y) = \min\{7x, 3x + 12y\}$, then if the price of whips were $20 and the price of leather jackets were $60, Kinko would demand *(a)* 6 times as many whips as leather jackets.

(b) 5 times as many leather jackets as whips.

(c) 3 times as many whips as leather jackets.

(d) 4 times as many leather jackets as whips.

(e) only leather jackets.

Revealed Preference

7.1 In Problem 7.1, if the only information we had about Goldie were that she chooses the bundle (6,6) when prices are (6,3) and she chooses the bundle (10, 0) when prices are (5,5), then we could conclude that

(a) The bundle (6,6) is revealed preferred to (10,0) but there is no evidence that she violates WARP.

(b) Neither bundle is revealed preferred to the other.

(c) Goldie violates WARP.

(d) The bundle (10,0) is revealed preferred to (6,6) and she violates WARP.

(e) The bundle (10,0) is revealed preferred to (6,6) and there is no evidence that she violates WARP.

7.2 In Problem 7.3, Pierre's friend Henri lives in a town where he has to pay 3 francs per glass of wine and 6 francs per loaf of bread. Henri consumes 6 glasses of wine and 4 loaves of bread per day. Recall that Bob has an income of $15 per day and pays $.50 per loaf of bread and $2 per glass of wine. If Bob has the same tastes as Henri, and if the only thing that either of them cares about is consumption of bread and wine, we can deduce

(a) nothing about whether one is better than the other.

(b) that Henri is better off than Bob.

(c) that Bob is better off than Henri.

(d) that both of them violate the weak axiom of revealed preferences.

(e) that Bob and Henri are equally well off.

7.3 Let us reconsider the case of Ronald in Problem 7.4. Let the prices and consumptions in the base year be as in Situation D, where $p_1 = 3$, $p_2 = 1$, $x_1 = 5$, and $x_2 = 15$. If in the current year, the price of good 1 is 1 and the price of good 2 is 3, and his current consumptions of good 1 and good 2 are 25 and 10 respectively, what is the Laspeyres price index of current prices relative to base-year prices? (Pick the most nearly correct answer.)

(a) 1.67

(b) 1.83

(c) 1

(d) 0.75

(e) 2.50

7.4 On the planet Homogenia, every consumer who has ever lived consumes only two goods x and y and has the utility function $U(x, y) = xy$. The currency in Homogenia is the fragel. On this planet in 1900, the price of good 1 was 1 fragel and the price of good 2 was 2 fragels. Per capita income was 120 fragels. In 1990, the price of good 1 was 5 fragels and the price of good 2 was 5 fragels. The Laspeyres price index for the price level in 1990 relative to the price level in 1900 is

(a) 3.75.

(b) 5.

(c) 3.33.

(d) 6.25.

(e) not possible to determine from this information.

7.5 On the planet Hyperion, every consumer who has ever lived has a utility function $U(x, y) = \min\{x, 2y\}$. The currency of Hyperion is the doggerel. In 1850 the price of x was 1 doggerel per unit, and the price of y was 2 doggerels per unit. In 1990, the price of x was 10 doggerels per unit and the price of y was 4 doggerels per unit. Paasche price index of prices in 1990 relative to prices in 1850 is

(a) 6.

(b) 4.67.

(c) 2.50.

(d) 3.50.

(e) not possible to determine without further information.

Slutsky Equation

8.1 In Problem 8.1, Charlie's utility function is $x_A x_B$. The price of apples used to be $1 per unit and the price of bananas was $2 per unit. His income was $40 per day. If the price of apples increased to $1.25 and the price of bananas fell to $1.25, then in order to be able to just afford his old bundle, Charlie would have to have a daily income of

(a) 37.50.

(b) 76.

(c) 18.75.

(d) 56.25.

(e) 150.

8.2 In Problem 8.1, Charlie's utility function is $x_A x_B$. The price of apples used to be $1 and the price of bananas used to be $2, and his income used to be $40. If the price of apples increased to 8 and the price of bananas stayed constant, the substitution effect on Charlie's apple consumption reduces his consumption by

(a) 17.50 apples.

(b) 7 apples.

(c) 8.75 apples.

(d) 13.75 apples.

(e) None of the other options are correct.

8.3 Neville, in Problem 8.2, has a friend named Colin. Colin has the same demand function for claret as Neville, namely $q = .02m - 2p$, where m is income and p is price. Colin's income is 6000 and he initially had to pay a price of 30 per bottle of claret. The price of claret rose to 40. The substitution effect of the price change

(a) reduced his demand by 20.

(b) increased his demand by 20.

(c) reduced his demand by 8.

(d) reduced his demand by 32.

(e) reduced his demand by 18.

8.4 Goods 1 and 2 are perfect complements and a consumer always consumes them in the ratio of 2 units of Good 2 per unit of Good 1. If a consumer has income 120 and if the price of good 2 changes from 3 to 4, while the price of good 1 stays at 1, then the income effect of the price change

(a) is 4 times as strong as the substitution effect.

(b) does not change demand for good 1.

(c) accounts for the entire change in demand.

(d) is exactly twice as strong as the substitution effect.

(e) is 3 times as strong as the substitution effect.

8.5 Suppose that Agatha in Problem 8.10 had $570 to spend on tickets for her trip. She needs to travel a total of 1500 miles. Suppose that the price of first-class tickets is $0.50 per mile and the price of second-class tickets is $0.30 per mile. How many miles will she travel by second class?

(a) 900

(b) 1050

(c) 450

(d) 1000

(e) 300

8.6 In Problem 8.4, Maude thinks delphiniums and hollyhocks are perfect substitutes, one-for-one. If delphiniums currently cost $5 per unit and hollyhocks cost $6 per unit, and if the price of delphiniums rises to $9 per unit,

(a) the income effect of the change in demand for delphiniums will be bigger than the substitution effect.

(b) there will be no change in the demand for hollyhocks.

(c) the entire change in demand for delphiniums will be due to the substitution effect.

(d) the fraction 1/4 of the change will be due to the income effect.

(e) the fraction 3/4 of the change will be due to the income effect.

Buying and Selling

9.1 In Problem 9.1, if Abishag owned 9 quinces and 10 kumquats, and if the price of kumquats is 3 times the price of quinces, how many kumquats could she afford if she spent all of her money on kumquats?

(a) 26

(b) 19

(c) 10

(d) 13

(e) 10

9.2 Suppose that Mario in Problem 9.2 consumes eggplant and tomatoes in the ratio of one bushel of eggplant per bushel of tomatoes. His garden yields 30 bushels of eggplant and 10 bushels of tomatoes. He initially faced prices of $10 per bushel for each vegetable, but the price of eggplant rose to $30 per bushel, while the price of tomatoes stayed unchanged. After the price change, he would

(a) increase his eggplant consumption by 5 bushels.

(b) decrease his eggplant consumption by at least 5 bushels.

(c) increase his consumption of eggplant by 7 bushels.

(d) decrease his consumption of eggplant by 7 bushels.

(e) decrease his tomato consumption by at least 1 bushel.

9.3 Suppose that in Problem 9.9(b), Dr. J. receives a lump sum payment of $50 per week. Suppose that the first $200 per week of his labor income is untaxed, but all labor income above $200 is taxed at a rate of 40 percent.

(a) Dr. J.'s budget line has a kink in it at the point where he takes 50 units of leisure.

(b) Dr. J.'s budget line has a kink where his income is 250 and his leisure is 40.

(c) The slope of Dr. J.'s budget line is everywhere −3.

(d) Dr. J.'s budget line has no kinks in the part of it that corresponds to a positive labor supply.

(e) Dr. J.'s budget line has a piece that is a horizontal straight line.

9.4 Dudley, in Problem 9.15, has a utility function $U(C, R) = C - (12 - R)^2$, where R is leisure and C is consumption per day. He has 16 hours per day to divide between work and leisure. If Dudley has a nonlabor income of $40 per day and is paid a wage of $6 per hour, how many hours of leisure will he choose per day?

(a) 6

(b) 7

(c) 8

(d) 10

(e) 9

9.5 Mr. Cog in Problem 9.7 has 18 hours a day to divide between labor and leisure If he has 16 dollars of nonlabor income per day and gets a wage rate of 13 dollars per hour when he works, his budget equation, expressing combinations of consumption and leisure that he can afford to have, can be written as

(a) $13R + C = 16$

(b) $13R + C = 250$

(c) $R + C/13 = 328$

(d) $C = 250 + 13R$

(e) $C = 298 + 13R$

9.6 Mr. Cog in Problem 9.7 has 18 hours per day to divide between labor and leisure. If he has a nonlabor income of 42 dollars per day and a wage rate of 13 dollars per hour, he will choose a combination of labor and leisure that allows him to spend

(a) 276 dollars per day on consumption.

(b) 128 dollars per day on consumption.

(c) 159 dollars per day on consumption.

(d) 138 dollars per day on consumption.

(e) 207 dollars per day on consumption.

Intertemporal Choice

10.1 If Peregrine in Problem 10.1 consumes (1000,1155) and earns (800,1365) and if the interest rate is 0.05, the present value of his endowment is

(a) 2165.

(b) 2100.

(c) 2155.

(d) 4305.

(e) 5105.

10.2 Suppose that Molly from Problem 10.2 had income $400 in period 1 and income 550 in period 2. Suppose that her utility function were $c_1^a c_2^{1-a}$, where $a = 0.40$ and the interest rate were 0.10. If her income in period 1 doubled and her income in period 2 stayed the same, her consumption in period 1 would

(a) double.

(b) increase by 160.

(c) increase by 80

(d) stay constant.

(e) increase by 400.

10.3 Mr. O. B. Kandle, of Problem 10.8 has a utility function $c_1 c_2$ where c_1 is his consumption in period 1 and c_2 is his consumption in period 2. He will have no income in period 2. If he had an income of 30,000 in period 1 and the interest rate increased from 10% to 12%,

(a) his savings would increase by 2% and his consumption in period 2 would also increase.

(b) his savings would not change, but his consumption in period 2 would increase by 300.

(c) his consumption in both periods would increase.

(d) his consumption in both periods would decrease.

(e) his consumption in period 1 would decrease by 12% and his consumption in period 2 would also decrease.

10.4 Harvey Habit in Problem 10.9 has a utility function $U(c_1, c_2) = \min\{c_1, c_2\}$. If he had an income of 1025 in period 1, and 410 in period 2, and if the interest rate were 0.05, how much would Harvey choose to spend on bread in period 1?

(a) 1087.50

(b) 241.67

(c) 362.50

(d) 1450

(e) 725

10.5 In the village in Problem 10.10, if the harvest this year is 3000 and the harvest next year will be 1100, and if rats eat 50% of any grain that is stored for a year, how much grain could the villagers consume next year if they consume 1000 bushels of grain this year.

(a) 2100

(b) 1000

(c) 4100

(d) 3150

(e) 1200

10.6 Patience has a utility function $U(c_1, c_2) = c_1^{1/2} + 0.83c_2^{1/2}$, c_1 is her consumption in period 1 and c_2 is her consumption in period 2. Her income in period 1 is 2 times as large as her income in period 2. At what interest rate will she choose to consume the same amount in period 1 as in period 2?

(a) 0.40

(b) 0.10

(c) 0.20

(d) 0

(e) 0.30

Asset Markets

11.1 Ashley, in Problem 11.6, has discovered another wine, Wine D. Wine drinkers are willing to pay 40 dollars to drink it right now. The amount that wine drinkers are willing to pay will rise by 10 dollars each year that the wine ages. The interest rate is 10%. How much would Ashley be willing to pay for the wine if he buys it as an investment? (Pick the closest answer.)

(a) 56

(b) 40

(c) 100

(d) 440

(e) 61

11.2 Chillingsworth, from Problem 11.10 has a neighbor, Shivers, who faces the same options for insulating his house as Chillingsworth. But Shivers has a larger house. Shivers' annual fuel bill for home heating is 1000 dollars per year. Plan A will reduce his annual fuel bill by 15%, plan B will reduce it by 20%, and plan C will eliminate his need for heating fuel altogether. The Plan A insulation job would cost Shivers 1000 dollars, Plan B would cost him 1900 and Plan C would cost him 11000 dollars. If the interest rate is 10% and his house and the insulation job last forever, which plan is the best for Shivers?

(a) Plan A.

(b) Plan B.

(c) Plan C.

(d) Plans A and B are equally good.

(e) He is best off using none of the plans.

11.3 The price of an antique is expected to rise by 2% during the next year. The interest rate is 6%. You are thinking of buying an antique and selling it a year from now. You would be willing to pay a total of 200 dollars for the pleasure of owning the antique for a year. How much would you be willing to pay to buy this antique. (See Problem 11.5.)

(a) 3333.33

(b) 4200

(c) 200

(d) 5000

(e) 2000

11.4 A bond has a face value of 9000 dollars. It will pay 900 dollars in interest at the end of every year for the next 46 years. At the time of the final interest payment, 46 years from now, the company that issued the bond will "redeem the bond at face value." That is, the company buys back the bond from its owner at a price equal to the face value of the bond. If the interest rate is 10% and is expected to remain at 10%, how much would a rational investor pay for this bond right now?

(a) 9000

(b) 50400

(c) 41400

(d) More than any of the above numbers

(e) Less than any of the above numbers

11.5 The sum of the infinite geometric series $1, 0.86, 0.86^2, 0.86^3, \ldots$, is closest to the following.

(a) infinity

(b) 1.86

(c) 7.14

(d) 0.54

(e) 116.28

11.6 If the interest rate is 11%, and will remain 11% forever, how much would a rational investor be willing to pay for an asset that will pay him 5550 dollars one year from now, 1232 dollars two years from now, and nothing at any other time.

(a) 6000

(b) 5000

(c) 54545.45

(d) 72000

(e) 7000

Uncertainty

12.1 In Problem 12.9, Billy has a von Neumann-Morgenstern utility function $U(c) = c^{1/2}$. If Billy is not injured this season, he will receive an income of 25 million dollars. If he is injured, his income will be only $10,000. The probability that he will be injured is .1 and the probability that he will not be injured is .9. His expected utility is

(a) 4510

(b) between 24 million and 25 million dollars.

(c) 100,000.

(d) 9020

(e) 18040

12.2 (See Prob 12.2) Willy's only source of wealth is his chocolate factory. He has the utility function $pc_f^{1/2} + (1-p)c_{nf}^{1/2}$ where p is the probability of a flood, $1-p$ is the probability of no flood and where c_f and c_nf are his wealth contingent on a flood and on no flood, respectively. The probability of flood is $p = 1/15$. The value of Willy's factory is $600,000 if there is no flood and 0 if there is a flood. Willy can buy insurance where if he buys $x worth of insurance, he must pay the insurance company $3x/17 whether there is a flood or not, but he gets back $x from the company if there is a flood. Willy should buy

(a) no insurance since the cost per dollar of insurance exceeds the probability of a flood.

(b) enough insurance so that if there is a flood, after he collects his insurance his wealth will be 1/9 of what it would be if there is no flood.

(c) enough insurance so that if there is a flood, after he collects his insurance, his wealth will be the same whether there is a flood or not.

(d) enough insurance so that if there is a flood, after he collects his insurance, his wealth will be 1/4 of what it would be if there is no flood.

(e) enough insurance so that if there is a flood, after he collects his insurance his wealth will be 1/7 of what it would be if there is no flood.

12.3 Sally Kink is an expected utility maximizer with utility function $pu(c_1) + (1-p)u(c_2)$ where for any $x < 4,000$, $u(x) = 2x$ and where $u(x) = 8,000 + x$ for x greater than or equal to 4,000.

(a) Sally will be risk averse if her income is less than 4,000 but risk loving if her income is more than 4,000.

(b) Sally will be risk neutral if her income is less than 4,000 and risk averse if her income is more than 4,000.

(c) For bets that involve no chance of her wealth exceeding 4,000, Sally will take any bet that has a positive expected net payoff.

(d) Sally will never take a bet if there is a chance that it leaves her with wealth less than 8,000.

(e) None of the above are true.

12.4 (See Problem 12.11) Martin's expected utility function is $pc_1^{1/2} + (1-p)c_2^{1/2}$ where p is the probability that he consumes c_1 and $1 - p$ is the probability that he consumes c_2. Wilbur is offered a choice between getting a sure payment of $\$Z$ or a lottery in which he receives $2500 with probability 0.40 and he receives $900 with probability 0.60. Wilbur will choose the sure payment if

(a) $Z > 1444$ and the lottery if $Z < 1444$.

(b) $Z > 1972$ and the lottery if $Z < 1972$.

(c) $Z > 900$ and the lottery if $Z < 900$.

(d) $Z > 1172$ and the lottery if $Z < 1172$.

(e) $Z > 1540$ and the lottery if $Z < 1540$.

12.5 Clancy has $4800. He plans to bet on a boxing match between Sullivan and Flanagan. He finds that he can buy coupons for $6 that will pay off $10 each if Sullivan wins. He also finds in another store some coupons that will pay off $10 if Flanagan wins. The Flanagan tickets cost $4 each. Clancy believes that the two fighters each have a probability of 1/2 of winning. Clancy is a risk averter who tries to maximize the expected value of the natural log of his wealth. Which of the following strategies would maximize his expected utility?

(a) Don't gamble at all.

(b) Buy 400 Sullivan tickets and 600 Flanagan tickets.

(c) Buy exactly as many Flanagan tickets as Sullivan tickets.

(d) Buy 200 Sullivan tickets and 300 Flanagan tickets.

(e) Buy 200 Sullivan tickets and 600 Flanagan tickets.

Risky Assets

13.1 Suppose that Ms Lynch in Problem 13.1 can make up her portfolio using a risk-free asset that offers a sure-fire rate of return of 15% and a risky asset with expected rate of return 30%, with standard deviation 5. If she chooses a portfolio with expected rate of return 18.75%, then the standard deviation of her return on this portfolio will be

(a) 0.63%.

(b) 4.25%.

(c) 1.25%.

(d) 2.50% .

(e) None of the other options are correct.

13.2 Suppose that Fenner Smith of Problem 13.2 must divide his portfolio between two assets, one of which gives him an expected rate of return of 15 with zero standard deviation and one of which gives him an expected rate of return of 30 and has a standard deviation of 5. He can alter the expected rate of return and the variance of his portfolio by changing the proportions in which he holds the two assets. If we draw a "budget line" with expected return on the vertical axis and standard deviation on the horizontal axis, depicting the combinations that Smith can obtain, the slope of this budget line is

(a) 3.

(b) −3.

(c) 1.50.

(d) −1.50.

(e) 4.50.

Consumer's Surplus

14.1 In Problem 14.1, Sir Plus has a demand function for mead that is given by the equation $D(p) = 100 - p$. If the price of mead is 75, how much is Sir Plus's net consumer surplus?

(a) 312.50

(b) 25

(c) 625

(d) 156.25

(e) 6000

14.2 Ms Quasimodo in Problem 14.3 has the utility function $U(x, m) = 100x - x^2/2 + m$ where x is his consumption of earplugs and m is money left over to spend on other stuff. If she has \$10,000 to spend on earplugs and other stuff, and if the price of earplugs rises from \$50 to \$95, then her net consumer's surplus

(a) falls by 1237.50.

(b) falls by 3237.50.

(c) falls by 225.

(d) increases by 618.75.

(e) increases by 2475.

14.3 Bernice in Problem 14.5 has the utility function $u(x, y) = \min\{x, y\}$ where x is the number of pairs of earrings she buys per week and y is the number of dollars per week she has left to spend on other things. (We allow the possibility that she buys fractional numbers of pairs of earrings per week.) If she originally had an income of \$13 per week and was paying a price of \$2 per pair of earrings, then if the price of earrings rose to \$4, the compensating variation of that price change (measured in dollars per week) would be closest to

(a) \$5.20.

(b) \$8.67.

(c) $18.33.

(d) $17.33.

(e) $16.33.

14.4 If Bernice (whose utility function is $\min\{x, y\}$ where x is her consumption of earrings and y is money left for other stuff) had an income of $16 and was paying a price of $1 for earrings when the price of earrings went up to $8, then the equivalent variation of the price change was

(a) $12.44.

(b) $56.

(c) $112.

(d) $6.22 .

(e) $34.22.

14.5 In Problem 14.7, Lolita's utility function is $U(x, y) = x - x^2/2 + y$ where x is her consumption of cow feed and y is her consumption of hay. If the price of cow feed is 0.40, the price of hay is 1, and her income is 4, and if Lolita chooses the combination of hay and cow feed that she likes best from among those combinations she can afford, her utility will be

(a) 4.18.

(b) 3.60.

(c) 0.18.

(d) 6.18.

(e) 2.18.

Market Demand

15.1 In Gas Pump, South Dakota, every Buick owner's demand for gasoline is $20 - 5p$ for p less than or equal to 4 and 0 for $p > 4$. Every Dodge owner's demand is $15 - 3p$ for p less than or equal to 5 and 0 for $p > 5$. Suppose that Gas Pump, S.D., has 100 Buick owners and 50 Dodge owners. If the price of gasoline is 4, what is the total amount of gasoline demanded in Gas Pump?

(a) 300

(b) 75

(c) 225

(d) 150

(e) None of the other options are correct.

15.2 In Problem 15.5, the demand function for drangles is given by $D(p) = (p + 1)^{-2}$. If the price of drangles is 10, then the price elasticity of demand is

(a) -7.27.

(b) -3.64.

(c) -5.45.

(d) -0.91.

(e) -1.82.

15.3 In Problem 15.6, the only quantities of good 1 that Barbie can buy are 1 unit or zero units. For x_1 equal to zero or 1 and for all positive values of x_2, suppose that Barbie's preferences were represented by the utility function $(x_1 + 4)(x_2 + 2)$. Then if her income were 28, her reservation price for good 1 would be

(a) 12.

(b) 1.50.

(c) 6.

(d) 2.

(e) 0.40.

15.4 In the same football conference as the university in Problem 15.9 is another university where the demand for football tickets at each game is $80,000 - 12,000p$. If the capacity of the stadium at that university is 50,000 seats, what is the revenue maximizing price for this university to charge per ticket.

(a) 3.33

(b) 2.50

(c) 6.67

(d) 1.67

(e) 10

15.5 In Problem 15.9, the demand for tickets is given by $D(p) = 200,000 - 10,000p$, where p is the price of tickets. If the price of tickets is 4, then the price elasticity of demand for tickets is

(a) −0.50.

(b) −0.38.

(c) −0.75.

(d) −0.13.

(e) −0.25.

Equilibrium

16.1 This problem will be easier if you have done Problem 16.3. The inverse demand function for grapefruit is defined by the equation $p = 296 - 7q$, where q is the number of units sold. The inverse supply function is defined by $p = 17 + 2q$. A tax of 27 is imposed on suppliers for each unit of grapefruit that they sell. When the tax is imposed, the quantity of grapefruit sold falls to

(a) 31.

(b) 17.50.

(c) 26.

(d) 28.

(e) 29.50

16.2 In a crowded city far away, the civic authorities decided that rents were too high. The long run supply function of two-room rental apartments was given by $q = 18 + 2p$ and the long run demand function was given by $q = 114 - 4p$ where p is the rental rate in crowns per week. The authorities made it illegal to rent an apartment for more than 10 crowns per week. To avoid a housing shortage, the authorities agreed to pay landlords enough of a subsidy to make supply equal to demand. How much would the weekly subsidy per apartment have to be to eliminate excess demand at the ceiling price?

(a) 9

(b) 15

(c) 18

(d) 36

(e) 27

16.3 Suppose that King Kanuta from Problem 16.11 demands that each of his subjects give him 4 coconuts for every coconut that they consume. The king puts all of the coconuts that he collects in a large pile and burns them. The supply of coconuts is given by $S(p_s) = 100p_s$, where p_s is the price received by suppliers. The demand for coconuts by the king's subjects is given by $D(p_d) = 8320 - 100p_d$, where p_d is the price paid by consumers. In equilibrium, the price received by suppliers will be

(a) 16.

(b) 24.

(c) 41.60.

(d) 208.

(e) None of the other options are correct.

16.4 In Problem 16.6, the demand function for Schrecklichs is $200 - 4P_S - 2P_L$ and the demand function for LaMerdes is $200 - 3P_L - P_S$, where P_S and P_L are respectively the price of Schrecklichs and LaMerdes. If the world supply of Schrecklichs is 100 and the world supply of Lamerdes is 90, then the equilibrium price of Schrecklichs is

(a) 8

(b) 25

(c) 42

(d) 34

(e) 16

Technology

17.1 This problem will be easier if you have done Problem 17.1. A firm has the production function $f(x_1, x_2) = x_1^{0.90} x_2^{0.30}$. The isoquant on which output is $40^{3/10}$ has the equation

(a) $x_2 = 40 x_1^{-3}$.

(b) $x_2 = 40 x_1^{3.33}$.

(c) $x_1/x_2 = 3$.

(d) $x_2 = 40 x_1^{-0.30}$.

(e) $x_1 = 0.30 x_2^{-0.70}$.

17.2 A firm has the production function $f(x, y) = x^{0.70} y^{-0.30}$. This firm has

(a) decreasing returns to scale and dimininishing marginal products for factor x.

(b) increasing returns to scale and decreasing marginal product of factor x.

(c) decreasing returns to scale and increasing marginal product for factor x.

(d) constant returns to scale.

(e) None of the other options are correct.

17.3 A firm uses 3 factors of production. Its production function is $f(x, y, z) = \min\{x^5/y, y^4, (z^6 - x^6)/y^2\}$. If the amount of each input is multiplied by 6, its output will be multiplied by

(a) 7776.

(b) 1296.

(c) 216 .

(d) 0.

(e) The answer depends on the original choice of x, y, and z.

17.4 A firm has a production function $f(x, y) = 1.20(x^{0.10} + y^{0.10})^1$ whenever $x > 0$ and $y > 0$. When the amounts of both inputs are positive, this firm has

(a) increasing returns to scale.

(b) decreasing returns to scale.

(c) constant returns to scale.

(d) increasing returns to scale if $x + y > 1$ and decreasing returns to scale otherwise.

(e) increasing returns to scale if output is less than 1 and decreasing returns to scale if output is greater than 1.

Profit Maximization

18.1 In Problem 18.1, the production function is given by $F(L) = 6L^{2/3}$. Suppose that the cost per unit of labor is 8 and the price of output is 8, how many units of labor will the firm hire?

(a) 128

(b) 64

(c) 32

(d) 192

(e) None of the other options are correct.

18.2 In Problem 18.2, the production function is given by $f(x) = 4x^{1/2}$. If the price of the commodity produced is 70 per unit and the cost of the input is 35 per unit, how much profits will the firm make if it maximizes profits?

(a) 560

(b) 278

(c) 1124

(d) 545

(e) 283

18.3 In Problem 18.11, the production function is $f(x_1, x_2) = x_1^{1/2} x_2^{1/2}$. If the price of factor 1 is 8 and the price of factor 2 is 16, in what proportions should the firm use factors 1 and 2 if it wants to maximize profits?

(a) $x_1 = x_2$.

(b) $x_1 = 0.50x_2$.

(c) $x_1 = 2x_2$.

(d) We can't tell without knowing the price of output.

(e) $x_1 = 16x_2$.

18.4 In Problem 18.9, when Farmer Hoglund applies N pounds of fertilizer per acre, the marginal product of fertilizer is $1 - (N/200)$ bushels of corn. If the price of corn is $4 per bushel and the price of fertilizer is $1.20 per pound, then how many pounds of fertilizer per acre should Farmer Hoglund use in order to maximize his profits?

(a) 140

(b) 280

(c) 74

(d) 288

(e) 200

Cost Minimization

19.1 Suppose that Nadine in Problem 19.1 has a production function $3x_1 + x_2$. If the factor prices are 9 for factor 1 and 4 for factor 2, how much will it cost her to produce 50 units of output?

(a) 1550

(b) 150

(c) 200

(d) 875

(e) 175

19.2 In Problem 19.2, suppose that a new alloy is invented which uses copper and zinc in fixed proportions, where one unit of output requires 3 units of copper and 3 units of zinc for each unit of alloy produced. If no other inputs are needed, if the price of copper is 2 and the price of zinc is 2, what is the average cost per unit when 4000 units of the alloy are produced?

(a) 6.33

(b) 666.67

(c) 0.67

(d) 12

(e) 6333.33

19.3 In Problem 19.3, the production function is $f(L, M) = 4L^{1/2}M^{1/2}$, where L is the number of units of labor and M is the number of machines used. If the cost of labor is $25 per unit and the cost of machines is $64 per unit, then the total cost of producing 6 units of output will be

(a) 120 .

(b) 267.

(c) 150 .

(d) 240.

(e) None of the other options are correct.

19.4 Suppose that in the short run, the firm in Problem 19.3 which has production function $F(L, M) = 4L^{1/2}M^{1/2}$ must use 25 machines. If the cost of labor is 8 per unit and the cost of machines is 7 per unit, the short run total cost of producing 200 units of output is

(a) 1500.

(b) 1400.

(c) 1600.

(d) 1950.

(e) 975.

19.5 In Problem 19.12, Al's production function for deer is $f(x_1, x_2) = (2x_1 + x_2)^{1/2}$ where x_1 is the amount of plastic and x_2 is the amount of wood used. If the cost of plastic is \$2 per unit and the cost of wood is \$4 per unit, then the cost of producing 8 deer is

(a) 64 .

(b) 70 .

(c) 256.

(d) 8.

(e) 32.

19.6 Two firms, Wickedly Efficient Widgets, and Wildly Nepotistic Widgets both produce widgets with the same production function $y = K^{1/2}L^{1/2}$ where K is the input of capital and L is the input of labor. Each company can hire labor at \$1 per unit and capital at \$1 per unit. WEW produces 10 widgets per week, choosing its input combination so as to produce these 10 widgets in the cheapest way possible. WNW also produces 10 widgets per week, but its dotty ceo requires it to use twice as much labor as WEW uses. Given that it must use twice as many laborers as WEW does, and must produce the same output, how much more larger are WNW's total costs than WEW's?

(a) \$10 per week

(b) \$20 per week

(c) \$15 per week

(d) \$5 per week

(e) \$2 per week

Cost Curves

20.1 In Problem 20.2, if Mr. Dent Carr's total costs were $4s^2 + 75s + 60$, then if he repairs 15 cars, his average variable costs will be

(a) 135.

(b) 139.

(c) 195.

(d) 270.

(e) 97.50.000

20.2 In Problem 20.3, Rex Carr could pay $10 for a shovel that lasts one year and pay $5 a car to his brother Scoop to bury the cars, or he could buy a low-quality car smasher that costs $200 a year to own and that smashes cars at a marginal cost of $1 per car. If it is also possible for Rex to buy a high-quality hydraulic car smasher that cost $300 per year to own and if with this smasher he could dispose of cars at a cost of $0.80 per car, it would be worthwhile for him to buy this high-quality smasher smasher if

(a) he plans to dispose of at least 500 cars per year.

(b) he plans to dispose of no more than 250 cars per year.

(c) he plans to dispose of at least 510 cars per year.

(d) he plans to dispose of no more than 500 cars per year.

(e) he plans to dispose of at least 250 cars per year.

20.3 Mary Magnolia in Problem 20.4 has variable costs equal to y^2/F where y is the number of bouquets she sells per month and where F is the number of square feet of space in her shop. If Mary has signed a lease for a shop with 1600 square feet and if she is not able to get out of the lease or to expand her store in the short run, and if the price of a bouquet is $3 per unit, how many bouquets per month should she sell in the short run?

(a) 1600

(b) 800

(c) 2400

(d) 3600

(e) 2640

20.4 Touchie MacFeelie's production function is $.1J^{1/2}L^{3/4}$, where J is the number of old jokes used and L is the number of hours of cartoonists' labor. Touchie is stuck with 900 old jokes for which he paid 6 dollars each. If the wage rate for cartoonists is 5, then the total cost of producing 24 comics books is

(a) 5480.

(b) 2740.

(c) 8220.

(d) 5504.

(e) 1370.

20.5 Recall that Touchie McFeelie's production function for comic books is $.1J^{1/2}L^{3/4}$. Suppose that Touchie can vary both jokes and cartoonists' labor. If old jokes cost \$2 each and cartoonists' labor costs \$18 per hour, then the cheapest way to produce comics books requires using jokes and labor in the ratio $J/L =$

(a) 9.

(b) 12.

(c) 3.

(d) 2/3.

(e) 6.

Firm Supply

21.1 Suppose that Dent Carr's long run total cost of repairing s cars per week is $c(s) = 3s^2 + 192$. If the price he receives for repairing a car is 36, then in the long run, how many cars will he fix per week if he maximizes profits?

(a) 6.

(b) 0.

(c) 12.

(d) 9.

(e) 18.

21.2 In Problem 21.9, suppose that Irma's production function is $f(x_1, x_2) = (\min\{x_1, 2x_2\})^{1/2}$. If the price of factor 1 is $w_1 = 6$ and the price of factor 2 is $w_2 = 4$, then her supply function is given by the equation

(a) $S(p) = p/16$.

(b) $S(p) = p \max\{w_1, 2 * w_2\}^2$.

(c) $S(p) = p \min\{w_1, 2w_2\}^2$.

(d) $S(p) = 8p$.

(e) $S(p) = \min\{6p, 8p\}$.

21.3 A firm has the long run cost function $C(q) = 2q^2 + 8$. In the long run, it will supply a positive amount of output, so long as the price is greater than

(a) 16.

(b) 24.

(c) 4.

(d) 8.

(e) 13.

NAME_____

Industry Supply

22.1 In Problem 22.1, if the cost of plaster and labor were $9 per gnome and everything else is as in the problem, what is the lowest price of gnomes at which there would be a positive supply in the long run?

(a) 9

(b) 18

(c) 11.20

(d) 9.90

(e) 10.80

22.2 Suppose that the garden gnome industry was in long run equilibrium given the circumstances described in Problem 22.1. Suppose, as in Problem 22.2, that it was discovered to everyone's surprise on January 1, 1993 after it was to late to change orders for gnome molds, that the cost of the plaster and labor needed to make a gnome had changed to 8. If the demand curve does not change, what will happen to the equilibrium price of gnomes?

(a) It rises by 1.

(b) It falls by 1.

(c) It stays constant.

(d) It rises by 8.

(e) It falls by 4.

22.3 Suppose that the garden gnome industry was in long run equilibrium as described in 22.1 and that on January 1, 1993, the cost of plaster and labor remained at $7 per gnome, and the government introduced a tax of $2 on every garden gnome sold. Then the equilibrium price of garden gnomes in 1993 would be

(a) 9.

(b) 9.20.

(c) 7.

(d) 10.

(e) 27.

22.4 Suppose that the cost of capturing a cockatoo and transporting him to the U. S. is about $40 per bird. Cockatoos are drugged and smuggled in suitcases to the U. S. Half of the smuggled cockatoos die in transit. Each smuggled cockatoo has a 10% probability of being discovered, in which case the smuggler is fined. If the fine imposed for each smuggled cockatoo is increased to $900, then the equilibrium price of cockatoos in the U. S. will be

(a) 288.89.

(b) 130.

(c) 85.

(d) 67.

(e) 200.

22.5 In Problem 22.13, in the absence of government interference, there is a constant marginal cost of $5 per ounce for growing marijuana and delivering it to buyers. If the probability that any shipment of marijuana is seized is 0.20 and the fine if a shipper is caught is $20 per ounce, then the equilibrium price of marijuana per ounce is

(a) 11.25.

(b) 9.

(c) 25.

(d) 4.

(e) 6.

22.6 In Problem 22.8, the supply curve of any firm is $S_i(p) = p/2$. If a firm produces 3 units of output, what is its total variable costs?

(a) $18

(b) $7

(c) $13.50

(d) $9

(e) There is not enough information given to determine total variable costs.

Monopoly

23.1 In Problem 23.1, if the demand schedule for Bong's book is $Q = 3000 - 100p$, the cost of having the book typeset is 10000, and the marginal cost of printing an extra book is \$4, then he would maximize his profits by

(a) having it typeset and selling 1300 copies.

(b) having it typeset and selling 1500 copies.

(c) not having it typeset and not selling any copies.

(d) having it typeset and selling 2600 copies.

(e) having it typeset and selling 650 copies.

23.2 In Problem 23.2, if the demand for pigeon pies is $p(y) = 70 - y/2$, then what level of output will maximize Peter's profits?

(a) 74

(b) 14

(c) 140

(d) 210

(e) None of the above

23.3 A profit-maximizing monopoly faces an inverse demand function described by the equation $p(y) = 70 - y$ and its total costs are $c(y) = 5y$, where prices and costs are measured in dollars. In the past it was not taxed, but now it must pay a tax of 8 dollars per unit of output. After the tax, the monopoly will

(a) increase its price by 8.

(b) increase its price by 12.

(c) increase its price by 4.

(d) leave its price constant.

(e) None of the other options are correct.

23.4 A firm has invented a new beverage called Slops. It doesn't taste very good, but it gives people a craving for Lawrence Welk's music and Professor Johnson's jokes. Some people are willing to pay money for this effect, so the demand for Slops is given by the equation $q = 14 - p$. Slops can be made at zero marginal cost from old-fashioned macroeconomics books dissolved in bathwater. But before any Slops can be produced, the firm must undertake a fixed cost of 54. Since the inventor has a patent on Slops, it can be a monopolist in this new industry.

(a) The firm will produce 12 units of Slops.

(b) A Pareto improvement could be achieved by having the government pay the firm a subsidy of 59 and insisting that the firm offer Slops at zero price.

(c) From the point of view of social efficiency, it is best that no Slops be produced.

(d) The firm will produce 14 units of Slops.

(e) None of the other options are correct.

Monopoly Behavior

24.1 (See Problem 24.1). If demand in the U.S. is given by $Q_1 = 23400 - 900p_1$, where p_1 is the price in the U.S. and if the demand in England is given by $2800 - 200p_2$ where p_2 is the price in England, then the difference between the price charged in England and the price charged in the U.S. will be

(a) 6.

(b) 12.

(c) 0.

(d) 14.

(e) 18.

24.2 (See Problem 24.2) A monopolist faces a demand curve described by p(y)=100-2y , has constant marginal costs of 16 and zero fixed costs. If this monopolist is able to practice perfect price discrimination, its total profits will be

(a) 1764.

(b) 21.

(c) 882.

(d) 2646.

(e) 441.

24.3 A price-discriminating monopolist sells in two separate markets such that goods sold in one market are never resold in the other. It charges 4 in one market and 8 in the other market. At these prices, the price elasticity in the first market is −1.50 and the price elasticity in the second market is −0.10. Which of the following actions is sure to raise the monopolists profits?

(a) Lower p_2.

(b) Raise p_2.

(c) Raise p_1 and lower p_2.

(d) Raise both p_1 and p_2.

(e) Raise p_2 and lower p_1.

24.4 The demand for Professor Bongmore's new book is given by the function $Q = 2000 - 100p$. If the cost of having the book typeset is 8000, if the marginal cost of printing an extra copy is 4, and if he has no other costs, then he would maximize his profits by

(a) having it typeset and selling 800 copies.

(b) having it typeset and selling 1000 copies.

(c) not having it typeset and not selling any copies.

(d) having it typeset and selling 1600 copies.

(e) having it typeset and selling 400 copies.

Factor Markets

25.1 Suppose that in Problem 25.2, the demand curve for mineral water is given by $p = 30 - 12q$, where p is the price per bottle paid by consumers and q is the number of bottles purchased by consumers. Mineral water is supplied to consumers by a monopolistic distributor, who buys from a monopolist producer who is able to produce mineral water at zero cost. The producer charges the distributor a price of c per bottle, where the price c maximizes the producer's total revenue. Given his marginal cost of c, the distributor chooses an output to maximize profits. The price paid by consumers under this arrangement is

(a) 15.

(b) 22.50.

(c) 2.50.

(d) 1.25.

(e) 7.50.

25.2 Suppose that the labor supply curve for a large university in a small town is given by $w = 60 + 0.08L$ where L is number of units of labor per week and w is the weekly wage paid per unit of labor. If the university is currently hiring 1000 units of labor per week, the marginal cost of an additional unit of labor

(a) equals the wage rate.

(b) is twice the wage rate.

(c) equals the wage rate plus 160.

(d) equals the wage rate plus 80.

(e) equals the wage rate plus 240

25.3 Rabelaisian Restaurants has a monopoly in the town of Upper Glutton. Its production function is $Q = 40L$ where L, is the amount of labor it uses and Q is the number of meals produced. Rabelaisian Restaurants finds that in order to hire L units of labor, it must pay a wage of $40 + .1L$ per unit of labor. The demand curve for meals at Rabelaisian Restaurants is given by $P = 30.75 - Q/1000$. The profit maximizing output for Rabelasian Restaurants is

(a) 14000.

(b) 28000.

(c) 3500.

(d) 3000.

(e) 1750.

Oligopoly

26.1 Suppose that the duopolists Carl and Simon in Problem 26.1 face a demand function for pumpkins of $Q = 13200 - 800P$, where Q is the total number of pumpkins that reach the market and P is the price of pumpkins. Suppose further that each farmer has a constant marginal cost of $0.50 for each pumpkin produced. If Carl believes that Simon is going to produce Q_s pumpkins this year, then the reaction function tells us how many pumpkins Carl should produce in order to maximize his profits. Carl's reaction function is $R_C(Q_s) =$

(a) $6400 - Q_s/2$.

(b) $13200 - 800Q_s$.

(c) $13200 - 1600Q_s$.

(d) $3200 - Q_s/2$.

(e) $9600 - Q_s$.

26.2 If in problem 26.4, the inverse demand for bean sprouts were given by $P(Y) = 290 - 4Y$ and the total cost of producing y units for any firm were $TC(Y) = 50Y$, and if the industry consisted of two Cournot duopolists, then in equilibrium each firm's production would be

(a) 30 units.

(b) 15 units.

(c) 10 units.

(d) 20 units.

(e) 18.13 units.

26.3 In Problem 26.5, suppose that Grinch and Grubb go into the wine business in a small country where wine is difficult to grow. The demand for wine is given by $p = \$360 - .2Q$ where p is the price and Q is the total quantity sold. The industry consists of just the two Cournot duopolists, Grinch and Grubb. Imports are prohibited. Grinch has constant marginal costs of $15 and Grubb has marginal costs of $75. How much is Grinch's output in equilibrium?

(a) 675

(b) 1350

(c) 337.50

(d) 1012.50

(e) 2025

26.4 In Problem 26.6, suppose that two Cournot duopolists serve the Peoria-Dubuque route, and the demand curve for tickets per day is $Q = 200 - 2p$ (so $p = 100 - Q/2$). Total costs of running a flight on this route are 700+40q where q is the number of passengers on the flight. Each flight has a capacity of 80 passengers. In Cournot equilibrium, each duopolist will run one flight per day and will make a daily profit of

(a) 100

(b) 350

(c) 200

(d) 200

(e) 2400

26.5 In Problem 26.4, suppose that the market demand curve for bean sprouts is given by $P = 880 - 2Q$, where P is the price and Q is total industry output. Suppose that the industry has two firms, a Stackleberg leader, and a follower. Each firm has a constant marginal cost of $80 per unit of output. In equilibrium, total output by the two firms will be

(a) 200.

(b) 100.

(c) 300.

(d) 400.

(e) 50.

26.6 There are two firms in the blastopheme industry. The demand curve for blastophemes is given by $p = 2100 - 3q$. Each firm has one manufacturing plant and each firm i has a cost function $C(q_i) = q_i^2$ where q_i is the output of firm i. The two firms form a cartel and arrange to split total industry profits equally. Under this cartel arrangement, they will maximize joint profits if

(a) and only if each firm produces 150 units in its plant.

(b) they produce a total of 300 units, no matter which firm produces them.

(c) and only if they each produce a total of 350 units.

(d) the produce a total of 233.33 units, no matter which firm produces them.

(e) they shut down one of the two plants, having the other operate as a monopoly, and splitting the profits.

Game Theory

27.1 (See Problem 27.1) Big Pig and Little Pig have two possible strategies, Press the Button, and Wait at the trough. If both pigs choose Wait, both get 4. If both pigs press the button then Big Pig gets 5 and Little Pig gets 5. If Little Pig presses the button and Big Pig waits at the trough, then Big Pig gets 10 and Little Pig gets 0. Finally, if Big Pig presses the button and Little Pig waits, then Big Pig gets 4 and Little Pig gets 2. In Nash equilibrium,

(a) Little Pig will get a payoff of 2 and Big Pig will get a payoff of 4.

(b) Little Pig will get a payoff of 5 and Big Pig will get a payoff of 5.

(c) Both pigs will wait at the trough.

(d) Little pig will get a payoff of zero.

(e) The pigs must be using mixed strategies.

27.2 (See Problem 27.6) Two players are engaged in a game of "chicken". There are two possible strategies. Swerve and Drive Straight. A player who chooses to Swerve is called "Chicken" and gets a payoff of zero, regardless of what the other player does. A player who chooses to Drive Straight gets a payoff of 32 if the other player swerves and a payoff of -48 if the other player also chooses to Drive Straight. This game has two pure strategy equilibria and

(a) a mixed strategy equilibrium in which each player swerves with probability 0.60 and drives straight with probability 0.40.

(b) two mixed strategies in which players alternate between swerving and driving straight.

(c) a mixed strategy equilibrium in which one player swerves with probability 0.60 and the other swerves with probability 0.40.

(d) a mixed strategy in which each player swerves with probability 0.30 and drives straight with probability 0.70.

(e) no mixed strategies.

27.3 The old Michigan football coach had only two strategies. Run the ball to the left side of the line. Run the ball to the right side. The defense can concentrate either on the left side or the right side of Michigan's line. If the opponent concentrates on the wrong side, Michigan is sure to gain at least 5 yards. If the defense defended the left side and Michigan ran left, Michigan would be stopped for no gain. But if the opponent defended the right side when Michigan ran right, Michigan would still gain at least 5 yards with probability 0.40. It is the last play of the game and Michigan needs to gain 5 yards to win. Both sides choose Nash equilibrium strategies. In Nash equilibrium, Michigan would

(a) be sure to run to the right side.

(b) run to the right side with probability 0.63.

(c) run to the right side with probability 0.77.

(d) run with equal probability to one side or the other.

(e) run to the right side with probability 0.60.

27.4 Suppose that in the Hawk-Dove game discussed in Problem 26.3, the payoff to each player is −4 if both play Hawk. If both play Dove, the payoff to each player is 1 and if one plays Hawk and the other plays Dove, the one that plays Hawk gets a payoff of 3 and the one that plays Dove gets 0. In equilibrium, we would expect Hawks and Doves to do equally well. This happens when the fraction of the total population that plays Hawk is

(a) 0.33.

(b) 0.17.

(c) 0.08.

(d) 0.67.

(e) 1.

27.5 (See Problem 27.11) If the number of persons who attend the club meeting this week is X, then the number of people who will attend next week is $27 + 0.70X$. What is a long run equilibrium attendance for this club?

(a) 27

(b) 38.57

(c) 54

(d) 90

(e) 63

Exchange

28.1 An economy has two people Charlie and Doris. There are two goods, apples and bananas. Charlie has an initial endowment of 3 apples and 12 bananas. Doris has an initial endowment of 6 apples and 6 bananas. Charlie's utility function is $U(A_C, B_C) = A_C B_C$ where A_C is his apple consumption and B_C is his banana consumption. Doris's utility function is $U(A_D, B_D) = A_D B_D$ where A_D and B_D are her apple and banana consumptions. At every Pareto optimal allocation,

(a) Charlie consumes the same number of apples as Doris.

(b) Charlie consumes 9 apples for every 18 bananas that he consumes.

(c) Doris consumes equal numbers of apples and bananas.

(d) Charlie consumes more bananas per apple than Doris does.

(e) Doris consumes apples and bananas in the ratio of 6 apples for every 6 bananas that she consumes.

28.2 In Problem 28.4, Ken's utility function is $U(Q_K, W_K) = Q_K W_K$ and Barbie's utility function is $U(Q_B, W_B) = Q_B W_B$. If Ken's initial endowment were 3 units of quiche and 10 units of wine and Barbie's endowment were 6 units of quiche and 10 units of wine, then at any Pareto optimal allocation where both persons consume some of each good,

(a) Ken would consume 3 units of quiche for every 10 units of wine.

(b) Barbie would consume twice as much quiche as Ken.

(c) Ken would consume 9 units of quiche for every 20 units of wine that he consumes.

(d) Barbie would consume 6 units of quiche for every 10 units of wine that she consumes.

(e) None of the other options are correct.

28.3 In Problem 28.1, suppose that Morris has the utility function $U(b, w) = 6b + 24w$ and Philip has the utility function $U(b, w) = bw$. If we draw an Edgeworth box with books on the horizontal axis and wine on the vertical axis and if we measure Morris' consumptions from the lower left corner of the box, then the contract curve contains

(a) a straight line running from the upper right corner of the box to the lower left.

(b) a curve that gets steeper as you move from left to right.

(c) a straight line with slope 1/4 passing through the lower left corner of the box.

(d) a straight line with slope 1/4 passing through the upper right corner of the box.

(e) a curve that gets flatter as you move from left to right.

28.4 In Problem 28.2, Astrid's utility function is $U(H_a, C_A) = H_A C_A$. Birger's utility function is $\min\{H_B, C_B\}$. Astrid's initial endowment is no cheese and 4 units of herring, and Birger's initial endowments are 6 units of cheese and no herring. Where p is a competitive equilibrium price of herring and cheese is the numeraire, it must be that demand equals supply in the herring market. This implies that

(a) $6/(p+1) + 2 = 4$.

(b) $6/4 = p$.

(c) $4/6 = p$.

(d) $6/p + 4/2p = 4$.

(e) $\min\{4, 6\} = p$.

28.5 Suppose that in Problem 28.8, Mutt's utility function is $U(m, j) = \max\{3m, j\}$ and Jeff's utility function is $U(m, j) = 2m + j$. Mutt is initially endowed with 4 units of milk and 2 units of juice. Jeff is initially endowed with 4 units of milk and 6 units of juice. If we draw an Edgeworth box with milk on the horizontal axis and juice on the vertical axis and if we measure goods for Mutt by the distance from the lower left corner of the box, then the set of Pareto optimal allocations includes the

(a) left edge of the Edgeworth box but no other edges.

(b) bottom edge of the Edgeworth box but no other edges.

(c) left edge and bottom edge of the Edgeworth box.

(d) right edge of the Edgeworth box but no other edges.

(e) right edge and top edge of the Edgeworth box.

28.6 In Problem 28.3, Professor Nightsoil's utility function, $U_N(B_N, P_N)$, is $B_N + 4P_N^{1/2}$ and Dean Interface's utility function is $U_I(B_I, P_I) == B_I + 2P_I^{1/2}$. If Nightsoil's initial endowment is 7 bromides and 15 platitudes and if Interface's initial endowment is 7 bromides and 25 platitudes, then at any Pareto efficient allocation where both persons consume positive amounts of both goods, it must be that

(a) Nightsoil consumes the same ratio of bromides to platitudes as Interface.

(b) Interface consumes 8 platitudes.

(c) Interface consumes 7 bromides.

(d) Interface consumes 3 bromides.

(e) Interface consumes 5 platitudes.

Quiz 29

Production

NAME_____

29.1 Suppose that in Problem 29.1, Tip can write 5 pages of term papers or solve 20 workbook problems in an hour, while Spot can write 2 pages of term papers or solve 6 workbook problems in an hour. If they each decide to work a total of 7 hours, and to share their output then if they produce as many pages of term paper as possible given that they produce 30 workbook problems,

(a) Spot will spend all of his time writing term papers and Tip will spend some time at each task.

(b) Tip will spend all of his time writing term papers and Spot will spend some time at each task.

(c) both students will spend some time at each task.

(d) Spot will write term papers only and Tip will do workbook problems only.

(e) Tip will write term papers only and Spot will do workbook problems only.

29.2 Al and Bill are the only workers in a small factory which makes geegaws and doodads. Al can make 3 geegaws per hour or 15 doodads per hour. Bill can make 2 geegaws per hour or 6 doodads per hour. Assuming that neither of them finds one task more odious than the other,

(a) Al has comparative advantage in producing geegaws, and Bill has comparative advantage in producing doodads.

(b) Bill has comparative advantage in producing geegaws, and Al has comparative advantage in producing doodads.

(c) Al has comparative advantage in producing both geegaws and doodads.

(d) Bill has comparative advantage in producing both geegaws and doodads.

(e) both persons have comparative advantage in producing doodads.

29.3 (See Problem 29.5.) Every consumer has a red-money income and a blue-money income and each commodity has a red price and a blue price. You can buy a good by paying for it either with blue money at the blue price, or with red money at the red price. Harold has 10 units of red money to spend and 18 units of blue money to spend. The red price of ambrosia is 1 and the blue price of ambrosia is 2. The red price of bubblegum is 1 and the blue price of bubblegum is 1. If ambrosia is on the horizontal axis, and bubblegum on the vertical, axis, then Harold's budget set is bounded

(a) by two line segments, one running from (0,28) to (10,18) and another running from (10,18) to (19,0).

(b) by two line segments one running from (0,28) to (9,10) and the other running from (9,10) to (19,0).

(c) by two line segments, one running from (0,27)to (10,18) and the other running from (10,18) to (20,0).

(d) a vertical line segment and a horizontal line segement, intersecting at (10,18).

(e) a vertical line segment and a horizontal line segment, intersecting at (9,10).

29.4 (See Problem 29.2.) Robinson Crusoe has exactly 12 hours per day to spend gathering coconuts or catching fish. He can catch 4 fish per hour or he can pick 16 coconuts per hour. His utility function is $U(F, C) = FC$ where F is his consumption of fish and C is his consumption of coconuts. If he allocates his time in the best possible way between catching fish and picking coconuts, his consumption will be the same as it would be if he could buy fish and coconuts in a competitive market where the price of coconuts is 1, and where

(a) his income is 192 and the price of fish is 4.

(b) his income is 48 and the price of fish is 4.

(c) his income is 240 and the price of fish is 4.

(d) his income is 192 and the price of fish is 0.25.

(e) his income is 120 and the price of fish is 0.25.

29.5 On a certain island there are only two goods, wheat and milk. The only scarce resource is land. There are 1000 acres of land. An acre of land will produce either 16 units of milk or 37 units of wheat. Some citizens have lots of land, some have just a little bit. The citizens of the island all have utility functions of the form $U(M, W) = MW$. At every Pareto optimal allocation,

(a) the number of units of milk produced equals the number of units of wheat produced.

(b) total milk production is 8000.

(c) all citizens consume the same commodity bundle.

(d) every consumer's marginal rate of substitution between milk and wheat is −1.

(e) None of the above is true at *every* Pareto optimal allocation.

Welfare

30.1 A Borda count is used to decide an election between 3 candidates, x, y, and z where a score of 1 is awarded to a first choice, 2 to a second choice and 3 to a third choice. There are 25 voters. 7 voters rank the candidates x first, y second, z third; 4 voters rank the candidates x first, z second, y third; 6 rank the candidates, z first, y second, x third; 8 voters rank the candidates, y first, z second, x third. Which candidate wins?

(a) Candidate x.

(b) Candidate y.

(c) Candidate z.

(d) There is a tie between x and y, with z coming in third.

(e) There is a tie between y and z, with x coming in third.

30.2 A parent has two children living in cities with different costs of living. The cost of living in city B is 3 times the cost of living in city A. The child in city A has an income of 3000 and the child in city B has an income of 9000. The parent wants to give a total of \$4000 to her two children. Her utility function is $U(C_A, C_B) = C_A C_B$, where C_A and C_B are the consumptions of the children living in cities A and B respectively. She will choose to

(a) give each child \$2000, even though this will buy less goods for the child in city B.

(b) give the child in city B 3 times as much money as the child in city B.

(c) Give the child in city A 3 times as much money as the child in city B.

(d) Give the child in city B 1.50 times as much money as the child in city A.

(e) Give the child in city A 1.50 times as much money as the child in city B.

30.3 Suppose that Paul and David from Problem 30.7 have utility functions $U = 5A_P + O_P$ and $U = A_D + 5O_D$, respectively, where A_P and O_P are Paul's consumptions of apples and oranges and A_D and O_D are David's consumptions of apples and oranges. The total supply of apples and oranges to be divided between them is 8 apples and 8 oranges. The "fair" allocations consist of all allocations satisfying the following conditions.

(a) $A_D = A_P$ and $O_D = O_P$.

(b) $10A_P + 2O_P$ is at least 48, and $2A_D + 10O_D$ is at least 48.

(c) $5A_P + O_P$ is at least 48, and $2A_D + 5O_D$ is at least 48

(d) $A_D + O_D$ is at least 8, and $A_S + O_S$ is at least 8.

(e) $5A_P + O_P$ is at least $A_D + 5O_D$, and $A_D + 5O_D$ is at least $5A_P + O_P$.

30.4 Suppose that Romeo in Problem 30.8 has the utility function $U = S_R^8 S_J^4$ and Juliet has the utility function $U = S_R^4 S_J^8$, where S_R is Romeo's spaghetti consumption and S_J is Juliet's. They have 96 units of spaghetti to divide between them.

(a) Romeo would want to give Juliet some spaghetti if he had more than 48 units of spaghetti.

(b) Juliet would want to give Romeo some spaghetti if she has more than 62 units.

(c) Romeo and Juliet would never disagree about how to divide the spaghetti.

(d) Romeo would want to give Juliet some spaghetti if he has more than 60 units of spaghetti.

(e) Juliet would want to give Romeo some spaghetti if she has more than 64 units of spaghetti.

30.5 Hatfield and McCoy burn with hatred for each other. They both consume corn whisky. Hatfield's utility function is $U = W_H - W_M^{2/8}$ and McCoy's utility is $U = W_M - W_H^{2/8}$, where W_H is Hatfield's whisky consumption and W_M is McCoy's whisky consumption, measured in gallons. The sheriff has a total of 28 units of confiscated whisky that he could give back to them. For some reason, the sheriff wants them both to be as happy as possible, and he wants to treat them equally. The sheriff should give them each

(a) 14 gallons.

(b) 4 gallons and spill 20 gallons in the creek.

(c) 2 gallons and spill 24 gallons in the creek.

(d) 8 gallons and spill the rest in the creek.

(e) 1 gallons and spill the rest in the creek.

Externalities

31.1 Suppose that in Horsehead, Massachusetts, the cost of operating a lobster boat is $3000 per month. Suppose that if X lobster boats operate in the bay, the total monthly revenue from lobster boats in the bay is $1000(23x - x^2)$. If there are no restrictions on entry and new boats come into the bay until there is no profit to be made by a new entrant, then the number of boats who enter will be $X1$. If the number of boats that operate in the bay is regulated to maximize total profitms, the number of boats in the bay will be $X2$.

(a) $X1 = 20$ and $X2 = 20$.

(b) $X1 = 10$ and $X2 = 8$.

(c) $X1 = 20$ and $X2 = 10$.

(d) $X1 = 24$ and $X2 = 14$.

(e) None of the other options are correct.

31.2 An apiary is located next to an apple orchard. The apiary produces honey and the apple orchard produces apples. The cost function of the apiary is $C_H(H, A) = H^2/100 - 1A$ and the cost function of the apple orchard is $C_A(H, A) = A^2/100$, where H and A are the number of units of honey and apples produced respectively. The price of honey is 8 and the price of apples is 7 per unit. Let $A1$ be the output of apples if the firms operate independently, and let $A2$ be the output of apples if the firms are operated by a single owner so that

(a) $A1 = 175$ and $A2 = 350$.

(b) $A1 = A2 = 350$.

(c) $A1 = 200$ and $A2 = 350$.

(d) $A1 = 350$ and $A2 = 400$.

(e) $A1 = 400$ and $A2 = 350$.

31.3 Martin's utility is $U(c, d, h) = 2c + 5d - d^2 - 2h$, where d is the number of hours per day that he spends driving around, h is the number of hours per day spent driving around by other people in his home town and c is the amount of money he has left to spend on other stuff besides gasoline and auto repairs. Gas and auto repairs cost \$.50 per hour of driving. All the people in Martin's home town have the same tastes. If each citizen believes that his own driving will not affect the amount of driving done by others, they will all drive $D1$ hours per day. If they are all drive the same amount, they would all be best off if each drove $D2$ hours per day, where

(a) $D1 = 2$ and $D2 = 1$.

(b) $D1 = D2 = 2$.

(c) $D1 = 4$ and $D2 = 2$.

(d) $D1 = 5$ and $D2 = 0$.

(e) $D1 = 24$ and $D2 = 0$.

31.4 (See Problems 31.8, 31.9.) An airport is located next to a housing development. Where X is the number of planes that land per day and Y is the number of houses in the housing development, profits of the airport are $22X - X^2$ and profits of the developer are $32Y - Y^2 - XY$. Let $H1$ be the number of houses built if a single profit-maximizing company owns the airport and the housing development. Let $H2$ be the number of houses built if the airport and the housing development are operated independently and the airport has to pay the developer the total "damages" XY done by the planes to developer's profits. Then

(a) $H1 = H2 = 14$.

(b) $H1 = 14$ and $H2 = 16$.

(c) $H1 = 16$ and $H2 = 14$.

(d) $H1 = 16$ and $H2 = 15$.

(e) H1=15 and H2=19.

31.5 (See Problem 31.5.) A clothing store and a jeweler are located side by side in a shopping mall. If the clothing store spend C dollars on advertising and the jeweler spends J dollars on advertising, then the profits of the clothing store will be $(48 + J)C - 2C^2$ and the profits of the jeweler will be $(42 + C)J - 2J^2$. The clothing store gets to choose his amount of advertising first, knowing that the jeweler will find out how much the clothing store advertised before deciding how much to spend. The amount spent by the clothing store will be *(a)* 23.

(b) 46.

(c) 69.

(d) 11.50.

(e) 34.50.

Law

32.1 Consider Madame Norrell, in problem 32.1. She gets $5 \log x$ if she delivers x buttons to her fence. She has to pay a fine Fx if she is caught, and she has a 10 percent chance of getting caught. If she is caught, she cannot collect anything from her fence. How big should the fine be if we want to limit Madam Norrell to taking 5 buttons?

(a) 4.5

(b) 5.5

(c) 9

(d) 11

(e) 12

32.2 Consider Jim and Dick, described in Problem 32.2. Jim rides at speed s and has money m; his utility function is $10s + m$. Dick walks at speed w and has money m; his utility function is $10w + m$. The cost of an accident to Jim is $c_J(s, w) = s^2 + w^2$, and the cost of an accident to Dick is also $c_D(s, w) = s^2 + w^2$. If there is no liability, how fast will Dick and Jim move?

(a) $s = 10$ and $w = 10$

(b) $s = 5$ and $w = 5$

(c) $s = 5$ and $w = 10$

(d) $s = 10$ and $w = 5$

(e) $s = 15$ and $w = 15$

Information Technology

33.1 If the demand function for the DoorKnobs operating system is related to perceived market share s and actual market share t by the equation $p = 512s(1 - x)$, then in the long run, the highest price at which DoorKnobs could sustain a market share of 3/4 is

(a) $156

(b) $64

(c) $96

(d) $128

(e) $256

33.2 Professor Kremepuff has published a new textbook. This book will be used in classes for two years, at which time it will be replaced by the new edition. The publisher charges a price of p_1 in the first year and p_2 in the second year. After the first year, bookstores will buy back copies from students for $p_2/2$ and resell them in the second year for p_2. (Students are indifferent between used and new copies of this book.) Students in the first year realize that they can resell it at the end of the year, so the cost of owning it for a year is just the new price minus the used price. In the first year of publication, the number of students who are willing to pay at least v to have the book while they are taking the class is $60,000 - 1000v$. The number of people who take the course in the first year and are willing to pay at least w to keep the book for reference (rather than resell it to the bookstores) is $60,000 - 5000w$. In the second year, the number of people who have not previously taken the course and are willing to pay at least p a copy of the book is $50,000 - 1000p$. If the publisher sets a price of p_1 in the first year and p_2 in the second year where $p_1 \geq p_2$, then the publisher's sales of new books in periods 1 and 2 are:

(a) $q_1 = 60,000 - 1000p_1$ and $q_2 = 60,000 - 1,000p_2$

(b) $q_1 = 60,000 - 1000(p_1 - (p_2/2))$ and $q_2 = 60,000 - 1,000p_2$

(c) $q_1 = (60,000 - 1000p_1) + (60,000 - 5000(p_2/2))$ and $q_2 = 60,000 - 1,000p_2$

(d) $q_1 = 60,000 - 1000(p_1 - (p_2/2))$ and $q_2 = (60,000 - 1,000p_2) - (60,000 - 1000(p_1 - (p_2/2))) + (60,000 - 5,000(p_2/2))$

(e) $q_1 = 60,000 - 1000(p_1 - (p_2/2))$ and $q_2 = (60,000 - 1,000p_2) - (60,000 - 5,000(p_2/2))$

Public Goods

34.1 Just north of the town of Muskrat, Ontario, is the town of Brass Monkey, population 500. Brass Monkey, like Muskrat, has a single public good, the town skating rink and a single private good, Labatt's ale. Everyone's utility function is $U_i(X_i, Y) = X_i - 64/Y$, where X_i is the number of bottles of ale consumed by i and Y is the size of the skating rink in square meters. The price of ale is \$1 per bottle. The cost of the skating rink to the city is \$5 per square meter. Everyone has an income of at least \$5000. What is the Pareto efficient size for the town skating rink?

(a) 80 square meters

(b) 200 square meters

(c) 100 square meters

(d) 165 square meters

(e) None of the other options are correct.

34.2 Recall Bob and Ray in Problem 34.4. They are thinking of buying a sofa. Bob's utility function is $U_B(S, M_B) = (1 + S)M_B$. and Ray's utility function is $U_R(S, M_R) = (4+S)M_R$, where $S = 0$ if they don't get the sofa and $S = 1$ if they do and where M_B and M_R are the amounts of money they have respectively to spend on their private consumptions. Bob has a total of \$800 to spend on the sofa and other stuff. Ray has a total of \$2000 to spend on the sofa and other stuff. The maximum amount that they could pay for the sofa and still arrange to both be better off than without it is

(a) 1200.

(b) 500.

(c) 450.

(d) 800.

(e) 1600.

34.3 Recall Bonnie and Clyde from Problem 34.5. Suppose that their total profits are $48H$, where H is the number of hours they work per year. Their utility functions are, respectively, $U_B(C_B, H) = C_B - 0.01H^2$ and $U_C(C_C, H) = C_C - 0.01H^2$, where C_B and C_C are their private goods consumptions and H is the number of hours they work per year. If they find a Pareto optimal choice of hours of work and income distribution, it must be that the number of hours they work per year is

(a) 1300.

(b) 1800.

(c) 1200.

(d) 550.

(e) 650.

34.4 Recall Lucy and Melvin from Problem 34.6. Lucy's utility function is $2X_L + G$, and Melvin's utility function is $X_M G$, where G is their expenditures on the public goods they share in their apartment and where X_L and X_M are their respective private consumption expenditures. The total amount they have to spend on private goods and public goods is 32,000. They agree on a Pareto optimal pattern of expenditures in which the amount that is spent on Lucy's private consumption is 8000. How much do they spent on public goods?

(a) 8000

(b) 16000

(c) 8050

(d) 4000

(e) There is not enough information here to be able to determine the answer.

Information

35.1 As in Problem 35.2, suppose that low-productivity workers all have marginal products of 10 and high-productivity workers have marginal products of 16. The community has equal numbers of each type of worker. The local community college offers a course in microeconomics. High-productivity workers think taking this course is as bad a wage cut of 4, and low-productivity workers think it is as bad as a wage cut of 7.

(a) There is a separating equilibrium in which high-productivity workers take the course and are paid 16 and low-productivity workers do not take the course and are paid 10.

(b) There is no separating equilibrium and no pooling equilibrium.

(c) There is no separating equilibrium, but there is a pooling equilibrium in which everybody is paid 13.

(d) There is a separating equilibrium in which high-productivity workers take the course and are paid 20 and low productivity workers do not take the course and are paid 10.

(e) There is a separating equilibrium in which high-productivity workers take the course and are paid 16 and low-productivity workers are paid 13.

35.2 Suppose that in Enigma, Ohio, Klutzes have productivity of $1000 and Kandos have productivity of $5000 per month. You can't tell Klutzes from Kandos by looking at them or asking them, and it is too expensive to monitor individual productivity. Kandos, however, have more patience than Klutzes. Listening to an hour of dull lectures is as bad as losing $200 for a Klutz and $100 for a Kando. There will be a separating equilibrium in which anybody who attends a course of H hours of lectures is paid 5000 per month and anybody who does not is paid $1000 per month

(a) if $H < 40$ and $H > 20$.

(b) if $H < 80$ and $H > 20$.

(c) for all positive values of H.

(d) only in the limit as H approaches infinity.

(e) if $H < 35$ and $H > 17.50$

35.3 In Rustbucket, Michigan, there are 200 used cars for sale. Half of them are good, and half of them are lemons. Owners of lemons are willing to sell them for $300. Owners of good used cars are willing to sell them for prices above $1100 but will keep them if the price is lower than $1100. There is a large number of potential buyers who are willing to pay $400 for a lemon and $2100 for a good car. Buyers can't tell good cars from bad, but original owners know.

(a) There will be an equilibrium in which all used cars sell for $1250.

(b) The only equilibrium is one in which all used cars on the market are lemons and they sell for 400.

(c) There will be an equilibrium in which lemons sell for 300 and good used cars sell for 1100.

(d) There will be an equilibrium in which all used cars sell for 700.

(e) There will be an equilibrium in which lemons sell for 400 and good used cars sell for 2100.

35.4 Suppose that in New Crankshaft, Pa., the quality distribution of the 1000 used cars on the market is such that the number of used cars of value less than V is $V/2$. Original owners must sell their used cars. Original owners know what their cars are worth, but buyers can't determine a car's quality until they buy it. An owner can either take his car to an appraiser and pay the appraiser $100 to appraise the car (accurately and credibly), or he can sell the car unappraised. In equilibrium, car owners will have their cars appraised if and only if their value is at least

(a) 100.

(b) 500.

(c) 300.

(d) 200.

(e) 400.

ANSWERS

1 The Market

1.2a. 18
1.2a. 18
1.2a. 18
1.2a. 18
1.2a. 25
1.2a. 25
1.2a. 25
1.2a. 25
1.2a. 15
1.2a. 15
1.2a. 15
1.2a. 15
1.2a. 18
1.2a. 15
1.2a. 18
1.2a. 18
1.2b. 18.
1.2b. Yes.
1.4a. E, who is willing to pay only \$10 for an apartment would sublet to F, who is willing to pay \$18.
1.4b. \$18.
1.4c. A, B, C, D, F.
1.4d. It's the same.

2 Budget Constraint

2.4a. \$100.
2.6a. $2P + 4M + 6J = 360$.
2.6c. 2.
2.6d. 3.
2.6e. 180.
2.6f. $P + 2M + 3J = 180$.
2.6f. No.
2.8a. $15X - 1P - 2A = 50$.
2.10a. 150 pages.
2.10b. 50 pages.
2.12b. The blue budget line lies strictly outside the red budget line, so to satisfy both budgets, one must be strictly inside the red budget line.

3 Preferences

3.2b. Yes.

3.2c. $-2/3$.

3.2d. -1.

3.2e. $-2/3$

3.2e. -1.

3.2f. Yes.

3.2g. Yes.

3.4a. 2.

3.4c. Yes.

3.4d. No.

3.4e. No.

3.4f. Line segments with slope -2.5.

3.6a. Yes.

3.8a. (20,70).

3.8c. No.

3.8d. (60,50).

3.8e. Yes.

3.10a. \$10.

3.10b. \$12.

3.14a. Goldilocks.

3.14b. Grubs.

3.14c. Grubs versus Goldilocks, then Honey versus the winner.

3.14d. No.

4 Utility

4.0. 2

4.0. 3

4.0. $-2/3$

4.0. 4

4.0. 6

4.0. $-2/3$

4.0. a

4.0. b

4.0. $-a/b$

4.0. $\frac{1}{\sqrt{x_1}}$

4.0. 1

4.0. $-\frac{1}{\sqrt{x_1}}$

4.0. $1/x_1$

4.0. 1

4.0. $-1/x_1$

4.0. $v'(x_1)$

4.0. 1

4.0. $-v'(x_1)$

4.0. x_2

4.0. x_1

4.0. $-x_2/x_1$

4.0. $ax_1^{a-1}x_2^b$

4.0. $bx_1^a x_2^{b-1}$

4.0. $-\frac{ax_2}{bx_1}$

4.0. $x_2 + 1$

4.0. $x_1 + 2$

4.0. $-\left(\frac{x_2+1}{x_1+2}\right)$

4.0. $x_2 + b$

4.0. $x_1 + a$

4.0. $-\left(\frac{x_2+b}{x_1+a}\right)$

4.0. ax_1^{a-1}

4.0. ax_2^{a-1}

4.0. $-\left(\frac{x_1}{x_2}\right)^{a-1}$

4.2a. 14.

4.2b. No.

4.2c. $-2/3$.

4.2c. $-2/3$.

4.2d. $-2/\sqrt{x_1}$.

4.2d. x_2

4.4b. 10.

4.4b. 10.

4.4c. No.

4.6a. $u(X,Y) = X + 2Y$.

4.6b. $u(X,Y) = X + Y$.

4.6c. Yes.

4.6c. Yes.

4.6c. No.

4.6d. Shirley prefers (0,2) to (3,0). Lorraine disagrees.

4.8a. $(10, 10)$.

4.8a. More women.

4.8a. More women.

4.8b. Worse.

4.8c. 22.

4.8c. 13.

4.8d. V.

4.10c. Yes.

4.10c. Yes.

4.10d. There is no difference.

4.10e. Their utility functions only differ by a monotonic transformation.

4.12a. -1.

4.12b. -1.

4.12c. Yes.

4.12c. Notice that $u(x_1, x_2) = [v(x_1, x_2)]^2$.

4.14a. $(x + y)(x + 4y)/100$.

4.14b. 20

4.14c. Greater than.

4.14c. Yes.

5 Choice

5.2a. $\frac{36}{X+2} - 1$.

5.2b. Yes.

5.2c. $-\frac{Y+1}{X+2}$.

5.2d. $\frac{Y+1}{X+2} = 1$.

5.2e. $X + Y = 11$.

5.2f. 5

5.2f. 6.

5.4b. $x_1 = x_2$.

5.4c. $10x_1 + 20x_2 = 1,200$.

5.4d. $(40, 40)$.

5.4e. 400

5.4e. 800

5.6a. 4.

5.6b. 4.

5.6c. 4.

5.6f. $x = y^2$.

5.6g. $(4,2)$.

5.6h. 1,150.

5.10a. $C + X = 70,000$.

5.10b. $(30,000, 40,000)$.

5.10c. $(30,000, 30,000)$

5.10d. $.5C + X = 60,000$.

5.10e. 20,000

5.10e. 50,000.

5.10f. $-.5$.

5.10f. -1.

5.12a. $(80, 8)$.

6 Demand

6.2a. $-2x_2/3x_1$.

6.2b. $2/3$.

6.2b. $2/5$.

6.2c. $a/(a+b)$.

6.4a. $1/t = p_t/p_s$.

6.4b. $t(p_s, p_t, m) = p_s/p_t$.

6.4c. p_s.

6.4d. $s = \frac{m}{p_s} - 1$.

6.4e. $s = 0$

6.4e. $t = m/p_t$.

6.4f. Yes.

6.6a. 8 units.

6.6a. 16 units.

6.6b. $\frac{m}{p_w + p_c/2}$.

6.8b. $2x/2 = 3/1$.

6.8b. 3

6.8b. 3.5

6.10a. A substitute. An increase in the price of ale increases demand for cakes.

6.10b. $q_c = 120 - 30p_c$.

6.10c. $p_c = 4 - q_c/30$.

6.10c. $3.

6.10d. $p_c = 5 - q_c/30$.

6.12a. Yes.

6.12a. $\frac{M}{P_1 + P_2}$.

6.12a. $P_1 S$

6.12a. $P_2 S$

6.12b. $\frac{1}{A(P_1 + P_2)}$.

6.12b. $\frac{1}{A(P_1 + P_2)^2}$.

6.12c. $\frac{1}{36,000}$.

6.12d. 1/2.

6.12d. Less than half.

7 Revealed Preference

7.2a. $30.

7.2b. Yes.

7.2b. $-1/2$.

7.2c. 45 pounds.

7.2d. $45.

7.2e. No.

7.4b. Yes.

7.6a. 30

7.6a. 33

7.6a. 16

7.6b. No.

7.6b. D

7.6b. I

7.6b. I

7.6b. D

7.6b. I

7.6c. Yes.

7.8b. McAfee.

7.8c. Falklands.

7.10a. 49.0

7.10a. 68.3

7.10a. 63.1

7.10a. 91.1

7.10b. Yes.

7.10c. 1.39.

7.10d. 1.44.

7.10e. 1.29.

7.10f. 1.39

7.10g. .69

7.12a. Exactly 2.

7.12a. Exactly 2.

7.12b. Yes.

7.12b. Yes, by 50%. Everybody's budget line shifted out by 50%. With homothetic preferences, the consumption of each good increases in the same proportion.

8 Slutsky Equation

8.2a. 90.

8.2b. 8,400 pounds.

8.2b. 88 bottles.

8.2c. 70 bottles.

8.2d. 20.

8.2d. reduced

8.2d. 2

8.2d. reduced

8.2d. 18 bottles.

8.4a. Yes.

8.4a. All due to income effect.

8.4d. $120.

8.4e. All substitution effect.

8.6.   80

8.6.   100.

8.6a. 920.

8.6a. 92.

8.6b. 80

8.6b. 92.

8.6b. 92

8.6b. 100.

8.8a. Worse off.

8.8a. Better off.

8.8b. He is better off in May than in February.

8.8c. No.

8.10b. $.2m_1 + .1m_2 = 200$, $m_1 + m_2 = 1,500$.

8.10c. 1,000.

8.10d. 666.66.

8.10d. No.

8.10d. Yes.

9 Buying and Selling

9.2a. $200.

9.2b. 20

9.2b. 20

9.2c. $300.

9.2c. 15

9.2c. 15

9.2d. 10

9.2d. 10

9.2e. 0.

9.2e. −10.

9.2e. +5.

9.2e. −5.

9.4. No. If p_1 falls, then with the new budget, she can still afford her old bundle. She could afford the bundles with less of good 1 than her endowment at the old prices. By WARP she won't choose them now.

9.6c. The same.

9.8a. 50

9.8a. $300.

9.8a. $5

9.8c. $150.

9.8d. 30

9.8d. 20

9.10b. shorter.

9.10c. longer

9.10c. more

9.10c. shorter

9.10c. endowment income

9.10c. Substitution and endowment income effects cancel each other out, so the work week stays roughly constant.

9.10d. 39

9.10d. 20

9.10d. understates

9.10d. more

9.12a. 40.

9.12b. 40

9.12b. 160.

9.12c. $c + 4r = 320.$

9.12c. $c + 6r = 400.$

9.12d. 40

9.12d. $160

9.12e. Yes.

9.12e. $(200, 33.3).$

9.12e. 46.6.

9.12f. Mac.

10 Intertemporal Choice

10.2a. $c_1 + c_2/(1 + r) = m_1 + m_2/(1 + r).$

10.2b. 1.

10.2b. $1/(1 + r).$

10.2b. $m_1 + m_2/(1 + r).$

10.2c. $.2m_1 + .2m_2/(1 + r).$

10.2c. $.8(1 + r)m_1 + .8m_2.$

10.2d. decrease

10.2d. increase

10.2d. increase

10.4a. False. Substitution effect makes him consume less in period 1 and save more. For a saver, income effect works in opposite direction. Either effect could dominate.

10.4b. True. The income and substitution effects both lead to more consumption in the second period.

10.6b. 710.8%.

10.6b. 7.1%.

10.6c. 6%

10.6c. 5.79%.

10.6c. −87.3%

10.6c. −21.57%.

10.6c. 677.7%

10.6c. 710.8%

10.6c. 5.7

10.6c. 5.5

10.6c. −21.57

10.6c. 109.4

10.6c. 0.5

10.6c. 3.33

10.6c. 3.0

10.6c. 4.4

10.6c. 5.6

10.6c. 7.6

10.8a. Stay the same. His demand for c_1 is $.5(m_1 + m_2/(1 + r))$ and $m_2 = 0$.

10.8b. More. He saves the same amount, but with higher interest rates, he gets more back next period.

10.8c. Less.

10.10b. 600 bushels.

10.10b. 100 bushels.

10.10b. 450 bushels.

10.10c. 568

10.10c. 624.

10.12a. Yes.

10.12c. No.

10.12c. Yes.

10.12c. No.

11 Asset Markets

11.0a. 1+r

11.0a. 1+r

11.0b. 1

11.0b. $1/(1 + r)$

11.0c. $X/(1 + r)$

11.0c. $X/(1 + r)$

11.0d. $-X/(1 + r)$

11.0e. $X/(1 + r)^2$

11.0f. $X_t/(1 + r)^t$

11.0g. $X_1/(1 + r) + X_2/(1 + r)^2 + X_{10}/(1 + r)^{10}$

11.0h. X/r

11.0h. X/r

11.0i. $\sum_{i=1}^{\infty} X/(1 + r)^i$.

11.0i. geometric

11.0i. X/r.

11.0j. $909.

11.0j. $10,000.

11.0k. $-550/(1.1) + 1,210/(1.1)^2 = 500$

11.2a.   The present value of $50,000 a year for 20 years is less than $1,000,000, since the present value of a dollar received in the future is less than $1.

11.2b. $10.

11.2c. $500,000.

11.2d. 500,000

11.2e. $75,000.

11.2f. $8.50 \times 50,000 = \$425,000$.

11.4.   75

11.4a. 75 years.

11.4b. 100 years.

11.6a. $200.

11.6b. $200.

11.6c. 6 years.

11.6d. $500 per case.

11.6e. $500/1.1^6$.

11.8a. $p_t - 5$.

11.8b. $p_{t+1} - 5$.

11.8c. $(p_{t+1} - 5)/(1 + r)^{t+1}$.

11.8c. $(p_t - 5)/(1 + r)^t$.

11.8d. The present values must be equal.

11.8d. $\frac{p_{t+1}-5}{(1+r)^{t+1}} = \frac{p_t-5}{(1+r)^t}$.

11.8e. $p_{t+1} = (1 + r)p_t - 5r$.

11.8f. The percent change in price is smaller.

11.10a. $450.

11.10a. $600.

11.10a. $3,000.

11.10b. $450 - 300 = 150$.

11.10b. $600 - 500 = 100$.

11.10b. $3,000 - 7,500 = -4,500$.

11.10c. A.

11.10d. B.

11.10e. B.

11.10e. C.

11.10f. $900.

11.10f. $1,200.

11.10f. $6,000.

11.10f. B.

11.10f. C.

11.12a.   Some might say that economics, like accounting or mortuary science, is so boring the pay has to be high to get you to do it. Others would suggest that the ability to do well in economics is scarce and is valued by the marketplace. Perhaps the English majors and psychology majors include disproportionately many persons who are not full-time participants in the labor force. No doubt there are several other good partial explanations.

11.12b. $596,000.

11.12b. $630,000.

12 Uncertainty

12.2a. $(50,000, 500,000)$.

12.2b. $50,000 + .9x$.

12.2b. $500,000 - .1x$.

12.2c. .1

12.2c. 455,000.

12.2d. $= -9$.

12.2d. $c_{NF}/c_F = 1$.

12.2e. $(455,000, 455,000)$.

12.2e. $450,000

12.2e. $45,000.

12.4a. 70.71

12.4a. 100.

12.4b. 122.5.

12.4b. 100.

12.4b. take

12.4c. $100 = \frac{1}{2}\sqrt{x}$.

12.4c. $40,000$.

12.4d. $40,000$.

12.4e. 40,000

12.4f. 6,715.73

12.6c. The slope is -1.

12.6e. The price is 1.

12.8a. $u = \frac{1}{2}\ln c_s + \frac{1}{2}\ln c_r$.

12.8b. Morgan's utility function is just the natural log of Sam's, so the answer is yes.

12.8c. 20

12.8c. 20

12.8c. This is the same as Sam's consumption.

12.10a. 300

12.10a. 150

12.10c. $250.

12.10c. $200.

12.12a. $498.

12.12b. $248,004.

12.12c. $248,400.

12.12d. $248,400

12.12d. $\sqrt{248,800}$.

13 Risky Assets

13.2a. $r_x = 30x + 10(1 - x)$.

13.2b. $\sigma_x = 10x$.

13.2c. The budget line is $r_x = 2\sigma_x + 10$.

13.2e. 20

13.2e. 5.

13.2g. Using the answer to Part (a), we find an x that solves $20 = r_x = 30x + 10(1 - x)$. The answer is $x = .5$.

13.4a. 10%.

13.4a. 10%.

13.4b. 10%.

13.4b. 0%.

13.4c. He should choose the second pasture since it has the same expected return and lower risk.

14 Consumer's Surplus

14.2a. A,B,C,D.

14.2b. 20.

14.2b. 5.

14.2c. 50.

14.2d. 130.

14.2e. 0.

14.2f. 4.

14.4a. 20.

14.4b. 30.

14.4c. 30.

14.4d. 40.

14.4e. Lower.

14.6a. $1/(x+1) = p_x$.

14.6b. quasilinear

14.6b. $x = 1/p_x - 1$.

14.6b. $y = m - 1 + p$.

14.6c. 3

14.6c. 9.25

14.6c. 10.64.

14.6d. $10.64.

14.6e. 1

14.6e. 9.5

14.6e. 10.19.

14.6f. $10.19.

14.6g. $-.45$

14.6g. $.25.

14.8a. $200.

14.8a. $100.

14.8b. At price $10, consumer's surplus is $100. At $14, he demands 8 burgers, for net consumer's surplus of $\frac{1}{2}(16 \times 8) = 64$. The change in consumer's surplus is $-$36.

14.10a. $15

14.10b. 10 hours.

14.10b. $20.

14.10c. 0 hours.

14.10c. $30.

15 Market Demand

15.0a. $-p/(60 - p)$.

15.0b. $-bp/(a - bp)$.

15.0c. -2.

15.0d. $-b$.

15.0e. $-2p/(p + 3)$.

15.0f. $-bp/(p+a)$.

15.2a. $p(q) = 5 - q/2$ if $q < 10$.

15.2b. $p(q) = 10,000/q^2$.

15.2c. $p(q) = (10 - \ln q)/4$.

15.2d. $p(q) = \sqrt{20/q}$.

15.4a. -2.

15.4a. -3.

15.4a. -4.

15.4b. 1.

15.4b. 1.

15.4b. 1.

15.4c. $-p$.

15.4c. 1.

15.6a. $(m - p_1 + 1)2 = m + 1$.

15.6a. $p = (m + 1)/2$.

15.6a. $1.

15.8a. $P = 5$.

15.8b. $Q = 5$.

15.10a. 9,900.

15.10b. $250,000.

15.10b. $250,000.

15.10c. 150,000 seats.

16 Equilibrium

16.2a. 15

16.2a. 25.

16.2b. 20.

16.2b. 30.

16.2b. $10.

16.2c. $10.

16.2d. $25.

16.4a. $20

16.4a. 100.

16.4b. $21

16.4b. $19.

16.4b. 95.

16.4c. $5 = 2 \times 5/2$.

16.6a. The equations are $200 - 4P_S - 2P_L = 100$ and $200 - 3P_L - P_S = 150$.

16.6b. 20

16.6b. 10.

16.6d. 23

16.6d. 9.

16.8a. It would rise by about 2% a year.

16.8b. 400.

16.8b. 400.

16.8c. 2

16.8c. 1.5 %.

16.8d. It would double if demand didn't change.

16.8e. Since the demand has elasticity of -1, the revenue would stay the same.

16.8f. They would recover to their old levels.

16.10a. 3.

16.10a. $9.

16.10b. 3.5.

16.10b. 9.5 cents.

16.10b. 7.5 cents.

16.10c. -16.66%.

16.10c. -8.33%.

17 Technology

17.0. 1

17.0. 2

17.0. $-1/2$

17.0. a

17.0. b

17.0. $-a/b$

17.0. $50x_2$

17.0. $50x_1$

17.0. $-\frac{x_2}{x_1}$

17.0. $\frac{3}{4}x_1^{1/4}x_2^{-1/4}$

17.0. $-\frac{x_2}{3x_1}$

17.0. $Cbx_1^a x_2^{b-1}$

17.0. $-\frac{ax_2}{bx_1}$

17.0. $x_1 + 2$

17.0. $-\left(\frac{x_2+1}{x_1+2}\right)$

17.0. $x_2 + b$

17.0. $x_1 + a$

17.0. $-\left(\frac{x_2+b}{x_1+a}\right)$

17.0. a

17.0. $\frac{b}{2\sqrt{x_2}}$

17.0. $-\frac{2a\sqrt{x_2}}{b}$

17.0. ax_1^{a-1}

17.0. ax_2^{a-1}

17.0. $-\left(\frac{x_1}{x_2}\right)^{a-1}$

17.0. $-\left(\frac{x_1}{x_2}\right)^{a-1}$

17.0. C

17.0. C

17.0. C

17.0. D

17.0. D

17.0. D

17.0. I

17.0. C

17.0. I

17.0. C
17.0. D
17.0. D
17.0. D
17.0. C
17.0. D
17.0. D
17.0. D
17.0. D
17.0. C
17.0. D
17.0. D
17.2a. 1
17.2a. remains constant
17.2a. 0
17.2a. remains constant
17.2a. infinity.
17.2a. constant
17.2b. 0.
17.2b. 0.
17.2b. increase
17.4a. decreasing
17.4a. constant
17.6a. $2A + 4B = 160$.
17.6b. $4A + 2B = 180$.
17.6d. $2A + 4B = 160$ and $4A + 2B = 180$.
17.6e. 45 units.
17.6e. Workers.
17.6e. 70.
17.8. For any $t > 1$, $f(tx_1, tx_2, tx_3) = A(tx_1)^a(tx_2)^b(tx_3)^c = t^{a+b+c}f(x_1, x_2, x_3) > tf(x_1, x_2, x_3)$.
17.10a. $ab < 1$.
17.10a. $ab = 1$.
17.10a. $ab > 1$.

18 Profit Maximization

18.2a. $\pi = 400\sqrt{x} - 50x$.
18.2b. 16.
18.2b. 16.
18.2b. $800.
18.2c. 16.
18.2c. 16.
18.2c. $640.
18.2d. $\pi = .50 \times (400\sqrt{x} - 50x)$.
18.2d. 16.
18.2d. $400.
18.4a. 200.
18.4a. 400.
18.4b. 300.

18.4b. 300.

18.4c. An infinite number.

18.4c. 250.

18.4e. 200

18.4e. 0

18.4e. $1,000.

18.6b. $80 million.

18.6b. $60 million.

18.6c. No. The data satisfy WAPM.

18.6d. Yes. When price of gas was $40, Golf could have made more money by acting as it did when price of gas was $20.

18.8a. Yes. If price of input doesn't change, $\Delta w = 0$, so WAPM says $\Delta p \Delta y \geq 0$.

18.8b. Yes. If price of output doesn't change, $\Delta p = 0$, so WAPM says $-\Delta w \Delta x \geq 0$.

18.8c. No. Sign pattern is $(+)(-) - (+)(+) \geq 0$, which cannot happen.

18.10a. $2x_1^{-1/2} x_2^{1/4} = w_1$

18.10a. $x_1^{1/2} x_2^{-3/4} = w_2$.

18.10a. $8/(w_1^3 w_2)$

18.10a. $4/(w_1^2 w_2^2)$.

18.10b. 1.

18.10b. 1.

18.10b. 1.

18.10b. 1.

18.12a. 0

18.12a. 16/9

18.12a. 8/3.

19 Cost Minimization

19.2b. Constant.

19.2c. 10 units.

19.2c. 5 units.

19.2d. It can *only* produce 10 units of output by using the bundle $(10, 5)$, so this is the cheapest way. It will cost $15.

19.2e. $c(w_1, w_2, 10) = 10w_1 + 5w_2$.

19.2f. $(w_1 + w_2/2)y$.

19.4a. Decreasing.

19.4b. w_1/w_2

19.4c. $w_2^{1/2} y^{3/2}/w_1^{1/2}$

19.4c. $w_1^{1/2} y^{3/2}/w_2^{1/2}$.

19.4d. $2w_1^{1/2} w_2^{1/2} y^{3/2}$.

19.6a. 1/2 unit of water.

19.6b. $(4, 2)$.

19.6c. h

19.6c. $h/2$.

19.6d. $w_1 h + \frac{w_2}{2} h$.

19.8b. $2,000.

19.8b. $2,500.

19.8b. $3,000.

19.8c. There is no such evidence, since the data satisfy WACM.

19.8d. $2,000.

19.8d. $3,500.

19.8d. $2,500.

19.8e. No. At prices $(20, 10)$, this bundle costs less than the bundle actually used at prices $(20, 10)$. If it produced as much as that bundle, the chosen bundle wouldn't have been chosen.

19.10a. Increasing.

19.10b. 12.

19.10b. 12w.

19.10c. $\sqrt{y}$.

19.10c. $w\sqrt{y}$.

19.10d. $w/\sqrt{y}$.

19.12b. Decreasing returns to scale.

19.12c. $(8, 0)$.

19.12c. $8.

19.12d. $(18, 0)$.

19.12d. $18.

19.12e. $y^2/2$.

19.12f. y^2.

20 Cost Curves

20.2. $2s^2$.

20.2. 10.

20.2. $2s$.

20.2. $10/s$.

20.2. $2s + 10/s$.

20.2. $4s$.

20.4a. $MC = \frac{y}{100}$

20.4a. $AC = \frac{200}{y} + \frac{y}{200}$.

20.4a. 200.

20.4a. 2.

20.4b. $MC = y/250$

20.4b. $AC = (500/y) + y/500$.

20.4b. 500.

20.4b. 2.

20.4c. $MC = y/500$

20.4c. $AC = (1,000/y) + y/1,000$.

20.4c. 1,000.

20.4c. 2.

20.6a. $Q^{4/3}$.

20.6b. $2Q^{4/3} + 100$.

20.6c. $8Q^{1/3}/3$.

20.6d. $2Q^{1/3} + 100/Q$.

20.8a. $AC = 4y + \frac{16}{y}$.

20.8b. $MC = 8y$.

20.8c. $y = 2$.

20.8d. $AVC = 4y$.

20.8e. At $y = 0$.

21 Firm Supply

21.2a. $3y^2 - 16y + 30$.

21.2b. $y^2 - 8y + 30$.

21.2d. 4

21.2d. 4.

21.2e. 4.

21.2f. 14.

21.2g. 4.

21.2g. 42.

21.4a. $2y$.

21.4a. $y + 10/y$.

21.4b. $\sqrt{10}$.

21.4b. $\sqrt{10}$.

21.4c. $2\sqrt{10}$.

21.4c. $\sqrt{10}$.

21.6a. 8.

21.6b. 8 hours.

21.6c. $p - 1$.

21.6d. $6.

21.6e. $S(p) = 8$ for $p > 6$, 0 otherwise.

21.8a. $(w_1 + w_2/2)y^2$.

21.8b. $3y$.

21.8b. $p/3$.

21.8b. $3y/2$.

21.8c. 16.

21.8c. 384.

21.8d. $(2w_1 + w_2)y$.

21.8d. $p/(2w_1 + w_2)$.

21.10a. $y + p_o$.

21.10b. $y + 5$

21.10b. $y + 15$

21.10d. 25 barrels.

21.10e. It would decrease to 15 barrels.

21.10f. $S(p) = p - 10$.

21.10f. 20 barrels.

22 Industry Supply

22.0a. $S(p) = 6p$.

22.0b. $S(p) = 2p$ for $p \leq 1$, $S(p) = 3p - 1$ for $p > 1$.

22.0c. $S(p) = 0$ for $p < 3$, $S(p) = 100p - 300$ for $3 \leq p \leq 4$, $S(p) = 500p - 1,900$ for $p > 4$.

22.0d. $S(p) = 6p - 24$ for $p > 4$.

22.2a. 14,000.

22.2a. $9.20.

22.2a. 2,100.

22.2a. Yes.

22.2a. 110%.

22.2b. 2,100

22.2b. No.

22.2b. $1,909.

22.2b. $1,909.

22.2c. Larger.

22.2c. $7.20.

22.4a. $p/2$.

22.4a. $Y = np/2$.

22.4b. $p^* = 2$.

22.4c. Guess at $p^* = 2$. This gives $D(p) = 52 - 2 = n2/2$, which says $n^* = 50$.

22.4d. $p^* = 2$.

22.4d. $y^* = 1$.

22.4e. $Y^* = 50$.

22.4f. If a new firm entered, there would be 51 firms. The supply-demand equation would be $52.5 - p = 51p/2$. Solve for $p^* = 105/53 < 2$. A new firm would lose money. Therefore in equilibrium there would be 50 firms.

22.4g. Solve $52.5 - p = 50p/2$ to get $p^* = 2.02$.

22.4g. $y^* = 1.01$.

22.4g. Around .02.

22.4h. 51.

22.4h. 2.

22.4i. $y = 1$.

22.4i. Zero.

22.6a. Profit per bushel $= 5 - .10t$.

22.6b. Rent $= 5,000 - 100t$.

22.6c. 50 miles.

22.8a. $3.50

22.8a. 3.5.

22.8a. 2.

22.8b. $3.20; 4.8.

22.8b. 3.

22.10. $15,000.

22.12b. Supply curve to the right.

22.12b. Increased.

22.12b. Decreased.

22.12b. Decreased.

23 Monopoly

23.2b. 50.

23.2b. 50.

23.2d. 75.

23.2d. 37.5 cents per pie.

23.4a. 3.

23.4b. 2.5.

23.4c. 3.

23.6a. At $y = 100$, $p = 100$.

23.6c. Larger.

24 Monopoly Behavior

24.2a. 20.

24.2b. $60.

24.2c. $20.

24.2d. 40.

24.2e. 400.

24.2f. 0.

24.4a. 30.

24.4a. $90.

24.4b. 30.

24.4c. 80.

24.4d. 40.

24.4e. 25.

24.6a. 100

24.6a. 80

24.6b. $50

24.6b. $32

24.6c. $32.

24.6d. $48.

24.6e. Solve $50 - p = 48 - 32$ to find $p = 34$.

24.6f. $30.

24.6g. $12.

24.6h. $38.

24.6i. 60.

24.8a. $p(x) = 1 - x/50$.

24.8b. 25.

24.8c. 50 cents.

24.8d. 12.5

24.8e. Zero.

24.8f. 50.

24.8g. 25.

24.8h. $25

24.8h. 0.

25 Factor Markets

25.2a. $p^* = \frac{1000+c}{2}$.

25.2b. $D(p^*) = \frac{1000-c}{2}$.

25.2c. $c^* = 500$.

25.2d. $D(c^*) = 250$.

25.2e. $\pi_b = (500 - 250)(750 - 500) = 250^2$.

25.2f. $\pi_p = 500 \cdot 250$.

25.2g. $CS_e = 250^2/2$.

25.2h. 10×250^2.

25.2i. $p^* = 500$ and $D(p^*) = 500$.

25.2j. $\pi_p = 500^2$.

25.2k. $CS_i = 500^2/2 > CS_e$.

26 Oligopoly

26.2a. $1,200 - q_C^t/2$.

26.2b. $1,200 - q_C^t/2$

26.2b. $1,200 + q_C^t/2$.

26.2b. $1.25 - q_C^t/3,200$.

26.2c. $1.25 q_C^t - (q_C^t)^2/3,200$.

26.2c. $1.25 - q_C^t/1,600$.

26.2d. $1,200$.

26.2d. 600.

26.2d. $7/8.

26.2d. $450.

26.2d. $225.

26.2d. Stackleberg

26.2e. No. Carl's profits in Stackleberg equilibrium are larger than in Cournot equilibrium. So if the output when neither knows the other's output this year until after planting time is a Cournot equilibrium, Carl will want Simon to know his output.

26.4a. 4.

26.4a. -2.

26.4b. 48

26.4b. $4.

26.4c. $y_1 = 24 - y_2/2$.

26.4c. $y_2 = 24 - y_1/2$.

26.4c. 32

26.4c. 16

26.4c. $36.

26.4e. 24

26.4e. $52.

26.4f. Profits increase by $22.

26.4g. $\max_{y_1} [100 - 2(y_1 + 24 - y_1/2)]y_1 - 4y_1$.

26.4g. 24

26.4g. 12.

26.4g. 36

26.4g. $28.

26.6b. 45

26.6b. 70

26.6b. $450 per day.

26.6c. About $1.6 million.

26.6d. No; losses would be about $900 per day.

26.6e. 60

26.6e. 2,000.

26.6f. $45

26.6f. 140.

26.6f. $900.

26.6f. No.

26.6g. $100/3

26.6g. 280/3

26.6g. $1,600/9.

26.8a. $y = p$.

26.8a. $50p$.

26.8b. $1,000 - 100p$.

26.8c. 500.

26.8c. $p = 5$.

26.8d. $50 \times 5 = 250$.

26.8d. $y_m + y_c = 750$.

26.10a. $2(120 - p)$.

26.10a. $2(120 - p)(p - 20) = 2(140p - p^2 - 2,400)$.

26.10b. $70.

26.10b. 50

26.10b. 100

26.10b. $5,000.

26.10c. $120.

26.10c. 200.

26.10c. $24,000

26.10c. $14,000.

26.10c. $10,000.

26.10c. If Ben pays for delivery, he can price-discriminate between nearby farmers and faraway ones. He charges a higher price, net of transport cost, to nearby farmers and a lower net price to faraway farmers, who are willing to pay less net of transport cost.

27 Game Theory

27.2a. e

27.2a. d

27.2a. c

27.2a. f

27.2b. $a > e; b > d$.

27.2c. Yes. A dominant strategy equilibrium is always a Nash equilibrium.

27.4a. The only one is (top, left).

27.4b. There are two: (top, left) and (bottom, right).

27.4c. Although (bottom, right) is a Nash equilibrium, it seems a silly one. If either player believes that there is any chance that the other will go to the party, he or she will also go.

27.4e. No.

27.4e. (1) Both go to the little party. (2) Both go to the big party.

27.4f. No.

27.4f. If both know the game matrix and each knows that the other knows it, then each might predict the other will choose the little party.

27.6a. No.

27.6a. The two outcomes where one teenager swervesand the does not.

27.6b. Play each strategy with probability $1/2$.

27.8. 1,0

27.8. 0,1

27.8. 0,1

27.8. 1,0

27.8a. Yes.

27.8a. There are none.

27.8b. Each person hides upstairs with probability 1/2, downstairs with probability 1/2.

27.8c. 2,0

27.8c. 0,1

27.8c. 0,1

27.8c. 1,0

27.8d. No.

27.8d. Ruth hides downstairs 2/3 of the time. Ned looks downstairs 1/2 the time.

27.8d. 1/2.

27.10a. $y = 10 + .8x$ and $x = y$.

27.10b. 50.

27.10d. $y = 11 + .8x$ and $y = x$, so $x = y = 55$.

27.10e. 4.

27.10f. 26.

27.10g. 30.8.

27.10h. 50.

27.12a. $1 - \frac{5}{8}\frac{I}{D}$.

27.12a. $8 - 5\frac{I}{D}$.

27.12b. 5.

27.12b. $8 - 5\frac{I}{D} = 5$.

27.12c. $\frac{3}{5}$.

27.12d. Black.

27.12d. Invade.

27.12d. Further away.

27.12e. Yes.

28 Exchange

28.2b. Pareto efficient allocations lie on the line with slope 1 extending from Birger's corner of the box.

28.4c. $W_B/Q_B = W_K/Q_K$.

28.4e. -2.

28.4e. 2.

28.4f. 2 quiche, 4 wine.

28.4f. 2 quiche, 4 wine.

28.6. 2.

28.10a. $c_1 + c_2/(1+r)$.

28.10a. I

28.10a. $I^*/(1+r)$.

28.10a. $c_1 + c_2/(1+r) = I$

28.10a. $c_1 + c_2/(1+r) = I^*/(1+r)$.

28.10b. $c_1 = aI$

28.10b. $c_2 = (1-a)I(1+r)$.

28.10b. $c_1 = aI^*/(1+r)$

28.10b. $c_2 = (1-a)I^*$.

28.10b. aI^*.

28.10b. $a = 1/2$.

28.10b. .22.

28.10c. N_2I^*.

28.10d. aI

28.10d. $aI^*/(1+r)$.

28.10d. $N_1aI + N_2aI^*/(1+r)$.

28.10e. $N_1aI + N_2aI^*/(1+r) = N_1I$.

28.10e. $r = \frac{N_2I^*a}{N_1I(1-a)} - 1$.

28.10e. $r = 10\%$.

28.10f. Supply = demand for period 2 if $N_1(1-a)I(1+r) + N_2(1-a)I^* = N_2I^*$. If $N_1 = N_2$ and $I = I^*$, then $(1-a)(1+r) + (1-a) = 1$. If $a = 11/21$, then $r = 10\%$.

29 Production

29.2. $F + C/2 = 8$.

29.2a. 4.

29.2a. 8.

29.2b. \$.50.

29.2b. \$.50

29.2b. 8

29.2c. 1

29.2c. 1

29.2c. 1

29.2c. \$.50.

29.4a. Specialize in milk.

29.4b. Specialize in wheat.

29.4c. No.

29.4e. In favor.

29.4e. Against.

29.4e. The change strictly enlarges the budget set for northerners and strictly shrinks it for southerners.

29.4f. Yes. Southerners would now switch to specializing in milk.

29.4f. In favor.

29.4f. Depends on their preferences about consumption.

29.4f. The two alternative budget lines for southerners are not nested.

30 Welfare

30.2a. 200

30.2a. 0.

30.2b. 66.66

30.2b. 66.66.

30.2c. 100

30.2c. 50.

30.4a. A.

30.4a. A.

30.4b. They get the same amount of money.

30.4b. A consumes more.

30.4c. B gets more money.

30.4c. They consume the same amount.

30.4d. A.

30.4d. A.

30.4e. B.

30.4e. They consume the same amount.

30.6b. See diagram.

30.8a. 16.

30.8a. 8.

30.8b. 16.

30.8b. 8.

30.8c. The Pareto optimal allocations are all of the allocations in which each person gets at least 8 units of spaghetti.

30.8f. 8.

30.8f. 8.

30.8g. Romeo wants to give spaghetti to Juliet, but she doesn't want to take it. Juliet wants to give spaghetti to Romeo, but he doesn't want to take it. Both like spaghetti for themselves, but would rather the other had it.

31 Externalities

31.2a. 100

31.2a. 150.

31.2b. 150.

31.2b. 150.

31.2c. 150.

31.2c. $1 per unit.

31.4b. Yes.

31.6a. 0.

31.6b. Better off.

31.6c. 1/2.

31.6d. No.

31.6e. No.

31.6f. 100.

31.8a. 24

31.8a. 18.

31.8a. 576

31.8a. 324

31.8a. 900.

31.8b. 30

31.8b. 900.

31.8c. 30

31.8c. 9

31.8c. 900

31.8c. 81.

31.8c. 981.

32 Law

32.2a. 4 miles per hour.

32.2a. 9 miles per hour.

32.2b. 1 miles per hour.

32.2b. 9 mile per hour.

32.2c. 4 miles per hour.

32.2c. 4 miles per hour.

32.2d. 1 mile per hour

32.2d. 4 miles per hour.

33 Information Technology

33.2a. .75

33.2a. .833

33.2a. .8529, 8534

33.2a. .853553

33.2b. This equation implies $x^2 - x + 1/8 = 0$. Solutions are $x = 0.85355$ and $x = 0.14645$. Both are equilibrium market shares with a price of \$32.

33.4a. $D_2(p_2) - D_1(p_1 - .4p_2) + D^k(.4p_2)$

33.4a.

33.4b. $D_1(p_1 - .4p_2) + D_2(p_2) - D_1(p_1 - .4p_2) + D^k(.4p_2)) = D_2(p_2) + D^k(.4p_2)$

33.4b.

33.4c. It would remain constant

33.4d. $p_1 D_1(p_1 - .4p_2) + p_2(D_2(p_2) - D_1(p_1 - .4p_2) + D^k(.4p_2)) = (p_1 - p_2)D_1(p_1 - .4p_2) + p_2(D_2(p_2) + D^k(.4p_2))$

33.4d.

33.4e. Variable cost is $c(D_2(p_2) + D^k(.4p_2))$. Subtract this from previous answer.

33.4e.

33.4e.

33.4f. $(p - c)(D_2(p) + D^k(.4p))$

33.4f.

33.6a. $200(90-p)$

33.6a. $200(p - 10)(90 - p)$

33.6b. \$50

33.6c. 4,000

33.6c. 4000

33.6d. \$320,000

33.6e. After two years

33.6e. After two years is better for students who take the course in the first year of publication and plan to sell. After one year is better for the other students.

34 Public Goods

34.2a. \$2.

34.2b. Each pays less than full cost of own meal, so all overindulge.

34.4a. Solve $W_B = 2(W_B - p_B)$ to get $p_B = W_B/2$.

34.4b. Solve $2W_R = 3(W_R - p_R)$, which gives $p_R = W_R/3$.

34.4c. \$75.

34.6a. 1/2.

34.6a. X_M/G.

34.6b. $1/2 + X_M/G = 1$.

34.6c. Yes.

34.6d. One example: Melvin gets \$2,500, Lucy gets \$500$G = \$5,000$.

34.6d. Lucy gets \$5,000, Melvin gets \$1,000$G = \$2,000$.

34.6e. The allocations that satisfy the equations $X_M/G = 1/2$ and $X_L + X_M + G = \$8,000$.

34.6f. Less of.

35 Information

35.2a. $12.50.

35.2b. $15

35.2b. $10.

35.2c. $2

35.2c. -$1

35.2c. will be

35.2d. $15

35.2d. $10.

35.2e. $4

35.2e. $1

35.2e. won't be

35.4a. 5.

35.4b. $5^2/10 = 2.50$.

35.4c. $5 - 2.50 = 2.50$.

35.4d. $3.50.

35.4e. $2.50.

35.6a. They'd all sell for $1,000 for total revenue of $1,000,000.

35.6b. $X/2$

35.6c. $X - 200$.

35.6c. $X/2$.

35.6d. Solve $X/2 = X - 200$ to get $X = \$400$.

35.6e. The worst 200 cars will be unappraised and will sell for $200.

35.6f. $\$1,000,000 - 800 \times 200 = 840,000$.

Answers to Quizzes

Chapter 2: Budget Constraint

    2.1 C
    2.2 A
    2.3 B
    2.4 C
    2.5 C
    2.6 A
    2.7 B

Chapter 3: Preferences

    3.1 E
    3.2 C
    3.3 B
    3.4 D
    3.5 B
    3.6 E

Chapter 4: Utility

4.1 E
4.2 B
4.3 C
4.4 C
4.5 E
4.6 C

Chapter 5: Choice

5.1 A
5.2 E
5.3 D
5.4 B
5.5 B
5.6 D

Chapter 6: Demand

6.1 A
6.2 D
6.3 D
6.4 A
6.5 E
6.6 B
6.7 C

Chapter 7: Revealed Preference

7.1 B
7.2 C
7.3 A
7.4 A
7.5 A

Chapter 8: Slutsky Equation

8.1 A
8.2 C
8.3 C
8.4 C
8.5 A
8.6 C

Chapter 9: Buying and Selling

9.1 D
9.2 A
9.3 B
9.4 E
9.5 B
9.6 D

Chapter 10: Intertemporal Choice

10.1 B
10.2 B
10.3 B
10.4 E
10.5 A
10.6 C

Chapter 11: Asset Markets

11.1 A
11.2 A
11.3 D
11.4 A
11.5 C
11.6 A

Chapter 12: Uncertainty

12.1 A
12.2 B
12.3 C
12.4 A
12.5 B

Chapter 13: Risky Assets

13.1 C
13.2 A

Chapter 14: Consumer's Surplus

14.1 A
14.2 A
14.3 B
14.4 A
14.5 A

Chapter 15: Market Demand

15.1 D
15.2 E
15.3 C
15.4 A
15.5 E

Chapter 16: Equilibrium

16.1 D
16.2 C
16.3 A
16.4 A

Chapter 17: Technology

17.1 A
17.2 A
17.3 B
17.4 B

Chapter 18: Profit Maximization

18.1 B
18.2 A
18.3 C
18.4 A

Chapter 19: Cost Minimization

19.1 B
19.2 D
19.3 A
19.4 E
19.5 A
19.6 D

Chapter 20: Cost Curves

20.1 A
20.2 A
20.3 C
20.4 A
20.5 E

Chapter 21: Firm Supply

21.1 B
21.2 A
21.3 D

Chapter 22: Industry Supply

22.1 C
22.2 C
22.3 A
22.4 A
22.5 A
22.6 D

Chapter 23: Monopoly

23.1 A
23.2 E
23.3 C
23.4 B

Chapter 24: Monopoly Behavior

24.1 A
24.2 A
24.3 B
24.4 C

Chapter 25: Factor Markets

25.1 B
25.2 D
25.3 A

Chapter 26: Oligopoly

26.1 A
26.2 D
26.3 A
26.4 A
26.5 C
26.6 A

Chapter 27: Game Theory

27.1 C
27.2 A
27.3 B
27.4 A
27.5 D

Chapter 28: Exchange

28.1 B
28.2 C
28.3 D
28.4 A
28.5 B
28.6 B

Chapter 29: Production

29.1 A
29.2 B
29.3 A
29.4 A
29.5 B

Chapter 30: Welfare

30.1 A
30.2 B
30.3 B
30.4 E
30.5 A

Chapter 31: Externalities

31.1 C
31.2 D
31.3 A
31.4 B
31.5 A

Chapter 32: Law

32.1 C
32.2 B

Chapter 33: Information Technology

33.1 C
33.2 D

Chapter 34: Public Goods

    34.1 A
    34.2 D
    34.3 C
    34.4 B

Chapter 35: Information

    35.1 A
    35.2 A
    35.3 B
    35.4 D